James Hunter Dec. 5
Finchale
1976.

WRITERS AT WORK

Fourth Series

Previously Published

WRITERS AT WORK
The *Paris Review* Interviews

FIRST SERIES

Edited, and with an Introduction, by MALCOLM COWLEY

E. M. Forster   Frank O'Connor
François Mauriac   Robert Penn Warren
Joyce Cary   Alberto Moravia
Dorothy Parker   Nelson Algren
James Thurber   Angus Wilson
Thornton Wilder   William Styron
William Faulkner   Truman Capote
Georges Simenon   Françoise Sagan

SECOND SERIES

Edited by GEORGE PLIMPTON and introduced by VAN WYCK BROOKS

Robert Frost   Aldous Huxley
Ezra Pound   Ernest Hemingway
Marianne Moore   S. J. Perelman
T. S. Eliot   Lawrence Durrell
Boris Pasternak   Mary McCarthy
Katherine Anne Porter Ralph Ellison
Henry Miller   Robert Lowell

THIRD SERIES

Edited by GEORGE PLIMPTON and introduced by ALFRED KAZIN

William Carlos Williams Saul Bellow
Blaise Cendrars   Arthur Miller
Jean Cocteau   James Jones
Louis-Ferdinand Céline   Norman Mailer
Evelyn Waugh   Allen Ginsberg
Lillian Hellman   Edward Albee
William Burroughs   Harold Pinter

Writers at Work

The *Paris Review* Interviews

FOURTH SERIES

Edited by George Plimpton
Introduced by Wilfrid Sheed

NEW YORK: THE VIKING PRESS

First published in 1976 by The Viking Press
625 Madison Avenue, New York, N.Y. 10022

Published simultaneously in Canada by
The Macmillan Company of Canada Limited

LIBRARY OF CONGRESS CATALOGING IN PUBLICATION DATA
Main entry under title: .
Writers at work.
1. Authors-Interviews.   I. Plimpton, George.
II. The Paris review.
PN453.W735   808.8   76–13918
ISBN 0–670–79097–4

Printed in the United States of America

ACKNOWLEDGMENTS

Farrar, Straus & Giroux, Inc.:
For The John Berryman interview.

Grove Press, Inc. and the Sterling Lord Agency, Inc.:
From "Mexico City Blues" by Jack Kerouac.
Copyright © 1959 by Jack Kerouac.
Reprinted by permission.

Macmillan, Inc. and Macmillan Administration (Basingstoke) Ltd.:
From "The Dynasts" by Thomas Hardy.

New Directions Publishing Corp.:
Delmore Schwartz, *Selected Poems: Summer Knowledge.*
Copyright 1938 by New Directions Publishing Corporation,
© 1966 by Delmore Schwartz.
Reprinted by permission of New Directions Publishing Corporation.

Random House, Inc. and Faber and Faber Ltd.:
From *Collected Poems* by W. H. Auden.

The Viking Press:
From *Journal of a Novel* by John Steinbeck.
Copyright © 1969 by the Estate of John Steinbeck.
From *Steinbeck: A Life In Letters,*
edited by Elaine Steinbeck and Robert Wallsten.
Copyright © 1975 by Elaine Steinbeck and Robert Wallsten.

Contents

Introduction

THIS IS partly an act of reparation. A few years back, I wrote a somewhat lofty piece about the second collection of *Paris Review* interviews, suggesting that the information therein was neither better nor worse than Hollywood gossip. I was mortally sick by then of hearing about Hemingway's number-two pencils, and I felt they had about as much to do with literature as, say, whether Aldous Huxley slept in pajama tops or bottoms.

It was a dishonest piece (I was too young to be honest) in that I artfully concealed how much I had enjoyed the volume—which meant it had some kind of value, if not the kind I was looking for. It was also an ingenuous piece because I did not yet realize that gossip is the very stuff of literature, the *materia prima* of which both books and their authors are made. From Homer to Bellow, gossip is simply what authors *do*, in books and out; and no fine distinctions are made between craft gossip and the wisdom of the keyhole. In fact, Aldous Huxley's sleeping arrangements would have interested Flaubert a good deal more than Hemingway's pencils. Literature is the one subject in the world one cannot be priggish about.

Can the interview as a form pass beyond the realm of necessary small talk into art itself? Perhaps. Whenever a good writer uses words, literature is a possibility, and in the interviews that follow, the subjects have a distinct interest in producing literature. Because the interviews represent the authors' contributions to their own gossip: These are their own fair copies of themselves, and this is the way they would like to be talked about. Hence, their idlest comments take on the urgency of missing pieces. If a movie star says that he sleeps with the windows open, we are probably getting a coarse reading of his present image. But if an author says so, he is adding a workmanlike stone to his monument. He is telling you for one thing that he is the kind of author who doesn't mind talking about the mundane personal—whether archly, as one might expect of Nabokov, mock eruditely à la Burgess ("the Elizabethans didn't even *have* windows, you know"), or with the exhaustive candor of a Jack Kerouac. In any event, he knows as movie actors do not that such details can immortalize a character for better or worse, and he is taking no chances. It is his business to know it. Novelists in particular spend a lifetime sabotaging their characters with one loathesome habit or ennobling them with a perfect gesture. So they are careful when they dress themselves for the public. As their own most important characters, they deserve the most attention.

This is not to suggest *The Paris Review*'s urbane corps of interviewers pepper their victims with inane questions—far from it. But as one moves from the artful table setting that introduces each interview through one's first glimpses of the great man into the actual questions, one senses a continuity of self-creation that would reveal itself equally in small or large matters. This author will be a grouch, that one generous; and they will not slip, unless intentionally. For these people are masters of disguise, of controlled performance, and this is the record they want to leave.

Which doesn't mean there are no real people in this book. The real person includes the magician *and* his tricks. Novelists begin life as liars. It is their apprenticeship (and I'm not sure that poets aren't even better at it); but by their maturity they don't need to lie anymore. The truth itself is a trick. The mask of a Vladimir Nabokov is welded seamlessly to his face: the persona in the interview is as real and unreal as Humbert Humbert himself.

I stress Nabokov because the greatest novelist gives the greatest performance. He is, to the tip of his tongue, the Nabokov man: a dispossessed nobleman whose blood runs irony and who will never stoop to being likable. (He is likable.) W. H. Auden, playing for the poets, is not far behind. His interviewing self is, or was, an extra person, like the Holy Ghost, generated by self-contemplation. Auden could apparently answer questions forever in a serene stream, without lapsing from character. He has given so many interviews that his answering service could give a perfect Auden response to anything.

Auden's self-monument was complete, and he wasn't about to tamper with it. Consider in contrast his old friend Christopher Isherwood, still trying on faces like a boy in a prop department. In fact his boyishness is his mask. He talks about his discovery of Eastern spirituality as if it had happened yesterday and not back in the thirties when he and the rest of the class, Aldous Huxley and Gerald Heard, discovered the East on the American Gold Coast. Yet who seems younger? The owlish, born-old Auden or Isherwood, the professional boy?

Novelists, since they need so many, perhaps settle less well into a single face than poets. Because the other quite spectacularly boyish interviewee is John Updike—still young, of course, and, as an American, full of vital blank spaces that are filled in for Europeans (prairie versus garden), yet earnest and eager for any age. Updike answers the questions as though it were for a very important exam and with a guileless sincerity that seems, like something in Henry James's *The American,* both provincially earnest and somehow more sophisticated than a European smartie like Nabokov. Like *The New Yorker* magazine at its best, he is beyond sophistication and even makes the latter seem rather a callow thing in itself, a trap for *arrivistes.* Of all the subjects, Updike gives the most honest day's work and worries the least about how he's doing.

For sheer vulgar performance that in no way cheapens the actor, Anthony Burgess remains something of a model for writers. He can go on the most rattle-brained talk show and make it sound exactly like a *Paris Review* interview, if you subtract the gibbering host. One feels he would be bored to hold the same opinion two nights in a row. These are his rules: It is a game, and Burgess is a game player. Just as Auden satisfies with his eternal Audenisms, Burgess could be interviewed nonstop for five years and continue to surprise.

Robert Graves takes this style to the end of the line; Graves is such a professional surpriser that only a conventional opinion from him could still shock us. It has been a unique privilege of our time to watch the building of Graves, from shell-shocked schoolboy in World War I to Mediterranean warlock, encanting at the Moon. As an expatriate in Majorca, Graves remains a bit of an Edwardian tease, as willful and unflaggingly facetious as a Sitwell; yet in another sense, he has grown more fully and richly than is given to most. His literary opinions are so quirky that they seem designed solely to start lengthy feuds in the London *Times;* yet in terms of his own art they are not quirky at all. As evaluations of other poets, one may find them arbitrary to the point of uselessness; but as definitions of himself and his task, they are as illuminating as his beloved Moon. Perhaps this is true whenever writers criticize other writers; from Tolstoy to Gore Vidal, they are simply telling us what they themselves plan to do next or defending what they've done last.

So understood, their crochets take on serious value. Writers make admirable critics (Vidal, since I've dragged him in from left field, is superb), but their subject is nearly always themselves, and how they reflect off others. "I wouldn't have done it like that" is their unspoken refrain; and what remains after they have chiseled away everyone else and every other possibility is a statue of themselves.

It is possible that the malice of writers has been overrated (by myself among others). Reading their ruminations on their craft, one sees why this writer could not possibly like that one, would indeed consider him a menace. Literature is a battleground of conflicting faiths, and nobler passions than envy are involved. Even those writers like Nabokov who are crabby by habit usually have a powerful aesthetic to back it up. (Nabokov's self-statue is chiseled so fine you can run your finger along the smirk.)

Concerning these craft ruminations: A beginner might alternately find them useful or fatal, depending on his own genius. Anne Sexton, for instance, was taught by Robert Lowell to make each line of verse perfect before going on to the next. Likewise, Anthony Burgess polishes as he goes and never looks back. I myself consider this practice deplorable, leading to fine sentence-by-sentence writing at the expense of form: but for writers like Sexton and Burgess, who have an innate sense of form, it seems to work. (When it doesn't, watch out.)

Hence, the value of a collection of discordant voices, each hawking its own dogmas. At the end, one wants to set up one's own stand. Where any one author might indeed be a menace, taken together they testify benignly to the richness of the enterprise. The Sexton interview, for instance, reminds one, so that you can almost feel it on your skin, of how the Spirit was blowing through Cambridge that year, for those who had the wit to use it. The confessional poetry she and Sylvia Plath learned from Lowell later turned in on itself like monoxide in a garage; yet at the time it had the scent of liberation. But the rambunctious George Seferis receives very different breezes in Greece. And Jorge Luis Borges, like a timeless satyr in a high-walled Roman garden, feels none at all.

It is not my aim to catalogue each interview and tap it on the head with my gavel but to indicate the range of meditation that each inspires. One could, as with a good novel, find a thousand other stories in the shadows, from the wistful reticences of Isak Dinesen to the desperate garrulity of John Steinbeck—so right when he's being funny and offhand, so wobbly and windy when he strains to be major (Nathaniel Benchley's introduction suggests a comedian trapped in a reputation). The interviews tell stories that even the watchful subjects may not have wanted told; but also, and really more valuably, they tell each subject's favorite story about him or herself.

The interviewers presumably prefer to remain faceless, and we'll leave them so. But it is worth noting how much this particular skill has refined itself since *The Paris Review* started (although these interviews are not necessarily the latest chronologically). It is not easy to play the straight man, with a touch of the D.A., to a famous writer; your own cunning must very nearly match his. And then at the end, you must be prepared to disappear altogether, leaving his answers standing alone on stage. Otherwise there is no art, only chat.

Having never attended one of these *corridas* myself, I cannot say whether the authors really talk as fluently and aptly as they appear to on the page. I'm sure some of them do, the inarticulate author being a romantic myth, like the deaf composer. But I fancy that for others, this is not so much how they talk as how they would like to talk: a further self-creation and self-concealment. Having been given the chance to revise their words and to erase the banalities of spontaneity, they are free to invent not only themselves but their way of presenting themselves: Stammers are ironed out, contradictions reconciled, mumbles turned into roars. A shy man like Dos Passos becomes airily confident; Conrad Aiken becomes young and John Berryman peaceful. This kind of magic is their stock in trade, and the rewritten interview gives them a rare chance to apply it to themselves—not in the rambling form of autobiography, which usually brings us yards of information that nobody asked for, but in the specific twentieth-century form of interrogation.

In a democracy, *we* ask the questions; *we* determine what is interesting. Within this cage of questions, the artist prowls, looks for exits, expresses himself somehow. The result (as with poets fettered by meter) is often better, or better for *us*, than their own mysterious wanderings would have been. That is what zoos are for. That is what art is for.

Most writer interviews are not art at all, but a sort of cultural packaging. The cages are too small, the questioner's powers too sweeping; what we want to know obliterates what the speaker wants to say. But in this case, where the subjects seem virtually to question themselves and to collaborate in their own limits, the zoo is at worst a low security one. And perhaps this amount of constraint enables them to show their plumage to better advantage. At any rate, several of the interviews that follow wander in and out of art (if I can use that impossible word one last time) and may even rank among their subjects' finer recent work, which is much more than I would have admitted in my *a priori* slumbers of a few years ago. Even the least ambitious of them constitute the finest in literary shop talk and exegesis. (No one should henceforth read Eudora Welty without consulting her carefully measured program notes.) And all sixteen of them are self-portraits of the artist of a kind scholars are lucky to piece together, much less satisfactorily, from diaries and letters. Speaking for my frivolous self, I would trade half of *Childe Harold* for such an interview with Byron and all of *Adam Bede* for the same with George Eliot. And if that is not precisely literature, it will do.

WILFRID SHEED

WRITERS AT WORK

Fourth Series

1. Isak Dinesen

Isak Dinesen was born Karen Dinesen in 1885 in Rungstedlund, Denmark, and spent her early years in the fashionable world of Copenhagen's upper class. In 1913 she became engaged to her Swedish cousin, Baron Bror von Blixen-Finecke, and they decided to emigrate to Africa and buy a farm. They were married in 1914 in Mombasa and moved onto a large plantation near Nairobi. The marriage was an unhappy one; they were separated after only a few years and divorced in 1921. Karen Blixen continued to live on the coffee plantation, which she developed and ran for seventeen years. When the coffee market collapsed in 1931, she was forced to leave Africa and return to her family home in Rungstedlund. There she dedicated herself to writing under the name of Isak Dinesen.

Seven Gothic Tales was published in England and America in 1934 and established her reputation. *Out of Africa,* about her years in Kenya, was published in 1937. Her later works include *Winter's Tales* (1942), *Last Tales* (1957), *Anecdotes of Destiny* (1958), *Shadows on the Grass* (1960), and *Ehrengard* (1963).

Isak Dinesen continued to live in Denmark for the rest of her life. Her increasing ill health has been attributed to a venereal disease, caught from her husband during the first year of their marriage, that was not properly treated. She spent long periods of time in the hospital, often too ill and weak to sit upright, dictating her later stories to her secretary. She died at the age of seventy-seven on September 7, 1962.

The road row Pisa.

Herman von Spiegelhausen, a
young poet of noble birth, was
travelling in Italy in the spring
of 1822. He was in a way
driving going from place to place
in search of peace of mind as
happiness which he was sr
far

One fine May eve he stopped
at a little inn on the road to
Pisa. - The air was clear as
glass as filled with sweet oan
as a golden damper light,
a lot of swallows were owing
about in it. While they made
his supper ready Herman
walked down the road alg which
a lot row of high poplars grew,

Isak Dinesen manuscript page

Isak Dinesen

It was, in a sense, typecasting, when a few years ago a film was planned that would have shown us Garbo playing the role of Isak Dinesen in a screen version of Out of Africa . . . *for the writer is, like the actress, a Mysterious Creature of the North. Isak Dinesen is really the Danish Baroness Karen Christentze Blixen-Finecke and is the daughter of Wilhelm Dinesen, author of a classic nineteenth-century work,* Boganis' Jagtbreve (A Hunter's—*or* Sportsman's—Letters). *Baroness Blixen has published under different names in various countries: usually Isak Dinesen, but also Tania Blixen and Karen Blixen. Old friends call her Tanne, Tanya, and Tania. Then there is a delightful novel she preferred not to acknowledge for a while, though any reader with half an eye could guess the baroness hiding behind the second pseudonym, Pierre Andrézel. Literary circles have buzzed with legends about her: She is really a man, he is really a woman, "Isak Dinesen" is really a brother-and-sister collaboration, "Isak Dinesen" came to*

3

America in the 1870s, she is really a Parisienne, he lives at El-
sinore, she stays mostly in London, she is a nun, he is very hospita-
ble and receives young writers, she is difficult to see and lives a
recluse, she writes in French; no, in English; no, in Danish; she
is really—and so the buzzing never stopped.

In 1934 the house of Haas and Smith (later absorbed by Ran-
dom House) brought out a book called Seven Gothic Tales *which*
Mr. Haas had accepted on first reading. It became a best-seller. A
favorite among writers and painters, the book was discussed from
first appearance as of some permanence.

Outside the canon of modern literature, like an oriole outside
a cage of moulting linnets, "Isak Dinesen" offers to her readers the
unending satisfaction of the tale told: "And then what happened?
. . . Well, then . . ." Her storyteller's, or ballad maker's, instinct,
coupled with an individual style of well-ornamented clarity, led
Hemingway, accepting the Nobel Prize, to protest it should have
gone to Dinesen.

SCENE ONE

Rome, Early Summer, 1956. *The first dialogue takes place in a*
sidewalk restaurant in the Piazza Navona, that long space, once
flooded, where mock naval battles raged. The twilight is darkening
the sky to an iris color; against it the obelisk that stands amidst
Bernini's figures seems pale and weightless. At a café table sit
Baroness Blixen, her secretary-traveling companion, Clara
Svendsen, and the Interviewer. The Baroness is like a personage
from one of her own tales. Slim, straight, chic, she is dressed in
black, with long black gloves and a black Parisian hat that comes
forward to shadow her remarkable eyes that are lighter in color at
the top than at the bottom. Her face is slender and distinguished;
around her mouth and eyes play the faint ghosts of smiles, chang-
ing constantly. Her voice is pleasing, being soft but with enough
force and timbre for one to hear at once that this is a lady with
opinions of both grave profundity and of most enchanting frivolity.

Her companion, Miss Svendsen, is a fresh-faced young person with a charming smile.

ISAK DINESEN: Interview? Oh, dear. . . . Well, yes, I suppose so . . . but not a list of questions or a third degree, I hope. . . . I was interviewed a short time ago. . . . Terrible. . . .

MISS SVENDSEN: Yes, there was a man who came for a documentary film. . . . It was like a catechism lesson. . . .

ISAK DINESEN: Couldn't we just talk together as we've been doing, you could write down what you like?

INTERVIEWER: Yes, then you could scratch out some things and scribble in others.

ISAK DINESEN: Yes. I ought not to undertake too much. I've been ill for over a year and in a nursing home. I really thought I should die. I planned to die, that is, I made preparations. I expected to.

MISS SVENDSEN: The doctor in Copenhagen told me: "Tania Blixen is very clever, but the cleverest thing she's ever done is to survive these two operations."

ISAK DINESEN: I even planned a last radio talk. . . . I have made a number of radio talks on all kinds of subjects, in Denmark. . . . They seem to enjoy me as a radio speaker there. . . . I planned a talk on how easy it was to die. . . . Not a morbid message, I don't mean that, but a message of, well, cheer . . . that it was a great and lovely experience to die. But I was too ill, you know, to get it done. Now, after being so long in the nursing home and so ill, I don't feel I do really belong to this life. I am hovering like a seagull. I feel that the world is happy and splendid and goes on but that I'm not part of it. I've come to Rome to try and get into the world again. Oh, look at the sky now!

INTERVIEWER: Do you know Rome well? How long since you've been here?

ISAK DINESEN: A few years ago, when I had an audience with the Pope. I first came in 1912 as a young girl, staying with my cousin and best friend, who was married to our Danish ambassa-

dor to Rome. We rode in the Borghese Gardens then, every day.
There were carriages with all the great beauties of the day in
them, and one stopped and chatted. It was delightful. Now look
at these motors and motor-bicycles and noise and rushing about.
It's what the young today want, though: Speed is the greatest
thing for them. But when I think of riding my horse—I always
had a horse when I was a girl—I feel that something very precious
is lost to them today. Children of my day lived differently. We
had little in the way of toys, even in great houses. Modern mechanical playthings, which furnish their own motion, had hardly
come into existence. We had simpler toys and had to animate
them. My love of marionettes springs from this, I think. I've tried
my hand at writing marionette plays. One might, of course, buy
a hobbyhorse, but we loved better a knotted stick personally
chosen in the woods, which our imagination could turn into
Bucephalus or Pegasus. Unlike children of today, who are content
from birth to be observers . . . we were creators. Young people
today are not acquainted with the elements or in touch with
them. Everything is mechanical and urban: Children are raised
up without knowing live fire, living water, the earth. Young people want to break with the past, they hate the past, they don't
want to even hear of it, and one can partly understand it. The near
past to them is nothing but a long history of wars, which to them
is without interest. It may be the end of something, of a kind of
civilization.

INTERVIEWER: But loathe leads to love: They may be led in a
circle back to a tradition. I should be frightened of indifference
more.

ISAK DINESEN: Perhaps. And I myself, you know, I should like
to love what they love. Now, I love jazz. I think it's the only new
thing in music in my lifetime. I don't prefer it to the old music,
but I enjoy it very much.

INTERVIEWER: Much of your work seems to belong to the last
century. For instance, *The Angelic Avengers.*

ISAK DINESEN *(laughing):* Oh, that's my illegitimate child!
During the German occupation of Denmark I thought I should

go mad with boredom and dullness. I wanted so to be amused, to amuse myself, and besides I was short of money, so I went to my publisher in Copenhagen and said, Look here, will you give me an advance on a novel and send me a stenographer to dictate it to? They said they would, and she appeared, and I started dictating. I had no idea at all of what the story would be about when I began. I added a little every day, improvising. It was very baffling to the poor stenographer.

MISS SVENDSEN: Yes, she was used to business letters, and when she'd type the story from her shorthand notes, she'd put numbers sometimes like "the 2 terrified girls" or "his 1 love."

ISAK DINESEN: I'd start one day by saying, "Then Mr. So-and-so entered the room," and the stenographer would cry out, "Oh dear, but he can't! He died yesterday in Chapter Seventeen." No, I prefer to keep *The Angelic Avengers* my secret.

INTERVIEWER: I loved it, and I remember it had excellent notices. Did many people guess that you had written it?

ISAK DINESEN: A few.

INTERVIEWER: And what about *Winter's Tales?* That came out in the midst of the war—how did you get the book to America?

ISAK DINESEN: I went to Stockholm—not in itself an easy thing to accomplish—and what was even more difficult took the manuscript with me. I went to the American embassy and asked them if they didn't have planes going to the United States every day, and if they couldn't take the manuscript, but they said they only carried strictly political or diplomatic papers, so I went to the British embassy and asked them, and they asked could I supply references in England, and I could (I had many friends in the Cabinet, among them Anthony Eden), so they cabled to check this then said yes they could, so started the manuscript on its way to America.

INTERVIEWER: I'm ashamed of the American embassy. They surely could have taken it.

ISAK DINESEN: Oh, don't be too hard on them. I owe a lot to my American public. Anyway, with the manuscript I sent a letter to my American publishers just telling them that everything was in their hands, and that I couldn't communicate with them at all, and I never knew anything of how *Winter's Tales* was received until after the war ended, when suddenly I received dozens of charming letters from American soldiers and sailors all over the world: The book had been put into *Armed Forces Editions*—little paper books to fit a soldier's pocket. I was very touched. They sent me two copies of it; I gave one to the King of Denmark and he was pleased to see that, after all, some voice had spoken from his silent country during that dark time.

INTERVIEWER: And you were saying about your American public?

ISAK DINESEN: Yes, I shall never forget that they took me in at once. When I came back from Africa in 1931, after living there since 1914, I had lost all the money I had when I married because the coffee plantation didn't pay, you know; I asked my brother to finance me for two years while I prepared *Seven Gothic Tales,* and I told him that at the end of two years I'd be on my own. When the manuscript was ready, I went to England, and one day at luncheon there was the publisher Huntington and I said, "Please, I have a manuscript and I wish you'd look at it." He said, "What is it?" and when I replied, "A book of short stories," he threw up his hands and cried, "No!" and I begged, "Won't you even look at it?" and he said, "A book of short stories by an unknown writer? No hope!" Then I sent it to America, and it was taken right away by Robert Haas, who published it, and the general public took it and liked it, and they have always been faithful. No, thank you, no more coffee. I'll have a cigarette.

INTERVIEWER: Publishers everywhere are bone-headed. It's the traditional lament of the author.

ISAK DINESEN: The amusing thing is that after the book was published in America, Huntington wrote to Robert Haas praising it and begging for the address of the author, saying he must have the book for England. He had met me as Baroness Blixen, while Mr. Haas and I had never seen one another. Huntington never connected me with Isak Dinesen. Later he did publish the book in England.

INTERVIEWER: That's delightful; it's like something from one of the tales.

ISAK DINESEN: How lovely to sit here in the open, but we must be going, I think. Shall we continue our discussion on Sunday? I should like to see the Etruscan things at the Villa Giulia: We might chat a little then. Oh, look at the moon!

INTERVIEWER: Splendid. I'll find a taxi.

SCENE TWO

Rainy, warm Sunday noon. The Etruscan Collection in the Villa Giulia is not too crowded because of the weather. The Baroness Blixen is now attired in a suit of reddish-brown wool and a conical ochre-colored straw hat that again shadows her extraordinary eyes. As she strolls through the newly arranged Etruscan figures, pottery, and jewelry, she seems as remote as they from the ordinary gallery-goers who are pattering through. She walks slowly, very erect, stopping to gaze lingeringly at those details that please her.

ISAK DINESEN: How could they get that blue, do you suppose? Powdered lazuli? Look at that pig! In the North we give a great mythological importance to the pig. He's a kind of minion of the sun. I suppose because his sweet fat helps to keep us warm in the darkest and coldest time. Very intelligent animal. . . . I love all animals. I have a huge dog in Denmark, an Alsatian; he's enormous. I take him walking. If I survive him, I think I shall get a very small dog—a pug. Though I wonder if it's possible to get a pug now. They used to be very fashionable. Look at the lions on that sarcophagus. How could the Etruscans have known the lion? In Africa it was the animal that I loved the most.

INTERVIEWER: You must have known Africa at its best. What made you decide to go?

ISAK DINESEN: When I was a young girl, it was very far from my thoughts to go to Africa, nor did I dream then that an African farm should be the place in which I should be perfectly happy. That goes to prove that God has a greater and finer power of imagination than we have. But at the time when I was engaged to be married to my cousin Bror Blixen, an uncle of ours went out to Africa big-game hunting and came back all filled with praise of the country. Theodore Roosevelt had been hunting there then, too; East Africa was in the news. So Bror and I made up our minds to try our luck there, and our relations on both sides financed us in buying the farm, which was in the highlands of Kenya, not far from Nairobi. The first day I arrived there, I loved the country and felt at home, even among unfamiliar flowers, trees, and animals, and changing clouds over the Ngong hills, unlike any clouds I had ever known. East Africa then was really a paradise, what the Red Indians called "happy hunting-grounds." I was very keen on shooting in my young days, but my great interest all through my many years in Africa was the African natives of all tribes, in particular the Somali and the Masai. They were beautiful, noble, fearless, and wise people. Life was not easy running a coffee plantation. Ten thousand acres of farmland, and locusts and drought . . . and too late we realized that the table land where we were located was really too high for raising coffee successfully. Life out there was, I believe, rather like eighteenth-century England: one might often be hard up for cash, but life was still rich in many ways, with the lovely landscape, dozens of horses and dogs, and a multitude of servants.

INTERVIEWER: I suppose that you began to write seriously there?

ISAK DINESEN: No, I really began writing before I went to Africa, but I never once wanted to be a writer. I published a few short stories in literary reviews in Denmark when I was twenty years old, and the reviews encouraged me, but I didn't go on— I don't know, I think I had an intuitive fear of being trapped. Also, when I was quite young, for a while I studied painting at the Danish Royal Academy; then I went to Paris in 1910 to study with Simon and Menard, but *(she chuckles)* . . . but I did little work. The impact of Paris was too great; I felt it was more

important to go about and see pictures, to see Paris, in fact. I
painted a little in Africa, portraits of the natives mostly, but every
time I'd get to work, someone would come up and say an ox has
died or something, and I'd have to go out in the fields. Later,
when I knew in my heart I should have to sell the farm and go
back to Denmark, I did begin to write. To put my mind to other
things I began to write tales. Two of the *Gothic Tales* were
written there. But earlier, I learned how to tell tales. For, you see,
I had the perfect audience. White people can no longer listen to
a tale recited. They fidget or become drowsy. But the natives have
an ear still. I told stories constantly to them, all kinds. And all
kinds of nonsense. I'd say, "Once there was a man who had an
elephant with two heads" . . . and at once they were eager to hear
more. "Oh? Yes, but Mem-Sahib, how did he find it, and how did
he manage to feed it?" or whatever. They loved such invention.
I delighted my people there by speaking in rhyme for them; they
have no rhyme, you know, had never discovered it. I'd say things
like "Wakamba na kula mamba" ("The Wakamba tribe eats
snakes"), which in prose would have infuriated them, but which
amused them mightily in rhyme. Afterwards they'd say, "Please,
Mem-Sahib, talk like rain," so then I knew they had liked it, for
rain was very precious to us there. Oh, here's Miss Svendsen.
She's Catholic, so she went off today to hear a special cardinal.
Now we'll go buy some post cards. Hope there is one of the lions.

MISS SVENDSEN: Good morning.

ISAK DINESEN: Clara, you must see the delightful lions; then
we'll get some post cards and go for lunch.

*Post cards are found, a taxi is summoned, umbrellas opened, the
party runs for taxi, drives off through the rainy Borghese Gardens.*

SCENE THREE

*The Casino Valadier is a fashionable restaurant in the Gardens,
just above the Piazza del Popolo, and commands a fine view of
Rome. After a brief glimpse of the rain-grayed city from the flooded
terrace, the party goes into a brocaded room, with considerately*

shaded girandoles, brightly colored carpets, and pictures.

ISAK DINESEN: I'll sit here so I can see everything. *(Lights cigarette)*

INTERVIEWER: Pleasant place, isn't it?

ISAK DINESEN: Yes, very pleasant, and I recognize it. I was here in 1912. Every now and again here in Rome I recognize very vividly a place I've visited then. *(Pause)* Oh, I shall go mad!

INTERVIEWER *(startled):* What is it?

ISAK DINESEN: Look how crooked that picture is! *(Indicates blackened portrait across room)*

INTERVIEWER: I'll straighten it. *(Goes to it)*

ISAK DINESEN: No, more to the right.

INTERVIEWER: Like this?

ISAK DINESEN: That's better. *(Two solemn gentlemen at table beneath portrait indicate bewilderment.)*

MISS SVENDSEN: It's like that at home. So much traffic passes, and I have always to straighten the pictures.

ISAK DINESEN: I live on the North Sea, halfway between Copenhagen and Elsinore.

INTERVIEWER: Perhaps halfway between Shiraz and Atlantis?

ISAK DINESEN: . . . Halfway between that island in *The Tempest* and wherever I am.

(Waiter takes order; luncheon is served.)

ISAK DINESEN: I'll have a cigarette now. Do you mind if we just stay here for a while? I hate to change once I'm installed in a décor I like. People are always telling me to hurry up or come on and do this or do that. Once when I was sailing around the Cape of Good Hope and there were albatrosses, people kept saying, "Why do you stay on deck? Come on in." They said, "It's time for lunch," and I said, "Damn lunch." I said, "I can eat lunch any day, but I shan't see albatrosses again." Such wingspread!

INTERVIEWER: Tell me about your father.

ISAK DINESEN: He was in the French army, as was my grandfather. After the Franco-Prussian War, he went to America and lived with the Plains Indians in the great middle part of your country. He built himself a little hut and named it after a place

in Denmark where he had been very happy as a young man—
Frydenlund ("Happy Grove"). He hunted animals for their skins
and became a fur trader. He sold his skins mostly to the Indians,
then used his profits to buy them gifts. A little community grew
up around him, and now Frydenlund is, I believe, the name of
a locality in the state of Wisconsin. When he returned to Denmark, he wrote his books. So you see, it was natural for me, his
daughter, to go off to Africa and live with the natives and after
return home to write about it. He also, incidentally, wrote a
volume of his war experiences called *Paris Under the Commune.*

INTERVIEWER: And how is it that you write in English?

ISAK DINESEN: It was quite natural to do so. I was partly
schooled in England after being taught always by governesses at
home. Because of that, I lack knowledge of plain facts which are
common coinage for others. But those governesses were ambitious: They did teach languages, and one of them put me to
translating *The Lady of the Lake* into Danish. Then, in Africa,
I had been seeing only English people, really. I had spoken English or Swahili for twenty years. And I read the English poets and
English novelists. I prefer the older writers, but I remember when
I first read Huxley's *Chrome Yellow*, it was like biting into an
unknown and refreshing fruit.

INTERVIEWER: Most of your tales are laid in the last century,
aren't they? You never write about modern times.

ISAK DINESEN: I do, if you consider that the time of our grand-
parents, that just-out-of-reach time, is so much a part of *us.* We
absorb so much without being aware. Also, I write about characters who together *are* the tale. I begin, you see, with a flavor of
the tale. Then I find the characters, and they take over. They
make the design, I simply permit them their liberty. Now, in
modern life and in modern fiction there is a kind of atmosphere
and above all an interior movement—inside the characters—
which is something else again. I feel that in life and in art people
have drawn a little apart in this century. Solitude is now the
universal theme. But I write about characters within a design,
how they act upon one another. Relation with others is important

to me, you see, friendship is precious to me, and I have been
blessed with heroic friendships. But time in my tales is flexible.
I may begin in the eighteenth century and come right up to
World War I. Those times have been sorted out, they are clearly
visible. Besides, so many novels that we think are contemporary
in subject with their date of publication—think of Dickens or
Faulkner or Tolstoy or Turgenev—are really set in an earlier
period, a generation or so back. The present is always unsettled,
no one has had time to contemplate it in tranquillity . . . I was
a painter before I was a writer . . . and a painter never wants the
subject right under his nose; he wants to stand back and study a
landscape with half-closed eyes.

INTERVIEWER: Have you written poetry?

ISAK DINESEN: I did as a young girl.

INTERVIEWER: What is your favorite fruit?

ISAK DINESEN: Strawberries.

INTERVIEWER: Do you like monkeys?

ISAK DINESEN: Yes, I love them in art: in pictures, in stories, in
porcelain, but not in life, they somehow look so sad. They make
me nervous. I like lions and gazelles. . . . Do you think I look like
a monkey?

*(The baroness refers to an earlier conversation where someone
had suggested that if the tale "The Monkey" were ever filmed, she
should play the character of the Chanoiness who turns into a
monkey.)*

INTERVIEWER: Of course. But you must understand that there
are many kinds of monkeys.

(The Interviewer has copied out a passage from Ivan Sanderson's
The Monkey Kingdom *for the baroness's delectation and now
reads it.)*

INTERVIEWER: "The definition of 'monkey' has not, however,
been satisfactorily resolved. This apparently simple question,
moreover, requires careful examination before we may proceed in
our story, for, although we are not solely or even primarily interested in mere monkeys, we cannot, without its resolution, attempt

the greater galaxy of life-forms to which they belong."

ISAK DINESEN *(laughs delightedly):* But no tale can proceed without examining apparently simple questions. And no tail, either.

SCENE FOUR

Now we are on the parapets of the central tower of the Castle of Sermonetta, perched on a hill amidst a clustering town, about an hour and a half south of Rome. We have crossed a moated drawbridge, climbed a rickety ladder-stair. We have seen remains of fourteenth-century frescoes, and in the tower stronghold seen scrawled phrases and drawings on the wall, fresh as new, from when Napoleonic soldiers were incarcerated here. Now the party comes out, shading their eyes. Below, the Pontine plain stretches green and gold to the sea, bathed in bright afternoon sunlight. We can see tiny figures miles below working amidst the bean fields and the peach orchards.

INTERVIEWER: I think it is curious that practically no critic nor reviewer in either America or England has pointed out the great comic element in your works. I hope we might speak a little of the comic spirit in your tales.

ISAK DINESEN: Oh, I'm glad you mentioned that! People are always asking me what is the significance of this or that in the tales —"What does this symbolize? What does that stand for?" And I always have a difficult time making them believe that I intend everything as it's stated. It would be terrible if the explanation of the work were outside the work itself. And I do often intend a comic sense, I love a joke, I love the humorous. The name "Isak" means "laughter." I often think that what we most need now is a great humorist.

INTERVIEWER: What humorists in the English language please you?

ISAK DINESEN: Well, Mark Twain, for example. But then all the writers I admire usually have a vein of comic spirit.

Writers of tales always do, at least.

INTERVIEWER: Who are writers of tales that appeal to you, or with whom you feel a kinship?

ISAK DINESEN: E. T. A. Hoffman, Hans Andersen, Barbey D'Aurevilly, La Motte Fouqué, Chamisso, Turgenev, Hemingway, Maupassant, Stendhal, Chekhov, Conrad, Voltaire . . .

MISS SVENDSEN: Don't forget Melville! She calls me Babu after the character in *Benito Cereno*, when she doesn't refer to me as Sancho Panza.

INTERVIEWER: Heavens, you've read them all!

ISAK DINESEN: I am really three thousand years old and have dined with Socrates.

INTERVIEWER: Pardon?

ISAK DINESEN *(laughing and lighting a cigarette)*: Because I was never told what I must read or what I mustn't read. I did read everything that fell into my hands. I discovered Shakespeare very early in life, and now I feel that life would be nothing without him. One of my new stories is about a company of actors playing *The Tempest*, incidentally. I love some of the Victorian novelists no one reads anymore: Walter Scott, for instance. Oh, and I like Melville very much, and the *Odyssey*, the Norse Sagas—Have you read the Norse Sagas? I love Racine, too.

INTERVIEWER: I remember your observation on the Norse mythology in one of the *Winter's Tales.* * It's very interesting to me, incidentally, how you have chosen the tale for your form.

ISAK DINESEN: It came naturally to me. My literary friends at home tell me that the heart of my work is not in the idea but in the line of the tale. Something you can tell, like one can TELL

---

* "And I have wondered, while I read," says the young nobleman in "Sorrow-Acre," "that we have not till now understood how much our Nordic mythology in moral greatness surpasses that of Greece and Rome. If it had not been for the physical beauty of the ancient gods, which has come down to us in marble, no modern mind could hold them worthy of worship. They were mean, capricious and treacherous. The gods of our Danish forefathers are as much more divine than they as the Druid is nobler than the Augur."

Ali Baba and the Forty Thieves but one could not TELL *Anna Karenina.*

INTERVIEWER: But there are some who find your tales "artificial" . . .

ISAK DINESEN *(smiling):* Artificial? Of course, they are artificial. They were meant to be, for such is the essence of the tale-telling art. And I felt I acknowledged that . . . or rather, pointed it out . . . by calling my first tales "Gothic." . . . When I used the word Gothic, I didn't mean the real Gothic, but the imitation of the Gothic, the Romantic age of Byron, the age of Horace Walpole, who built Strawberry Hill, the age of the Gothic Revival . . . you know Walpole's *Castle of Otranto,* of course?

INTERVIEWER: Yes, indeed. In a tale, the plot is all important, isn't it?

ISAK DINESEN: Yes, it is. I start with a tingle, a kind of feeling of the story I will write. Then come the characters, and they take over, they make the story. But all this ends by being a plot. For other writers, that seems an unnatural thing. But a proper tale has a shape and an outline. In a painting the frame is important. Where does the picture end? What details should one include? Or omit! Where does the line go that cuts off the picture? People always ask me, they say, "In 'The Deluge at Norderney,' were those characters drowned or saved at the end?" (You remember they are trapped in a loft during a flood and spend the night recounting their stories while awaiting rescue.) Well, what can I reply? How can I tell them? That's outside the story. I really don't know!

INTERVIEWER: Do you rewrite your tales very much?

ISAK DINESEN: Oh, I do, I do. It's hellish. Over and over again. Then when I think I'm finished, and Clara copies them out to send to the publishers, I look over them, and have a fit, and rewrite again.

MISS SVENDSEN: In one tale there was a lesser character called "Mariana the Rat" who ran an inn called The Lousing-Comb. The publishers mentioned her in the text for the book jacket, but by the time they had the final proofs, she had been removed from the tale. It must have caused mystification.

INTERVIEWER: Many people are mystified by the tale "The Monkey."

ISAK DINESEN: Yes, I grow weary from the questions people ask me about that particular tale. But that is a fantastic story; it should be interpreted that way. The principle is this: Let the monkey resolve the mess when the plot has got too complicated for the human characters. But people say, "What does it mean?" *That's* what it means. . . . *(She pauses, with a little laugh.)* It would be a bad thing if I could explain the tale better than what I have already said in the tale. As I never tire of pointing out, the story should be *all*.

INTERVIEWER: Everyone would be interested to know just how one of your tales takes shape. Especially those with tales within the tale. Take "The Deluge at Norderney," for instance . . . it seems so inevitable and ordered, but if one studies it, the design is amazing . . . How did . . . ?

ISAK DINESEN *(interrupting, smiling mischievously):* Read it, read it, and you'll see how it's written!

For Epilogue here, let's append a passage from the Baroness Blixen's Albondocani, *a long series of connected tales still unfinished at the time of the author's death in 1962. This excerpt is from* "The Blank Page," *published in* Last Tales *(1957). An old woman who earns her living by storytelling is speaking:*

"With my grandmother," she said, "I went through a hard school. 'Be loyal to the story,' the old hag would say to me, 'Be eternally and unswervingly loyal to the story.' 'Why must I be that, Grandmother,' I asked her. 'Am I to furnish you with reasons, baggage?' she cried. 'And you mean to be a story-teller! Why, you are to become a story-teller, and I shall give you the reasons! Hear then: Where the story-teller is loyal, eternally and unswervingly loyal to the story, there, in the end, silence will speak. Where the story has been betrayed, silence is but emptiness. But we, the faithful, when we have spoken our last word, will hear the voice of silence. Whether a small snotty lass understands it or not.'

"Who then," she continues, "tells a finer tale than any of us? Silence does. And where does one read a deeper tale than upon the most perfectly printed page of the most precious book? Upon the blank page. When a royal, and gallant pen, in the moment of its highest inspiration, has written down its tale with the rarest ink of all—where, then, may one read a still deeper, sweeter, merrier, and more cruel tale than that? Upon the blank page."

EUGENE WALTER

2. Conrad Aiken

Born in Savannah, Georgia, on August 5, 1889, Conrad Aiken was taken to New Bedford, Massachusetts, in 1900 to be brought up by his great-great-aunt after a violent disagreement between his parents ended with his father killing his mother and then himself. After attending Harvard, where he was a member and later president of the *Harvard Advocate*, he lived in England for many years before returning to Brewster, Massachusetts, to make his permanent home.

His first collections of poems were published in 1914 and 1916. Among his early volumes of verse are *The Jig of Forslin: A Symphony* (1916), *Nocturne of Remembered Spring* (1917), *The Charnel Rose* (1918), and *Senlin: A Biography and Other Poems* (1918). His more important volumes include *Preludes for Memnon* (1931); *The Kid* (1947); *Skylight One* (1949); *Collected Poems* (1953), for which he won the 1954 National Book Award; *Selected Poems* (1961); and *Preludes* (1966). He also wrote five novels, including the highly acclaimed *Great Circle* (1933); many short stories, which were gathered together in *Bring! Bring! and Other Stories* (1925), *Costumes by Eros* (1928), *Among the Lost People* (1934), and *Collected Short Stories* (1960); an experimental autobiography, *Ushant: An Essay* (1952); and a great deal of literary criticism, much of which was written at the suggestion of Marianne Moore when she was editor of *The Dial*. Aiken collected the best of his criticism in *A Reviewer's ABC* (1958).

From 1950 to 1952 he held the chair of poetry at the Library of Congress. Among his other honors were the Pulitzer Prize for the best volume of verse in 1929; the Bollingen Prize (1956); a Gold Medal for poetry from the National Institute of Arts and Letters (1958); the Huntington Hartford Foundation Award in Literature (1961); the Brandeis medal for poetry (1967); and membership in the American Academy of Arts and Letters. In 1969 he won the National Medal of Literature.

He lived in his Brewster home until his death on August 17, 1973.

by these translated
and made an ecstasy.
Thus in our transient and translunar love
translate the love to you and me.
Now that is gone,
and love undone.

                    He   *against*   *IV*

curve
    I invoke,then,a particular day.The clock strikes one.
    Now the first snowflake floats upon the stone
    and perishes in the same. Our eyes are filled
    with immortal light,clear recognition,clear knowledge
    of all that's past and to come:
    yes,those histories and prophecies you speak of,the secret
    tangents of sense thrust against sense
    but only to illumine: the I and You.
    opposed in a compelled counterpoint
    which willy nilly joins them. Of all this
    what shall we remember? Simply,the first snowflake falling:
    while,from the distance of a breath,for the first time,
    I observe the pale and delicate shape of a closed eyelid
    closed on the vulnerable secret of the flower   *Secret*
and shall   (yourself the flower) ——— *Secret*
we say.   and yet inviolable as death.

                    She

I saw your head   Yes. Remember that.
building against the   And I too will remember something.
(now unbroken   When my eyes opened,your hand was holding the umbrella
And then [green] and the green transparent shadow changed your face.
translucent light These shall be time and place.
shifted across
your submarine   He
face
                And now,since there's no help,without a kiss we'll part.

                    She

Each with a separate but remembering heart.

Early draft of the concluding lines of "Love's Grammarians"

Karl Bissinger

Conrad Aiken

The interview took place in two sessions of about an hour each in September 1963, at Mr. Aiken's house in Brewster, Massachusetts. The house, called Forty-one Doors, dates largely from the eighteenth century; a typical old Cape Cod farmhouse, the rooms are small but many, opening in all directions off what must originally have been the most important room, the kitchen. The house is far enough from the center of town to be reasonably quiet even at the height of the summer, and it is close enough to the North Cape shore for easy trips to watch the gulls along the edges of relatively unspoiled inlets.

Mr. Aiken dresses typically in a tweed sports coat, a wool or denim shirt, and a heavy wool tie. A fringe of sparse white hair gives him a curiously friarly appearance, belied by his irreverence and love of bawdy puns.

He answered the questions about his own work seriously and carefully but did not appear to enjoy them; not that he seemed to find them too pressing or impertinent, rather as if answering them was simply hard work. He enjoyed far more telling anecdotes about himself and his friends and chuckled frequently in recalling these stories.

By the end of each hour Mr. Aiken, who had been seriously ill the previous winter, was visibly tired; but once the tape recorder was stilled and the martinis mixed and poured into silver cups—old sculling or tennis trophies retrieved from some pawn or antique shop—he quickly revived. He was glad to be interviewed, but more glad still when it was over.

Later, shortly before the interview went to press, a dozen or so follow-up questions were sent to him at the Cape; the answers to these are spliced into the original interview. "You may find you will need to do a bit of dovetailing here and there," he wrote; "the old mens isn't quite, may never be, as sana *as before, if indeed it ever was." But there was no real problem; his mind and memory remain clear and precise despite the physical frailties that age has brought.*

INTERVIEWER: In *Ushant* you say that you decided to be a poet when you were very young—about six years old, I think.

AIKEN: Later than that. I think it was around nine.

INTERVIEWER: I was wondering how this resolve to be a poet grew and strengthened?

AIKEN: Well, I think *Ushant* describes it pretty well, with that epigraph from *Tom Brown's School Days:* "I'm the poet of White Horse Vale, Sir, with Liberal notions under my cap." For some reason those lines stuck in my head, and I've never forgotten them. This image became something I *had* to be.

INTERVIEWER: While you were at Harvard, were you constantly aware that you were going to be a poet; training yourself in most everything you studied and did?

AIKEN: Yes. I compelled myself all through to write an exercise in verse, in a different form, every day of the year. I turned out my page everyday, of some sort—I mean I didn't give a damn about the meaning, I just wanted to master the form—all the way from free verse, Walt Whitman, to the most elaborate of villanelles and ballad forms. Very good training. I've always told everybody who has ever come to me that I thought that was the first thing to do. And to study all the vowel effects and all the consonant effects and the variation in vowel sounds. For example, I gave Malcolm Lowry an exercise to do at Cuernavaca, of writing ten lines of blank verse with the caesura changing one step in each line. Going forward, you see, and then reversing on itself.

INTERVIEWER: How did Lowry take to these exercises?

AIKEN: Superbly. I still have a group of them sent to me at his rented house in Cuernavaca, sent to me by hand from the bar with a request for money, and in the form of a letter—and unfortunately not used in his collected letters; very fine, and very funny. As an example of his attention to vowel sounds, one line still haunts me: "Airplane or aeroplane, or just plain plane." Couldn't be better.

INTERVIEWER: What early readings were important to you? I gather that Poe was.

AIKEN: Oh, Poe, yes. I was reading Poe when I was in Savannah, when I was ten, and scaring myself to death. Scaring my brothers and sisters to death, too. So I was already soaked in him, especially the stories.

INTERVIEWER: I see you listed occasionally as a Southern writer. Does this make any sense to you?

AIKEN: Not at all. I'm not in the least Southern; I'm entirely New England. Of course, the Savannah *ambiente* made a profound impression on me. It was a beautiful city and so wholly different from New England that going from South to North every year, as we did in the summers, provided an extraordinary counterpoint of experience, of sensuous adventure. The change was so violent, from Savannah to New Bedford or Savannah to Cambridge, that it was extraordinarily useful. But no, I never was connected with any of the Southern writers.

INTERVIEWER: In what way was the change from Savannah to New England "useful" to you?

AIKEN: Shock treatment, I suppose: the milieu so wholly different, and the social customs, and the mere *transplantation;* as well as having to change one's accent twice a year—all this quite apart from the astonishing change of landscape. From swamps and Spanish moss to New England *rocks*.

INTERVIEWER: What else at Harvard was important to your development as a poet, besides the daily practice you described?

AIKEN: I'm afraid I wasn't much of a student, but my casual reading was enormous. I did have some admirable courses, especially two years of English 5 with Dean Briggs, who was a great teacher, I think, and that was the best composition course I ever had anywhere.

INTERVIEWER: How did Briggs go about teaching writing?

AIKEN: He simply let us write, more or less, what we wanted to. Then discussion (after his reading aloud of a chosen specimen) and his own marvelous comments: He had genius, and emanated it. Then, at the end of class, we had ten minutes in which to write a short critique of the piece that had been read. This was so helpful to *me* that I took the course for two years.

INTERVIEWER: Was Copeland still teaching then? What did you think of him?

AIKEN: Brilliant reader, not a profound teacher. Vain. At the end of the year he asked me, "Aiken, do you think this course has benefited you?" I was taken aback and replied, "Well, it has made me write often." He replied, "Aiken, you're a very *dry* young man."

INTERVIEWER: Eliot mentioned in an interview with *The Paris Review* that while he was reading French poetry at Harvard, you were reading Italian and Spanish poets.

AIKEN: Yes, I had begun to read Spanish poetry, come to think of it, and Italian, that's true. I'd begun reading Leopardi in 1911, and the French poets I didn't get around to until senior year at Harvard when I discovered Symond's *Symbolist Poets* and swallowed that in one gulp.

INTERVIEWER: None of these foreign readings had anything like the same effect on your work that Eliot's reading of the French symbolists had on his, did they?

AIKEN: I don't think so.

INTERVIEWER: You kept rather to the English Romantic tradition—

AIKEN: Yes, and Whitman had a profound influence on me. That was during my sophomore year when I came down with a bad attack of Whitmanitis. But he did me a lot of good, and I think the influence is discoverable.

INTERVIEWER: What was the good he did? Mainly enabling you to get away from Victorian forms?

AIKEN: General loosening up, yes. He was useful to me in the perfection of form, as a sort of compromise between the strict and the free.

INTERVIEWER: Was William James still at Harvard when you were there?

AIKEN: No, he retired the year I got there, or the year before, but was still around, and you felt his presence very much. But Santayana was the real excitement for me at Harvard, especially "Three Philosophical Poets," which he was inventing that year as he went along—so we were getting the thing right off the fire.

INTERVIEWER: Santayana's insistence that philosophical content—the "vision" of philosophy—is one of the things that can give the greatest effect to poetry—this, I gather, impressed you quite highly at the time?

AIKEN: Oh, much. Tremendously. It really fixed my view of what poetry should ultimately be.

INTERVIEWER: That it was greatest if it thought most deeply?

AIKEN: That it really had to begin by *understanding*, or trying to understand.

INTERVIEWER: Did you know Eliot quite well at Harvard?

AIKEN: Eliot and I must have met at the end of my freshman year, when I was elected to the *Harvard Advocate*. We saw a great deal of each other, in spite of the fact that we were a year apart, and remained very close.

INTERVIEWER: Was your conversation largely about poetry, or did you share other interests and activities?

AIKEN: Of course, at the beginning, on the *Advocate*, we talked chiefly about poetry, or literature in general. But as the friendship,

or kinship developed—for in a way I became his younger brother
—it widened to take in everything. And we met on very, very
many quite frivolous occasions. Sports, comics, everything. We
developed a shorthand language of our own which we fell into for
the rest of our lives whenever we met, no holds barred—all a
matter of past reference, a common language, but basically *affec-
tion,* along with humor, and appreciation of each other's minds,
and of Krazy Kat. Faced with England, and the New World, and
Freud and all, we always managed to *relax,* and go back to the
kidding, and bad punning, and drinking, to the end. It really was
marvelous.

INTERVIEWER: Did you see Eliot much after the war brought
you back to the States?

AIKEN: Only when he paid his infrequent visits here, when we
invariably met to get drunk together. There was a splendid occasion when he and I and our wives dined at "The Greeks' " after
he'd received a silver bowl from the Signet Society; he was wearing a cowboy hat, and we all got plastered. We went on to the
Red Lion Grill, after many drinks at the Silver Dollar Bar, the two
toughest and *queerest* joints in Boston. He couldn't walk, for his
ankles were crossed, so Valerie *lifted* him into the taxi.

INTERVIEWER: Did Eliot's early work—such as "Prufrock"—
help you in developing your own style?

AIKEN: Oh, "Prufrock" had a tremendous influence on me.
You can see it all through the verse symphonies.

INTERVIEWER: The use of the interior monologue in particular?

AIKEN: I don't know whether that came from him. In fact, the
whole complex of our relationship is a very subtle thing. I think
there was a lot of interchange. For example, I did for English 5
in my extra year at Harvard—the fall of 1911—a poem called
"The Clerk's Journal," which was about the life of a little stool-
sitting clerk in a bank and his mundane affairs, his little love affair,
his worry about clothes . . . and telephone wires in the moonlight.
This was three years before "Prufrock."

INTERVIEWER: Do you still have this poem?

AIKEN: Yes, I've still got it, with Briggs' comment on the back of it. This was an anticipation. In other words, I was thinking in this direction before "Prufrock," and I have no doubt that Tom saw this poem, "The Clerk's Journal." The juices went both ways.

INTERVIEWER: There's a lot of what we now think of as *"The Waste Land* attitude" in your verse symphonies, isn't there? In *Forslin* and *The House of Dust,* which came well before *The Waste Land?*

AIKEN: Yes, there's a lot in *The Waste Land* that owes something, I think, to *The House of Dust* and *Forslin.*

INTERVIEWER: Did you ever see *The Waste Land* in manuscript?

AIKEN: No, I never did. Not as a whole. But I had seen whole sections which prior to *The Waste Land* existed as separate small poems, I believe not then intended for any other purpose, which were later conglomerated into *The Waste Land.*

INTERVIEWER: How did Pound come across "Prufrock"? Did you take it to him, or did Eliot do that after he came to England himself?

AIKEN: In 1914 I persuaded Tom to let me take "Prufrock" to England; he wasn't at all sure of it. I tried it everywhere—not even Harold Monro of the famous Poetry Bookshop could see it, thought it crazy; many years later he said it was the Kubla Khan of the twentieth century. Then I met Pound, showed it to him, and he was at once bowled over. He sent it to *Poetry.* So, when Tom had to retreat from Germany, when the war started, one of his first moves was to go and see Ezra.

Of course, Tom insisted all his life that I had made him cut a whole page or more out of "Prufrock." I don't remember this, but he claimed it was so—that there was a page or something like that that I thought didn't belong, so he took it out. It may be true, or he may have been confusing it with the major operation that Ezra performed on *The Waste Land.* I'm sorry about it, if so, because there's thirty lines lost!

INTERVIEWER: You knew Maxwell Bodenheim, didn't you? *(A new paperback copy of Bodenheim's* My Life and Loves in Greenwich Village *was on the coffee table.)*

AIKEN: Oh, very well. He was a great friend of mine. He used to catch me now and then, touring the country. I don't know how he managed it, but periodically he'd show up in Boston on his way to or from Chicago or New York. He was quite a fascinating creature. He really was a *dedicated* bum and poet.

INTERVIEWER: Did he have an effect on other poets that we've lost sight of?

AIKEN: Yes, I think so. He was a fascinating talker, in spite of the stammer, and he knew everybody. He was a great friend of Bill Williams. You must have heard the story of his broken arm? He called up Williams at Rutherford and said, "I've broken my arm. Can I come and stay with you till it heals?" Bill said, "Certainly." About a month or two went by, and Max did nothing about having the cast examined or changed, so finally Bill insisted on looking at it and discovered that there had never been any broken arm.

INTERVIEWER: Did you see a good bit of Pound in the early days?

AIKEN: I saw a lot of him for about six weeks in 1914 in London. I had a letter of introduction to him from Herman Hagedorn, who, it turned out, really didn't know Pound at all. But Pound was extraordinarily kind to me and really took pains to take me around and introduce me to people and to publishers, not always with luck.

INTERVIEWER: Was he any help to you in your own work?

AIKEN: Not a bit. We agreed to disagree about that right off, and I felt right off, too, that he was not for me, that he would become the old man of the sea and be on my shoulders in no time —which is exactly the experience that Williams had with him. I remember Williams describing how when he walked with Pound in London, Pound was always one step ahead. This gradually annoyed Williams to death, so he made a point of being right beside Pound. Very typical that—tells a lot, I think.

INTERVIEWER: How about John Gould Fletcher? You worked with him, were very close to him, in Boston and Cambridge, weren't you?

AIKEN: Yes, just after the war began, about 1915, he came back to Boston, and we lived next door to each other for three years. I saw a great deal of him, and we swapped notes and what-not; and agreed to disagree about many things because he was more involved in imagism or "Amy" gism than I proposed to be. But I think he had great talent which didn't quite come off somehow.

INTERVIEWER: He's practically unread now.

AIKEN: I know. He wrote me a tragic letter in 1949, I think it was, saying, "You know, Aiken, we are forgotten. We might as well face it." This was only a year or two before he jumped into the lake.

INTERVIEWER: Did Fletcher's organization of material, the sort of thing he was experimenting with in the color symphonies, bear any relation to the work you were doing with music in your verse symphonies?

AIKEN: I don't know. I don't think we influenced each other, but we were interested in the same sort of thing, in a very different way, of course. He was going for this abstract color business and, I think, with more French influence behind him than I had.

INTERVIEWER: When did you first meet Malcolm Lowry?

AIKEN: In 1929. He came to Cambridge to work with me one summer on *Ultramarine*.

INTERVIEWER: How old was he then?

AIKEN: Barely nineteen, I think. He went back to matriculate at Cambridge that autumn.

INTERVIEWER: Later you moved back to England yourself?

AIKEN: Yes, the next year. Then it was that his father turned him over to me *in loco parentis*.

INTERVIEWER: To keep him out of trouble or to teach him poetry?

AIKEN: To take care of him and to work with him. So he spent all his holidays with us in Rye or went with us if we went abroad. During his years at Cambridge, he was with me constantly.

INTERVIEWER: What was he working on at this time?

AIKEN: He was finishing *Ultramarine*. I've still got about a third of one version of *Ultramarine*. An interesting specimen of his deliberate attempt to absorb me came to light because there was a page recounting the dream of eating the father's skeleton which comes into my own novel, *Great Circle*. He was going to put this in his book and it didn't seem to matter at all that *I'd* had the dream and written it out.

INTERVIEWER: He doesn't put that in the final version?

AIKEN: No. I said, "No, Malcolm, this is carrying it *too* far."

INTERVIEWER: What about *Under the Volcano?* Did you work with him on that also?

AIKEN: No. The first version was already finished when I arrived in Mexico in 1937. He'd been there two or three years. The extraordinary thing is that it was not published for another ten years, during which time he was constantly revising and rewriting. He changed the end, I think entirely, from the version I saw. But the book was already finished and so was another novel called *In Ballast to the White Sea,* which was lost. I think it was in his shack that burnt down at Dollarton, Vancouver.

That was a remarkable thing, too, although very derivative. You could swim from one influence to another as you went from chapter to chapter. Kafka and Dostoevsky and God knows what all. But it was a brilliant thing, had some wonderful stuff in it, including, I remember, a description of a drunken steamboat ride up the Manchester Canal from Liverpool to Manchester.

INTERVIEWER: He lived through a lot that he was able to use very effectively.

AIKEN: Oh, he didn't miss a trick. He was a born observer.

INTERVIEWER: Was Lowry a disciplined writer? His life seems to have been so undisciplined.

AIKEN: Yes, when it came to writing, Malcolm was as obsessed with style as any Flaubert and read enormously to *feed* himself. As I mentioned, he wrote and rewrote *Volcano* for ten years. He once chided me for not taking more pains to "decorate the page."

INTERVIEWER: Do you think writers—fiction writers, particularly—should try deliberately to get out and live through the sort of thing he did? Search for experience? I doubt if he did it quite so consciously, but he lived a very active and varied life.

AIKEN: No, I don't think that was the intention, or not wholly the intention in his case. He really had a yen for the sea. And he came by it naturally; I think his mother's father had something to do with the sea. Of course, that's how we met, through his reading *Blue Voyage*. And he always assumed that in some mystic way the fact I had dedicated *Blue Voyage* to C. M. L. was a dedication to him. Those are his initials. Actually these were the initials of my second wife. But he always thought this was the finger pointing.

The very first night he arrived in Hampton Hall, on Plympton Street where I was living, next door to the Crimson Building, he and I and my youngest brother Robert had a sort of impromptu wrestling match. In the course of this I suggested we use the lid of the w.c. tank and each take hold of one end of it and wrestle for possession of this thing. So I got it all right; I got it away from Malcolm but fell right over backward into the fireplace and went out like a light; and when I came to, all I could see was red. I was stripped to the waist and lying in bed by myself. They'd disappeared, of course—we'd been imbibing a little bit—and I galloped down the hall to the elevator not knowing what to do. I thought I'd better get a doctor because blood was pouring down my face. It turned out I had a fracture of the skull, and I was in bed for the next two or three weeks. Malcolm would sometimes remember to bring me a bottle of milk, and sometimes not. And during all this we were working on *Ultramarine*. That was the day's work, always.

INTERVIEWER: To turn to your own work—and the prototypical *Paris Review* question: How do you write? You've told me before that you compose on the typewriter.

AIKEN: Yes, ever since the early twenties. I began by doing book reviews on the typewriter and then went over to short stories on the machine, meanwhile sticking to pencil for poetry.

INTERVIEWER: So your verse symphonies were all written in long hand?

AIKEN: They were all written in little exercise books, with pencil.

INTERVIEWER: When did you start writing poetry on the typewriter?

AIKEN: About the middle of the twenties, I think. It was largely in the interests of legibility because my handwriting was extremely small and not very distinct, and the pencil *faded.* And so this was a great advantage and saved me the pains of copying because in many instances the short stories in *Bring! Bring!* were sent out exactly as written. They were composed straight off my head. I didn't change anything. It's a great labor-saving device—with some risks, because if you lost a copy in the mails it was gone!

INTERVIEWER: You didn't make carbons?

AIKEN: I never used a carbon because that made me self-conscious. I can remember discussing the effect of the typewriter on our work with Tom Eliot because he was moving to the typewriter about the same time I was. And I remember our agreeing that it made for a slight change of style in the prose—that you tended to use more periodic sentences, a little shorter, and a rather choppier style—and that one must be careful about that. Because, you see, you couldn't look ahead quite far enough, for you were always thinking about putting your fingers on the bloody keys. But that was a passing phase only. We both soon discovered that we were just as free to let the style throw itself into the air as we had been writing manually.

INTERVIEWER: Did writing on the typewriter have any comparable effect on the style of the poetry?

AIKEN: I think it went along with my tendency to compress the poetry that began about the midtwenties, '23 or '24, thereabouts. But revision was always done manually. I preferred yellow paper because it's not so responsible looking, and I would just let fly and then put the thing away after it was written and not look at it until the next day. Then go to work on it with a pencil—chop and change and then copy that off again on the yellow paper—and this would go on for days sometimes. There are some instances, especially in later work, when there have been something like twenty versions of a poem.

INTERVIEWER: In the verse symphonies, you did less revising?

AIKEN: Much less. It came out like a ribbon and lay flat on the brush.

INTERVIEWER: Did you often work on two or three poems at once? Particularly when you were doing the shorter poems, like the ones in the two series of *Preludes?*

AIKEN: No, not so much. I usually stayed with the individual item until it was satisfactory. Although sometimes I would do two or three preludes in a day, first drafts. And then all three would come in for retooling, so to speak, the next day or the day after. Those happened very fast, the preludes—especially the *Time in the Rock* ones. They were outpourings as I've only really known during that period. Didn't matter when or where I was. I remember in "Jeake's House" in Rye when carpenters were going through the kitchen and the dining room all the time, which is where I worked at a long refectory table, and I would just go cheerfully on turning out preludes while hammering and sawing and what-not happened about me.

INTERVIEWER: But most of your other poems have come much more slowly?

AIKEN: Yes, much. Things like *A Letter from Li Po* and "The Crystal" were immensely labored over. Months. Very different procedure entirely. I had the idea, but it had to be developed very slowly.

INTERVIEWER: In revising, say, the shorter poems like the *Preludes,* did you usually find it possible to revise so that you were eventually satisfied with the poem, or have you often discarded poems along the way?

AIKEN: Oh, I've discarded a great many. And occasionally I've discarded and then resurrected. I would find a crumpled yellow ball of paper in the wastebasket, in the morning, and open it to see what the hell I'd been up to; and occasionally it was something that needed only a very slight change to be brought off, which I'd missed the day before.

INTERVIEWER: Do you tend now to look on the two series of *Preludes* as your major poetry?

AIKEN: I think those two books are central, along with *Osiris*

Jones and *Landscape West of Eden,* but I still don't think the symphonies are to be despised. They've got to be looked at in an entirely different way; and allowances must be made for the diffuseness and the musical structure, which I think I overdid sometimes. Although *Senlin* I think stands up fairly well. And *Festus,* too.

INTERVIEWER: You speak of your "verse symphonies." Where did you get the idea of adapting musical structures to poetry?

AIKEN: For one thing, I always hankered to be a composer— I was mad about music, though I never studied seriously, and can't read a note. But I learned to play the piano and became pretty skillful at improvisation, especially after a drop or two. And from the beginning I'd thought of the two realms as really one: They were saying the same thing but in two voices. Why not marry them? A young composer named Bainbridge Crist, whom I met in London in 1913, introduced me to the tone poems of Strauss, and out of this came an early poem, "Disenchantment," now disavowed (though I still like parts of it). And then the symphonies. They had the tone of the time, and they married the unlikely couple of Freud and music.

INTERVIEWER: What about your new poem, *Thee?* Is it related to some of this earlier work?

AIKEN: No, *Thee* is something else again. This is nearer to some of the *Preludes*—not so much aimed at music *(pace* the title *Preludes)* as at meaning. But this poem, like "Blues for Ruby Matrix," for another example, just came like Topsy. It seized me at lunch, the first section, and I had to leave the table to put it down. Then it finished itself. In a way I had little to do with it. The theme is much like that of the *Preludes,* but the style very different: I think I'd learned a trick or two from my children's book, *Cats and Bats and Things with Wings.* Short lines, no adjectives, and, for its purpose, *very* heavy rhyming. None of which was in the least calculated. Who dunnit?

INTERVIEWER: You stress in *Ushant* that about the time you were writing *Landscape West of Eden* and the *Preludes* you were beginning to formulate a view of poetry, or of a poetic comprehension of the world, as the only religion any longer tenable or viable. Should we be seeing this more clearly in the two series of *Preludes* than we have, or than most critics have?

AIKEN: Yes, it was there, all right. Actually Houston Peterson in *The Melody of Chaos* got a little close to it although he had only seen the first ten or twelve of *Memnon*. But he, I think, detected the novelty of this approach to the world, or something.

INTERVIEWER: What about your later poems—are *Li Po* and "The Crystal," for example, related to the work you did in the thirties?

AIKEN: Yes, I think you can see their roots in the *Preludes*. But again, of course, it's a more expanded thing, as the earlier work was more expansive, in a different way. "The Crystal" and the poem about my grandfather, "Halloween," and *Li Po* and "A Walk in the Garden"—I think you can see how that whole group grew out of the *Preludes*.

INTERVIEWER: You mention "Halloween"—this has an emphasis on the American past, as does *The Kid*, which is quite a bit different from the work you did in England. Is *The Kid*—

AIKEN: That's a sort of *sport* in my career, I would say. And the vaudeville poems are another sort of deliberate divagation.

INTERVIEWER: You mean the ones you were doing very early, in the 1910s?

AIKEN: Yes. Those were based on observation; I was an addict of vaudeville, and Boston was marvelous for it. You had about three levels of vulgarity or refinement, whichever way you want to put it. The refinement being Keiths at the top, of course, and the bottom being Waldron's Casino, and in between Loews Theatre. And Loews was really the best. It was a wonderful mixture of vulgarity and invention, of high spirits and dirty cracks.

INTERVIEWER: When you started writing fiction—I suppose in the early twenties—what made you turn away from poetry, which you'd been doing up until then? Were you looking for a wider public?

AIKEN: No, it was almost wholly financial. Our income wasn't quite sufficient, and I thought maybe if I could turn out some short stories, I could make a little money. But of course that proved to be an illusion because the sort of stories I wrote could only be sold to things like *The Dial* or *The Criterion,* and I didn't make any more than I would have out of poetry. But then I got involved in it and found that it was fun, in its different way, and that in fact the short story is a kind of poem, or for *my* purposes it was. And so on it went, *pari passu* with the poetry.

INTERVIEWER: Some of your stories, like "Mr. Arcularis" and "Silent Snow, Secret Snow," have become classics. Where did you get the ideas for these stories? Dreams? Did reading Freud have anything to do with them?

AIKEN: Of course Freud was in everything I did, from 1912 on. But there was no special influence on these. "Arcularis" *did* come out of a dream, plus a meeting with a man of that name on a ship. "Silent Snow" was a complete invention; or, let's say, a projection of my own inclination to insanity.

INTERVIEWER: Then you started working with the longer fiction—*Blue Voyage* and *Great Circle?*

AIKEN: Yes, and that was another reason for going into the short stories. Because I actually wrote one chapter of *Blue Voyage* and then stopped dead. I thought no, I really don't know enough about the *structure* of fiction—perhaps I'd better play with the short story for a while and learn something about this. And also make a little money. So it was after *Bring! Bring!* was finished that I went back to *Blue Voyage.*

Blue Voyage was another matter. I really wanted, sort of in midcareer, to make a statement about the predicament of the would-be artist and just what made him tick, and what was wrong with him, and why he went fast or slow. Just as *Ushant* was the other end of that statement. "D." of *Ushant* is Demarest of *Blue Voyage,* grown fatter and balder. That was always planned—that I should, as it were, give myself away, to such extent as I could bear it, as to what made the wheels go round. Feeling that this was one of the responsibilities of a writer—that he should take off the mask.

INTERVIEWER: Show just exactly how his own mind and his

own experience go into his work—

AIKEN: Yes, and to what extent accidents helped him, and mistakes even, and failures in character, and so forth.

INTERVIEWER: Did you ever meet Freud? Wasn't H.D. trying for a while to get you to go and work with him?

AIKEN: Freud's influence—*and* along with his, that of Rank, Ferenczi, Adler, and (somewhat less) Jung—was tremendous. And I wrote one letter to Freud, to which he never replied. I was being groomed by H.D. and Bryher to go to Vienna and take over what H.D. had been doing, that is, observer: observing: reciprocal analysis. Freud had read *Great Circle*, and I'm told kept a copy on his office table. But I didn't go, though I started to. Misgivings set in, and so did poverty.

INTERVIEWER: You've spoken a couple of times—in *Ushant* and more guardedly or more subtly in the poetry—of your faith in consciousness. You speak of the "teleology of consciousness" at one point. This sounds almost as if you're looking for a new spiritual attitude toward life, a new religion not based on religious dogma or revelation or a conventional God. Is there anything to this?

AIKEN: Possibly. I don't know whether I'd put it quite like that. Of course I do believe in this evolution of consciousness as the only thing which we can embark on, or in fact, willy-nilly, *are* embarked on; and along with that will go the spiritual discoveries and, I feel, the inexhaustible wonder that one feels, that opens more and more the more you know. It's simply that this increasing knowledge constantly enlarges your kingdom and the capacity for admiring and loving the universe. So in that sense I think what you say is correct. *Ushant* says this.

INTERVIEWER: One statement that's always impressed me is the preface you recreated for *The House of Dust* in 1948 in which you wrote that "implicit in this poem was the theory that was to underlie much of the later work—namely, that in the evolution of man's consciousness, ever widening and deepening and subtil-izing his awareness, and in his dedication of himself to this su-preme task, man possesses all that he could possibly require in the way of a religious credo: when the halfgods go, the gods arrive; he can, if he only will, become divine." Is that too extreme a statement, do you feel, now?

AIKEN: No, I would stand by that. Which is really, in sum, more or less what my Grandfather Potter preached in New Bedford.

INTERVIEWER: When did you first come across your Grandfather Potter's sermons?

AIKEN: I've been carrying the *corpus* of my grandfather—to change the famous saying—with me all my life. I was given very early two volumes of his sermons; and I never go anywhere without them.

INTERVIEWER: What is it in them that's been so important to you?

AIKEN: Well, the complete liberation from dogma; and a determined acceptance of Darwin and all the rest of the scientific fireworks of the nineteenth century.

INTERVIEWER: This was toward the end of the nineteenth century?

AIKEN: Middle of the century. He actually took his parish out of the Unitarian Church. As he put it, "They have defrocked not only me, but my church." For thirty years he and the church, the New Bedford parish, were in the wilderness. Then the Unitarians, about 1890, caught up with him and embraced him. By this time he was president of the Free Religious Association and was lecturing all over the country on the necessity for a religion without dogma.

And this inheritance has been my guiding light: I regard myself simply as a continuance of my grandfather, and primarily, therefore, as a teacher and preacher, and a distributor, in poetic terms, of the *news* of the world, by which I mean new knowledge. This is gone into at some length in *Ushant.* And elsewhere I have said repeatedly that as poetry is the highest speech of man, it can not only accept and contain, but in the end express best everything in the world, or in himself, that he discovers. It will absorb and transmute, as it always has done, and glorify, all that we can know.

This has always been, and always will be, poetry's office.

INTERVIEWER: You once wrote, speaking of the great writers of the American nineteenth century—Whitman, Melville, Hawthorne, James, Poe: "We isolate, we exile our great men, whether by ignoring them or praising them stupidly. And perhaps this isolation we offer them is our greatest gift." It seems to me you didn't receive much attention from the time of your Pulitzer Prize in 1930 until, at best, fairly recently—that you were ignored in the way you speak of for almost thirty years. "This isolation we offer" as "our greatest gift"—would this be true of yourself also?

AIKEN: I think so. I think it's very useful to be insulated from your surrounds, and this gives it to you because it gives you your inviolate privacy, without pressures, so that you can just be yourself. I think that what's happening today, with all the young poets rushing from one college to another, lecturing at the drop of a hat and so on, is not too good; I think it might have a bad effect on a great many of the young poets. They—to quote Mark Twain —"swap juices" a little too much, so that they are in danger of losing their own identity and don't give themselves time enough in which to work out what's really of importance to them— they're too busy. I think Wordsworth and Coleridge had the right idea, too—they deliberately sequestered themselves.

INTERVIEWER: What do you think of the state of poetry today? We sometimes think of the period from 1910 to 1940 or so as being the Golden Era of modern American poetry. Do you think there is anything being done now comparable to the work that was done in those years?

AIKEN: No, I don't think there is. I think we've come to a kind of splinter period in poetry. These tiny little bright fragments of observation—and not produced under sufficient pressure—some of it's very skillful, but I don't think there's anywhere a discernible major poet in the process of emerging; or if he is, I ain't seen him. But I think there's an enormous lot of talent around, and somewhere amongst these I'm sure that something will emerge, given time.

INTERVIEWER: In an interview for *The Paris Review* Robert

Lowell said: "Poets of my generation and particularly younger
ones . . . write a very musical, difficult poem with tremendous skill,
perhaps there's never been such skill. Yet the writing seems divorced from culture somehow. It's become too much something
specialized that can't handle much experience. It's become a
craft, purely a craft, and there must be some breakthrough back
into life." He speaks almost as if there's *too* much skill, that it's
become something that's holding younger poets back; as if they're
concentrating so much on finding the perfect line or the perfect
image that they aren't thinking or feeling—

AIKEN: Well, I don't think that's so, and I think possibly there
Lowell is really reflecting one of his own defects, because he *is* a
little awkward. What really astonished me in that interview with
him is his description of his method of writing verse nowadays—
writing out a prose statement first and then trying to translate it
to metrics without sacrificing the phrases. Well, this is really the
damnedest way of writing a poem that I ever heard of, and I don't
think it's any wonder that sometimes his things sound so—so
prosaic—if I may go so far.

INTERVIEWER: Poets now seem so wrapped up in the short
poem and the perfect small statement; this seems to grow out of
the early experiments of Pound and Williams, imagism also. Do
you think that these tendencies have taken poets' minds away
from larger subjects—from really *thinking* about what they're
going to write about?

AIKEN: I think quite likely. That's a little apropos of what I
called the "splinter" stage of poetry. And I think this does go
back to the imagists and Pound, T. E. Hulme, and H.D., primarily. And of course that, as a lot of us were quick to see at the
time, did impose limitations and very serious ones. That's why I
suppose you could say that Williams, for all his power, never
really came out with a *final* thing. In fact, I think one of his
completest statements is in one of his earliest poems, "The
Wanderer," which is much better than *Paterson* because in that
he has a real continuing line which goes from one section to

another, and it isn't so fragmented.

INTERVIEWER: What about Pound's later works? Do you think that in the *Cantos* he's found a way to give a larger organization, make a larger statement, from the earlier techniques?

AIKEN: No, I don't think so. I think that's a majestic failure. There, too, it's—he described it himself in one of his own lines: "A broken bundle of mirrors." That's exactly what it is—brilliant fragments here and there, and beautiful—but it doesn't work; there isn't sufficient mind behind it, or organizing theme. He's said this himself—but I take that with a grain of salt.

INTERVIEWER: What do you think about the contemporary poets who talk about "mind expanding" or "consciousness expanding"—Ginsberg and his group? Do you think drugs can expand a writer's awareness or perceptions?

AIKEN: I've tried it long ago, with hashish and peyote. Fascinating, yes, but no good, no. This, as we find in alcohol, is an *escape* from awareness, a cheat, a momentary substitution, and in the end a destruction of it. With luck, someone might have a fragmentary Kubla Khan vision. But with no meaning. And with the steady destruction of the observing and remembering mind.

INTERVIEWER: Do you still waver between the view of the artist as simply supplying vicarious experience and your later view that the artist is the leader in the expansion of man's awareness and consciousness?

AIKEN: I think they can function together. I think they do. It's like two parts of the same machine; they go on simultaneously.

INTERVIEWER: When you speak of the artist as the creator and purveyor of new knowledge, doesn't this, to be effective, demand a fairly wide audience?

AIKEN: To be effective?

INTERVIEWER: Yes, socially effective.

AIKEN: No, not necessarily. I mean that can come serially, with time. A small but brilliant advance made today by someone's awareness may for the moment reach a very small audience, but insofar as it's valid and beautiful, it will make its way and become part of the whole world of consciousness. So in that sense it's all working toward this huge audience, and all working toward a better man.

ROBERT HUNTER WILBUR

3. Robert Graves

Born in London in 1895 to parents of Anglo-Irish and German descent, Robert Graves attended Charterhouse school before joining the Royal Welch Fusiliers in France in World War I. He served with them until he was wounded in 1917. After the war was over, he attended Oxford; in 1926 he began a brief term as professor of English at the Egyptian University in Cairo. Written during this time, *Goodbye to All That* (1929), an account of his war experiences, was so commercially successful that it allowed him to settle in Deyá, Majorca, and pursue his writing. Except for absences during the Spanish Civil War and World War II, he has lived there ever since.

Graves's earliest collection of poetry was *Poems 1914–1927* (1927). His poems were collected again in 1938 and 1961. Since then he has published *New Poems* (1963), *Poems 1965–68* (1969), and *Poems About Love* (1969). He has made his living, however, largely by his prose, including a number of historical novels such as *I, Claudius* (1934), *Wife to Mr. Milton* (1943), *The Golden Fleece* (1944), *King Jesus* (1946), and *Homer's Daughter* (1955). Graves is also the author of a number of volumes of literary criticism, including *A Survey of Modernist Poetry* (1927), *The White Goddess* (1948), and *Oxford Addresses on Poetry* (1962).

Robert Graves won the Russell Loines Award for Poetry in 1958 and the Gold Medal of the National Poetry Society of America in 1960. In 1961 he was appointed to the Professorship of Poetry at Oxford, where he served until 1966, when he returned to Majorca.

but that is a long argument

One strange feature of the Indiana school is their ~~adoption~~ *(whole-hearted adoption)*
~~of~~ Max Müller's Aryan creed. They seem unaware that ~~the British Isles~~
were first civilized from Africa, not from Central Asia,
~~by the~~ ~~Iberian~~ people ~~whose natural mathematic genius has~~ *it is now apparent* ~~never since been excelled~~

Professor Dorson's copious
index of sources omits our wisest and most *Kandiroth line*
folklorist, George Ewart Evans, whose ~~books~~ *The Horse and The*
Furrow and *Ask the Fellows Who Cut the Hay*, are now followed
by ~~his~~ even more remarkable *The Pattern Under the Plough*, a single
page of which is worth a wilderness of folk motifs

~~ho~~ *especially his* ~~extraordinary~~ *accounts* *of* smiths and
horses.

Smiths were so closely connected with magic from the earliest
times that they *refused* ~~accepted~~ ~~have never taken~~ a Catholic patron saint longer
than any other craft, and ~~cannot~~ ~~take~~ *This Ste Eligius* Saint Eloi
too seriously. ~~being*~~ Bishop of Noyon, had been
a mere goldsmith, not a blacksmith, and ~~was~~ *we* therefore wholly
unversed in horse-lore, ~~~~ ~~un~~privileged to mount
a horseshoe on his wall ~~with~~ points downwards,

as any member of the Worshipful Company of Farriers may do.

farrier was the only craftsman admitted to the secrets of the
the Horsemans Word *(still active)*
Society of ~~~~, which seems, like early Scottish
Freemasonry, to have been ~~~~ *~~breed~~* *returning* by ~~~~ Crusaders.
So many extra remarkable
~~ordinary~~ details of East Anglian horse magic, plough magic,
as are given here have never (even) in my knowledge
seed magic, smithcraft and leech-craft ~~~~
been printed before in such small space.
~~~~ the most

Robert Graves

Dressed in corduroys, mariner's sweater, black horsehide jacket, and with a blanket wrapped around his middle, Robert Graves rolled his own cigarettes and chain-smoked throughout the interview. Reading glasses hung from his neck on a ribbon, which frequently became tangled in his hair. Tall, loosely built, Graves has always been physically powerful, but as result of a climbing accident during his schooldays he cannot swivel his head and therefore uses a reading stand—fidgeting it into strategic positions on the desk in front of him while he talks. Tins of small Dutch cigars, jars of tobacco, marbles, pencils, and porcelain clown heads are on the desk. There is a carton brimming with press clippings on the floor. Over the fireplace is a shelf with the works of T. E. Lawrence; on the mantel, Greek, Roman, Oriental, and African figurines. "This dial of wood? From a tree hewn in Shakespeare's yard." He fingered it, spoke of continuity. He knew Hardy, and Hardy knew—

Gertrude Stein first told Robert Graves about Majorca. Except for the Civil War years, he has lived in Deyá since 1929. He and Laura Riding built the stone house he now occupies, and they lived in it together until 1936. There is an orchard with fifteen kinds of fruit trees, a large vegetable garden, and an English-style lawn of Bermuda grass.

Robert Graves is the author of over one hundred books, besides a number of anonymous rewrite jobs for friends. His most important prose work is The White Goddess, *a history of poetic myth —"the language of poetic myth . . . was a magical language bound up with popular religious ceremonies in honour of the Moon Goddess, or Muse . . . and this remains the language of 'true' poetry . . . in the sense of being the unimprovable original, not a synthetic substitute." The true poet worships the White Goddess, or goddess of creation; unswerving and absolute devotion to her is the poet's only path. He "falls in love, absolutely, and his true love for her is the Muse's embodiment." The present Muse is fifty-two years younger than Graves—"but we are the same age" . . . "I am at the top of my manic cycle because good things are happening to her just now." She is a classical dancer performing in a far-off city.*

At various times during the following interview (which appeared in the Summer 1969 issue of The Paris Review*), he was setting the table, correcting a manuscript, checking references, cutting his nails with an enormous pair of scissors, picking carrots, singing folk songs, and slicing beans. He was not an easy man to keep up with.*

GRAVES: Do you notice anything strange about this room?

INTERVIEWER: No.

GRAVES: Well, everything is made by hand—with one exception: this nasty plastic triple file which was given me as a present. I've put it here out of politeness for two or three weeks, then it will disappear. Almost everything else is made by hand. Oh yes, the books have been printed, but many have been printed by hand —in fact some I printed myself. Apart from the electric light fixtures, everything else is handmade; nowadays very few people live in houses where anything at all is made by hand.

INTERVIEWER: Does this bear directly on your creative work?

GRAVES: Yes: one secret of being able to think is to have as little as possible around you that is not made by hand.

INTERVIEWER: You once wrote that "the Muse-poet must die for the Goddess as the Sacred King did when a divine victim." In spite of all you've survived, do you still hold to this?

GRAVES: Yes. What nearly always happens is that the Muse finds it impossible to sustain the love of a poet and allies herself with a pretended poet who she knows is not a real one. Someone she can mother. I have given a picture of it in a poem called "Lack." The process starts again each time that there's a death of love, which is as painful as a real death. There's always a murderer about, always a "Lack" character. The King or poet represents growth, and the rival or tanist represents drought.

INTERVIEWER: Surely long years of service to the Muse are rewarded.

GRAVES: The reward is becoming eventually attached to somebody who's not a murderess. I don't want to talk about it because I don't want to tempt my luck.

INTERVIEWER: By definition, your pursuit of the Muse cannot bring satisfaction. What has it given you?

GRAVES: It has brought me nearer and nearer to the center of the fire, so to speak.

INTERVIEWER: Your poems, especially your love poems, get more intense as you go on. Is that a function of age or experience?

GRAVES: One gets to the heart of the matter by a series of experiences in the same pattern, but in different colors.

INTERVIEWER: In other words, you don't learn anything new, but you get a deeper understanding.

GRAVES: That's about it. An understanding of what the poet's ordeals are. Love poems must be bounced back off a moon. Moons vary. Love a different Muse-woman and you get a different poem.

INTERVIEWER: What about that simple appetite, lust, which you have attacked?

GRAVES: Lust involves a loss of virtue, in the sense of psychic power. Lust is giving away something that belongs to somebody else. I mean the act of love is a metaphor of spiritual togetherness, and if you perform the act of love with someone who means little to you, you're giving away something that belongs to the person you do love or might love. The act of love belongs to two people, in the way that secrets are shared. Hugs and kisses are permissible, but as soon as you start with what's called the mandalot—I invented the word, from the Greek; it comes from *mandalós* (which is the bolt you put in the socket) and means the tongue-kiss or by dictionary definition "a lecherous and erotic kiss"—you should reserve such familiarities only for those whom you really love. I'm on simple hugs-and-kisses terms with several friends. That's all right. But promiscuity seems forbidden to poets, though I do not grudge it to any nonpoet.

INTERVIEWER: Can the experience of the Muse give felicity?

GRAVES: Not really. But what does? Felicity and pain always alternate. She serves as a focus and challenge. She gives happiness. Here I use the English language precisely—hap: happening. She gives hap; provides happening. Tranquility is of no poetic use. (The first to use Muse in the sense of White Goddess was Ben Jonson—then it dropped down into weakly meaning self-inspiration of young men.)

After experience of the untranquil Muse one may move on to the Black Goddess—for black is positive in the East and stands for wisdom. Can a white Muse become a black one, or must it be another Muse? That is difficult . . .

INTERVIEWER: They are all about of an age—

GRAVES: As a rule the Muse is one whose father has deserted her mother when she was young and for whom therefore the patriarchal charm is broken, and who hates patriarchy. She may grow to be very intelligent, but emotionally she is arrested at about the age of fourteen or fifteen.

INTERVIEWER: What is the Muse's reaction to the poet?

GRAVES: It's embarrassing in a way for a well-known poet to write poems to a girl. She may resent being made a part of literary history. In France it is different. Many a woman wants to be known as the last girl Victor Hugo slept with . . . I'm all against literary history. Sometimes that's the reason why a "great poem," one that occurs in all the anthologies, is bad. It is usually interesting to examine its history.

INTERVIEWER: You mean it's been manufactured for an event?

GRAVES: Yes.

INTERVIEWER: *The White Goddess* is a handbook and a shelter behind which all questions can be answered. Do you feel the need for a final definition of what you're up to?

GRAVES: *The White Goddess* and *The Nazarene Gospel Restored* are curious: I wrote the first to define the non-Jewish element in Christianity, especially the Celtic. And I wrote the second, with the help of the late Joshua Podro, to drive the Greek and Roman element out of what was a purely Jewish event. The curious result was that a special Early Christian Society got founded at Cambridge, based on the *Nazarene Gospel,* and various White Goddess religions started in New York State and California. I'm today's hero of the love-and-flowers cult out in the Screwy State, so they tell me: where hippies stop policemen in the street and say, "I adore you, officer." Also I get a number of letters from witches' covens, requesting flying ointment, magical recipes, and esoteric information.

INTERVIEWER: In the "Colophon to Love Respelt" you talk of the battlefield being deserted. Who won?

GRAVES: I meant that there was no occasion for further poems on the subject . . . The historical sequence of a man's poems has a general resemblance to the order in which they are written. Yet often one writes a poem a long time before, or long after, a thing happens. Autobiography doesn't correspond exactly with poetic sequence.

INTERVIEWER: You get the idea for a poem and then life catches up with it?

GRAVES: Or alternatively, you have omitted recording a poetic experience sometime, and it occurs later. The words are already fixed in the storehouse of the memory. The poem is there at the origin, but at the seventh level of consciousness, and rises up gradually through each repeated revision. The rereading touches off the original hypnotic state, but expression is amplified.

INTERVIEWER: In what way amplified?

GRAVES: For example, by the dreams of the night, which are the real interpretations in the primitive mind of the events of the previous day. A poem is nonetheless present from the conception, from the first germ of it crossing the mind—it must be scratched for and exhumed. There is an element of timelessness. The leading atomic scientist in Australia agreed with me the other day that time does not really exist. The finished poem is present before it is written and one corrects it. It is the final poem that dictates what is right, what is wrong.

INTERVIEWER: Why did you not write war poems—of your trench experience in World War I like your friend Sassoon, and like Owen?

GRAVES: I did. But I destroyed them. They were journalistic. Sassoon and Wilfred Owen were homosexuals; though Sassoon tried to think he wasn't. To them, seeing *men* killed was as horrible as if you or I had to see fields of corpses of women.

INTERVIEWER: Your poems are very complete and personal statements. Are you not at all reticent about what you reveal?

GRAVES: You tell things to your friends that you don't put into print.

INTERVIEWER: But your audience . . .

GRAVES: Never use the word "audience." The very idea of a public, unless a poet is writing for money, seems wrong to me. Poets don't have an "audience": They're talking to a single person all the time. What's wrong with someone like Yevtushenko is that he's talking to thousands of people at once. All the so-called "great artists" were trying to talk to too many people. In a way, they were talking to nobody.

INTERVIEWER: Hence your estimate of the English poets, whom you've criticized pretty heavily from the Poetry Chair at Oxford?

GRAVES: There are fifteen English poets—I am speaking precisely—in the history of listed literature who were real poets and not playing at it.

INTERVIEWER: Would you care to name them?

GRAVES: That wouldn't be polite.

INTERVIEWER: What do they have in common?

GRAVES: A source in the primitive. In the prerational.

INTERVIEWER: As you work at a poem, do you feel that you are in some sense matching?

GRAVES: What happens is this—if a hypnotist says, "Look at this ring," and you are hypnotized by looking at the ring, then if he produces that ring again any time afterward, you go down. So also if you're writing a poem, and you come back to it the next day, you're immediately rehypnotized and at it again at that level.

INTERVIEWER: Is it the physical circumstance? This room?

GRAVES: No, it's not the ambiance. The ambiance may help. It's the actual draft, which is yourself. That's the hypnotic ring.

INTERVIEWER: And what happens if you don't "go down"?

GRAVES: That happened to me only yesterday. You can't force it intellectually. You spoil the poem. You mess it up. When you've worked through to the real poetic level, the connections webbing together every single word are quite beyond intellectual arrangement. A computer couldn't do it. You've got not merely sound and sense to deal with but the histories of the words, cross rhythms, the interrelation of all the meanings of the words—a complete microcosm. You never get it quite right, but if you get it almost right, it insulates itself in time. That's why real poems travel.

INTERVIEWER: One feels your poetry has become more and more urgent, especially in the love lyrics which begin late.

GRAVES: Don't forget that I began in the Victorian era; I had a lot to throw off. My poetic system accords with the Irish of the eighth century A.D., which was untinctured by Rome and which passed over eventually into Wales. Where did it come from? From the East. The correspondence with Sufic poetry is immense. That accounts for my interest in Omar Khayyám—a very noble poet so mishandled by FitzGerald. Besides, one gradually ceases to take critics into account.

INTERVIEWER: Who got you to come to the Balearic Islands?

GRAVES: Gertrude Stein.

INTERVIEWER: What did you think of her?

GRAVES: She had an *eye*. She used to say she had been the only woman in Picasso's life, that she had formed him. Maybe this was true; the other females were only round and about.

INTERVIEWER: The poem you've shown me just now, "The Thing to Be Said," seems to sum up so much.

GRAVES: Even in "The Thing to Be Said," which I am working on now, which is about the necessity of first statement and that treats obsessive revision as a disease of age, there are ten successive versions. To date. Yes. The thing to be said, *say* it.

INTERVIEWER: This immense, abrupt change. The late poetry—

GRAVES: Yes, that came when I was writing *The White Goddess*. (I wrote it in six weeks. It took me ten years to revise it. And I about tripled its length.) Suddenly I was answering ancient Welsh and Irish questions that had never been answered, and I didn't know how or why. It terrified me. I thought I was going mad. But those solutions haven't been disproved. Then someone sent me an article on the Irish tree alphabet, and the footnote referred to Graves but not to me. It was my grandfather! And I hadn't even known he had investigated such things. I believe in the inheritance of skills and crafts—the inheritance of memory. They find now that if a snail eats another snail it gets that second snail's memory.

INTERVIEWER: How did you sum up such vast detail into your conclusions?

GRAVES: I didn't. I knew it at the outset, and then checked.

INTERVIEWER: You certainly write Muse poetry and express great contempt for the Apollonian, which I take it is the logical or utilitarian stuff, but aren't your novels Apollonian?

GRAVES: My writing of prose was always thematically in line with my thought. Always myself, I never left that. That was always the background. For example, *They Hanged My Saintly Billy* was to show how Victorian England really was: how rotten, how criminal in contrast to the received version. I had a couple of good characters, too, besides the bad.

INTERVIEWER: You write novels when stimulated by some historical problem. How do you go on from there?

GRAVES: I don't know. Some people have gifts, like a friend of mine who can balance a glass on his finger and make it turn round by just looking at it. I have the gift of being occasionally able to put myself back in the past and see what's happening. That's how historical novels should be written. I also have a very good memory for anything I want to remember and none at all for what I don't want to remember. *Wife to Mr. Milton*—my best novel—started when my wife and I were making a bed in 1943 and I suddenly said: "You know, Milton must have been a trichomaniac"—meaning a hair fetishist. The remark suddenly sprang out of my mouth. I realized how often his imagery had been trichomaniac. So I read all I could find about him and went into the history of his marriages. I'd always hated Milton, from earliest childhood; and I wanted to find out the reason. I found it. His jealousy. It's present in all his poems . . . Marie Powell had long hair with which he could not compete.

INTERVIEWER: I think you describe that precisely in the novel, when they are riding on the heath . . .

GRAVES: He had the schoolmaster's disease. Constipation.

INTERVIEWER: You mean that literally?

GRAVES: Yes! Of course I mean it literally! It shows in all his poetry. We know all about what he was given for it. Well, I had always smelt something, and then it all came to me more or less at once, and I wrote *Wife to Mr. Milton.* I found out a lot of things about him, heaven knows how, which have never been disproved.

INTERVIEWER: Did he inherit the constipation?

GRAVES: He was a scrivener's son. He well may have.

INTERVIEWER: How long did *I, Claudius* take to write?

GRAVES: *I, Claudius* and *Claudius the God* took me eight months. I had to get the job done quickly because I was £4000 in debt. I got so close to him that I was accused of doing a lot of research that I had never done at all.

INTERVIEWER: Did you dictate any of it?

GRAVES: No. I had a typist here in the village, but I didn't dictate. If you only use the main sources, and you know the period, a book writes itself.

INTERVIEWER: About how many hours per day did it take you?

GRAVES: I don't know. It must have been seven or eight. The story came to about 250,000 words in all. I had mortgaged the house and didn't want to lose it.

INTERVIEWER: Why did you choose the historical novel?

GRAVES: Well, with that one I had noted in my diary, a year or two before, that the Roman historians—Tacitus, Suetonius, and Dion Cassius, but especially Tacitus—had obviously got Claudius wrong, and that one day I'd have to write a book about it. If I hadn't done so, you wouldn't be here drinking in this house.

INTERVIEWER: What did you have in mind at the end of *Claudius the God?* There's a distinct change in Claudius. One wonders what you were getting at as a novelist?

GRAVES: I didn't think I was writing a novel. I was trying to find out the truth of Claudius. And there was some strange confluent feeling between Claudius and myself. I found out that I was able to know a lot of things that happened without having any basis except that I knew they were true. It's a question of reconstructing a personality.

INTERVIEWER: There is not much direct source extant, though he wrote voluminously.

GRAVES: There's his speech to the Aeduans, his letter to the Alexandrians, and a number of records of what he said in Suetonius and elsewhere. We know now exactly what disease he suffered from: Little's disease. The whole scene is so solid, really, that you feel you knew him personally, if you're sympathetic with him. The poor man—only now, at last, people have begun to forget the bad press he was given by contemporary historians. And he's now regarded as one of the very few good emperors between Julius Caesar and Vespásian.

INTERVIEWER: In the end, though, he was disenchanted—

GRAVES: He saw he could do nothing. He had to give up.

INTERVIEWER: He disintegrated and became very nearly another Caligula or Tiberius . . .

GRAVES: Well, now—Caligula was born bad. Tiberius was a marvelous man. But too much pressure was put on him, and he warned the Senate of what was going to happen. He foresaw a severe psychological breakdown. If you've always been extremely clean—always brushed your teeth and made your bed—and you get to a point of intolerable stress, you break down and display what is called paradoxical behavior: You mess your bed, you do the most disgusting things. Tiberius had been noted for his chastity and manly virtues, and then he broke down. I now feel the greatest possible sympathy for Tiberius.

INTERVIEWER: Weren't you getting at Livy a bit in the novel as a manipulator of truth for effect?

GRAVES: It's a sort of habit in my family, you know. My granduncle was Leopold von Ranke, the so-called "father of modern history." He was always held up to me by my mother as the first modern historian who decided to tell the truth in history.

INTERVIEWER: Did that instigate your quest, the shibboleths you've upset to the consternation of many?

GRAVES: You see, there are many people who believe things of which they can't get rid. Suddenly they are faced by some strange fact—such as that God, in the Holy of Holies, had a wife. My friend Raphael Patai has worked it all out in his *Hebrew Goddess.* It's more than they can stand. But you've got to admit it.

INTERVIEWER: That God had a wife? Did you really mean that?

GRAVES: Indeed he did. It's in the Talmud. Of course the Jews had always kept it rather quiet. At first he was One—but then came the division. You've got to find the focal point. God was a male deity and the focal point was obviously a woman. He couldn't do without one.

INTERVIEWER: How many books have you published?

GRAVES: One hundred and twenty-one—but many of those are revised collections. Then I've written books for other people.

INTERVIEWER: Why have you done that?

GRAVES: Because they had something to say, and they couldn't write it down.

INTERVIEWER: Have you given up writing fiction?

GRAVES: It might happen again. I doubt it, but I don't know. One never knows.

INTERVIEWER: After writing *The Reader Over Your Shoulder* with Alan Hodge in 1942—your handbook for writers of English prose—you say that your own style changed completely. Why, or rather how?

GRAVES: Whoever thinks about the English language and tries to discover its principles, and also pulls a whole lot of writers to pieces to show how badly they write, can't afford to write badly himself. In 1959 I entirely rewrote *Goodbye to All That*—every single sentence—but no one noticed. Some said: "What a good book this is, after all. How well it's lasted." It hasn't lasted at all. It's an entirely new product. One of those computer analyses of style couldn't possibly decide that my historical novels were all written by the same hand. They're completely different in vocabulary, syntax, and language level.

INTERVIEWER: Considering this vast output and all the revision, how much time do you spend writing? Do you write everything by hand?

GRAVES: Yes. Now let me see, *Nazarene Gospel Restored* took me two years. Now that is eight hundred pages of close writing. Yes, it's about—two books a year for fifty years. That's not so much. I have nothing else to do. The score this year is six.

INTERVIEWER: Do you find you can remember the vast research you have collected?

GRAVES: I know where to look.

INTERVIEWER: Isn't it difficult to be here so far from libraries?

GRAVES: I have never worked in a library.

INTERVIEWER: Where do you get all this information?

GRAVES: I don't know. It comes. I am not erudite. In the normal way of being I am not even well read. I am simply well informed in certain areas of my interest.

INTERVIEWER: You have to know the dates of history—the spelling of the Welsh words—

GRAVES: I've got a Welsh dictionary. I've got quite a big classical library.

INTERVIEWER: Would you say the core ideas come first and then you research?

GRAVES: One has the whole vision of the thing—and then one just checks. Cause may not necessarily ordain effect; it may equally be that effect ordains cause—once one has got the whole time thing under control.

INTERVIEWER: What do you do exactly?

GRAVES: Revise the manuscript till I can't read it any longer, then get somebody to type it. Then I revise the typing. Then it's retyped again. Then there's a third typing, which is the final one. Nothing should then remain that offends the eye.

INTERVIEWER: This is for prose?

GRAVES: Yes. But that's no proof that in ten years' time it may not read badly. One doesn't know about prose at the time.

INTERVIEWER: And poetry?

GRAVES: Sometimes you know: "This is right, this is one of the things that stands." You feel there are a certain number of poems that have got to be written. You don't know what they are, but you feel: This is one, and that is one. It is the relation between jewels and the matrix—the jewels come from the matrix, then there's the matrix to prove it. A lot of poems are matrix rather than jewels.

INTERVIEWER: What do you mean?

GRAVES: The matrix is partly jewel, partly not jewel. And lots of poems are like that. Those are the ones that usually the public likes best: ones that are not wholly jewels.

INTERVIEWER: Is that because these poems are transitional between generalized views and your personal attitude?

GRAVES: Something like that.

INTERVIEWER: More accessible?

GRAVES: Yes.

INTERVIEWER: Do you still experiment with hallucinogens?

GRAVES: I had two trips on the Mexican mushroom back in 1954 or so. None since. And never on LSD. First of all it's dangerous, and secondly, ergot, from which LSD is made, is the enemy of mankind. Ergot is a minute black fungus that grows on rye, or did in the Middle Ages, and people who ate rye bread got manic visions, especially Germans. They now say that ergot affects the genes and might disorder the next generation. It occurs to me that this may explain the phenomenon of Nazism, a form of mass hysteria. Germans were rye eaters, as opposed to wheat eaters like the English. LSD reminds me of the minks that escape from mink farms and breed in the forest and become dangerous and destructive. It has escaped from the drug factory and gets made in college laboratories.

INTERVIEWER: You have spoken of a vision of total knowledge that you once had at twelve—

GRAVES: You probably had a similar vision, and you've forgotten it. It needn't be a vision of anything; so long as it's a foretaste of Paradise. Blake had one. All poets and painters who have that extra "thing" in their work seem to have had this vision and never let it be destroyed by education. Which is all that matters.

INTERVIEWER: You've just finished a new translation of the *Rubáiyát* of Omar Khayyám. Why did you choose the *Rubáiyát* rather than the work of a purer Sufic poet such as Rumi or Sa'adi?

GRAVES: I was invited to cooperate in the task by Omar Ali-Shah, whose family has possessed the original manuscript since A.D. 1153. That's why. I was in the hospital and very glad of the job to take my mind off hospital routine. Khayyám's original poem was written in honor of God's love and spiced with satires against the Moslem puritans of the day. FitzGerald got it all wrong: he believed Khayyám really was a drunkard, and an unbeliever, not a man who was satirizing unbelievers. It's amazing how many millions have been fooled by FitzGerald. Most of them will hate being undeceived.

INTERVIEWER: You have said that the critics now writing about your *Rubáiyát* fail to understand it because they are not Sufis.

GRAVES: As I said, I can take no credit for the job. I worked from a literal crib by Omar Ali-Shah, who is a Sufi. Not only a Sufi, but his family is in the direct line of descent from the Prophet—and they claim that Mohammed was a Sufi and delivered this secret doctrine to them.

INTERVIEWER: It seems to me your Khayyám is more clear and incisive intellectually, whereas FitzGerald—

GRAVES: FitzGerald, you see, was one of those Irishmen at a time when people were ashamed of being Irish and so kept it quiet. And he became a sort of dilettante Englishman. And broke with the poetic tradition of Ireland, which is one of the strongest in the world. I should think after the Persian it is the strongest.

INTERVIEWER: You are talking about the original Irish poetic tradition?

GRAVES: There is only one!

INTERVIEWER: You explained to me once that that was originally Sufi—

GRAVES: Before that it was Milesian Greek superimposed on the archaic Libyan culture of about 2500 B.C. The Milesians came to Ireland via Spain and brought with them the Ogham tradition —which is an early form of alphabet, taking us back toward the day when letters originated in the observation of flights of cranes, and so on. But Ireland always remained in contact with Greek-speaking Antioch and not Rome, which was important.

INTERVIEWER: Is the important thing that Ogham was preclassical?

GRAVES: That's right. Before Plato. Before the Greeks went wrong. You know, the Jews had a saying—"of the ten measures of folly the Greeks have nine." They were all right until about the sixth century B.C. By the time of Alexander the Great they'd gone to pieces altogether.

INTERVIEWER: In what way?

GRAVES: They tried to decry myth. They tried to put in its place what we would now call scientific concepts. They tried to give it a literal explanation. Socrates jokes about myths, and Horace makes fun of them. When put to it, Socrates could clarify a myth in a way that deprived it of all sense. They simply had no use for poetic thought. Logic works at a very high level in consciousness. The academic never goes to sleep logically, he always stays awake. By doing so, he deprives himself of sleep. And he misses the whole thing, you see. Sleep has seven levels, topmost of which is the poetic trance—in it you still have access to conscious thought while keeping in touch with dream . . . with the topmost fragments of dream . . . you own memory . . . pictorial imagery as children know it and as it was known to primitive man. No poem is worth anything unless it starts from a poetic trance, out of which you can be wakened by interruption as from a dream. In fact, it is the same thing.

INTERVIEWER: But where does this itself come from?

GRAVES: From yourself, under the direction of the more-than-you formed by your relation with the person with whom you are in rapport at the time. If anybody were really observant, he'd be able to take a poem and draw a picture of the person it was addressed to.

INTERVIEWER: In looking at the beloved, do you then see yourself most clearly—as distinct from looking at yourself?

GRAVES: Yes. Otherwise it's not you.

INTERVIEWER: How do you feel about honors and laureateships? Will you accept if the laureateship is offered to you?

GRAVES: I don't answer questions about conjectures. I don't want any honors, but I wouldn't so much mind being honored for writing novels which sell abroad and earn money for England. Writing poems is different. To get a C.B.E. for being a poet would be absurd. But the government always tries to coax well-known writers into the Establishment; it makes them feel educated . . . I refuse doctorates because they suggest that one has passed some sort of academic test. Accepting the Professorship of Poetry at Oxford was different—it's a free election.

INTERVIEWER: In your last and most violent lecture at Oxford you said there were no poetic standards left. It is rare for you to make generalizations of this sort. Do you feel that "pop" poetry is inconsistent with dedication to the Muse?

GRAVES: There are no standards of verse-craft left, I think I said. Genuine folk songs are welcome, but why those artificial songs of protest? There are few now, if any, who go to the real root of the thing. Fewer, since Frost and Cummings died.

INTERVIEWER: What about your own poetic influences, apart from the Tudor poet Skelton and Laura Riding?

GRAVES: "Influence" is a very loose term. It sounds as though one is being dominated by someone. I never wrote anything in Laura Riding's style as far as I know. I learnt from her a general attitude to things, rather than verse-craft.

INTERVIEWER: Is it that what you get from successive incarnations of the Muse?

GRAVES: Yes, but in the form of warnings rather than instructions.

INTERVIEWER: May I ask you about the way you work? You don't have a routine, do you?

GRAVES: None. I admit only to a certain sense of priority in things. This morning, for instance, I got up at seven. I felt drawn to the ash pit where I burn waste paper and sieved out all the tins and things which have been mistakenly put there. Then I put the ash on the compost heap. Then I soaked the carrot patch so that I could thin it out a bit. Then I revised my "Monsters" piece.

INTERVIEWER: You write in longhand, on a sort of lectern . . .

GRAVES: That's because I broke my neck once. When the doctor asked me how, I couldn't remember until just the other day. It was when I was climbing Snowdon in 1913. I was belayed in a gully when the leader dislodged a large stone: It fell on my head and knocked me out. The other day I had almost exactly the same experience and so remembered the occasion. Now my neck is—well, I wrote a poem about it: "Broken Neck."

INTERVIEWER: Does most of your income come from royalties on your novels?

GRAVES: I don't know, really. I never study my royalty returns.

INTERVIEWER: You said you only read for information. What do you read, and when do you get time?

GRAVES: I used to read at night; now I go straight to sleep. I don't read for pleasure. The other day I had to revise *The Naza-rene Gospel Restored* for publication in Hungary, which meant a good deal of research.

INTERVIEWER: You said, "I foresee no change for the better in the world until everything gets worse." Well, now it *is* worse. Can we do anything about it?

GRAVES: Poets can't march in protest or do that sort of thing. I feel that it's against the rules, and pointless. If mankind wants a great big final bang, that's what it'll get. One should never protest against anything unless it's going to have an effect. None of those marches do. One should either be silent or go straight to the top. Once this village was without electricity for three months because the local system had broken down and the provincial company was scared of putting a pylon on the land of an old noblewoman, whose son was a Captain-General and who said that the spot was sacred to St. Catalina Tomás, the island's patron saint. I went to Madrid to see the Minister of Information and National Tourism and told him: "The local hotels will be empty this summer for lack of electricity." He kindly informed our Civil Governor that the pylon should be put up regardless of the Saint's feelings. But it's different if one can't go to the top. I regret the war in Vietnam, but marching won't stop it, and there is no one person, like our Minister in Madrid, who can control this complex situation.

INTERVIEWER: Does this disturb you?

GRAVES: Civilization has got further and further from the so-called "natural" man, who uses all his faculties: perception, invention, improvisation. It's bound to end in the breakdown of society and the cutting down of the human race to manageable size. That's the way things work; they always have. My hope is that a few cultural reservations will be left undisturbed. A suitable place might be certain Pacific Islands and tracts in Siberia and Australia, so that when the present mess is over, the race of man can restore itself from these centers.

INTERVIEWER: Who will be on the reservations? Who'll decide?

GRAVES: The people who are already there. They should be left. The Melanesians, for instance, and the palaeo-Siberians.

INTERVIEWER: Has your living here in Deyá, isolated from what you call the modern mechanarchic civilization, gradually led to what you call handcraft in your poetry?

GRAVES: I once lived here for six years without moving out. That was in the years 1930–1936. Didn't even go to Barcelona. Apart from that, I've always made a point of traveling. One's got to go out because one can't live wholly in oneself or wholly in the traditional past. One's got to be aware of how really nasty urban life is.

INTERVIEWER: But you take in much less by osmosis than if you were T. S. Eliot at the bank?

GRAVES: Obviously I do.

INTERVIEWER: You are constantly revising your collected poems. Why?

GRAVES: I realize from time to time that certain poems were written for the wrong reasons and feel obliged to remove them; they give me a sick feeling. Only the few necessary poems should be kept. There's no mystery about them: If one is a poet, one eventually learns which they are. Though, of course, a perfect poem is impossible. Once it had been written, the world would end.

PETER BUCKMAN
WILLIAM FIFIELD

4. John Dos Passos

Born on January 14, 1896, John Dos Passos was brought up in Chicago and educated at Choate and Harvard. In 1916 he went to Spain to study architecture, but World War I intervened, and he abandoned his studies to join the French Ambulance Service. Out of his war experience came his first book, *One Man's Initiation: 1917* (1920).

Among the books he wrote in the 1920s were the novels *Three Soldiers* (1921) and *Manhattan Transfer* (1925), in which he arrived at the techniques he later utilized in *U.S.A.*, and three plays remembered for their "movie" technique, *The Moon Is a Gong* (1926), *Airways, Inc.* (1928), and *Fortune Heights* (1933). His famous trilogy *U.S.A.* (1938), a sweeping criticism of cultural decay, employed "newsreel" and "camera eye" techniques to deal with hundreds of characters, constantly changing scenes, and vast social history. The three volumes are *The 42nd Parallel* (1930), *1919* (1932), and *The Big Money* (1936).

His next trilogy, *District of Columbia* (1952) was, in contrast, a defense of the free-enterprise system. His later work, including *The Theme Is Freedom* (1956), *The Great Days* (1958), *Midcentury* (1961), *Mr. Wilson's War* (1963), and *Occasions and Protests* (1964) continued his conservative trend. *The Best Times* (1966), his last book, was a reminiscence of his boyhood and early manhood.

Although he traveled a great deal when he was young, in his middle years he led a simple, quiet life on Cape Cod. Later, he and his wife moved to his father's Virginia farm, where they were living when he died in 1970.

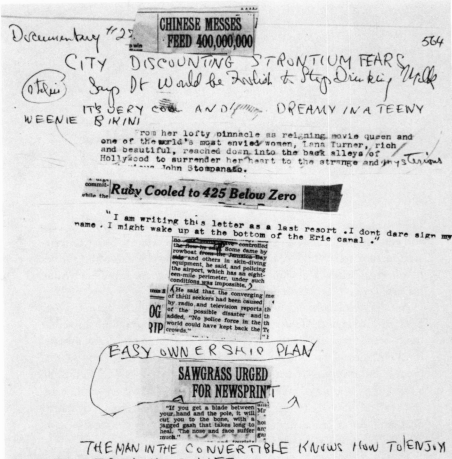

Documentary #27

564

CHINESE MESSES FEED 400,000,000

CITY DISCOUNTING STRONTIUM FEARS

(title) Says It Would be Foolish to Stop Drinking Milk

IT'S VERY COOL AND _____ DREAMY IN A TEENY
WEENIE BIKINI

From her lofty pinnacle as reigning movie queen and
one of the world's most envied women, Lana Turner, rich
and beautiful, reached down into the back alleys of
Hollywood to surrender her heart to the strange and mysterious
____ John Stompanato.

commit-
while the **Ruby Cooled to 425 Below Zero**

"I am writing this letter as a last resort. I dont dare sign my
name. I might wake up at the bottom of the Erie canal."

no ____ controlled
the flow he said. Some came by
rowboat from the Jamaica Bay
side and others in skin-diving
equipment, he said, and policing
the airport, which has an eight-
een-mile perimeter, under such
conditions was impossible.

He said that the converging
of thrill seekers had been caused
by radio and television reports
of the possible disaster and
added, "No police force in the
world could have kept back the
crowds."

me
t
th
th
th
Te

OG
RTP

EASY OWNERSHIP PLAN

**SAWGRASS URGED
FOR NEWSPRINT**

"If you get a blade between
your hand and the pole, it will
cut you to the bone, with a
jagged gash that takes long to
heal. The nose and face suffer
much."

Mr.
hou
an
ga

THE MAN IN THE CONVERTIBLE KNOWS HOW TO ENJOY
THE BETTER THINGS OF LIFE

"evidence makes it reasonably
certain that the ancestors of
the group had to pass through
a stage of existence underground as deaf, half-blind and
legless burrowing lizards."

"Is this what I fought for in World War II ? is this the world
my children are growing up into ?"

Manuscript page of *Midcentury*. From originals in the University of Virginia Library

John Dos Passos

Shortly after John Dos Passos had completed the three volumes of
U.S.A. *in 1936, Jean-Paul Sartre observed that he was "the greatest
living writer." In 1939, a* New Masses *reviewer attacked his novel,*
Adventures of a Young Man, *as "Trotskyist agitprop." Neither
statement set a pattern for later estimates of Dos Passos, although
they suggested the extremes with which his earlier novels* (Three
Soldiers, Manhattan Transfer, *and* U.S.A.) *and then his later ones*
(District of Columbia, Midcentury) *have been accepted. Dos
Passos has also run to extremes in his experiences: from the* New
Masses *to the* National Review, *from the Norton-Harjes Ambu-
lance Service to an assignment for* Life *in the Pacific Theater, from
Versailles to Nuremberg, from incessant travel to the quiet of his
grandfather's farm.*

*Despite all these contradictions and despite even the autobio-
graphical thread in his work, he has been a writer of unusual
detachment. He is still asked, as he was in the twenties: "Are you*

*for us or against us?" He has also been unusually industrious,
having published eighteen books since U.S.A. He works too hard
and too steadily to spare much time for answering questions about
himself.*

*Dos Passos was interviewed in 1968 on his farm, Spence's Point,
on the Northern Neck of Virginia, a sandy, piney strip of land
between the Rappahannock and the Potomac. The state highway
in from U.S. 301 passes turnoffs to the birthplaces of Washington
and Monroe. The windy, overcast June day didn't hold enough
threat of a storm to keep the writer, his strikingly handsome wife,
and the interviewer from swimming in the Potomac before proceed-
ing to anything else. He spoke easily about what he was doing
currently or was soon about to do but turned talk away from what
he had done years before by short, muffled answers, a nod or
chuckle, and a quick switch back to fishing in the Andes and flying
down the Amazon from Iquitos. The interview took place in a
small parlor of the late eighteenth-century house.*

*He is a tall man, conspicuously fit. He is round-faced, bald,
wears steel-rimmed glasses, and is much younger than he appears
to be in recent photographs. Characteristically, his head is pitched
forward at a slight angle in an attitude of perpetual attention. He
speaks a little nervously and huskily, with a trace of the cultivated
accent his schoolmates once thought "foreign." Although it
seemed that nothing could ruffle his natural courtesy, he was un-
comfortable about what he called "enforced conversation." The
tape recorder had something to do with this, but it was more
obvious that he simply did not enjoy talking about himself. Hesita-
tions aside, he was completely willing to say exactly what he
thought about individuals and events.*

INTERVIEWER: Is this the same farm where you spent your
summers as a boy?

DOS PASSOS: This is a different part of the same farm. When
my father was alive, we had a house down at the other end, a
section that has been sold, which is now part of a little development called Sandy Point, that string of cottages you saw along the

shore. We've been here for more than ten years now, but I don't get to spend as much time here as I would like to because I still have a good deal of unfinished traveling.

INTERVIEWER: Has this polarity between Spence's Point and your traveling had any particular effect on your writing?

DOS PASSOS: I don't know. Of course anything that happens to you has some bearing upon what you write.

INTERVIEWER: Perhaps it once led you to write that the novelist was a truffle dog going ahead of the social historian?

DOS PASSOS: I don't know how true that is. It's the hardest thing in the world to talk about your own work. You stumble along, and often the truffle dog doesn't get to eat the truffle . . . he just picks it up.

INTERVIEWER: Have you become the social historian at the expense of the artist?

DOS PASSOS: There's just no way that I can tell. I have to do what I'm interested in at the time, and I don't think there's anything necessarily inartistic about being the historian. I have great admiration for good history. All of my work has some certain historical connotation. Take *Three Soldiers*. I was trying to record something that was going on. I always felt that it might not be any good as a novel, but that it would at least be useful to add to the record. I had that idea when I began writing—with *One Man's Initiation*—and I've had it right along.

INTERVIEWER: Always, then, you have been observing for the record?

DOS PASSOS: Very much, I think.

INTERVIEWER: It must have been difficult to remain simply an objective observer.

DOS PASSOS: Possibly, but I think I've tended to come back to center. I'm often carried away by emotions and enthusiasms for various ideas at one time or another, but I think the desire to observe, to put down what you see as accurately as possible, is still paramount. I think the critics never understand that because they always go on the basis that if a man writes about Mormonism he must be a Mormon, that if he writes about Communism he must be Communist, which is not necessarily true. I've usually been on the fence in partisan matters. I've often been partisan for particular people, usually people who seem to be getting a raw deal, but that's a facet I share with many others.

INTERVIEWER: You've said that when you began observing you were a "half-baked young man" out of Harvard. Have you had any recent thoughts about that education?

DOS PASSOS: I got quite a little out of being at Harvard, although I was kicking all of the time I was there, complaining about the "ethercone" atmosphere I described in camera eye. I probably wouldn't have stayed if it hadn't been for my father, who was anxious for me to go through. At that time, the last of the old New Englanders were still at Harvard. They were really liberal-minded people, pretty thoroughly independent in their ideas, and they all had a sort of basic Protestant ethic behind them. They really knew what was what. I didn't agree with them then, but looking back on them now, I think more highly of them than I once did. But that essentially valid cast of mind was very much damaged by the strange pro-Allied and anti-German delusion that swept through them. You couldn't talk to people about it. When the war started in the summer of my sophomore year, I was curious to see it, even though theoretically I disapproved of war as a human activity. I was anxious to see what it was like. Like Charley Anderson in *42nd Parallel*, I wanted to go over before everything "went bellyup." When I got out of college in the summer of 1916, I was anxious to get started in architecture, but at the same time I was so restless that I had already managed to sign myself up in the volunteer ambulance service. My father was determined to put that off, so we kind of compromised on a Spanish expedition, and I went to Madrid to study architecture. Then my father died in January of 1917, and I went ahead into the ambulance service. I suppose that World War I then became my university.

INTERVIEWER: Especially because you were in the ambulance service?

DOS PASSOS: . . . You *saw* the war. I don't know if it was on the more or less seamier side of combat, but in the ambulance service you did have a more objective point of view toward war. After all, the infantryman must be carried away by the spirit of combat, which is quite different from sitting around and dragging off the wreckage.

INTERVIEWER: What remains with you now about the First War—thinking back on it?

DOS PASSOS: Much of it I don't remember, really because I wrote about it; when you write about something you often never think of it again. I do remember little snatches of experience. The smells. They seem to linger on in the memory—the gas smells, the almond smell of high explosive, latrine and body odors. A terrible time, there has never been such a series of massacres, but all of us were glad to have seen it and survived it. In the ambulance corps, my capacities were largely concerned with driving a car without dumping people into ditches. As for the troops, they had an ambivalent feeling about the corps. Where they saw us in greatest volume was where an attack had been planned and was going to be mounted and a lot of people were going to be killed. They must have thought us a collection of scavenger crows.

INTERVIEWER: Did you go through this time thinking of yourself as a writer?

DOS PASSOS: I never felt I wanted to be a writer . . . I didn't much like the literary world as I knew it. I studied architecture. I've always been a frustrated architect. But there are certain periods of life when you take in an awful lot of impressions. I kept a good diary—very usual sort of thing—and I was consistent about putting down my impressions. But I had no intention, really, of being a writer then. It may have been Barbusse that got me going. Or more likely something to keep the dry rot from settling in the brain. Robert Hillyer and I began what we called the Great Novel, or more simply the GN. Our schedule then at the front was twenty-four hours on, twenty hours off, and I remember we worked on the novel in a cement tank that protected us from the shelling. We wrote alternate chapters. I sent the manuscript up to the University of Virginia the other day. I didn't dare look at it.

INTERVIEWER: You mention the novels of Barbusse. Was it *Le Feu,* in particular, which made an impression?

DOS PASSOS: It impressed us a good deal at the time. It was the first of the novels that gave a picture of the massacres of World War I. He had a very good ear for the conversations of those involved. His other things weren't really very much. They were cultish works, like Rolland's *Jean-Christophe,* which impressed so many of us in our college days. One had to make a reassessment. I met Barbusse a number of times in Russia afterward. It was rather horrible: he was a combination of evangelist and Communist, and by that time he had become a mere mouthpiece for the Party.

INTERVIEWER: Then, after the war, you were at the Versailles peace conference?

DOS PASSOS: Not really. Sometime in the winter after the armistice they established a thing very much like the G.I. Bill. If you were a college student or a recent graduate, you could go to any university you picked over there, and I picked the Sorbonne. So I was around in Paris, I guess, from February to June of 1919. Of course, that was the peace-conference period, and I talked to a lot of people connected with it in various ways. Most of them were observers. No, I wasn't taking notes on it.

INTERVIEWER: The question of combining politics and fiction has engaged a good many critics, often drawing from them the notion that it's very difficult to mix the two.

DOS PASSOS: Well, I don't know. Recently, I've been calling my novels contemporary chronicles, which seems to fit them rather better. They have a strong political bent because after all—although it isn't the only thing—politics in our time has pushed people around more than anything else. I don't see why dealing with politics should harm a writer at all. Despite what he said about politics in the novel being "the pistol shot at the opera," Stendhal also wrote contemporary chronicles. Or look at Thucydi-

des. I don't think his history was at all damaged by the fact that
he was a political writer. A lot of very good writing has been more
or less involved in politics, although it's always a dangerous terri-
tory. It's better for some people to keep out unless they're willing
to learn how to observe. It is the occupation of a special kind of
writer. His investigation—using blocks of raw experience—must
be balanced. Sartre in his straight, plain reporting was wonderful.
I can't read him now. A writer in this field should be both engaged
and disengaged. He must have passion and concern and anger—
but he must keep his emotions at arm's length in his work. If he
doesn't, he's simply a propagandist, and what he offers is a
"preachment."

INTERVIEWER: Let's recall how you observed things when you
were among the first American writers to see the results of the
Soviet revolution. Did you speak the language?

DOS PASSOS: I learned French at an early age, and Spanish, and
Portuguese. I tried Russian, but I didn't do very well with it. I
used to get a special kind of headache over their verbs.

INTERVIEWER: Just how impressed were you on those first visits?

DOS PASSOS: My first glimpse of the Red Army was in 1921–22
when I was with the Near East Relief in the Caucasus. At that
time it still seemed very hopeful that they would develop something that would be leaning forward instead of backward. You
may remember having read in *Orient Express* how hopeful I felt
upon observing that the pawnshop in Baku seemed to be going
out of business. And, then, probably the period when I was in
Leningrad and Moscow in 1928 was the time when I was very
much on the fence because I tried to avoid politics entirely on
that visit. I'd been working with the New Playwrights—Gold,
Lawson—in New York, and I was very much interested in the
theater. The Russian theater was still quite good, and so there was
a great deal to see. I didn't know at that time that its development
was just about coming to its end. Often things you think are just
beginning are coming to an end. I spent about six months there
in 1928. Even then it was a much more open period than any they

had since except possibly the early part of the Khrushchev regime. People were still being introduced as Trotskyites, although Trotsky was in exile. Stalin hadn't really attained power the way he did after the purges. Most of the Russians I knew then were connected with the theater, and a few of them would shake their fists when they passed his picture. This was in '28. They already hated him. They knew more about him than I did. All those people disappeared in the purges.

INTERVIEWER: Would it be fair to say that at first you thought the Soviet experiment held some sort of promise for the individual?

DOS PASSOS: Yes, I thought it might. I always felt at that time that the Soviets might develop into something like the New England town meeting, but of course they became entirely different, something more like the boss-controlled conventions at home.

INTERVIEWER: What were your literary influences at this time —during the twenties?

DOS PASSOS: The futurists, Ungaretti in Italy in particular. I wasn't taken at all by D'Annunzio. He was a little too rhetorical for my taste. Then I admired Pío Baroja, the Spanish novelist, and Rimbaud, of course, and Stephen Crane, particularly *Maggie, Girl of the Streets*, in which Crane has a terribly good ear for conversation and the way people put things.

INTERVIEWER: Did Hemingway read Barbusse?

DOS PASSOS: Not as far as I know. Ernest and I used to read the Bible to each other. He began it. We read separate little scenes. From Kings, Chronicles. We didn't make anything out of it—the reading—but Ernest at that time talked a lot about style. He was crazy about Stephen Crane's "The Blue Hotel." It affected him very much. I was very much taken with him. He took me around to Gertrude Stein's. I wasn't quite at home there. A Buddha sitting up there, surveying us. Ernest was much less noisy then than he was in later life. He felt such people were instructive.

INTERVIEWER: Was Hemingway as occupied with the four-letter word problem as he was later?

DOS PASSOS: He was *always* concerned with four-letter words. It never bothered me particularly. Sex can be indicated with asterisks. I've always felt that was as good a way as any.

INTERVIEWER: Do you think Hemingway's descriptions of those times were accurate in *A Moveable Feast?*

DOS PASSOS: Well, it's a little sour, that book. His treatment of people like Scott Fitzgerald—the great man talking down about his contemporaries. He was always competitive and critical, overly so, but in the early days you could kid him out of it. He had a bad heredity. His father was very overbearing apparently. His mother was a very odd woman. I remember once when we were in Key West Ernest received a large unwieldy package from her. It had a big, rather crushed cake in it. She had put in a number of things with it, including the pistol with which his father had killed himself. Ernest was terribly upset.

INTERVIEWER: Have you ever had an equivalent sense of competition with your fellow writers?

DOS PASSOS: No, not at all. I've always thought you should concentrate on paddling your own canoe. Ernest's jealousy of Scott was really embarrassing—because much of it was at a time when Scott was going through a horrible experience in his own life. He was writing stories like "A Diamond As Big As The Ritz" —out of a state of mind which had so little to do with his literary energies.

INTERVIEWER: If we may return to your novels, is characterization particularly difficult in such a novel as *42nd Parallel* where J. Ward Moorehouse, who seems to personify the whole system being indicted, might be taken—I believe he has been taken— as based on Ivy Lee, the man who actually started the field of public relations?

DOS PASSOS: Well, Ivy Lee did have something to do with Moorehouse because I met Ivy Lee in Moscow—I've forgotten what he was doing there—when I was writing the book. We were at the same hotel. I was trying to learn Russian, a very painful process, and so it was quite a relief to find someone to talk English to. I had several rather interesting conversations with him. I think it was in the fall of '28, but I'm not sure what hotel it was. The Metropole? Anyway, I had done the first few chapters of *42nd Parallel* before I went, and then J. Ward Moorehouse was just emerging. I think those conversations with Ivy Lee probably had something to do with his completed portrait. Then, also, I knew quite a few advertising men in New York.

INTERVIEWER: I suppose a much more direct characterization of an actual figure occurs in *The Great Days,* doesn't it, with Roger Thurloe modeled as he is on Forrestal?

DOS PASSOS: That's closer to being an effort to produce a characterization of a living person, I think, than most of the others. I had met Forrestal a couple of times, but even so the characterization is pretty far off. I think if I had actually intended to do Forrestal, I would have done him as one of those portraits in *Midcentury.*

INTERVIEWER: Do you find it difficult to read anything written about your work?

DOS PASSOS: I never do, if I can help it. I know it has a bad effect on fellow writers. People sometimes send me articles about myself, and I bundle them off after a while to the University of Virginia for the professors to mull over. Occasionally I look at things, but I've generally managed to avoid stuff written about my work because there just isn't time to fuss with it. I don't think I've lost very much sleep by what you would call the critical reception of my work. I've been very fortunate in a way. If a thing is knocked in one place, somebody else may like it somewhere else. *The Great Days* was very much ignored in this country, but it went quite well in England and in Germany. I wouldn't have been able to make a living without the international market.

INTERVIEWER: What do you think of the considerable disparity between criticisms here and in Europe of your work over the past twenty years, or at least since *U.S.A.* was so well received in both places?

DOS PASSOS: I haven't followed it very much. I think there are a lot of American critics who try to pretend that I don't exist at all. They haven't read much of the stuff, and so they really don't know. When you do historical things, say, like *The Men Who Made the Nation*, a totally different set of people review it from those who review so-called fiction. There's this strange schizophrenia in American publishing between fiction and nonfiction, and so people who review nonfiction have never read any of the fiction. It works both ways.

INTERVIEWER: How much of the hostile American reception dated from *Adventures of a Young Man* in 1939, with the cues from left-wing reviewers?

DOS PASSOS: A certain amount, but still *Three Soldiers* was greeted with hostility all the way back in 1921. Of course I think they were wrong on *Adventures of a Young Man* because I don't think my position was so much changed. Politically it was, but from a human point of view I don't think it was so different.

INTERVIEWER: How have these differed in your orientation? The political and the human point of view? In going from *U.S.A.* to *District of Columbia* to *Midcentury*, have you, in effect, gone from big money to big government to big labor?

DOS PASSOS: To a certain extent, I think, yes. At different periods one seems more drastic than the other.

INTERVIEWER: It's a procession which points, perhaps, to this human consistency in your work.

DOS PASSOS: I think it probably does because I think that's what motivates it. It's a fact that I have tried to look at it from the point of view of the ordinary man, the ordinary woman, struggling to retain some dignity and to make a decent life in these vast organizations.

INTERVIEWER: In almost all of your work, then, there has been some opposition between individuals and systems?

DOS PASSOS: Always, yes. We've gone through a period when the industrial society has been very rapidly solidified. The Communist way is just one way of solidifying. What it seems to me they have done is to take the capitalist system and kind of freeze it, including a great many of its less agreeable characteristics, freeze it and turn it over completely to bureaucratic control.

INTERVIEWER: I've always wanted to know how *Manhattan*

Transfer was written—more than *Three Soldiers* or the other two early novels which more directly follow your experiences. When you wrote *Manhattan Transfer*, were you trying to create an entirely new kind of novel? Or were you building from definite precedents?

DOS PASSOS: *Three Soldiers* had just raised quite a stir and had quite a considerable sale. I seem to remember writing some of *Manhattan Transfer* in Brooklyn, in a room on Columbia Heights that looked out on the harbor. I don't know how this question can be answered. I was trying to get a great many things in to give a picture of the city of New York because I had spent quite a while there. I was trying also to get a certain feeling in. Precedents? I don't think so. I never went in much for theories of that sort. At the time I did *Manhattan Transfer*, I'm not sure whether I had seen Eisenstein's films. The idea of montage had an influence on the development of this sort of writing. I may have seen *Potemkin*. Then, of course, I must have seen *The Birth of a Nation*, which was the first attempt at montage. Eisenstein considered it the origin of his method. I don't know if there were any particular origins for *Manhattan Transfer* in my reading. *Vanity Fair* isn't at all like it, but I'd read *Vanity Fair* a great deal, and I'd read eighteenth-century English stuff. Perhaps *Tristram Shandy* has certain connections. It's all subjective, while, in my stuff, I was trying to be all objective. Sterne made up his narrative out of a great many different things. It doesn't seem to have much cohesion, but if you read the whole book, it adds up to a very cohesive picture.

INTERVIEWER: What about the reception of *Manhattan Transfer?*

DOS PASSOS: One critic called it "an explosion in a sewer." Probably the person who helped the book most was Sinclair Lewis, who wrote a very favorable review.

INTERVIEWER: What sort of plan did you have for *U.S.A.* when you began writing it?

DOS PASSOS: I was trying to develop what I had started, possibly somewhat unconsciously, in *Manhattan Transfer*. By that time I was really taken with the idea of montage. I had tried it out in *Manhattan Transfer*—using pieces of popular songs. By the time it evolved into such compartments as the camera eye of the *U.S.A.* trilogy it served a useful function—which in that case was to distill my subjective feelings about the incidents and people described. My hope was to achieve the objective approach of a Fielding, or a Flaubert, particularly as one sees it in Flaubert's letters, which are remarkable. In the biographies, in the newsreels, and even the narrative, I aimed at total objectivity by giving conflicting views—using the camera eye as a safety valve for my own subjective feelings. It made objectivity in the rest of the book much easier.

INTERVIEWER: You eventually closed down the camera eye— though *Midcentury* is the same as *U.S.A.* in its other formal aspects.

DOS PASSOS: After a while, you feel more in control of your subjective feelings. I didn't think that I needed it by then.

INTERVIEWER: Was *U.S.A.* a trilogy to begin with?

DOS PASSOS: No, it started to be one book, but then there was so much that I wanted to get in that it got to be three books very soon . . . before *42nd Parallel* was finished.

INTERVIEWER: Did you begin with the idea of just taking the years up to the war?

DOS PASSOS: No, I had the basic idea for the whole thing. It started with what I didn't then call a contemporary chronicle; I do call it that now because it seems a useful label. I think, if I can remember back, I started *42nd Parallel* with the idea of publishing a series of reportages of the times. I don't think I thought of the book as any sort of a novel. I thought of it as a series of reportages in which characters appeared and reappeared. It was to cover quite a long period.

INTERVIEWER: I've often wondered why some of them, like Richard Ellsworth Savage or Vag, didn't reappear in *District of Columbia* or *Midcentury*.

DOS PASSOS: I decided to try to close that group down. You have to make a fresh start every now and then.

INTERVIEWER: How did you come to add the portraits to *U.S.A.?* Did you get much editorial advice on this book?

DOS PASSOS: Eugene Saxton, first at Doran and then at Harpers, was a very friendly editor, but I don't think anybody gave me any advice. If they did, I doubt if I took it—I guess because I've been very hard to convince. I've always been very grateful for what they've been able to point out about misspellings and bad construction, but as far as the *gist* of things is concerned I've not been much moved. It's awfully hard to say how I came to add the portraits. I was trying to get different facets of my subject and trying to get something a little more accurate than fiction, at the same time to work these pieces into the fictional picture. The aim was always to produce fiction. That's why I was completely unable to understand the fiction, nonfiction dichotomy. I was sort of on the edge between them, moving from one field to the other very rapidly.

INTERVIEWER: Critics might drop labels altogether when they take up *U.S.A.?*

DOS PASSOS: It would be a good idea to look at it a little more objectively without preconceived ideas. That wouldn't mean that they would necessarily have to like it, but I think they would have a better basis for criticism.

INTERVIEWER: In connection with research, is a social life with literary people useful?

DOS PASSOS: Almost never. I hear a good deal more nonliterary conversation. Certainly useful to me in my line of work. I read very little. Yet the language does change—mostly through television and teenage jargon—and it's very hard to keep up with it. Knowing a younger generation helps. An academic community is pretty dreary, but the students, of course, are an interesting quantity. They come down from the University of Virginia and deliver themselves of the current doctrine. As do my daughter and stepson. It's very valuable. Word of mouth provides the great texture, not research.

INTERVIEWER: Incidentally, what is your opinion of the students of the New Left?

DOS PASSOS: Many of them seem to be going through something rather like a tantrum. An odd paranoia sweeping the country, I don't know exactly why . . . a mass hysteria . . . a combination of the St. Vitus' dance of medieval times and the Children's Crusade . . .

INTERVIEWER: What about other forms of activity? In the twenties you maintained a great interest in the theater.

DOS PASSOS: The theater didn't suit me really. I can't sit up all night. Everything in the theater is done after midnight. I lived in Brooklyn at the time, and we always finished so late that I had to walk back home across the Brooklyn Bridge. I never got home before three A.M. and being someone who's never been able to sleep later than seven in the morning, I just couldn't keep up the schedule.

INTERVIEWER: Did you ever run across Hart Crane on those walks?

DOS PASSOS: He was very much a night animal. I used to try to get him to go home to his bed for a change. I'd get him there all right, but then he'd hide in the entry and dart out again.

INTERVIEWER: He used to prod his creative impulse by writing to the noise of a phonograph turned up full volume.

DOS PASSOS: Yes, I've heard that. For me it would be too distracting . . . pleasure and pain equally divided. I find that simpler things get me going—diaries, for instance, especially if they turn up in old trunks . . .

INTERVIEWER: What is your ideal set of working conditions?

DOS PASSOS: All you need is a room without any particular interruptions. Some things I've done entirely in longhand, but now I tend to start chapters in longhand and then finish them on the typewriter, and that becomes such a mess that nobody can transcribe it except my wife. I find it easier to get up early in the morning, and I like to get through by one or two o'clock. I don't do very much in the afternoon. I like to get out of doors then if I can.

INTERVIEWER: You get all of your work done before you go swimming?

DOS PASSOS: Yes. Down here that's my regular routine.

INTERVIEWER: How much revising do you go through?

DOS PASSOS: I do a lot of revising. Certain chapters six or seven times. Occasionally you can hit it right the first time. More often, you don't. George Moore rewrote entire novels. In my own case I usually write to a point where the work is getting worse rather than better. That's the point to stop and the time to publish.

INTERVIEWER: How did *District of Columbia* become a trilogy?

DOS PASSOS: *Adventures of a Young Man* came by itself, and the Spottswood family seemed to need more development. I began with the younger brother, went on to the older brother, and finished with the father. It worked out backwards.

INTERVIEWER: Was Glenn Spottswood's predicament in *Adventures of a Young Man* anything like your own in the later thirties? By his predicament I mean Glenn's feeling that he had been deceived while he worked on the Harlan County Defense Committee, the Scottsboro Boys Defense Committee, all of his encounters with the Communists.

DOS PASSOS: I wouldn't have known about conditions in Harlan County or what was behind either Defense Committee if I hadn't been through those experiences. I wouldn't have known how to describe them. Of course, I think you always have to have a little seed of personal experience, although it's often a very small seed, to produce the real verisimilitude, which is what you are looking for.

INTERVIEWER: In *Number One,* the novel about Glenn's older brother Tyler, there is an account of the third-term convention. Had you admired Roosevelt before that occasion?

DOS PASSOS: Yes, I certainly did. I thought he did very well all of his first term. I voted for him a second term, and then I regret to say that I voted for him for his third term. Now I think it would probably have been better for the country if Willkie had been elected, if anybody else had been elected, because it would have broken up the continuity of Roosevelt's extraordinary machine in Washington. I think Roosevelt would have come down as a really great president if he had only served two terms. I think he had done all the good he had in him, and there was only harm left. In that third term, the consolidation of the federal government really was the rebirth of bureaucracy, which had shown its head under Wilson and then faded away. That's what *The Grand Design* is about.

INTERVIEWER: It seemed to me that Roosevelt dominated that book, if not all of *District of Columbia,* in much the same way that Wilson did *1919.*

DOS PASSOS: I think so, although I fairly intentionally kept him behind the scenes. At that time I had done quite a bit of reporting around Washington. Reporting has always been an important part of my career. Between books, I've always done a few reporting jobs.

INTERVIEWER: One political question seems inescapable. In many of your books since the war, you write of the "abominable snowman" of international Communism, of having been among the first to see him, and having kept on seeing him through all of the crises, alliances, and thaws. Do you see him as clearly today?

DOS PASSOS: It's very hard to tell. It's almost impossible to have any view of present-day international politics without having a double standard of judgment. Our development and that of the Soviet Union have many things in common except that the Soviet Union is motivated by this tremendous desire for world conquest, more active sometimes and at other times less active. It may be that the people of Russia are not very much motivated by this passion for expansion any more. I'm not sure whether they ever were. I would like to know. I mean I don't think the mass of people is motivated at all because it's so hard for them to reach any conclusion. They are doped with ideology.

INTERVIEWER: Have you ever thought of going back there to check on it?

DOS PASSOS: It would be hard to. There might come a time when it would be interesting to go to Russia, but I don't think that time has come yet. I think there are certain phases of the development of Russian society which are on our side.

Some Russians might be among our best allies because some of them really want much the same things that we do. But those particular people are helpless in the bureaucratic setup. Pasternak was a good example, I think, with his curious book, *Doctor Zhivago.* It seemed so much a voice from the past, like something of Turgenev's coming back to life. It was very attractive to me because it showed a side of the Russian people which I've had great sympathy with. It showed that that side of the Russian mind, that nineteenth-century humanism, still existed. Of course, Pasternak was quite an old man. Still, as long as they teach people to read and write and allow them to read nineteenth-century Russian literature, there are going to be more Pasternaks.

INTERVIEWER: Do you read many contemporary American writers?

DOS PASSOS: I don't get time for very much because I do so much reading of a research type in connection with things I am doing—documents. It's very hard for me to get time. I read Salinger with a great deal of pleasure, and I mention him simply because he has given me pleasure. *The Catcher in the Rye* and *Frannie and Zooey* were very entertaining books. I read a certain amount of Faulkner, and I'm very, very fond of some of his writing. "The Bear" and *As I Lay Dying.* "The Bear" is a marvelous hunting story. I liked *Intruder in the Dust.* He reminds me very much of the old storytellers I used to listen to down here when I visited summers as a boy, when I would hide in the shadows so that I wouldn't be sent off to bed. I'd listen till my ears would burst. I suppose what I like best in Faulkner is the detail. He is a remarkably accurate observer and builds his narratives—which sometimes strike me as turgid—out of the marvelous raw material of what he has seen.

INTERVIEWER: And Cummings' poetry?

DOS PASSOS: Oh, I've always enjoyed Cummings' poetry. I was very fond of Cummings personally. He was in college at the same time I was, I think a class ahead of me, and I saw quite a little bit of him there. We always met on much the same terms, although sometimes a year would go by when I didn't see him. He was the last of the great New Englanders.

INTERVIEWER: How does the work of some of the more committed left-wing writers of the thirties seem to you now? Michael Gold and Howard Fast, for example.

DOS PASSOS: Somebody credited me with a wisecrack about that time: Writers of the world unite, you have nothing to lose but your brains. Mike Gold wrote quite well. His first book, *Jews Without Money*, was a warm, human thing, very much influenced by Gorky, whom Gold admired greatly. Fast never interested me. His book on Tom Paine irritated me very much because I thought he completely falsified the picture. Generally, though, the writers who became CP members either stopped writing or became so boring nobody could read them.

INTERVIEWER: Have you known any of the Communist politicians, rather than the writers?

DOS PASSOS: I had a long conversation with Earl Browder, to whom I took a great dislike. He was a horrible fellow. I've met Foster and didn't dislike him.

INTERVIEWER: Did you discover a great disparity between Browder and Foster, on the one hand, and John Reed on the other?

DOS PASSOS: Of course, I had a great deal of sympathy with John Reed. I thought he wrote very well, and I think I liked his writings better than I did him. The only time I ever met him he was giving a talk, maybe about Mexico. It was at Harvard when I was an undergraduate. There was something indefinably Harvard Brahmin in his manner that threw me off at the time. I was a very intolerant young man in a bashful and retiring sort of way in those days. I hated college boys. From what Louise Bryant said privately, I suspect that John Reed was pretty discouraged before he died.

INTERVIEWER: Have *you* been more optimistic about the world situation in the last five years or less so?

DOS PASSOS: It would be hard to say. I think I have probably become more so as I get older and a little less passionately involved, but then when they pull something like the operation in the Bay of Pigs, I become extremely pessimistic, particularly when nobody seems to understand its significance.

INTERVIEWER: What do you think of the academic treatment of modern literature?

DOS PASSOS: It seems to be rather confused, although I haven't followed it very much. The academic community is more likely to suffer from mass delusions than the general public. I don't know exactly why, but I suppose it's always been the case.

INTERVIEWER: Do you feel that your own most recent writing is generally misunderstood in this country?

DOS PASSOS: I wouldn't say that. Some people misunderstand it, naturally. They always will. It would be absurd to expect them to understand things. Also, if you deal with matters that touch people, you must expect to cause pain; particularly, if you hit at some target that is close to the truth. It always causes pain, agony. Naturally, they resent it.

INTERVIEWER: Have you ever thought that you have what has been called a Wayne Morse complex, an unwillingness to go along with a major party or major tendency?

DOS PASSOS: There is a type of mind that does tend to say, as Ibsen did, that the minority is always right. Perhaps I agree with Ibsen in that.

INTERVIEWER: Have you tried other artistic forms? Poetry, for instance.

DOS PASSOS: I did quite a lot of that . . . but it took a different form . . . it got into certain rhythmic passages in *U.S.A.* I do a little painting, a watercolor or so. The prose can get too high-colored; a watercolor gets that drained off.

INTERVIEWER: Do you enjoy writing?

DOS PASSOS: That depends. Sometimes I do, and sometimes I don't.

INTERVIEWER: What is its particular pleasure?

DOS PASSOS: Well, you get a great deal off your chest—emotions, impressions, opinions. Curiosity urges you on—the driving force. What is collected must be got rid of. That's one thing to be said about writing. There is a great sense of relief in a fat volume.

DAVID SANDERS

5. Vladimir Nabokov

The son of a distinguished jurist and statesman, Vladimir Nabokov learned to read English before mastering Russian. Born in St. Petersburg on April 23, 1899, he and his family left Russia in 1919, following the Bolshevik Revolution, and he began studies in French and Russian literature at Trinity College, Cambridge. Mr. Nabokov was graduated from Cambridge in 1922 and rejoined his family in Berlin, where he remained until 1937. During that time he wrote his first novels: *Mashenka* (1926), *King, Queen, Knave* (1928), *The Defense* (1930), and *Despair* (1936). He also wrote short stories, criticism, and poems. He was a frequent contributor to the émigré journal *Contemporary Annals*, and to *Rudder*, a liberal émigré newspaper.

After a brief period of residence in Paris (1937–1940), during which he wrote *The Eye* (1938) and *Invitation to a Beheading* (1938), Nabokov came to the United States with his wife, the former Vera Slonim, and his son, Dmitri. At that time he decided to start writing in English. Mr. Nabokov became an American citizen in 1945 and taught Russian literature and creative writing at Stanford, Wellesley, Cornell, and Harvard.

Nabokov first achieved popular fame in the United States in 1958 with the publication of *Lolita*. His other novels and short stories in English include *The Real Life of Sebastian Knight* (1941), *Bend Sinister* (1947), *Pnin* (1957), *Nabokov's Dozen* (1958), *Pale Fire* (1962), *The Defense* (1964), *Ada* (1969), *Mary* (1970), *Glory* (1972), *Transparent Things* (1972), *A Russian Beauty and Other Stories* (1973), *Strong Opinions* (1973), and *Look at the Harlequins!* (1974). He was awarded the 1973 National Medal for Literature.

peace, and of nights with her, the red blaze of her hair spreading all over the pillow, and, in the morning, again her quiet laughter, the green dress, the coolness of her bare arms.

In the middle of a square stood a black wigwam: ~~they were~~ _were being repaired_ ~~working on~~ the tram tracks. He remembered how he had got today under her short sleeve, and kissed the touching scar from her small-pox vaccination. And now he was walking home, unsteady on his feet from too much happiness and too much drink, swinging his slender cane, and among the dark houses on the opposite side of the empty street a night echo clop-clopped in time with his footfalls; but grew silent when he turned at the corner where the same man as always, in apron and peaked cap, stood by his grill, selling frankfurters, crying out in a tender and sad bird-like whistle: "Würstchen, würstchen..."

Mark felt a sort of delicious pity for the frankfurters, the moon, the blue spark that had receded along the wire and, as he tensed his body against a friendly fence, he was overcome with laughter, and, bending, exhaled into a little round hole in the boards the words "Klara, Klara, oh my darling!"

On the other side of the fence, in a gap between the buildings, was a rectangular vacant lot. Several moving vans stood there like enormous coffins. They were bloated from their loads. Heaven knows what was piled inside them. Oakwood trunks, probably, and chandeliers like iron spiders, and the heavy skeleton of a double bed. The moon

Vladimir Nabokov

Vladimir Nabokov lives with his wife Vera in the Montreux-Palace Hotel in Montreux, Switzerland, a resort city on Lake Geneva which was a favorite of Russian aristocrats of the last century. They dwell in a connected series of hotel rooms that, like their houses and apartments in the United States, seem impermanent, places of exile. Their rooms include one used for visits by their son Dmitri, and another, the chambre de debarras, *where various items are deposited—Turkish and Japanese editions of* Lolita, *other books, sporting equipment, an American flag.*

Nabokov arises early in the morning and works. He does his writing on filing cards, which are gradually copied, expanded, and rearranged until they become his novels. During the warm season in Montreux he likes to take the sun and swim at a pool in a garden near the hotel. His appearance at sixty-eight is heavy, slow, and powerful. He is easily turned to both amusement and annoyance, but prefers the former. His wife, an unequivocally devoted col-

laborator, is vigilant over him, writing his letters, taking care of business, occasionally even interrupting him when she feels he is saying the wrong thing. She is an exceptionally good-looking, trim, and sober-eyed woman. The Nabokovs still go off on frequent butterfly-hunting trips, though the distances they travel are limited by the fact that they dislike flying.

The interviewer had sent ahead a number of questions. When he arrived at the Montreux-Palace, he found an envelope waiting for him—the questions had been shaken up and transformed into an interview. A few questions and answers were added later, before the interview's appearance in the 1967 Summer/Fall issue of The Paris Review. *In accordance with Nabokov's wishes, all answers are given as he wrote them down. He claims that he needs to write his responses because of his unfamiliarity with English; this is a constant serio-comic form of teasing. He speaks with a dramatic Cambridge accent, very slightly nuanced by an occasional Russian pronunciation. Spoken English is, in fact, no hazard to him. Misquotation, however, is a menace. There is no doubt that Nabokov feels as a tragic loss the conspiracy of history that deprived him of his native Russia, and that brought him in middle life to doing his life's work in a language that is not that of his first dreams. However, his frequent apologies for his grasp of English clearly belong in the context of Nabokov's special mournful joking: he means it, he does not mean it, he is grieving for his loss, he is outraged if anyone criticizes his style, he pretends to be just a poor lonely foreigner, he is as American "as April in Arizona."*

Nabokov is now at work on a long novel that explores the mysteries and ambiguities of time. When he speaks of this book, his voice and gaze are those of a delighted and bemused young poet eager to get to the task.

INTERVIEWER: Good morning. Let me ask forty-odd questions.

NABOKOV: Good morning. I am ready.

INTERVIEWER: Your sense of the immorality of the relationship between Humbert Humbert and Lolita is very strong. In Hollywood and New York, however, relationships are frequent between men of forty and girls very little older than Lolita. They marry— to no particular public outrage; rather, public cooing.

NABOKOV: No, it is not *my* sense of the immorality of the Humbert Humbert-Lolita relationship that is strong; it is Humbert's sense. *He* cares, I do not. *I* do not give a damn for public morals, in America or elsewhere. And, anyway, cases of men in their forties marrying girls in their teens or early twenties have no bearing on Lolita whatever. Humbert was fond of "little girls"— not simply "young girls." Nymphets are girl-children, not starlets and "sex kittens." Lolita was twelve, not eighteen when Humbert met her. You may remember that by the time she is fourteen, he refers to her as his "aging mistress."

INTERVIEWER: One critic (Pryce-Jones) has said about you that "his feelings are like no one else's." Does this make sense to you? Or does it mean that you know your feelings better than others know theirs? Or that you have discovered yourself at other levels? Or simply that your history is unique?

NABOKOV: I do not recall that article; but if a critic makes such a statement, it must surely mean that he has explored the feelings of literally millions of people, in at least three countries, before reaching his conclusion. If so, I am a rare fowl indeed. If, on the other hand, he has merely limited himself to quizzing members of his family or club, his statement cannot be discussed seriously.

INTERVIEWER: Another critic has written that your "worlds are static. They may become tense with obsession, but they do not break apart like the worlds of everyday reality." Do you agree? Is there a static quality in your view of things?

NABOKOV: Whose "reality"? "Everyday" where? Let me suggest that the very term "everyday reality" is utterly static since it presupposes a situation that is permanently observable, essentially objective, and universally known. I suspect you have invented that expert on "everyday reality." Neither exists.

INTERVIEWER: *He* does *(names him)*. A third critic has said that you "diminish" your characters "to the point where they become ciphers in a cosmic farce." I disagree; Humbert, while comic, retains a touching and insistent quality—that of the spoiled artist.

NABOKOV: I would put it differently: Humbert Humbert is a vain and cruel wretch who manages to appear "touching." That epithet, in its true, tear-iridized sense, can only apply to my poor little girl. Besides, how can I "diminish" to the level of ciphers, et cetera, characters that I have invented myself? One can "diminish" a biographee, but not an eidolon.

INTERVIEWER: E. M. Forster speaks of his major characters sometimes taking over and dictating the course of his novels. Has this ever been a problem for you, or are you in complete command?

NABOKOV: My knowledge of Mr. Forster's works is limited to one novel, which I dislike; and anyway, it was not he who fathered that trite little whimsy about characters getting out of hand; it is as old as the quills, although of course one sympathizes with *his* people if they try to wriggle out of that trip to India or wherever he takes them. My characters are galley slaves.

INTERVIEWER: Clarence Brown of Princeton has pointed out striking similarities in your work. He refers to you as "extremely repetitious" and that in wildly different ways you are in essence saying the same thing. He speaks of fate being the "muse of Nabokov." Are you consciously aware of "repeating yourself," or to put it another way, that you strive for a conscious unity to your shelf of books?

NABOKOV: I do not think I have seen Clarence Brown's essay, but he may have something there. Derivative writers seem versatile because they imitate many others, past and present. Artistic originality has only its own self to copy.

INTERVIEWER: Do you think literary criticism is at all purposeful? Either in general, or specifically about your own books? Is it ever instructive?

NABOKOV: The purpose of a critique is to say something about a book the critic has or has not read. Criticism can be instructive in the sense that it gives readers, including the author of the book, some information about the critic's intelligence, or honesty, or both.

INTERVIEWER: And the function of the editor? Has one ever had literary advice to offer?

NABOKOV: By "editor" I suppose you mean proofreader. Among these I have known limpid creatures of limitless tact and tenderness who would discuss with me a semicolon as if it were a point of honor—which, indeed, a point of art often is. But I have also come across a few pompous avuncular brutes who would attempt to "make suggestions" which I countered with a thunderous "stet!"

INTERVIEWER: Are you a lepidopterist, stalking your victims? If so, doesn't your laughter startle them?

NABOKOV: On the contrary, it lulls them into the state of torpid security which an insect experiences when mimicking a dead leaf. Though by no means an avid reader of reviews dealing with my own stuff, I happen to remember the essay by a young lady who attempted to find entomological symbols in my fiction. The essay might have been amusing had she known something about Lepidoptera. Alas, she revealed complete ignorance, and the muddle of terms she employed proved to be only jarring and absurd.

INTERVIEWER: How would you define your alienation from the so-called White Russian refugees?

NABOKOV: Well, historically I am a "White Russian" myself since all Russians who left Russia as my family did in the first years of the Bolshevist tyranny because of their opposition to it were and remained White Russians in the large sense. But these refugees were split into as many social fractions and political factions as was the entire nation before the Bolshevist coup. I do not mix with "black-hundred" White Russians and do not mix with the so-called "bolshevizans," that is "pinks." On the other hand, I have friends among intellectual Constitutional Monarchists as well as among intellectual Social Revolutionaries. My father was an old-fashioned liberal, and I do not mind being labeled an old-fashioned liberal, too.

INTERVIEWER: How would you define your alienation from present-day Russia?

NABOKOV: As a deep distrust of the phony thaw now advertised. As a constant awareness of unredeemable iniquities. As a complete indifference to all that moves a patriotic Sovetski man of today. As the keen satisfaction of having discerned as early as 1918 (nineteen eighteen) the *meshchantsvo* (petty bourgeois smugness, Philistine essence) of Leninism.

INTERVIEWER: How do you now regard the poets Blok and Mandelshtam and others who were writing in the days before you left Russia?

NABOKOV: I read them in my boyhood, more than a half century ago. Ever since that time I have remained passionately fond of Blok's lyrics. His long pieces are weak, and the famous *The Twelve* is dreadful, self-consciously couched in a phony "primitive" tone, with a pink cardboard Jesus Christ glued on at the end. As to Mandelshtam, I also knew him by heart, but he gave me a less fervent pleasure. Today, through the prism of a tragic fate, his poetry seems greater than it actually is. I note incidentally that professors of literature still assign these two poets to different schools. There is only one school: that of talent.

INTERVIEWER: I know your work has been read and is attacked in the Soviet Union. How would you feel about a Soviet edition of your work?

NABOKOV: Oh, they are welcome to my work. As a matter of fact, the Editions Victor are bringing out my *Invitation to a Beheading* in a reprint of the original Russian of 1935, and a New York publisher (Phaedra) is printing my Russian translation of *Lolita*. I am sure the Soviet Government will be happy to admit officially a novel that seems to contain a prophecy of Hitler's regime, and a novel that condemns bitterly the American system of motels.

INTERVIEWER: Have you ever had contact with Soviet citizens? Of what sort?

NABOKOV: I have practically no contact with them, though I did once agree, in the early thirties or late twenties, to meet—out of sheer curiosity—an agent from Bolshevist Russia who was trying hard to get émigré writers and artists to return to the fold. He had a double name, Lebedev something, and had written a novelette entitled *Chocolate*, and I thought I might have some sport with him. I asked him would I be permitted to write freely and would I be able to leave Russia if I did not like it there. He said that I would be so busy liking it there that I would have no time to dream of going abroad again. I would, he said, be perfectly free to choose any of the many themes Soviet Russia bountifully allows a writer to use, such as farms, factories, forests in Fakistan —oh, lots of fascinating subjects. I said farms, et cetera, bored me, and my wretched seducer soon gave up. He had better luck with the composer Prokofiev.

INTERVIEWER: Do you consider yourself an American?

NABOKOV: Yes, I do. I am as American as April in Arizona. The flora, the fauna, the air of the Western states, are my links with Asiatic and Arctic Russia. Of course, I owe too much to the Russian language and landscape to be emotionally involved in, say, American regional literature, or Indian dances, or pumpkin pie on a spiritual plane; but I do feel a suffusion of warm, light-hearted pride when I show my green U.S.A. passport at European frontiers. Crude criticism of American affairs offends and distresses me. In home politics I am strongly antisegregationist. In foreign policy, I am definitely on the government's side. And when in doubt, I always follow the simple method of choosing that line of conduct which may be the most displeasing to the Reds and the Russells.

INTERVIEWER: Is there a community of which you consider yourself a part?

NABOKOV: Not really. I can mentally collect quite a large number of individuals whom I am fond of, but they would form a very disparate and discordant group if gathered in real life, on a real island. Otherwise, I would say that I am fairly comfortable in the company of American intellectuals who have read my books.

INTERVIEWER: What is your opinion of the academic world as a milieu for the creative writer? Could you speak specifically of the value or detriment of your teaching at Cornell?

NABOKOV: A first-rate college library with a comfortable campus around it is a fine milieu for a writer. There is, of course, the problem of educating the young. I remember how once, between terms, not at Cornell, a student brought a transistor set with him into the reading room. He managed to state that (1) he was playing "classical" music; that (2) he was doing it "softly"; and that (3) "there were not many readers around in summer." I was there, a one-man multitude.

INTERVIEWER: Would you describe your relationship with the contemporary literary community? With Edmund Wilson, Mary McCarthy, your magazine editors and book publishers?

NABOKOV: The only time I ever collaborated with any writer was when I translated with Edmund Wilson Pushkin's *Mozart and Salieri* for the *New Republic* twenty-five years ago, a rather paradoxical recollection in view of his making such a fool of himself last year when he had the audacity of questioning my understanding of *Eugene Onegin*. Mary McCarthy, on the other hand, has been very kind to me recently in the same *New Republic*, although I do think she added quite a bit of her own angelica to the pale fire of Kinbote's plum pudding. I prefer not to mention here my relationship with Girodias, but I have answered in *Evergreen* his scurvy article in the Olympia anthology. Otherwise, I am on excellent terms with all my publishers. My warm friendship with Catharine White and Bill Maxwell of *The New Yorker* is something the most arrogant author cannot evoke without gratitude and delight.

INTERVIEWER: Could you say something of your work habits? Do you write to a preplanned chart? Do you jump from one section to another, or do you move from the beginning through to the end?

NABOKOV: The pattern of the thing precedes the thing. I fill in the gaps of the crossword at any spot I happen to choose. These bits I write on index cards until the novel is done. My schedule is flexible, but I am rather particular about my instruments: lined Bristol cards and well sharpened, not too hard, pencils capped with erasers.

INTERVIEWER: Is there a particular picture of the world which you wish to develop? The past is very present for you, even in a novel of the "future," such as *Bend Sinister*. Are you a "nostalgist"? In what time would you prefer to live?

NABOKOV: In the coming days of silent planes and graceful aircycles, and cloudless silvery skies, and a universal system of padded underground roads to which trucks shall be relegated like Morlocks. As to the past, I would not mind retrieving from various corners of spacetime certain lost comforts, such as baggy trousers and long, deep bathtubs.

INTERVIEWER: You know, you do not have to answer *all* my Kinbote-like questions.

NABOKOV: It would never do to start skipping the tricky ones. Let us continue.

INTERVIEWER: Besides writing novels, what do you, or would you, like most to do?

NABOKOV: Oh, hunting butterflies, of course, and studying them. The pleasures and rewards of literary inspiration are nothing beside the rapture of discovering a new organ under the microscope or an undescribed species on a mountainside in Iran or Peru. It is not improbable that had there been no revolution in Russia, I would have devoted myself entirely to lepidopterology and never written any novels at all.

INTERVIEWER: What is most characteristic of poshlust in contemporary writing? Are there temptations for you in the sin of poshlust? Have you ever fallen?

NABOKOV: "Poshlust," or in a better transliteration *poshlost,* has many nuances, and evidently I have not described them clearly enough in my little book on Gogol, if you think one can ask anybody if he is tempted by *poshlost.* Corny trash, vulgar clichés, Philistinism in all its phases, imitations of imitations, bogus profundities, crude, moronic, and dishonest pseudo-literature—these are obvious examples. Now, if we want to pin down *poshlost* in contemporary writing, we must look for it in Freudian symbolism, moth-eaten mythologies, social comment, humanistic messages, political allegories, overconcern with class or race, and the journalistic generalities we all know. *Poshlost* speaks in such concepts as "America is no better than Russia" or "We all share in Germany's guilt." The flowers of *poshlost* bloom in such phrases and terms as "the moment of truth," "charisma," "existential" (used seriously), "dialogue" (as applied to political talks between nations), and "vocabulary" (as applied to a dauber). Listing in one breath Auschwitz, Hiroshima, and Vietnam is seditious *poshlost*. Belonging to a very select club (which sports *one* Jewish name—that of the treasurer) is genteel *poshlost*. Hack reviews are frequently *poshlost*, but it also lurks in certain highbrow essays. *Poshlost* calls Mr. Blank a great poet and Mr. Bluff a great novelist. One of *poshlost*'s favorite breeding places has always been the Art Exhibition; there it is produced by so-called sculptors working with the tools of wreckers, building crankshaft cretins of stainless steel, zen stereos, polystyrene stinkbirds, objects *trouvés* in latrines, cannon balls, canned balls. There we admire the *gabinetti* wall patterns of so-called abstract artists, Freudian surrealism, roric smudges, and Rorschach blots—all of it as corny in its own right as the academic "September Morns" and "Florentine Flowergirls" of half a century ago. The list is long, and, of course, everybody has his *bête noire*, his black pet, in the series. Mine is that airline ad: the snack served by an obsequious wench to a young couple—she eyeing ecstatically the cucumber canapé, he admiring wistfully the hostess. And, of course, *Death in Venice*. You see the range.

INTERVIEWER: Are there contemporary writers you follow with great pleasure?

NABOKOV: There are several such writers, but I shall not name them. Anonymous pleasure hurts nobody.

INTERVIEWER: Do you follow some with great pain?

NABOKOV: No. Many accepted authors simply do not exist for me. Their names are engraved on empty graves, their books are dummies, they are complete nonentities insofar as my taste in reading is concerned. Brecht, Faulkner, Camus, many others, mean absolutely nothing to me, and I must fight a suspicion of conspiracy against my brain when I see blandly accepted as "great literature" by critics and fellow authors Lady Chatterley's copulations or the pretentious nonsense of Mr. Pound, that total fake. I note he has replaced Dr. Schweitzer in some homes.

INTERVIEWER: As an admirer of Borges and Joyce you seem to share their pleasure in teasing the reader with tricks and puns and puzzles. What do you think the relationship should be between reader and author?

NABOKOV: I do not recollect any puns in Borges, but then I read him only in translation. Anyway, his delicate little tales and miniature Minotaurs have nothing in common with Joyce's great machines. Nor do I find many puzzles in that most lucid of novels, *Ulysses.* On the other hand, I detest *Punningans Wake* in which a cancerous growth of fancy word-tissue hardly redeems the dreadful joviality of the folklore and the easy, too easy, allegory.

INTERVIEWER: What have you learned from Joyce?

NABOKOV: Nothing.

INTERVIEWER: Oh, come.

NABOKOV: James Joyce has not influenced me in any manner whatsoever. My first brief contact with *Ulysses* was around 1920 at Cambridge University, when a friend, Peter Mrozovski, who had brought a copy from Paris, chanced to read to me, as he stomped up and down my digs, one or two spicy passages from Molly's monologue, which, *entre nous soit dit,* is the weakest chapter in the book. Only fifteen years later, when I was already well formed as a writer and reluctant to learn or unlearn anything, I read *Ulysses* and liked it enormously. I am indifferent to *Finnegans Wake* as I am to all regional literature written in dialect— even if it be the dialect of genius.

INTERVIEWER: Aren't you doing a book about James Joyce?

NABOKOV: But not only about him. What I intend to do is publish a number of twenty-page essays on several works— *Ulysses, Madame Bovary,* Kafka's *Transformation, Don Quixote,* and others—all based on my Cornell and Harvard lectures. I remember with delight tearing apart *Don Quixote*, a cruel and crude old book, before six hundred students in Memorial Hall, much to the horror and embarrassment of some of my more conservative colleagues.

INTERVIEWER: What about other influences? Pushkin?

NABOKOV: In a way—no more than, say, Tolstoy or Turgenev were influenced by the pride and purity of Pushkin's art.

INTERVIEWER: Gogol?

NABOKOV: I was careful *not* to learn anything from him. As a teacher, he is dubious and dangerous. At his worst, as in his Ukranian stuff, he is a worthless writer; at his best, he is incomparable and inimitable.

INTERVIEWER: Anyone else?

NABOKOV: H. G. Wells, a great artist, was my favorite writer when I was a boy. *The Passionate Friends, Ann Veronica, The Time Machine, The Country of the Blind,* all these stories are far better than anything Bennett, or Conrad or, in fact, any of Wells' contemporaries could produce. His sociological cogitations can be safely ignored, of course, but his romances and fantasias are superb. There was an awful moment at dinner in our St. Petersburg house one night when Zinaïda Vengerov, his translator, informed Wells, with a toss of her head: "You know, *my* favorite work of yours is *The Lost World.*" "She means the war the Martians lost," said my father quickly.

INTERVIEWER: Did you learn from your students at Cornell? Was the experience purely a financial one? Did teaching teach you anything valuable?

NABOKOV: My method of teaching precluded genuine contact with my students. At best, they regurgitated a few bits of my brain during examinations. Every lecture I delivered had been carefully, lovingly handwritten and typed out, and I leisurely read it out in class, sometimes stopping to rewrite a sentence and sometimes repeating a paragraph—a mnemonic prod which, however, seldom provoked any change in the rhythm of wrists taking it down. I welcomed the few shorthand experts in my audience, hoping they would communicate the information they stored to their less fortunate comrades. Vainly I tried to replace my appearances at the lectern by taped records to be played over the college radio. On the other hand, I deeply enjoyed the chuckle of appreciation in this or that warm spot of the lecture hall at this or that point of my lecture. My best reward comes from those former students of mine who, ten or fifteen years later, write to me to say that they now understand what I wanted of them when I taught them to visualize Emma Bovary's mistranslated hairdo or the arrangement of rooms in the Samsa household or the two homosexuals in *Anna Karenina*. I do not know if I learned anything from teaching, but I know I amassed an invaluable amount of exciting information in analyzing a dozen novels for my students. My salary as you happen to know was not exactly a princely one.

INTERVIEWER: Is there anything you would care to say about the collaboration your wife has given you?

NABOKOV: She presided as adviser and judge over the making of my first fiction in the early twenties. I have read to her all my stories and novels at least twice; and she has reread them all when typing them and correcting proofs and checking translations into several languages. One day in 1950, at Ithaca, New York, she was responsible for stopping me and urging delay and second thoughts as, beset with technical difficulties and doubts, I was carrying the first chapters of *Lolita* to the garden incinerator.

INTERVIEWER: What is your relation to the translations of your books?

NABOKOV: In the case of languages my wife and I know or can read—English, Russian, French, and to a certain extent German and Italian—the system is a strict checking of every sentence. In the case of Japanese or Turkish versions, I try not to imagine the disasters that probably bespatter every page.

INTERVIEWER: What are your plans for future work?

NABOKOV: I am writing a new novel, but of this I cannot speak. Another project I have been nursing for some time is the publication of the complete screenplay of *Lolita* that I made for Kubrick. Although there are just enough borrowings from it in his version to justify my legal position as author of the script, the film is only a blurred skimpy glimpse of the marvelous picture I imagined and set down scene by scene during the six months I worked in a Los Angeles villa. I do not wish to imply that Kubrick's film is mediocre; in its own right, it is first-rate, but it is not what I wrote. A tinge of *poshlost* is often given by the cinema to the novel it distorts and coarsens in its crooked glass. Kubrick, I think, avoided this fault in his version, but I shall never understand why he did not follow my directions and dreams. It is a great pity; but at least I shall be able to have people read my *Lolita* play in its original form.

INTERVIEWER: If you had the choice of one and only one book by which you would be remembered, which one would it be?

NABOKOV: The one I am writing or rather dreaming of writing. Actually, I shall be remembered by *Lolita* and my work on *Eugene Onegin*.

INTERVIEWER: Do you feel you have any conspicuous or secret flaw as a writer?

NABOKOV: The absence of a natural vocabulary. An odd thing to confess, but true. Of the two instruments in my possession, one —my native tongue—I can no longer use, and this not only because I lack a Russian audience, but also because the excitement of verbal adventure in the Russian medium has faded away gradually after I turned to English in 1940. My English, this second instrument I have always had, is however a stiffish, artificial thing, which may be all right for describing a sunset or an insect, but which cannot conceal poverty of syntax and paucity of domestic diction when I need the shortest road between warehouse and shop. An old Rolls Royce is not always preferable to a plain jeep.

INTERVIEWER: What do you think about the contemporary competitive ranking of writers?

NABOKOV: Yes, I have noticed that in this respect our professional book reviewers are veritable bookmakers. Who's in, who's out, and where are the snows of yesteryear. All very amusing. I am a little sorry to be left out. Nobody can decide if I am a middle-aged American writer or an old Russian writer—or an ageless international freak.

INTERVIEWER: What is your great regret in your career?

NABOKOV: That I did not come earlier to America. I would have liked to have lived in New York in the thirties. Had my Russian novels been translated then, they might have provided a shock and a lesson for pro-Soviet enthusiasts.

INTERVIEWER: Are there significant disadvantages to your present fame?

NABOKOV: *Lolita* is famous, not I. I am an obscure, doubly obscure, novelist with an unpronounceable name.

HERBERT GOLD

6. Jorge Luis Borges

Born on August 24, 1899, Jorge Luis Borges spent his boyhood in Switzerland and Spain, and remained as a student in Switzerland during World War I. He returned to his native Argentina after the war, founded the leading intellectual magazine *Sur,* and began writing.

His many books include *Ficciones* (1962), *Labyrinths* (1962), *Dream-tigers* (1964), *Personal Anthology* (1967), *The Aleph and Other Stories 1933–1969* (1970), *Doctor Brodie's Report* (1971), and *Selected Poems 1923–1967* (1972).*

Over the years, Borges' eyesight diminished until in 1955 his blindness halted his teaching at the University of Buenos Aires, where he was professor of English and American Literature, and necessitated dictating all his work to his secretary for transcription.

Dr. Borges was Charles Eliot Norton Professor of Poetry at Harvard from 1967 to 1968. From 1955 (when Perón fell from power) until 1973, he was director of the Argentine National Library. In 1961 he shared the Prix Internationale des Editeurs (Prix Formentor) with Samuel Beckett. His other honors include the first Inter-American Literature Prize (1970) and the Jerusalem Book Prize (1971); Honorary Memberships in the American Academy of Arts and Letters and the National Institute of Arts and Letters; and Honorary Doctor of Letters degrees from Oxford and Columbia.

He and his wife, the former Elsa Astete de Albarracen, whom he married in 1967, live in Buenos Aires.

---

*All parenthetical dates above indicate American publication in translation.

Jorge Luis Borges manuscript page

Jill Krementz

Jorge Luis Borges

This interview was conducted in July 1966, in conversations I held with Borges at his office in the Biblioteca Nacional, of which he is the director. The room, recalling an older Buenos Aires, is not really an office at all but a large, ornate, high-ceilinged chamber in the newly renovated library. On the walls—but far too high to be easily read, as if hung with diffidence—are various academic certificates and literary citations. There are also several Piranesi etchings, bringing to mind the nightmarish Piranesi ruin in Borges' story, "The Immortal." Over the fireplace is a large portrait; when I asked Borges' secretary, Miss Susana Quinteros, about the portrait, she responded in a fitting, if unintentional echo of a basic Borgesean theme: "No importa. It's a reproduction of another painting."

At diagonally opposite corners of the room are two large, revolving bookcases that contain, Miss Quinteros explained, books Borges frequently consults, all arranged in a certain order and never

*varied so that Borges, who is nearly blind, can find them by position
and size. The dictionaries, for instance, are set together, among
them an old, sturdily rebacked, well-worn copy of* Webster's Ency-
clopedic Dictionary of the English Language *and an equally well-
worn Anglo-Saxon dictionary. Among the other volumes, ranging
from books in German and English on theology and philosophy
to literature and history, are the complete* Pelican Guide to English Literature, *the* Modern Library Francis Bacon, *Hollander's*
The Poetic Eddas, The Poems of Catullus, *Forsyth's* Geometry
of Four Dimensions, *several volumes of* Harrap's English Classics,
Parkman's The Conspiracy of Pontiac, *and the Chambers edition
of* Beowulf. *Recently, Miss Quinteros said, Borges had been reading* The American Heritage Picture History of the Civil War,
*and just the night before he had taken to his home, where his
mother, who is in her nineties, reads aloud to him, Washington
Irving's* Life of Mahomet.

*Each day, late in the afternoon, Borges arrives at the library
where it is now his custom to dictate letters and poems, which Miss
Quinteros types and reads back to him. Following his revisions, she
makes two or three, sometimes four copies of each poem before
Borges is satisfied. Some afternoons she reads to him, and he
carefully corrects her English pronunciation. Occasionally, when
he wants to think, Borges leaves his office and slowly circles the
library's rotunda, high above the readers at the tables below. But
he is not always serious, Miss Quinteros stressed, confirming what
one might expect from his writing: "Always there are jokes, little
practical jokes."*

*When Borges entered the library, wearing a beret and a dark gray
flannel suit hanging loosely from his shoulders and sagging over
his shoes, everyone stopped talking for a moment, pausing, perhaps
out of respect, perhaps out of empathetic hesitation for a man who
is not entirely blind. His walk is tentative, and he carries a cane,
which he uses like a divining rod. He is short, with hair that looks
slightly unreal in the way it rises from his head. His features are
vague, softened by age, partially erased by the paleness of his skin.
His voice, too, is unemphatic, almost a drone, seeming, possibly*

because of the unfocused expression of his eyes, to come from another person behind the face, and his gestures and expressions are lethargic—characteristic is the involuntary droop of one eyelid. But when he laughs—and he laughs often—his features wrinkle into what actually resembles a wry question mark; and he is apt to make a sweeping or clearing gesture with his arm and to bring his hand down on the table. Most of his statements take the form of rhetorical questions, but in asking a genuine question, Borges displays now a looming curiosity, now a shy, almost pathetic incredulity. When he chooses, as in telling a joke, he adopts a crisp, dramatic tone, and his quotation of a line from Oscar Wilde would do justice to an Edwardian actor. His accent defies easy classification: a cosmopolitan diction emerging from a Spanish background, educated by correct English speech and influenced by American movies. (Certainly no Englishman ever pronounced piano *as* pie-ano, *and no American says* a-nee-hilates *for* annihilates.) *The predominant quality of his articulation is the way his words slur softly into one another, allowing suffixes to dwindle so that* couldn't *and* could *are virtually indistinguishable. Slangy and informal when he wants to be, more typically he is formal and bookish in his English speech, relying, quite naturally, on phrases like "that is to say" and "wherein." Always his sentences are linked by the narrative "and then" or the logical "consequently."*

But most of all, Borges is shy. Retiring, even self-obliterating, he avoids personal statement as much as possible and obliquely answers questions about himself by talking of other writers, using their words and even their books as emblems of his own thought.

In this interview it has been attempted to preserve the colloquial quality of his English speech—an illuminating contrast to his writings and a revelation of his intimacy with a language that has figured so importantly in the development of his writing.

INTERVIEWER: You don't object to my recording our conversations?

BORGES: No, no. You fix the gadgets. They are a hindrance, but I will try to talk as if they're not there. Now where are you from?

INTERVIEWER: From New York.

BORGES: Ah, New York. I was there, and I liked it very much—I said to myself: "Well, I have made this; this is my work."

INTERVIEWER: You mean the walls of the high buildings, the maze of streets?

BORGES: Yes. I rambled about the streets—Fifth Avenue—and got lost, but the people were always kind. I remember answering many questions about my work from tall, shy young men. In Texas they had told me to be afraid of New York, but I liked it. Well, are you ready?

INTERVIEWER: Yes, the machine is already working.

BORGES: Now, before we start, what kind of questions are they?

INTERVIEWER: Mostly about your own work and about English writers you have expressed an interest in.

BORGES: Ah, that's right. Because if you ask me questions about the younger contemporary writers, I'm afraid I know very little about them. For about the last seven years I've been doing my best to know something of Old English and Old Norse. Consequently, that's a long way off in time and space from the Argentine, from Argentine writers, no? But if I have to speak to you about the "Finnsburg" fragment or the elegies or the "Battle of Brunanburg" . . .

INTERVIEWER: Would you like to talk about those?

BORGES: No, not especially.

INTERVIEWER: What made you decide to study Anglo-Saxon and Old Norse?

BORGES: I began by being very interested in metaphor. And then in some book or other—I think in Andrew Lang's *History of English Literature*—I read about the kennings, metaphors of Old English, and in a far more complex fashion of Old Norse poetry. Then I went in for the study of Old English. Nowadays, or rather today, after several years of study, I'm no longer interested in the metaphors because I think that they were rather a weariness of the flesh to the poets themselves—at least to the Old English poets.

INTERVIEWER: To repeat them, you mean?

BORGES: To repeat them, to use them over and over again and to keep on speaking of the *hronrad, waelrad,* or "road of the whale" instead of "the sea"—that kind of thing—and "the sea-wood," "the stallion of the sea" instead of "the ship." So I decided finally to stop using them, the metaphors, that is; but in the meanwhile I had begun studying the language, and I fell in love with it. Now I have formed a group—we're about six or seven students—and we study almost every day. We've been going through the highlights in *Beowulf,* the "Finnsburg" fragment, and "The Dream of the Rood." Also, we've gotten into King Alfred's prose. Now we've begun learning Old Norse, which is rather akin to Old English. I mean the vocabularies are not really very different: Old English is a kind of halfway house between the Low German and the Scandinavian.

INTERVIEWER: Epic literature has always interested you very much, hasn't it?

BORGES: Always, yes. For example, there are many people who go to the cinema and cry. That has always happened: It has happened to me also. But I have never cried over sob stuff, or the pathetic episodes. But, for example, when I saw the first gangster films of Sternberg, I remember that when there was anything epic about them—I mean Chicago gangsters dying bravely—well, I felt that my eyes were full of tears. I have felt epic poetry far more than lyric or elegy. I *always* felt that. Now that may be, perhaps, because I come from military stock. My grandfather, Colonel Borges, fought in the border warfare with the Indians, and he died in a revolution; my great grandfather, Colonel Suarez, led a Peruvian cavalry charge in one of the last great battles against the Spaniards; another great uncle of mine led the vanguard of San Martin's army—that kind of thing. And I had, well, one of my great-great-grandmothers was a sister of Rosas*—I'm not especially proud of that relationship because I think of Rosas as being

---

*Rosas, Juan Manuel de (1793–1877), an Argentinian military dictator.

a kind of Perón in his day; but still all those things link me with Argentine history and also with the idea of a man's having to be brave, no?

INTERVIEWER: But the characters you pick as your epic heroes —the gangster, for example—are not usually thought of as epic, are they? Yet you seem to find the epic there?

BORGES: I think there is a kind of, perhaps, of low epic in him —no?

INTERVIEWER: Do you mean that since the old kind of epic is apparently no longer possible for us, we must look to this kind of character for our heroes?

BORGES: I think that as to epic poetry or as to epic literature, rather—if we except such writers as T. E. Lawrence in his *Seven Pillars of Wisdom* or some poets like Kipling, for example, in "Harp Song of the Dane Women" or even in the stories—I think nowadays, while literary men seem to have neglected their epic duties, the epic has been saved for us, strangely enough, by the Westerns.

INTERVIEWER: I have heard that you have seen the film *West Side Story* many times.

BORGES: Many times, yes. Of course, *West Side Story* is not a Western.

INTERVIEWER: No, but for you it has the same epic qualities?

BORGES: I think it has, yes. During this century, as I say, the epic tradition has been saved for the world by, of all places, Hollywood. When I went to Paris, I felt I wanted to shock people, and when they asked me—they knew that I was interested in the films, or that I had been, because my eyesight is very dim now —and they asked me, "What kind of film do you like?" And I said, "Candidly, what I most enjoy are the Westerns." They were all Frenchmen; they fully agreed with me. They said, "Of course we see such films as *Hiroshima, mon amour* or *L'Année dernière à Marienbad* out of a sense of duty, but when we want to amuse ourselves, when we want to enjoy ourselves, when we want, well, to get a real kick, then we see American films."

INTERVIEWER: Then it is the content, the "literary" content of the film, rather than any of the technical aspects of the movies that interests you?

BORGES: I know very little about the technical part of movies.

INTERVIEWER: If I may change the subject to your own fiction, I would like to ask about your having said that you were very timid about beginning to write stories.

BORGES: Yes, I was very timid because when I was young I thought of myself as a poet. So I thought: If I write a story, everybody will know I'm an outsider, that I am intruding in forbidden ground. Then I had an accident. You can feel the scar. If you touch my head here, you will see. Feel all those mountains, bumps? Then I spent a fortnight in a hospital. I had nightmares and sleeplessness—insomnia. After that they told me that I had been in danger, well, of dying, that it was really a wonderful thing that the operation had been successful. I began to fear for my mental integrity—I said, "Maybe I can't write anymore." Then my life would have been practically over because literature is very important to me. Not because I think my own stuff particularly good, but because I know that I can't get along without writing. If I don't write, I feel, well, a kind of remorse, no? Then I thought I would try my hand at writing an article or a poem. But I thought: I have written hundreds of articles and poems. If I can't do it, then I'll know at once that I am done for, that everything is over with me. So I thought I'd try my hand at something I hadn't done: If I couldn't do it, there would be nothing strange about it because why should I write short stories?—It would prepare me for the final overwhelming blow: knowing that I was at the end of my tether. I wrote a story called let me see, I think, *"Hombre de la esquina rosada,"** and everyone enjoyed it very much. It was a great relief to me. If it hadn't been for that particular knock on the

---

*This is, perhaps, a slip of memory: The story was *"Pierre Menard, autor del Quijote,"* published in *Sur,* number 56 (May 1959).

head I got, perhaps I would never have written short stories.

INTERVIEWER: And perhaps you would never have been translated?

BORGES: And no one would have thought of translating me. So it was a blessing in disguise. Those stories, somehow or other, made their way: They got translated into French, I won the Formentor Prize, and then I seemed to be translated into many tongues. The first translator was Ibarra. He was a close friend of mine, and he translated the stories into French. I think he greatly improved upon them, no?

INTERVIEWER: Ibarra, not Caillois, was the first translator?

BORGES: He and Roger Caillois. At a ripe old age, I began to find that many people were interested in my work all over the world. It seems strange: Many of my writings have been done into English, into Swedish, into French, into Italian, into German, into Portuguese, into some of the Slav languages, into Danish. And always this comes as a great surprise to me because I remember I published a book—that must have been way back in 1932, I think—and at the end of the year I found out that no less than thirty-seven copies had been sold!

INTERVIEWER: Was that the *Universal History of Infamy?*

BORGES: No, no. *History of Eternity.* At first I wanted to find every single one of the buyers to apologize because of the book and also to thank them for what they had done. There is an explanation for that. If you think of thirty-seven people—those people are real, I mean every one of them has a face of his own, a family, he lives in his own particular street. Why, if you sell, say two thousand copies, it is the same thing as if you had sold nothing at all because two thousand is too vast—I mean, for the imagination to grasp. While thirty-seven people—perhaps thirty-seven are too many, perhaps seventeen would have been better or even seven—but still thirty-seven are still within the scope of one's imagination.

INTERVIEWER: Speaking of numbers, I notice in your stories that certain numbers occur repeatedly.

BORGES: Oh, yes. I'm awfully superstitious. I'm ashamed about it. I tell myself that after all, superstition is, I suppose, a slight form of madness, no?

INTERVIEWER: Or of religion?

BORGES: Well, religion, but . . . I suppose that if one attained one hundred and fifty years of age, one would be quite mad, no? Because all those small symptoms would have been growing. Still, I see my mother, who is ninety, and she has far fewer superstitions than I have. Now, when I was reading for the tenth time, I suppose, Boswell's *Johnson,* I found that he was full of superstition, and at the same time, that he had a great fear of madness. In the prayers he composed, one of the things he asked God was that he should not be a madman, so he must have been worried about it.

INTERVIEWER: Would you say that it is the same reason— superstition—that causes you to use the same colors—red, yellow, green—again and again?

BORGES: But do I use green?

INTERVIEWER: Not as often as the others. But you see I did a rather trivial thing, I counted the colors in . . .

BORGES: No, no. That is called *estilística;* here it is studied. No, I think you'll find yellow.

INTERVIEWER: But red, too, often moving, fading into rose.

BORGES: Really? Well, I never knew that.

INTERVIEWER: It's as if the world today were a cinder of yesterday's fire—that's a metaphor you use. You speak of "Red Adam," for example.

BORGES: Well, the word *Adam,* I think, in the Hebrew means "red earth." Besides it sounds well, no? *"Rojo Adan."*

INTERVIEWER: Yes it does. But that's not something you intend to show: the degeneration of the world by the metaphorical use of color?

BORGES: I don't intend to show anything. *(Laughter)* I have no intentions.

INTERVIEWER: Just to describe?

BORGES: I describe. I write. Now as for the color yellow, there is a physical explanation of that. When I began to lose my sight, the last color I saw, or the last color, rather, that stood out, because of course now I know that your coat is not the same color as this table or of the woodwork behind you—the last color to stand out was yellow because it is the most vivid of colors. That's why you have the Yellow Cab Company in the United States. At first they thought of making the cars scarlet. Then somebody found out that at night or when there was a fog that yellow stood out in a more vivid way than scarlet. So you have yellow cabs because anybody can pick them out. Now when I began to lose my eyesight, when the world began to fade away from me, there was a time among my friends . . . well they made, they poked fun at me because I was always wearing yellow neckties. Then they thought I really liked yellow, although it really was too glaring. I said, "Yes, to you, but not to me, because it is the only color I can see, practically!" I live in a gray world, rather like the silver-screen world. But yellow stands out. That might account for it. I remember a joke of Oscar Wilde's: a friend of his had a tie with yellow, red, and so on in it, and Wilde said, "Oh, my dear fellow, only a deaf man could wear a tie like that!"

INTERVIEWER: He might have been talking about the yellow necktie I have on now.

BORGES: Ah, well. I remember telling that story to a lady who missed the whole point. She said, "Of course, it must be because being deaf he couldn't hear what people were saying about his necktie." That might have amused Oscar Wilde, no?

INTERVIEWER: I'd like to have heard his reply to that.

BORGES: Yes, of course. I never heard of such a case of something being so perfectly misunderstood. The perfection of stupidity. Of course, Wilde's remark is a witty translation of an idea; in Spanish as well as English you speak of a "loud color." A "loud color" is a common phrase, but then the things that are said in literature are always the same. What is important is the way they are said. Looking for metaphors, for example: When I was a young man I was always hunting for new metaphors. Then I found out that really good metaphors are always the same. I mean you compare time to a road, death to sleeping, life to dreaming, and those are the great metaphors in literature because they correspond to something essential. If you invent metaphors, they are apt to be surprising during the fraction of a second, but they strike no deep emotion whatever. If you think of life as a dream, that is a thought, a thought that is real, or at least that most men are bound to have, no? "What oft was thought but ne'er so well expressed." I think that's better than the idea of shocking people, than finding connections between things that have never been connected before, because there is no real connection, so the whole thing is a kind of juggling.

INTERVIEWER: Juggling just words?

BORGES: Just words. I wouldn't even call them real metaphors because in a real metaphor both terms are really linked together. I have found one exception—a strange, new, and beautiful metaphor from Old Norse poetry. In Old English poetry a battle is spoken of as the "play of swords" or the "encounter of spears." But in Old Norse, and I think, also, in Celtic poetry, a battle is called a "web of men." That is strange, no? Because in a web you have a pattern, a weaving of men, *un tejido*. I suppose in medieval battle you got a kind of web because of having the swords and spears on opposite sides and so on. So there you have, I think, a new metaphor; and, of course, with a nightmare touch about it, no? The idea of a web made of living men, of living things, and still being a web, still being a pattern. It is a strange idea, no?

INTERVIEWER: It corresponds, in a general way, to the metaphor George Eliot uses in *Middlemarch*, that society is a web and one cannot disentangle a strand without touching all the others.

BORGES: *(with great interest):* Who said that?

INTERVIEWER: George Eliot, in *Middlemarch*.

BORGES: Ah, *Middlemarch!* Yes, of course! You mean the whole universe is linked together; everything linked. Well that's one of the reasons the Stoic philosophers had for believing in omens. There's a paper, a very interesting paper, as all of his are, by De Quincey on modern superstition, and there he gives the Stoic theory. The idea is that since the whole universe is one living thing, then there is a kinship between things that seem far off.

For example, if thirteen people dine together, one of them is bound to die within the year. Not merely because of Jesus Christ and the Last Supper, but also because *all* things are bound together. He said—I wonder how that sentence runs—that everything in the world is a secret glass or secret mirror of the universe.

INTERVIEWER: You have often spoken of the people who have influenced you, like De Quincey . . .

BORGES: De Quincey greatly, yes, and Schopenhauer in German. Yes, in fact, during the First World War, I was led by Carlyle—Carlyle: I rather dislike him: I think he invented Nazism and so on: one of the fathers or forefathers of such things—well, I was led by Carlyle to a study of German, and I tried my hand at Kant's *Critique of Pure Reason.* Of course, I got bogged down as most people do—as most Germans do. Then I said, "Well, I'll try their poetry, because poetry has to be shorter because of the verse." I got hold of a copy of Heine's *Lyrisches Intermezzo* and an English-German dictionary, and at the end of two or three months I found I could get on fairly well without the aid of a dictionary.

I remember the first English novel I read through was a Scottish novel called *House with the Green Shutters.*

INTERVIEWER: Who wrote that?

BORGES: A man called Douglas. Then that was plagiarized by the man who wrote *Hatter's Castle*—Cronin—there was the same plot, practically. The book was written in the Scots dialect —I mean, people instead of saying *money* speak of *baubees* or instead of *children, bairns*—that's an Old English and Norse word also—and they say *nicht* for *night:* that's Old English.

INTERVIEWER: And how old were you when you read that?

BORGES: I must have been about—there were many things I didn't understand—I must have been about ten or eleven. Before that, of course, I had read the *Jungle Books,* and I had read Stevenson's *Treasure Island,* a very fine book. But the first real novel was that novel. When I read that, I wanted to be Scotch, and then I asked my grandmother, and she was very indignant about it. She said, "Thank goodness that you're not!" Of course, maybe she was wrong. She came from Northumberland; they must have had some Scottish blood in them. Perhaps even Danish blood way back.

INTERVIEWER: With this long interest in English and your great love of it . . .

BORGES: Look here, I'm talking to an American: There's a book I *must* speak about—nothing unexpected about it—that book is *Huckleberry Finn*. I thoroughly dislike *Tom Sawyer*. I think that Tom Sawyer spoils the last chapters of *Huckleberry Finn*. All those silly jokes. They are all pointless jokes; but I suppose Mark Twain thought it was his duty to be funny even when he wasn't in the mood. The jokes had to be worked in somehow. According to what George Moore said, the English always thought: "Better a bad joke than no joke."

I think that Mark Twain was one of the really great writers, but I think he was rather unaware of the fact. But perhaps in order to write a really great book, you *must* be rather unaware of the fact. You can slave away at it and change every adjective to some other adjective, but perhaps you can write better if you leave the mistakes. I remember what Bernard Shaw said, that as to style, a writer has as much style as his conviction will give him and not more. Shaw thought that the idea of a game of style was quite nonsensical, quite meaningless. He thought of Bunyan, for example, as a great writer because he was convinced of what he was saying. If a writer disbelieves what he is writing, then he can hardly expect his readers to believe it. In this country, though, there is a tendency to regard any kind of writing—especially the writing of poetry—as a game of style. I have known many poets here who have written well—very fine stuff—with delicate moods and so on—but if you talk with them, the only thing they tell you is smutty stories or speak of politics in the way that everybody does, so that really their writing turns out to be kind of sideshow. They had learned writing in the way that a man might learn to play chess or to play bridge. They were not really poets or writers at all. It was a trick they had learned, and they had learned it thoroughly. They had the whole thing at their finger ends. But most of them—except four or five, I should say—seemed to think of life as having nothing poetic or mysterious about it. They take things for granted. They know that when they have to write, then, well, they have to suddenly become rather sad or ironic.

INTERVIEWER: To put on their writer's hat?

BORGES: Yes, put on the writer's hat and get into a right mood, and then write. Afterward, they fall back on current politics.

SUSANA QUINTEROS *(entering):* Excuse me. Señor Campbell is waiting.

BORGES: Ah, please ask him to wait a moment. Well, there's a Mr. Campbell waiting; the Campbells are coming.

INTERVIEWER: When you wrote your stories, did you revise a great deal?

BORGES: At first I did. Then I found out that when a man reaches a certain age, he has found his real tone. Nowadays, I try to go over what I've written after a fortnight or so, and of course there are many slips and repetitions to be avoided, certain favorite tricks that should not be overworked. But I think that what I write nowadays is always on a certain level and that I can't better it very much, nor can I spoil it very much, either. Consequently I let it go, forget all about it, and think about what I'm doing at the time. The last things I have been writing are *milongas,* popular songs.

INTERVIEWER: Yes, I saw a volume of them, a beautiful book.

BORGES: Yes, *Para Seis Cuerdas,* meaning, of course, the guitar. The guitar was a popular instrument when I was a boy. Then you would find people strumming the guitar, not too skillfully, at nearly every street corner of every town. Some of the best tangos were composed by people who couldn't write them nor read them. But of course they had music in their souls, as Shakespeare might have said. So they dictated them to somebody: They were played on the piano, and they got written down, and they were published for the literate people. I remember I met one of them —Ernesto Poncio. He wrote "Don Juan," one of the best tangos before the tangos were spoiled by the Italians in La Boca and so on: I mean, when the tangos came from the *criolla.* He once said to me: "I have been in jail many times, Señor Borges, but always for manslaughter!" What he meant to say was that he wasn't a thief or a pimp.

INTERVIEWER: In your *Antología Personal* . . .

BORGES: Look here, I want to say that that book is full of misprints. My eyesight is very dim, and the proofreading had to be done by somebody else.

INTERVIEWER: I see, but those are only minor errors, aren't they?

BORGES: Yes, I know, but they creep in, and they worry the writer, not the reader. The reader accepts anything, no? Even the starkest nonsense.

INTERVIEWER: What was your principle of selection in that book?

BORGES: My principle of selection was simply that I felt the stuff was better than what I had left out. Of course, if I had been cleverer, I would have insisted on leaving out those stories, and then after my death someone would have found out that what had been left out was really good. That would have been a cleverer thing to do, no? I mean, to publish all the weak stuff, then to let somebody find out that I had left out the real things.

INTERVIEWER: You like jokes very much, don't you?

BORGES: Yes, I do, yes.

INTERVIEWER: But the people who write about your books, your fiction in particular . . .

BORGES: No, no—they write far too seriously.

INTERVIEWER: They seldom seem to recognize that some of them are very funny.

BORGES: They are meant to be funny. Now a book will come out called *Crónicas de H. Bustos Domecq,* written with Adolpho Bioy Casares. That book will be about architects, poets, novelists, sculptors, and so on. All the characters are imaginary, and they are all very up-to-date, very modern; they take themselves very seriously; so does the writer, but they are not actually parodies of anybody. We are simply going as far as a certain thing can be done. For example, many writers from here tell me: "We would like to have your message." You see, we have no message at all.

When I write, I write because a thing has to be done. I don't think a writer should meddle too much with his own work. He should let the work write itself, no?

INTERVIEWER: You have said that a writer should never be judged by his ideas.

BORGES: No, I don't think ideas are important.

INTERVIEWER: Well, then, what should he be judged by?

BORGES: He should be judged by the enjoyment he gives and by the emotions one gets. As to ideas, after all it is not very important whether a writer has some political opinion or other because a work will come through despite them, as in the case of Kipling's *Kim*. Suppose you consider the idea of the empire of the English—well, in *Kim* I think the characters one really is fond of are not the English, but many of the Indians, the Mussulmans. I think they're nicer people. And that's because he thought them —No! No! not because he thought them nicer—because he *felt* them nicer.

INTERVIEWER: What about metaphysical ideas, then?

BORGES: Ah, well, metaphysical ideas, yes. They can be worked into parables and so on.

INTERVIEWER: Readers very often call your stories parables. Do you like that description?

BORGES: No, no. They're not meant to be parables. I mean if they are parables . . . *(long pause)* . . . that is, if they are parables, they have *happened* to be parables, but my intention has never been to write parables.

INTERVIEWER: Not like Kafka's parables, then?

BORGES: In the case of Kafka, we know very little. We only know that he was very dissatisfied with his own work. Of course, when he told his friend Max Brod that he wanted his manuscripts to be burned, as Vergil did, I suppose he knew that his friend wouldn't do that. If a man wants to destroy his own work, he throws it into a fire, and there it goes. When he tells a close friend of his: "I want all the manuscripts to be destroyed," he knows that the friend will never do that, and the friend knows that he knows and that he knows that the other knows that he knows and so on and so forth.

INTERVIEWER: It's all very Jamesian.

BORGES: Yes, of course. I think that the whole world of Kafka is to be found in a far more complex way in the stories of Henry James. I think that they both thought of the world as being at the same time complex and meaningless.

INTERVIEWER: Meaningless?

BORGES: Don't you think so?

INTERVIEWER: No, I don't really think so. In the case of James . . .

BORGES: But in the case of James, yes. In the case of James, yes. I don't think he thought the world had any moral purpose. I think he disbelieved in God. In fact, I think there's a letter written to his brother, the psychologist William James, wherein he says that the world is a diamond museum, let's say a collection of oddities, no? I suppose he meant that. Now in the case of Kafka, I think Kafka was looking for something.

INTERVIEWER: For some meaning?

BORGES: For some meaning, yes; and not finding it, perhaps. But I think that they both lived in a kind of maze, no?

INTERVIEWER: I would agree to that. A book like *The Sacred Fount*, for example.

BORGES: Yes, *The Sacred Fount* and many short stories. For example, "The Abasement of the Northmores," where the whole story is a beautiful revenge, but a revenge that the reader never knows will happen or not. The woman is very sure that her husband's work, which nobody seems to have read or cares about, is far better than the work of his famous friend. But maybe the whole thing is untrue. Maybe she was just led by her love for him. One doesn't know whether those letters, when they are published, will really come to anything. Of course James was trying to write two or three stories at one time. That's the reason why he never gave any explanation. The explanation would have made the story poorer. He said: *"The Turn of the Screw* was just a pot-boiler, don't worry about it." But I don't think that was the truth. For instance, he said, "Well, if I give explanations, then the story will be poorer because the alternative explanations will be left out." I think he did that on purpose.

INTERVIEWER: I agree; people shouldn't know.

BORGES: People shouldn't know, and perhaps he didn't know himself!

INTERVIEWER: Do you like to have the same effect on your readers?

BORGES: Oh, yes. Of course I do. But I think the stories of Henry James are far above his novels. What's important in the stories of Henry James are the situations created, not the characters. *The Sacred Fount* would be far better if you could tell one character from the other. But you have to wade through some three hundred pages in order to find out who Lady So-and-so's lover was, and then at the end you may guess that it was So-and-so and not What's-his-name. You can't tell them apart; they all speak in the same way; there are no real characters. Only the American seems to stand out. If you think of Dickens, well, while the characters don't seem to stand out, they are far more important than the plot.

INTERVIEWER: Would you say that your own stories have their point of origin in a situation, not in a character?

BORGES: In a situation, right. Except for the idea of bravery, of which I'm very fond. Bravery, perhaps, because I'm not very brave myself.

INTERVIEWER: Is that why there are so many knives and swords and guns in your stories?

BORGES: Yes, that may be. Oh, but there are two causes there: first, seeing the swords at home because of my grandfather and my great-grandfather and so on. Seeing all those swords. Then I was bred in Palermo; it all was a slum then, and people always thought of themselves—I don't say that it was true but that they always thought of themselves—as being better than the people who lived on a different side of the town—as being better fighters and that kind of thing. Of course, that may have been rubbish.

I don't think they were especially brave. To call a man, or to think of him, as a coward—that was the last thing; that's the kind of thing he couldn't stand. I have even known of a case of a man coming from the southern side of the town in order to pick a quarrel with somebody who was famous as a knifer on the north side and getting killed for his pains. They had no real reason to quarrel: They had never seen each other before; there was no question of money or women or anything of the kind. I suppose it was the same thing in the West in the States. Here the thing wasn't done with guns, but with knives.

INTERVIEWER: Using the knife takes the deed back to an older form of behavior?

BORGES: An older form, yes. Also, it is a more personal idea of courage. Because you can be a good marksman and not especially brave. But if you're going to fight your man at close quarters, and you have knives . . . I remember I once saw a man challenging another to fight, and the other caved in. But he caved in, I think, because of a trick. One was an old hand, he was seventy, and the other was a young and vigorous man, he must have been between twenty-five and thirty. Then the old man, he begged your pardon, he came back with two daggers, and one was a span longer than the other. He said: "Here, choose your weapon." So he gave the other the chance of choosing the longer weapon, and having an advantage over him; but that also meant that he felt so sure of himself that he could afford that handicap. The other apologized and caved in, of course. I remember that a brave man, when I was a young man in the slums, he was always supposed to carry a *short* dagger, and it was worn here. Like this *(pointing to his armpit)*, so it could be taken out at moment's notice, and the slum word for the knife—or one of the slum words—well, one was *el fierro*, but of course that means nothing special. But one of the names, and that has been quite lost—it's a pity—was *el vaivén*, the "come and go." In the word *come-and-go (making gesture)* you see the flash of the knife, the sudden flash.

INTERVIEWER: It's like a gangster's holster?

BORGES: Exactly, yes, like a holster—on the left side. Then it could be taken out at a moment's notice, and you scored *el vaivén*. It was spelled as one word and everyone knew it meant *knife*. *El fierro* is rather poor as a name because to call it *the iron* or *the steel* means nothing, while *el vaivén* does.

SUSANA QUINTEROS *(entering again):* Señor Campbell is still waiting.

BORGES: Yes, yes, we know. The Campbells are coming!

INTERVIEWER: Two writers I wanted to ask you about are Joyce and Eliot. You were one of the first readers of Joyce, and you even translated part of *Ulysses* into Spanish, didn't you?

BORGES: Yes, I'm afraid I undertook a very faulty translation of the last page of *Ulysses*. Now as to Eliot, at first I thought of him as being a finer critic than a poet; now I think that sometimes he is a very fine poet, but as a critic I find that he's too apt to be always drawing fine distinctions. If you take a great critic, let's say, Emerson or Coleridge, you feel that he has read a writer, and that his criticism comes from his personal experience of him, while in the case of Eliot you always think—at least I always feel —that he's agreeing with some professor or slightly disagreeing with another. Consequently, he's not creative. He's an intelligent man who's drawing fine distinctions, and I suppose he's right; but at the same time after reading, to take a stock example, Coleridge on Shakespeare, especially on the character of Hamlet, a new Hamlet had been created for you, or after reading Emerson on Montaigne or whoever it may be. In Eliot there are no such acts of creation. You feel that he has read many books on the subject —he's agreeing or disagreeing—sometimes making slightly nasty remarks, no?

INTERVIEWER: Yes, that he takes back later.

BORGES: Yes, yes, that he takes back later. Of course, he took those remarks back later because at first he was what might be called nowadays "an angry young man." In the end, I suppose he thought of himself as being an English classic, and then he found that he had to be polite to his fellow classics, so that afterwards he took back most of the things he had said about Milton or even against Shakespeare. After all, he felt that in some ideal way they were all sharing the same academy.

INTERVIEWER: Did Eliot's work, his poetry, have any effect on your own writing?

BORGES: No, I don't think so.

INTERVIEWER: I have been struck by certain resemblances between *The Waste Land* and your story "The Immortal."

BORGES: Well, there may be something there, but in that case I'm quite unaware of it because he's not one of the poets I love. I should rank Yeats far above him. In fact, if you don't mind my saying so, I think Frost is a finer poet than Eliot. I mean, a finer *poet*. But I suppose Eliot was a far more intelligent man; however, intelligence has little to do with poetry. Poetry springs from something deeper; it's beyond intelligence. It may not even be linked with wisdom. It's a thing of its own; it has a nature of its own. Undefinable. I remember—of course I was a young man— I was even angry when Eliot spoke in a slighting way of Sandburg. I remember he said that Classicism is good—I'm not quoting his words, but the drift of them—because it enabled us to deal with such writers as Mister Carl Sandburg. When one calls a poet "Mister" *(laughter)*, it's a word of haughty feelings; it means Mister So-and-so who has found his way into poetry and has no right to be there, who is really an outsider. In Spanish it's still worse because sometimes when we speak of a poet we say, "El Doctor So-and-so." Then that annihilates him, that blots him out.

INTERVIEWER: You like Sandburg, then?

BORGES: Yes, I do. Of course, I think Whitman is far more important than Sandburg, but when you read Whitman, you think of him as a literary, perhaps a not too learned man of letters, who is doing his best to write in the vernacular, and who is using slang as much as he can. In Sandburg the slang seems to come naturally. Now of course there are two Sandburgs: There is the *rough;* but there is also a very delicate Sandburg, especially when he deals with landscapes. Sometimes when he is describing the fog, for example, you are reminded of a Chinese painting. While in other poems of Sandburg you rather think of, well, gangsters, hoodlums, that kind of people. But I suppose he could be both, and I think he was equally sincere: when he was doing his best to be the poet of Chicago and when he wrote in quite a different mood. Another thing that I find strange in Sandburg is that in Whitman—but of course Whitman is Sandburg's father—Whitman is full of hope, while Sandburg writes as if he were writing in the two or three centuries to come. When he writes of the American expeditionary forces, or when he writes about empire or the War or so on, he writes as if all those things were dead and gone by.

INTERVIEWER: There is an element of fantasy in his work, then —which leads me to ask you about the fantastic. You use the word a great deal in your writing, and I remember that you call *Green Mansions*, for example, a fantastic novel.

BORGES: Well, it is.

INTERVIEWER: How would you define *fantastic*, then?

BORGES: I wonder if you *can* define it. I think it's rather an intention in a writer. I remember a very deep remark of Joseph Conrad—he is one of my favorite authors—I think it is in the foreword to something like *The Dark Line*, but it's not that . . .

INTERVIEWER: *The Shadow Line?*

BORGES: *The Shadow Line*. In that foreword he said that some people have thought that the story was a fantastic story because of the captain's ghost stopping the ship. He wrote—and that struck me because I write fantastic stories myself—that to deliberately write a fantastic story was not to feel that the whole universe is fantastic and mysterious; nor that it meant a lack of sensibility for a person to sit down and write something deliberately fantastic. Conrad thought that when one wrote, even in a realistic way, about the world, one was writing a fantastic story because the world itself is fantastic and unfathomable and mysterious.

INTERVIEWER: You share this belief?

BORGES: Yes. I found that he was right. I talked to Bioy Casares, who also writes fantastic stories—very, very fine stories —and he said, "I think Conrad is right. Really, nobody knows whether the world is realistic or fantastic, that is to say, whether the world is a natural process or whether it is a kind of dream, a dream that we may or may not share with others."

INTERVIEWER: You have often collaborated with Bioy Casares, haven't you?

BORGES: Yes, I have always collaborated with him. Every night I dine at his house, and then after dinner we sit down and write.

INTERVIEWER: Would you describe your method of collaboration?

BORGES: Well, it's rather queer. When we write together, when we collaborate, we call ourselves H. Bustos Domecq. Bustos was a great-great-grandfather of mine, and Domecq was a great-great-grandfather of his. Now, the queer thing is that when we write, and we write mostly humorous stuff—even if the stories are tragic, they are told in a humorous way, or they are told as if the teller hardly understood what he was saying—when we write together, what comes of the writing, if we are successful, and sometimes we are—why not? after all, I'm speaking in the plural, no?—when our writing is successful, then what comes out is something quite different from Bioy Casares' stuff and my stuff, even the jokes are different. So we have created between us a kind of third person; we have somehow begotten a third person that is quite unlike us.

INTERVIEWER: A fantastic author?

BORGES: Yes, a fantastic author with his likes, his dislikes, and a personal style that is meant to be ridiculous; but still, it is a style of his own, quite different from the kind of style I write when I try to create a ridiculous character. I think that's the only way of collaborating. Generally speaking, we go over the plot together before we set pen to paper—rather, I should talk about typewriters because he has a typewriter. Before we begin writing, we discuss the whole story; then we go over the details, we change them, of course, we think of a beginning, and then we think the beginning might be the end or that it might be more striking if somebody said nothing at all or said something quite outside the mark. Once the story is written, if you ask us whether this adjective or this particular sentence came from Bioy or from me, we can't tell.

INTERVIEWER: It comes from the third person.

BORGES: Yes. I think that's the only way of collaborating because I have tried collaborating with other people. Sometimes it works out all right, but sometimes one feels that the collaborator is a kind of rival. Or, if not—as in the case of Peyrou—we began collaborating, but he is timid and a very courteous, a very polite kind of person, and consequently, if he says anything, and you make any objections, he feels hurt, and he takes it back. He says: "Oh, yes, of course, of course, yes, I was quite wrong. It was a blunder." Or if you propose anything, he says: "Oh, that's wonderful!" Now that kind of thing can't be done. In the case of me and Casares, we don't feel as if we are two rivals, or even as if we were two men who play chess. There's no case of winning or losing. What we're thinking of is the story itself, the stuff itself.

INTERVIEWER: I'm sorry, I'm not familiar with the second writer you named.

BORGES: Peyrou. He began by imitating Chesterton and writing stories, detective stories, not unworthy, and even worthy of Chesterton. But now he's struck a new line of novels whose aim is to show what this country was like during Perón's time and after Perón took to flight. I don't care very much for that kind of writing. I understand that his novels are fine; but, I should say, from the historical, even the journalistic point of view. When he began writing stories after Chesterton, and then he wrote some very fine stories—one of them made me cry, but of course, perhaps it made me cry because he spoke of the quarter I was bred in, Palermo, and of hoodlums of those days—a book called *La Noche Repetida*, with very, very fine stories about gangsters, hoodlums, holdup men, that kind of thing. And all that way back, let's say, well, at the beginning of the century. Now he has started this new kind of novel wherein he wants to show what the country was like.

INTERVIEWER: Local color, more or less?

BORGES: Local color and local politics. Then his characters are very interested, well, in graft, in loot, making money, and so on. As I am less interested in those subjects, maybe it's my fault, not his, if I prefer his early stuff. But I always think of him as a great writer, an important writer, and an old friend of mine.

INTERVIEWER: You have said that your own work has moved from, in the early times, *expression,* to, in the later times, *allusion.*

BORGES: Yes.

INTERVIEWER: What do you mean by *allusion?*

BORGES: Look, I mean to say this: When I began writing, I thought that everything should be defined by the writer. For example, to say "the moon" was strictly forbidden; that one had to find an adjective, an epithet for the moon. (Of course, I'm simplifying things. I know it because many times I have written "la luna," but this is a kind of symbol of what I was doing.) Well, I thought everything had to be defined and that no common turns of phrase should be used. I would never have said, "So-and-so came in and sat down," because that was far too simple and far too easy. I thought I had to find out some fancy way of saying it. Now I find out that those things are generally annoyances to the reader. But I think the whole root of the matter lies in the fact that when a writer is young he feels somehow that what he is going to say is rather silly or obvious or commonplace, and then he tries to hide it under baroque ornament, under words taken from the seventeenth-century writers; or, if not, and he sets out to be modern, then he does the contrary: He's inventing words all the time, or alluding to airplanes, railway trains, or the telegraph and telephone because he's doing his best to be modern. Then as time goes on, one feels that one's ideas, good or bad, should be plainly expressed, because if you have an idea you must try to get that idea or that feeling or that mood into the mind of the reader. If, at the same time, you are trying to be, let's say, Sir Thomas Browne or Ezra Pound, then it can't be done. So that I think a writer always begins by being too complicated: He's playing at several games at the same time. He wants to convey a peculiar mood; at the same time he must be a contemporary and if not a contemporary, then he's a reactionary and a classic. As to the vocabulary, the first thing a young writer, at least in this country, sets out to do is to show his readers that he possesses a dictionary, that he knows all the synonyms; so we get, for example, in one line, *red,* then we get *scarlet,* then we get other different words, more or less, for the same color: *purple.*

INTERVIEWER: You've worked, then, toward a kind of classical prose?

BORGES: Yes, I do my best now. Whenever I find an out-of-the-way word, that is to say, a word that may be used by the Spanish classics or a word used in the slums of Buenos Aires, I mean, a word that is different from the others, then I strike it out, and I use a common word. I remember that Stevenson wrote that in a well-written page all the words should look the same way. If you write an uncouth word or an astonishing or an archaic word, then the rule is broken; and what is far more important, the attention of the reader is distracted by the word. One should be able to read smoothly in it even if you're writing metaphysics or philosophy or whatever.

INTERVIEWER: Dr. Johnson said something similar to that.

BORGES: Yes, he must have said it; in any case, he must have agreed with that. Look, his own English was rather cumbersome, and the first thing you feel is that he is writing in a cumbersome English—that there are far too many Latin words in it—but if you reread what is written, you find that behind those involutions of phrase there is always a meaning, generally an interesting and a new meaning.

INTERVIEWER: A personal one?

BORGES: Yes, a personal one. So even though he wrote in a Latin style, I think he is the most English of writers. I think of him as—this is a blasphemy, of course, but why not be blasphemous while we're about it?—I think that Johnson was a far more English writer than Shakespeare. Because if there's one thing typical of Englishmen, it's their habit of understatement. Well, in the case of Shakespeare, there are no understatements. On the contrary, he is piling on the agonies, as I think the American said. I think Johnson, who wrote a Latin kind of English, and Wordsworth, who wrote more Saxon words, and there is a third writer whose name I can't recall—well—let's say Johnson, Wordsworth, and Kipling also, I think they're far more typically English than Shakespeare. I don't know why, but I always feel something Italian, something Jewish about Shakespeare, and perhaps Englishmen admire him because of that, because it's so unlike them.

INTERVIEWER: And why the French dislike him to the extent that they do; because he's so bombastic.

BORGES: He *was* very bombastic. I remember I saw a film some days ago—not too good a film—called *Darling*. There some verses of Shakespeare are quoted. Now those verses are always better when they are quoted because he is defining England, and he calls it, for example, "This other Eden, demi-paradise . . . This precious stone set in the silver sea" and so on, and in the end he says something like, "this realm, this England." Now when that quotation is made, the reader stops there, but in the text I think the verses go on so that the whole point is lost. The real point would have been the idea of a man trying to define England, loving her very much and finding at the end that the only thing he can do is to say "England" outright—as if you said "America." But if he says "this realm, this land, this England," and then goes on "this demi-paradise" and so on, the whole point is lost because *England* should be the last word. Well, I suppose Shakespeare always wrote in a hurry, as the player said to Ben Jonson, and so be it. You've no time to feel that that would have been the last word, the word England, summing up and blotting out all the others, saying: "Well, I've been attempting something that is impossible." But he went on with it, with his metaphors and his bombast, because he was bombastic. Even in such a famous phrase as Hamlet's last words, I think: "The rest is silence." There is something phony about it; it's meant to impress. I don't think anybody would say anything like that.

INTERVIEWER: In the context of the play, my favorite line in

Hamlet occurs just after Claudius's praying scene when Hamlet enters his mother's chamber and says: "Now, Mother, what's the matter?"

BORGES: "What's the matter?" is the opposite of "The rest is silence." At least for me, "The rest is silence" has a hollow ring about it. One feels that Shakespeare is thinking: "Well, now Prince Hamlet of Denmark is dying: He must say something impressive." So he ekes out that phrase "The rest is silence." Now that may be impressive, but it is not true! He was working away at his job of poet and not thinking of the real character, of Hamlet the Dane.

INTERVIEWER: When you are working, what kind of reader do you imagine you are writing for, if you do imagine it? Who would be your ideal audience?

BORGES: Perhaps a few personal friends of mine. Not myself because I never reread what I've written. I'm far too afraid to feel ashamed of what I've done.

INTERVIEWER: Do you expect the many people who read your work to catch the allusions and references?

BORGES: No. Most of those allusions and references are merely put there as a kind of private joke.

INTERVIEWER: A *private* joke?

BORGES: A joke not to be shared with other people. I mean, if they share it, all the better; but if they don't, I don't care a hang about it.

INTERVIEWER: Then it's the opposite approach to allusion from, say, Eliot in *The Waste Land*.

BORGES: I think that Eliot and Joyce wanted their readers to be rather mystified and so to be worrying out the sense of what they had done.

INTERVIEWER: You seem to have read as much, if not more, nonfiction or factual material as fiction and poetry. Is that true? For example, you apparently like to read encyclopedias.

BORGES: Ah, yes. I'm very fond of that. I remember a time when I used to come here to read. I was a very young man, and I was far too timid to ask for a book. Then I was rather, I won't say poor, but I wasn't too wealthy in those days—so I used to come every night here and pick out a volume of the *Encyclopaedia Britannica,* the old edition.

INTERVIEWER: The eleventh?

BORGES: The eleventh or twelfth because those editions are far above the new ones. They were meant to be *read.* Now they are merely reference books. While in the eleventh or twelfth edition of the *Encyclopaedia Britannica,* you had long articles by Macaulay, by Coleridge; no, not by Coleridge by . . .

INTERVIEWER: By De Quincey?

BORGES: Yes, by De Quincey, and so on. So that I used to take any volume from the shelves—there was no need to ask for them: They were reference books—and then I opened the book till I found an article that interested me, for example, about the Mormons or about any particular writer. I sat down and read it because those articles were really monographs, really books or short books. The same goes for the German encyclopedias— Brockhaus or Meyers. When we got the new copy, I thought that was what they call the *Shorter Brockhaus,* but it wasn't. It was explained to me that because people live in small flats there is no longer room for books in thirty volumes. Encyclopedias have suffered greatly; they have been packed in.

SUSANA QUINTEROS *(interrupting):* I'm sorry. *Está esperando el* Señor Campbell.

BORGES: Ah, please ask him to wait just a moment more. Those Campbells keep coming.

INTERVIEWER: May I ask just a few more questions?

BORGES: Yes, please, of course.

INTERVIEWER: Some readers have found that your stories are cold, impersonal, rather like some of the newer French writers. Is that your intention?

BORGES: No. *(Sadly)* If that has happened, it is out of mere clumsiness. Because I have felt them very deeply. I have felt them so deeply that I have told them, well, using strange symbols so that people might not find out that they were all more or less autobiographical. The stories were about myself, my personal experiences. I suppose it's the English diffidence, no?

INTERVIEWER: Then a book like the little volume called *Everness* would be a good book for someone to read about your work?

BORGES: I think it is. Besides the lady who wrote it is a close friend of mine. I found that word in *Roget's Thesaurus*. Then I thought that word was invented by Bishop Wilkins, who invented an artificial language.

INTERVIEWER: You've written about that.

BORGES: Yes, I wrote about Wilkins. But he also invented a wonderful word that strangely enough has never been used by English poets—an awful word, really, a terrible word. *Everness*, of course, is better than eternity because eternity is rather worn now. Ever-r-ness is far better than the German *Ewigheit*, the same word. But he also created a beautiful word, a word that's a poem in itself, full of hopelessness, sadness, and despair: the word *neverness*. A beautiful word, no? He invented it, and I don't know why the poets left it lying about and never used it.

INTERVIEWER: Have you used it?

BORGES: No, no never. I used *everness*, but *neverness* is very beautiful. There is something hopeless about it, no? And there is no word with the same meaning in any other language, or in English. You might say *impossibility*, but that's very tame for *neverness:* the Saxon ending in *-ness. Neverness.* Keats uses *nothingness:* "Till world and fame to nothingness do sink;" but *nothingness*, I think, is weaker than *neverness.* You have in Spanish *nadería*—many similar words—but nothing like *neverness.* So if you're a poet, you should use that word. It's a pity for that word to be lost in the pages of a dictionary. I don't think it's ever been used. It may have been used by some theologian; it might. I suppose Jonathan Edwards would have enjoyed that kind of word or Sir Thomas Browne, perhaps, and Shakespeare, of course, because he was very fond of words.

INTERVIEWER: You respond to English so well, you love it so much, how is it you have written so little in English?

BORGES: Why? Why, I'm afraid. Fear. But next year, those

lectures of mine that I shall deliver, I'll write them in English. I already wrote to Harvard.

INTERVIEWER: You're coming to Harvard next year?

BORGES: Yes. I'm going to deliver a course of lectures on poetry. And as I think that poetry is more or less untranslatable, and as I think English literature—and that includes America—is by far the richest in the world, I will take most, if not all of my examples, from English poetry. Of course, as I have my hobby, I'll try to work in some Old English verses, but that's English also! In fact, according to some of my students, it's far more English than Chaucer's English!

INTERVIEWER: To get back to your own work for a moment: I have often wondered how you go about arranging works in those collections. Obviously the principle is not chronological. Is it similarity of theme?

BORGES: No, not chronology; but sometimes I find out that I've written the same parable or story twice over, or that two different stories carry the same meaning, and so I try to put them alongside each other. That's the only principle. Because, for example, once it happened to me to write a poem, a not too good poem, and then to rewrite it many years afterwards. After the poem was written, some of my friends told me: "Well, that's the same poem you published some five years ago." And I said: "Well, so it is!" But I hadn't the faintest notion that it was. After all, I think that a poet has maybe five or six poems to write and not more than that. He's trying his hand at rewriting them from different angles and perhaps with different plots and in different ages and different characters, but the poems are essentially and innerly the same.

INTERVIEWER: You have written many reviews and journal articles.

BORGES: Well, I had to do it.

INTERVIEWER: Did you choose the books you wanted to review?

BORGES: Yes, I generally did.

INTERVIEWER: So the choice does express your own tastes?

BORGES: Oh yes, yes. For example, when somebody told me to write a review of a certain *History of Literature*, I found there were so many howlers and blunders, and as I greatly admire the author as a poet, I said: "No, I don't want to write about it, because if I write about it I shall write against it." I don't like to attack people, especially now—when I was a young man, yes, I was very fond of it—but as time goes on, one finds that it is no good. When people write in favor or against anybody, that hardly helps or hurts them. I think that a man can be helped, well, the man can be done or undone by his *own* writing, not by what other people say of him, so that even if you brag a lot and people say that you are a genius—well, you'll be found out.

INTERVIEWER: Do you have any particular method for the naming of your characters?

BORGES: I have two methods: One of them is to work in the names of my grandfathers, great-grandfathers, and so on. To give them a kind of, well, I won't say immortality, but that's one of the methods. The other is to use names that somehow strike me. For example, in a story of mine, one of the characters who comes and goes is called Yarmolinsky because the name struck me—it's a strange word, no? Then another character is called Red Scharlach because Scharlach means *scarlet* in German, and he was a murderer; he was doubly red, no? Red Scharlach: Red Scarlet.

INTERVIEWER: What about the princess with the beautiful name who occurs in two of your stories?

BORGES: Faucigny Lucinge? Well, she's a great friend of mine. She's an Argentine lady. She married a French prince, and as the name is very beautiful, as most French titles are, especially if you cut out the Faucigny, as she does. She calls herself La Princesse de Lucinge. It's a beautiful word.

INTERVIEWER: What about Tlön and Uqbar?

BORGES: Oh, well, those are merely meant to be uncouth. *Sou-q-b-a-r.*

INTERVIEWER: Unpronounceable, in a way?

BORGES: Yes, more or less unpronounceable, and then *Tlön: t-l* is rather an uncommon combination, no? Then ö. The Latin *Orbis Tertius*—one can say that swimmingly, no? Perhaps in Tlön I may have been thinking of *traum,* the same word as the English *dream.* But then it would have to be *Tröme,* but *Tröme* might remind the reader of a railway train: *t-l* was a queerer combination. I thought I had invented a word for imagined objects called *hrön.* Yet when I began learning Old English, I found that *hron* was one of the words for whale. There were two words, *wael* and *hron,* so the *hronrad* is the "whale road," that is to say "the sea" in Old English poetry.

INTERVIEWER: Then the word you invented to describe an object perpetrated on reality by the imagination, that word had already been invented and was, in fact, a *hrön?*

BORGES: Yes, yes, it came to me. I would like to think that it came from my ancestors of ten centuries ago—that's a probable explanation, no?

INTERVIEWER: Would you say that in your stories you have tried to hybridize the short story and the essay?

BORGES: Yes—but I have done that on purpose. The first to point that out to me was Casares. He said that I had written short stories that were really sort of halfway houses between an essay and a story.

INTERVIEWER: Was that partly to compensate for your timidity about writing narratives?

BORGES: Yes, it may have been. Yes; because nowadays, or at least today, I began writing that series of stories about hoodlums of Buenos Aires: Those are straightforward stories. There is nothing of the essay about them or even of poetry. The story is told in a straightforward way, and those stories are in a sense sad, perhaps horrible. They are always understated. They are told by people who are also hoodlums, and you can hardly understand them. They may be tragedies, but tragedy is not felt by them. They merely tell the story, and the reader is, I suppose, made to feel that the story goes deeper than the story itself. Nothing is said of the sentiments of the characters—I got that out of the Old

Norse saga—the idea that one should know a character by his words and by his deeds, but that one shouldn't get inside his skull and say what he was thinking.

INTERVIEWER: So they are nonpsychological rather than impersonal?

BORGES: Yes, but there is a hidden psychology behind the story because, if not, the characters would be mere puppets.

INTERVIEWER: What about the Kabbala? When did you first get interested in that?

BORGES: I think it was through De Quincey, through his idea that the whole world was a set of symbols, or that everything meant something else. Then when I lived in Geneva, I had two personal, two great friends—Maurice Abramowicz and Seymour Jichlinski—their names tell you the stock they sprang from: They were Polish Jews. I greatly admired Switzerland and the nation itself, not merely the scenery and the towns; but the Swiss are very standoffish; one can hardly have a Swiss friend because as they have to live on foreigners, I suppose they dislike them. That would be the same case with the Mexicans. They chiefly live on Americans, on American tourists, and I don't think anybody likes to be a hotel keeper even though there's nothing dishonorable about it. But if you are a hotel keeper, if you have to entertain many people from other countries, well, you feel that they are different from you, and you may dislike them in the long run.

INTERVIEWER: Have you tried to make your own stories Kabbalistic?

BORGES: Yes, sometimes I have.

INTERVIEWER: Using traditional Kabbalistic interpretations?

BORGES: No. I read a book called *Major Trends in Jewish Mysticism.*

INTERVIEWER: The one by Scholem?

BORGES: Yes, by Scholem and another book by Trachtenberg on Jewish superstitions. Then I have read all the books of the Kabbala I have found and all the articles in the encyclopedias and so on. But I have no Hebrew whatever. I may have Jewish ancestors, but I can't tell. My mother's name is Acevedo: Acevedo may be a name for a Portuguese Jew, but again, it may not. Now if you're called Abraham, I think there is no doubt whatever about it, but as the Jews took Italian, Spanish, Portuguese names, it does not necessarily follow that if you have one of those names you come from Jewish stock. The word *acevedo*, of course, means a kind of tree; the word is not especially Jewish, though many Jews are called Acevedo. I can't tell. I wish I had some Jewish fore-fathers.

INTERVIEWER: You once wrote that all men are either Plato-nists or Aristotelians.

BORGES: I didn't say that. Coleridge said it.

INTERVIEWER: But you quoted him.

BORGES: Yes, I quoted him.

INTERVIEWER: And which are you?

BORGES: I think I'm Aristotelian, but I wish it were the other way. I think it's the English strain that makes me think of particu-lar things and persons being real rather than general ideas being real. But I'm afraid now that the Campbells are coming.

INTERVIEWER: Before I go, would you mind signing my copy of *Labyrinths?*

BORGES: I'll be glad to. Ah yes, I know this book. There's my picture—but do I really look like this? I don't like that picture. I'm not so gloomy? So beaten down?

INTERVIEWER: Don't you think it looks pensive?

BORGES: Perhaps. But so dark? So heavy? The brow . . . oh, well.

INTERVIEWER: Do you like this edition of your writings?

BORGES: A good translation, no? Except that there are too many Latin words in it. For example, if I wrote, just say, *habita-ción oscura* (I wouldn't, of course, have written *that*, but *cuarto oscuro*, but just say that I did), then the temptation is to translate *habitación* with *habitation*, a word which sounds close to the original. But the word I want is *room:* It is more definite, simpler, better. You know, English is a beautiful language, but the older languages are even more beautiful: They had *vowels*. Vowels in modern English have lost their value, their color. My hope for

English—for the English language—is America. Americans speak clearly. When I go to the movies now, I can't see much, but in the American movies, I understand every word. In the English movies I can't understand as well. Do you ever find it so?

INTERVIEWER: Sometimes, particularly in comedies. The English actors seem to speak too fast.

BORGES: Exactly! Exactly. Too fast with too little emphasis. They blur the words, the sounds. A fast blur. No, America must save the language; and, do you know, I think the same is true for Spanish? I prefer South American speech. I always have. I suppose you in America don't read Ring Lardner or Bret Harte much anymore?

INTERVIEWER: They are read, but mostly in the secondary schools.

BORGES: What about O. Henry?

INTERVIEWER: Again, mostly in the schools.

BORGES: And I suppose there mostly for the technique, the surprise ending. I don't like that trick, do you? Oh, it's all right in theory; in practice, that's something else. You can read them only once if there is just the surprise. You remember what Swift said: "the art of sinking." Now in the detective story, that's different. The surprise is there, too, but there are also the characters; the scene or the landscape to satisfy us. But now I remember that the Campbells are coming, the Campbells are coming. They are supposed to be a ferocious tribe. Where are they?

RONALD CHRIST

7. George Seferis

During World War I Giorgos Seferiadis fled from Smyrna (where he was born on February 29, 1900) to Athens. In 1926 he entered the diplomatic service of Greece and was appointed Vice Consul in London in 1931. He returned to Athens in 1934 to serve as head of the Press and Information Department for the Greek Foreign Ministry. When the Germans invaded Greece in the Second World War, he escaped to Egypt. Seferiadis continued to serve the Free Greek government as a diplomat in South Africa (1941) and as Press Spokesman (1942). He returned to Greece for the liberation of Athens in 1944 and subsequently continued his diplomatic career as Ambassador to Turkey, Lebanon, and Great Britain. In 1963 he retired to Athens to devote his time to his writing.

His first volume was *The Turning Point* (1931), which he published himself under his pen name, George Seferis. Among his other volumes are *Poems* (1961), *On the Greek Style: Selected Essays on Poetry and Hellenism* (1966) and *Collected Poems 1924–1955* (1968).*

Among Dr. Seferis's many awards and honors are the Nobel Prize (1963); honorary doctorates from Cambridge (1960), Oxford (1964), and Princeton (1965); the William Foyle Poetry Prize (1961); and Honorary Membership in the American Academy of Arts and Letters (1971). Dr. Seferis died of pneumonia in Athens in 1971.

---

*Parenthetical dates indicate publication in translation.

Edmund Keeley

George Seferis

Seferis was nearing the end of his longest visit to the United States at the time of this interview, which took place in late December of 1968. He had just completed a three-month term as fellow of the Institute for Advanced Study in Princeton, and he was in particularly good spirits because he felt that his visit had served for a kind of rejuvenation: an interlude free from the political tensions that had been building up for some months in Athens and the occasion for both reflection and performance. The latter included a series of readings—at Harvard, Princeton, Rutgers, Pittsburgh, Washington, D.C., and the YMHA Poetry Center in New York —Seferis reading in Greek and the interviewer in English, each appearance with its distinct qualities of excitement and response. In Pittsburgh, for example, the audience (composed mostly of local Greek-Americans) seemed bewildered by the poetry during the reading but responded to the poet during the reception afterward as they might to Greece's exiled king. The New York reading began

*with an introduction by Senator Eugene McCarthy. During the
discussion period several questions from the audience had to do
specifically with the political situation in Greece. Seferis refused
to answer them. He was thought to be evasive by some in the
audience, but he held his ground, and during the dinner following
the reading he gave his reasons in private: He didn't consider it
proper to criticize his government while a guest on foreign soil,
safely outside the boundaries of the government's displeasure. He
saved his answers for his return to Greece: an uncompromising
statement against the dictatorship presented to local and foreign
correspondents in defiance of martial law and at obvious personal
risk* (The New York Times, *March 29, 1969*).

*The combination of diplomatic tact and high conscience that
defines the political character of Seferis also colors his presence and
personal style. He is a heavy man, his voice gentle when disengaged, his movements slow, almost lethargic at times; yet he has
a habit of gripping your arm as he moves, and the grip, though
amiable in the old-fashioned European manner, remains young
and firm enough to give you word of the strength still in him. And
the voice has a second edge that cuts sharply when he senses
something dubious or facile challenging it. Then, on the diplomatic side again, comes a sense of humor: a love of nonsense, of
the risqué joke, of kidding himself and others with a wry little moon
of a smile that appears unexpectedly in his oval face—especially
after he's trapped his listener with the question: "Why are you
laughing?" An American poet once referred to him as a "Middle-
Eastern troglodyte" in a poem about his first reading in New York
some years ago. When the interviewer finally got up the courage
to show him the poem, Seferis fixed him with a sharp, uncompromising look. "Middle-Eastern troglodyte. Ridiculous and inaccu-
rate. I once called myself a Cappadocian troglodyte, and that is
what I plan to remain. Why are you laughing?" Then the smile.*

*The interview took place in the Seferis temporary home at the
Institute for Advanced Study, an unpretentious second-floor apartment with three rooms, with a large window overlooking the
grounds, the bookcase almost empty, none of the modern Greek*

paintings and classical treasures that set the style of the Seferis home in Athens. Yet the poet was delighted with the place because it gave him access to a number of exotic things: changing trees, and squirrels, and children crossing the lawn from school. His wife Maro—hair still gold and braided like a girl's—was present throughout the interview, sometimes listening with apparent amusement, sometimes preparing food or drinks in the background. There were three recording sessions. Seferis would take a while to warm up with the microphone watching him from the coffee table, but whenever he began to reminisce about friends from the war years and before—Henry Miller, Durrell, Katsimbalis—or the years of his childhood, he would relax into his natural style and talk easily until the tape died out on him.

INTERVIEWER: Let me start by asking you about the Institute for Advanced Study and how you feel, only recently retired from the diplomatic service, about beginning a new career as a student.

SEFERIS: My dear, the problem which puzzles me is: What is advanced study? Should one try to forget, or to learn more, when one is at my stage of advanced study? Now I must say, on a more prosaic level, that I enjoy very much the whole situation here because there are very nice people, very good friends, and I enjoy—how shall I put it?—their horizons. There are many horizons around me: science, history, archaeology, theology, philosophy . . .

INTERVIEWER: But don't you feel out of place among so many scientists? So many historians?

SEFERIS: No, because I am attracted by people whose interests are not in my own area.

INTERVIEWER: Do you think there's an advantage—as I think Cavafy would probably have thought—to being in dialogue with historians? In other words, do you feel that history has something particular to say to the poet?

SEFERIS: If you remember, Cavafy was *proud* of having a sense of history. He used to say: "I am a man of history"—something like that, I don't remember the exact quotation. I am not that way; but still, I feel the pressure of history. In another way, perhaps: more mythological, more abstract, or more concrete . . . I don't know.

INTERVIEWER: How about the relation of the Greek poet to his particular historical tradition? You once said that there is no ancient Greece in Greece. What did you mean by that exactly?

SEFERIS: I meant Greece is a continuous process. In English the expression "ancient Greece" includes the meaning of "finished," whereas for us Greece goes on living, for better or for worse; it is *in* life, has not expired yet. That is a fact. One can make the same argument when one discusses the pronunciation of ancient Greek. Your scholars in America or in England or in France may be quite right in adopting the Erasmic pronunciation: for them Greek is a dead language; but for us it is another story. The fact is, you consider that ancient Greek has terminated its function at a certain point, and this enables you to pronounce it —with my regrets—in an arbitrary way.

INTERVIEWER: Then you obviously see the Greek tradition in language, as well as in other things, as a continuous process. That is not the belief of some classical and Byzantine scholars in this country—and, I suppose, elsewhere.

SEFERIS: You know why that happens? Because the subject, the history, of Greece is so large that each scholar limits himself to a certain period or branch, and nothing exists outside of it. For example, Gibbon considered that a thousand years of life were a decline. How can a people be in decline for a thousand years? After all, between the Homeric poems and the birth of Christ eight hundred years elapsed—or something like that—and then presumably there were a thousand years of decline.

INTERVIEWER: On the question of the Greek poet's relation to his tradition, it has always seemed to me that the Greek poet has an advantage over his Anglo-Saxon counterpart who makes use of Greek mythology and sometimes even of Greek landscape. I remember years ago when I was writing a thesis on what I thought were English influences in the poetry of Cavafy and Seferis, I asked you about certain images that crop up in your landscape, for example, the symbolic meaning of the statues that appear in your work. You turned to me and said: "But those are real statues. They existed in a landscape I had seen." What I think you were saying is that you always start with the fact of a living, actual setting and move from there to any universal meaning that might be contained in it.

SEFERIS: An illustration of that from someone who is a specialist in classical statues came the other day from an English scholar who was lecturing about the statuary of the Parthenon. I went up to congratulate him after his lecture, and he said to me, as I remember: "But you have a line which expresses something of what I meant when you say 'the statues are not the ruins—*we* are the ruins.' " I mean I was astonished that a scholar of his caliber was using a line from me to illustrate a point.

INTERVIEWER: The imagery that a poet gets from his childhood is something we've discussed before. You once distinguished yourself from the average Englishman by suggesting that donkeys probably did for you what footballs and cars might do for them. I remember you also talked about the sea and the sailors of your native village near Smyrna.

SEFERIS: You know, the strange thing about imagery is that a great deal of it is subconscious, and sometimes it appears in a poem, and nobody knows wherefrom this emerged. But it is rooted, I am certain, in the poet's subconscious life, often of his childhood, and that's why I think it is decisive for a poet: the childhood that he has lived.

I think there are two different things functioning: conscious and subconscious memory. I think the way of poetry is to draw from the subconscious. It is not the way you write your memoirs, let's say, or the way you try to remember your past, your early life. I remember many things from my childhood which *did* impress me. For instance, when I was a child I discovered somewhere in a corner of a sort of bungalow we had in my grandmother's garden —at the place where we used to spend our summers—I discovered a compass from a ship which, as I learned afterwards, belonged to my grandfather. And that strange instrument—I think

I destroyed it in the end by examining and re-examining it, taking it apart and putting it back together and then taking it apart again —became something mythical for me. Or again, when autumn approached, when there would be a rather strong wind, and the fishing barges would have to sail through rough weather, we would always be glad when they were at last anchored, and my mother would say to someone among the fishermen who'd gone out: "Ah, bravo, you've come through rough weather"; and he would answer: "Madam, you know, we always sail with Charon at our side." That's moving to me. Perhaps when I wrote about Ulysses in that early poem you've commented on ["Upon a Foreign Verse"]—perhaps I had in mind somebody like that fisherman. Those "certain old sailors from my childhood" who would recite the *Erotocritos*. In any case, I think it is always a bit dangerous to make unconscious images conscious, to bring them out into the light, because, you know, they dry out immediately.

INTERVIEWER: Have you felt any burden from having spent so many years writing for a tiny audience—an audience so small in the early years of your career that you had to publish your work at your own expense and issued something under three hundred copies of each volume. That is a situation quite unfamiliar to an established American poet.

SEFERIS: I'll give you an example. When I published my first volume, *Strophe* [*Turning Point*], I issued 150 copies. That was in 1931. And I remember that in 1939 there were still copies available at the bookseller—copies that I withdrew from circulation so that I could bring out a new edition of the volume in 1940. But I must say that soon after that things began to change a bit. When I left for Egypt after the collapse of Greece in the war against Germany, I left behind me three editions of my work— *Logbook I, Mythistorima,* and *Book of Exercises,* besides the earlier volumes *Cistern* and *Strophe*—left them there all brand new, without having sold a single copy before I sailed for Crete and Cairo with the Greek government in exile, as you know. During my absence everything was sold out. When I came back, no copies remained. The foreign occupation—enemy occupation

—had given the Greek public the opportunity of concentration and reading. And I reckoned that when I returned at the end of the occupation I was much better known in Greece than before.

INTERVIEWER: It's a very strange phenomenon, the revival of interest in poetry during the period of the occupation in Greece. I've heard about this from other poets: Gatsos and Elytis, for example. Poetry became an activity that brought together the Athenian intellectuals for readings and discussion, so that in a way it became the richest period for poetry in this century after the period of the thirties.

SEFERIS: Elytis published his book during the occupation, and Gatsos his: I mean the famous *Amorgos* came out during the occupation!

INTERVIEWER: What happened after the occupation? Why was there silence for so long among the leading poets?

SEFERIS: It wasn't silence. Times had changed, and horizons had widened, and everybody tried to see more of life outside the country; they were trying to find new modes of expression.

INTERVIEWER: I wonder if you have felt anything new and interesting through reading to large public audiences in this country. The evidence of friends of mine who have no knowledge at all of Greek is that they have captured, from your reading in Greek, a different sense of the poetry's rhythm from what they get out of my reading in English.

SEFERIS: That is very important. But I can say something more about this experience of reading in America. The other day another poet reacted by sending me a poem about my reading. That is a new kind of response. But still, the important thing is to see reactions, not to be applauded or not applauded.

INTERVIEWER: After your reading at Rutgers this fall, someone in the audience asked you what you thought of the English translations of your poetry, and you went on to make generous gestures towards your English translators, but then you added: "Of course the best translation of my poetry is in Chinese, a language which I don't understand at all."

SEFERIS: It isn't difficult to elaborate on that because, you know, I feel in languages that I know, perhaps because I know them too well (not English, but in French, for example, which I know really well) that there are other possibilities in the translation. For Chinese there are no other possibilities. But translating —I'm changing the question a little bit—is interesting always because it is a means of controlling your own language. Now of course the English language is a more stable language than ours; we have to create ours, so to speak, all the time we are writing.

INTERVIEWER: Pound said that translation is a means for a writer to sharpen continually his awareness of his own language, and he advised young poets to translate whenever they could.

SEFERIS: Provided you don't overdo it, I think it is always useful.

INTERVIEWER: You are a poet who writes in a language which few people know outside Greece. I wonder if you feel any resentment of the fact that you are known in the world of poetry outside your own country largely through translation.

SEFERIS: There are compensations. For example, about a year ago, I received a letter from an American saying to me: "Well, I have learned modern Greek in order to read Seferis." That's a great compliment, I think. It is much more personal than the case of a man who learns a foreign language at school, isn't it? I've heard other people say: "Well, you know, we learned our Greek from your poems." A great reward. And then I should add, perhaps, this situation of not having a very large audience has something good in it, too. I mean, that it educates you in a certain way: not to consider that great audiences are the most important reward on this earth. I consider that even if I have three people who read me, I mean really read me, it is enough. That reminds me of a conversation I had once upon a time during the only glimpse I ever had of Henri Michaux. It was when he had a stopover in Athens, coming from Egypt, I think. He came ashore while his ship was in Piraeus just in order to have a look at the Acropolis. And he told me on that occasion: "You know, my dear, a man who has only one reader is not a writer. A man who has two readers is not a writer, either. But a man who has *three* readers (and he pronounced "three readers" as though they were three million), that man is *really* a writer."

INTERVIEWER: You said earlier there is a problem in Greek of establishing a language. That's something which most American readers naturally don't understand. We have a language. Our problem is always to stretch the language which we have so that it somehow shows a new vitality. When you talk about establishing or creating a language, you mean something quite different.

SEFERIS: We've had the calamity of academic intervention. Mark you, I mean from both the left and the right. In the beginning we had the intervention of professors who wanted to transform our living language into something abstract in order to reach some sort of "idea" of a pure language. On the other side, we had the fight for *demotiki,* as we call the popular spoken language. But this tradition—the professorial tradition—was so strong that there was a sort of academic mind which fought actively for both the puristic and the vernacular language. The best way to progress is by forgetting all that academic intervention. For example, I admire very much the Cretan Renaissance. In that period you find a whole poem—ten thousand lines, an enormous poem—where there is no strain at all, no effort at all; the language functions quite naturally, without any flagrant tendency to be learned.

INTERVIEWER: It's interesting that you take an effortless poem for a model because I remember that, in another context, you described style as the difficulty one encounters in expressing himself.

SEFERIS: I said that in lecturing about Makriyannis, who, as you know, never learned how to write or read until the age of thirty-five. When you see his manuscript, it is like a wall—a wall built up out of stones, one placed on top of the other. It is very strange. For example, he never uses punctuation at all. No paragraphs. Nothing. It goes on like that. And you see that each word is added to another word like a stone on top of another stone. I mean, in any case, that when you really feel something, you face the difficulty of expressing it. And that, after all, forms your style.

INTERVIEWER: What are the difficulties you've encountered in establishing your own style?

SEFERIS: That's another story. In my youth I worked very much over the Greek language. Glossaries, old texts, medieval texts, and things of that kind. But the difficulty wasn't only in studying them; the difficulty was how to forget them and be natural. I had the blessing, perhaps, of being natural, I don't know. That's for others to say . . .

INTERVIEWER: I know you always considered it the first order of business for a poet to try for economy in style. This seems to be in contrast to the dominant mode of your predecessors—at least the mode of Palamas and Sikelianos.

SEFERIS: That's perhaps a local characteristic. I felt at the time of my early efforts that in Greece they were too rhetorical, and I reacted against it. That was my feeling. And I reacted against it in many ways. For example, in the use of words, of adjectives —especially compound adjectives, which I avoided. To avoid certain things is deliberate with me, you know. My interest in expression was not so much in the color of the language, which Greek has plenty of, but in precision above all; and in order to be precise, you have to be spare in the use of your material. You remember that Valery said lyricism is, after all, the development of an exclamation, of an "Ah." For me "Ah" is quite enough. I never try to elaborate on the exclamation.

INTERVIEWER: Let me pursue the matter of style as process of using language sparingly. Do you agree that in your own work there is a development, a further economy of means, between *Strophe* and everything that followed it?

SEFERIS: Of course. It is not so much a stylistic development as a sort of evolution. Everything evolves. I mean, one *has* to evolve—one *has* to see new things. One has to see other aspects and express these other aspects. Certainly there is an evolution, but I don't see it as a "development" in inverted commas. If I had years more in front of me, I would perhaps write in another way, even in another style. I might again use the strict line or rhymed verse, perhaps. In poetry you change the base of things from time to time in order to have a fresh expression. The main thing you are looking for in poetry is to avoid worn-out expressions. That's the great problem.

INTERVIEWER: Now what about the problem of developing a prose style. You are one of the very few poets in Greece who has had almost as strong an impact on the language of prose criticism as you've had on the language of poetry. Developing a live yet careful prose style must have been part of your struggle from the beginning.

SEFERIS: Yes, but, you know, my struggle was always for precision. That is at the base of it. And of course in prose it appears more obvious—I mean the matter of economy.

INTERVIEWER: This tape machine seems to have stopped recording. Say something and let's see if it's still working properly.

SEFERIS: Wallace Stevens was in an insurance company.

INTERVIEWER: Let's hope it will go on with us for a while. One of your remarks which has interested me is about the question of the relation between poetry and public service; I think you said that the important thing was for the poet not to have a job which was directly connected with that of being a poet.

SEFERIS: I didn't say the "important" thing. I don't know, really, because I can't speak for other people; but for me at least, I suppose that it is a help not to be in a job where I have to write as I write in my notebooks or poetry books. For example, I am not a professor or a teacher or even a newspaperman. I prefer to have another occupation.

INTERVIEWER: Was there anything in your professional career —that is, the experience you had as a diplomat—which may have influenced in some way the imagery of your poetry or affected the particular themes you chose to express?

SEFERIS: I don't believe that any themes or any imagery were created by my job, though I might mention—how did you translate it?—the lines from "Last Stop": "souls shriveled by public sins, each holding office like a bird in its cage." I mean that is one of the few images I have drawn directly from my public service. But I could have felt that even if I had not been in the diplomatic service. But it was important for me that I had a job which was not related to my creative work. And the other thing is that I was not—how shall I put it?—not obliged to deal with models which belonged to literature. Of course, there are troubles in that career. The main thing I suffered from was not having enough time. Although others might tell you that it is better not to have time because it is the subconscious which is doing the poetical work. That's the point of view of Tom Eliot. I remember once, when I was transferred from London to Beirut (this was after just one and a half years of service in London), I told him: "My dear Mr. Eliot, I think I am fed up with my career and I shall give up all this." I remember his saying: "Be careful, be careful if you do that," and then he mentioned the subconscious—the subconscious working for poetry. And I told him: "Yes, but if I have a job, an official job which is interfering with my subconscious, then I prefer not to have a job. I mean I would prefer to be a carpenter and to be where my subconscious is quite free to do whatever it likes, dance or not dance." And I added: "You know, I can tell you when my public life began to interfere with my subconscious. It was on the eve of the war with the Italians—in September '40—when I started having political dreams. Then I knew quite well that my subconscious was suffering the onslaught of my official job. 'In dreams responsibilities begin.' "

INTERVIEWER: You once made a comment about the connection between poetry and politics . . .

SEFERIS: You mean what I've said about propaganda writing, or "engaged" writing, or whatever you call that kind of writing in our times. I believe that something real, as far as feeling is concerned, should be elaborated as feeling. I don't consider that Aeschylus was making a propaganda play by putting the suffering Persians on stage, or desperate Xerxes, or the ghost of Darius, and so forth. On the contrary, there was human compassion in it. For his enemies. Not that he's not of course glad that the Greeks won the battle of Salamis. But even then he showed that Xerxes' defeat was a sort of divine retribution: a punishment for the hubris that Xerxes committed in flagellating the sea. Since his hubris was to flagellate the sea, he was punished exactly *by* the sea in the battle of Salamis.

INTERVIEWER: Is it possible to compare poetry across national lines? Or do we always have to make qualitative comparisons strictly within a single tradition?

SEFERIS: I feel a sort of reluctance about comparing poets. It is very difficult—even within the same tradition. Try to compare Dante and Alfred, Lord Tennyson, for example: What that would lead to, I don't know. Or, in the French tradition, how can you compare Racine and Victor Hugo? You have to go very deep, to the bottom of the tradition, in order to find some sort of common ground where the comparison can fairly take place. On the other hand, for example, I myself used Yeats in my Stockholm acceptance speech because I had been reading, just a few months before my trip to Stockholm, "The Bounty of Sweden," where he recounts the whole affair of his election to the Nobel Prize: his trip to Stockholm, the ceremony, and everything. And there I felt a sort of relation with him as a human being—not as a poet but as a human being; because Yeats belonged to a small country with a great folklore tradition, a country which, after all, had political turmoil. By the way, there's another example of a public poet who doesn't write propaganda. He writes, for example, a poem about an Irish airman which isn't at all propaganda. "Those I fight I do not hate—" etc. Or he writes "The Second Coming." That, too, is not propaganda: "The center cannot hold," etc., which after all starts somewhere in Irish political life; but it goes deeper, and that's the whole point, I think.

INTERVIEWER: You've mentioned at your readings, in talking about "The King of Asine," the fact that it had taken you two years to find a way of writing about that particular experience, and then, at some point, after having given your notes for that poem to a friend, you completed the final draft in one long evening. Eliot has implied that you finished the poem (between ten P.M. and three in the morning) exactly because you didn't have your notes before you.

SEFERIS: I had no notes. And he may have been right. I don't know. In my home in Athens, I have all my papers and my books. And I wonder if that's a helpful thing or not, if it's not better to have just a blank writing desk without any papers or any books at all, where you can sit at regular hours every day.

INTERVIEWER: Do you normally make notes on the experience of a poem before you write it?

SEFERIS: Oh, there are many ways. Sometimes I do. Sometimes I do not. There are things which you have to remember, and I have to record these somewhere, so of course I make notes. For example, there is a poem where I have used the chronographer Makhairas, where it was impossible to avoid referring to that story about the demon of fornication.

INTERVIEWER: I didn't mean notes once the poem has been composed in your mind, but notes on the experience which, in effect, becomes the poem.

SEFERIS: No, I don't do that. When I say notes, I mean there are those on the material, notes which are needed because they are descriptive. And there are notes that are ideas, poetical ideas. For example, poetical expressions, poetical utterances, that is the kind of notes I mean. If I were to write a poem about you—I might make a note that "Mike has ceased to smoke for many years." I mean if the things sound well in Greek to my ear, I could write it. That's all—things which are indifferent to other people. These I call poetical notes. Sometimes I disregard them altogether, and sometimes I go back to them. Sometimes, when they are quite forgotten, by having a glimpse at them, I say: "Oh, that poem was rather interesting," although they don't say anything at all to the ordinary person. Still, they take me back to a certain atmosphere which, in the meantime, has been working, elaborating, a form in my mind.

INTERVIEWER: Do you keep these notes or do you destroy them?

SEFERIS: Oh, I destroy a lot. Some months ago in Athens— there was somebody, a sort of Hellenist, who was interested in photographing notes. And I had the impression that I had kept my notes on *The Cistern*. I looked for them in all my files, and it appeared to me then that I had destroyed them. The only thing that I found was the "Notes for a 'Week' " which have been published quite recently—that is, the two missing poems from that group.

INTERVIEWER: I'm sorry about that, in a way, because I think *The Cistern* is a poem that all of us have found obscure in places, and the notes might have helped—might have helped *me,* anyway.

SEFERIS: Don't complain about it. They might have made the poem much more obscure, you know. For example, the general idea about my evolution in poetry is: "Ah, you see, Seferis started with regular lines, rhymes, strict versification, and then he moved to free verse." When I see my notes, I see that the main poem of *Strophe,* the "Erotikos Logos," appears to be in very strict versification; but my notes show me that this poem was also written in free verse. I have found some of the first drafts.

INTERVIEWER: Would you ever consider publishing them?

SEFERIS: By God, no.

INTERVIEWER: Do you think that's the reason Eliot was so careful about not rediscovering the lost parts of *The Waste Land,* which have now been rediscovered?

SEFERIS: When he told me the story about the writing of *The Waste Land,* he seemed quite desperate about the manuscripts being lost. On the other hand, he also told me how useful—he stressed that point—how *useful* the intervention of Pound had really been.

INTERVIEWER: Do you approve of publishing discarded things?

SEFERIS: I don't know; it depends. It needs a great deal of tact. Not by the poet himself but by his editors. If they publish them, they tend to stress that they are all-important discoveries, and I think this is bad. Overplaying it. The editors and the philologists are always overdoing things, I think.

INTERVIEWER: I know from a section of your diary which my wife and I translated that your relationship with Eliot was an important one in your life in various ways. I wonder if any other literary figures who are known in the West have also been important to you. I'm thinking particularly of Henry Miller and Lawrence Durrell and maybe others I don't know about. I'm thinking also of your own compatriots: Theotokas and Katsimbalis, for example.

SEFERIS: Durrell was much younger than me, you know. He was a very interesting young man when I met him. He was in his mid-twenties. I met him with Henry Miller. They came to Athens to see the Colossus of Maroussi, Katsimbalis. It was on the day —if my memory is correct—of the declaration of war.

INTERVIEWER: But of course Katsimbalis wasn't the Colossus at that point.

SEFERIS: No, but Miller was threatening to make him something very colossal.

INTERVIEWER: Well, he did.

SEFERIS: It was nice to meet them; they were, let's say, the first —or if not exactly the first, then the second or third—readers with an understanding of what I was doing. For example, one of them, Miller or Larry, told me after reading my poems: "You know what I like about you is that you turn things inside out. And I mean that in the *good* sense." That was a very nice compliment for me at that time.

INTERVIEWER: How did they come to know your poetry?

SEFERIS: How. Hm. There were then in English only the translations of Katsimbalis. Manuscript translations, I mean.

INTERVIEWER: When they came to Athens, why did they go directly to Katsimbalis? Why was he the man whom they approached? Was he well known as a literary figure outside Greece?

SEFERIS: I don't know. It was a matter of common friends, perhaps. He became a bigger literary figure after *The Colossus of Maroussi.* At that time he was more in contact than I was with the English and American literary circles. There was a sort of international bohemia, I might say, by then in Athens. I mean on the eve of the war. I must add that Katsimbalis has that wonderful quality of being without evil intention in his heart. He might criticize somebody, but in a good-hearted way. And he believed

that our country, our little country, was able to do something. He
had that sort of belief.

INTERVIEWER: What about Henry Miller? How did you respond to him?

SEFERIS: I like Miller because he is a very good-hearted man,
and I think—excuse me for saying so, but this is not a criticism:
It is great praise to say about a writer that he is a good man—
Miller has a great deal of generosity in him. For example, when
the moment came for him to go back to America (he was advised
to do so by the American consul; as an American national, he had
to go back home because the war was coming near), he said to
me one day: "My dear George, you've been so kind to me, and
I want to give you something." And he produced a diary which
he had been keeping during his stay in Greece. I said: "Look here,
Henry. But after all, I know that you are going to write a book,
and you can't write the book—I mean you might need your
notes." He said: "No. All those things are here," pointing to his
head. I offered to make a typescript copy for him to give him.
"No," he said, "a gift must be whole." Well, that's a splendid way
of behaving, I think. And I shall never forget that. The diary was
a sort of first draft of the *Colossus*. But with more personal
explosions. And more jokes, of course.

INTERVIEWER: There are quite a few jokes in the book, too.

SEFERIS: The trip to Hydra is splendid and the channel of
Poros. Remember? My feeling about Miller is this: Of course it's
a great thing to have an understanding of the ancient authors; but
the first man I admired for not having any classical preparation
on going to Greece is Miller. There is such a freshness in him.

INTERVIEWER: The freshness of being ready to take it all in for
the first time, you mean?

SEFERIS: I suppose I was the first man to give him a text of
Aeschylus, when he decided to go to Mycenae. But of course he
doesn't see anything from Aeschylus; he sees, in the plain of
Argos, *redskins* while he hears a jazz trumpeter. That is spontaneous behavior. And I admire it.

INTERVIEWER: Jazz trumpeter?

SEFERIS: The jazz trumpeter was inspired, I suppose, by Louis Armstrong. Because he had heard Armstrong on a small gramophone—a quite elementary gramophone—that I had then in my home in Athens. I myself had discovered jazz eight or ten years earlier . . .

INTERVIEWER: Before Miller's arrival in Greece. So you taught *him* about jazz?

SEFERIS: I was thirty-two or thirty-three at that time. And I became a jazz addict. I said to myself, after all, you have discovered at the same time the importance of Bach—the great Bach —*and* the importance of jazz. I remember once I said to Mitropoulos: "For me, my dear maestro, jazz is one of the few ways left for us to express feeling without embarrassment." That was in '35. No, '34.

INTERVIEWER: Was there any other writer abroad or in Greece with whom you had a particularly close relationship?

SEFERIS: Its depends on what period you are referring to. For example, I had very close relations with Sikelianos once upon a time. I met him first in 1929, though it did not become a close relationship until after his illness and my return to Greece in 1944. During his illness, Sikelianos was really remarkable, when he had all those crises in his health. While I was serving abroad, I would take advantage of my trips to Athens to go and see him. One time I heard that he had just been through a sort of cerebral hemorrhage. I found him at the theater wearing dark glasses—a première at the National Theatre. I said: "Oh Angelo, I am so glad you are here, because I had heard that you were not so well." "My dear," he said, "it is such a splendid thing to have a little ruby on the top of your brain." He meant the hemorrhage. I said to him: "It is a splendid thing that you can talk about it that way. I am so glad." He said: "George, look here. I shall tell you a story during the next intermission." I approached him during the next intermissiion. He said: "Have you read *Rocambol?*" It's a sort of French thriller. Sikelianos went on: "Once upon a time a woman had thrown vitriol against the face of Rocambol, and Rocambol was in danger of losing his eyesight; so he was taken by one of his henchmen to the best specialist in Paris, and the specialist examined him very carefully while the friend of Rocambol was sitting in the waiting room overhearing the conversation of the doctor. And the doctor's conclusion was: 'Sir, you have to choose between two things: either lose your eyesight or be disfigured.' There was a moment of heavy silence; then the voice from the waiting room, the voice of the friend of Rocambol, was heard: 'Rocambol has no need of his eyesight.'

INTERVIEWER: Tell me more about Sikelianos. So little is known about him outside Greece.

SEFERIS: Another thing which I have mentioned in writing, at the time of his death. He had a great crisis in Athens, and I rushed to see him; I was very anxious; he had collapsed in the house of a friend. And again, the same splendid reaction. I said to him: "My dear Angelo, are you all right?" He said: "I'm all right. But I had a splendid experience. I saw the absolute dark. It was so beautiful."

INTERVIEWER: Did you know Palamas? What kind of man was he?

SEFERIS: You know, it is strange the memories I have kept of people. For example, other people admire Sikelianos for their own special reasons; myself, I was attracted by those tragic and splendid moments of Sikelianos' last years. Now Palamas: One of my last memories of him was when I went to tell him good-by because I was leaving shortly. During our conversation he referred to various crazy people mentioned in his poetry and added: "You know, we have many mad people in my family. I wanted once upon a time to write a book called 'To Genos ton Loxon.' " How can we translate that into English? "The breed of . . ."

INTERVIEWER: Of madmen.

SEFERIS: Not quite of madmen. Of "oblique" men.

INTERVIEWER: *Oblique* men?

SEFERIS: I'm trying to get the precise translation of the word.

INTERVIEWER: Unbalanced men, perhaps.

SEFERIS: I said to him: "Mr. Palamas, it is a pity you *didn't* write such a book." Because I thought it would be a good book. He had an interesting sense of humor.

INTERVIEWER: What do you consider Palamas' most significant contribution to Greek literature?

SEFERIS: Well, I said it in *Dokimes,* but I would repeat: his very important contribution to the Greek language. I mean compared to his, Cavafy's expression seems rather faint, although at certain moments more real.

INTERVIEWER: But the minute you say "although more real" . . .

SEFERIS: Again, what I appreciate very much in Cavafy is his having started with terrifically unreal poems, and then, by insistence and work, he found at last his own personal voice. He wrote very bad poems up to his thirty-fourth year. The failure of those poems cannot be translated or communicated to a foreign reader because the language of the translation is always bound to improve them. There is no possibility of translating that sort of thing faithfully.

You know, what I admire—let me put it my own way—what I admire about Cavafy was this: He was a man who starts at a certain age with all signs showing that he's unable to produce anything of importance. And then, by refusing and refusing things which are offered him, in the end he *finds,* he *sees,* as they say; he becomes certain that he's found his own expression. It's a splendid example of a man who, through his refusals, finds his way.

INTERVIEWER: What did he refuse precisely?

SEFERIS: Expressions, and the easy things, verbosity—that sort of thing. Take his poem on ancient tragedy, for example. It is very bad. It is something unbelievable. By putting aside things like that, Cavafy improves his expression up to the end of his life, even up to the last poem he wrote on the outskirts of Antioch: the happenings between the Christians and Julian. And I admire him for going on to the end like that. He's a great example. He had the courage, up to the end of his life, not to admit certain things, to reject them. And that's why I have doubts about all these people who are trying to put into circulation all the rejected writings of Cavafy, unless one is very careful in reading him. You know, that needs a great deal of discernment.

INTERVIEWER: To turn now to the other well-known writer of the older generation, what about Kazantzakis? In the U. S., Cavafy is the poet who's respected by those who are themselves poets—Auden, for instance, and many of the important younger American poets; most of them know Cavafy, and most of them have a sympathetic attitude towards him. But among students and among those who are just beginning to learn about literature, Kazantzakis is by far the most popular Greek writer, both as poet and as novelist. Increasingly my job is to try to discuss Kazantzakis' work—whether poetry or fiction—without diminishing him.

SEFERIS: I don't wonder. The thing is that one must have a possibility of being in contact with a writer, and that I cannot do in the case of Kazantzakis—a terrible thing for me, you know. I must give you a warning as far as Kazantzakis is concerned. On the one hand, there is his poetry—what is called poetry—and that's the *Odyssey* sequel, of course, and his plays in verse; and on the other hand, there is his prose: the novels. Now, as far as the novels are concerned, I am not competent to judge. I don't know how to speak about the novels. I have not read all of them. I hear from people whom I trust that they are very good, and they may well *be* very good. But the *Odyssey* sequel is another matter. There, although you have interesting passages, I'm afraid there is no poetry in them. I say interesting passages—passages that are informative about the man Kazantzakis; but I don't believe that's poetry, at least not the poetry I believe in.

INTERVIEWER: What about as "idea," quite aside from poetic considerations? As statement of a philosophical or religious position.

SEFERIS: I don't know. I have no idea about philosophical positions and world views. You know, whenever world views begin interfering with writing—I don't know. I prefer world views in the sort of dry, repulsive, and (I don't know how to put it) prosaic way. I don't like people who try to express world views in writing poetry. I remember once I had a reading in Thessalonike, and a philosopher stood up and asked: "But what, after all, Mr. Seferis, is your world view?" And I said: "My dear friend, I'm sorry to say that I have no world view. I have to make this public confession to you that I am writing without having any world view. I don't know, perhaps you find that scandalous, sir, but may I ask you to tell me what Homer's world view is?" And I didn't get an answer.

INTERVIEWER: To move on to a more general subject, you said during one of our conversations in Athens that a circumstance which is notable about Greek writers in this century was that so many of them were outside the Kingdom of Greece proper. You mentioned yourself as an instance, having been brought up in Smyrna. Could you comment on the ways your Smyrna origin may have influenced your work or your general role as a man of letters.

SEFERIS: Let me say that I am interested in everything which finds expression in the Greek language and in Greek lands—I mean, taking Greek lands as a whole. For example, I was terribly interested, as you know, in what happened in Crete in the seventeenth century. And in another way, people in Rumania, for example, the principalities of Moldavia and Wallachia, interested me very much—even odd minor people like Kaisarios Dapontes, if you know who he is. I think he was from somewhere in the northern islands, Skopelos of the Sporades, and he lived a long part of his life in the principalities, then Constantinople, and finally he retired to Mt. Athos under the name of Kaisarios. I don't mean that he is a great poet, simply that his way of expressing himself interests me. I don't say that he writes great poetry, but after all, one feels that in those countries in the eighteenth century, there was such a flourishing of Greek letters. Another monk of Mt. Athos—I'm trying to remember his name—yes, his name was Pamberis, wrote a poem, not a very long one because it would be an impossible achievement to write a long poem under the system he decided to use. He called it "Poiema Karkinikon," so to say, "Poem Cancerous." It was devised so that it could be read from left to right or from right to left, and still attempting to make sense—but a sense so remote that he had to put notes explaining what each line meant. These small details amuse me, you know. And I think that they add to the too professorial image we have of Greek literature. Or again, another text: "The Mass of the Beardless Man." It is a text written in the form of a mock Mass that parodies the Mass in a rather shocking way. It amuses me especially because I don't see enough light comic texts in our literature. Either people refrained from writing such texts, or such texts were eliminated by somber-minded academics.

INTERVIEWER: That's an interesting remark. You've said on another occasion that one thing which you find that the Anglo-Saxon tradition has and no other tradition has is that element of nonsense—an element which is fairly continuous in our literature and which seems always to have existed in some form.

SEFERIS: The Anglo-Saxon tradition is certainly different from ours in that respect; and I believe that no continental country can claim the same kind of nonsense that Edward Lear and Lewis Carroll offer.

INTERVIEWER: You've spent three periods of service in England, spread over the best part of your literary career. Did you find it an especially congenial climate for work?

SEFERIS: Not really. A very good place for me for writing was when I was in Albania because I was quite unknown there, and very isolated; at the same time I was near Greece, I mean, from the language point of view, and I could use my free time to advantage. There were no exhausting social functions.

INTERVIEWER: What about your acquaintance with English men of letters during your early years in England? You met Eliot, of course.

SEFERIS: No, I had a letter of introduction to Eliot, and I rang his office, but the secretary informed me that Eliot was in the United States. It was the time when he was Charles Eliot Norton Professor at Harvard. I never met Eliot nor any other writer in the beginning. First of all, I was rather shy as a person; then, it was a period when I was groping to find my own further expression. In contrast, when I came to England after World War II, my period in the Middle East had created a great many friends among the English, and when I came back to England as Counselor at the Embassy, I had no difficulty at all because by then I was quite well known in England. It was just after the publication of my first translation into English, *The King of Asine and Other Poems*, in 1948.

INTERVIEWER: During the period of your first official visit to England, I wonder whether you had any contact with English or American literature that you found particularly exciting along with Eliot's work.

SEFERIS: I think a very instructive man for me, as I found out afterwards, was W. B. Yeats. But I'm talking about Yeats's early period. After all, you see, I had endeavored to exploit folklore much as Yeats did.

INTERVIEWER: What about American literature? Did you have any favorite American authors in your formative years?

SEFERIS: It is an odd thing for us—I suppose that happens to everybody abroad—I mean, one gets into literature and art by chance. For example, I don't remember on what occasion I came to know Archibald MacLeish. And I translated him, as a matter of fact. I think I am the first man to have translated him in Greece. Then there was Marianne Moore. I had translated Marianne Moore before the war also. "The Monkeys," "To a Snail."

INTERVIEWER: You say you encountered them by accident. What was the accident?

SEFERIS: Oh, I don't know. Some review where I saw the poems, I don't remember which one. And again, Ezra Pound. I had already translated three *Cantos* before the war.

INTERVIEWER: When I brought up American literature, I was really thinking about the older American poets: Walt Whitman and Emily Dickinson, for example.

SEFERIS: I knew Walt Whitman. Because I started with French literature, and Walt Whitman was translated into French early enough to be available to me. And then Henry Miller had an admiration for Whitman. He gave me many hints about him.

That was quite near the outbreak of the war, of course. But I keep reading Whitman, as, in my youth, I was reading Edgar Allan Poe.

INTERVIEWER: Now that you're about to go back to Greece, do you have anything that you can say about this particular visit to the United States—which is your third visit, if I'm not mistaken —anything about your impressions of this country.

SEFERIS: My third visit to America has been the most important of all, this visit; it has been more substantial than the others. I don't believe that visiting New York helps you to understand America. Curiously enough, I am now in the middle of a wood in a remote place, Princeton, yet I have been able to see and understand more of America from this remote place than if I were in a great center.

INTERVIEWER: Of course Princetonians don't think Princeton is all that remote.

SEFERIS: Well, I mean for others who are trying, when they are traveling, to see cosmopolitan centers, it might look remote. And after all, we travelers do not attend courses at the university.

INTERVIEWER: What have you seen in particular during this visit that has impressed you?

SEFERIS: I don't want to mention things which impress me, you know. Nobody knows what impresses him on the spot. I mean it takes time to be elaborated somehow by memory.

INTERVIEWER: Did you get some work done?

SEFERIS: Yes, I think I did. I can't say. I don't know how to speak about work done. I have the impression that one can speak about work done only when the work is finished. I am not inclined to speak about my work during the period of elaboration. But in any case, there is an inner feeling that you have not lost your time. Which is something. I mean, I want to be honest with you: I cannot mention anything really done. The only thing I can mention to you—and I'm not going to mention the substance of it —is that I wrote a poem of two lines.

INTERVIEWER: You just received a volume of Eugene McCar-

thy's poems. I found that rather moving: to discover that he had
in fact written a volume of poems, and apparently during his
campaign last year.

SEFERIS: Yes, why not? I mean I can very well understand that.
If there was a period of euphoria, there is no reason why it
shouldn't happen in poetry at the same time that it happens in
a chapter of politics. One of my poems, "Thrush," was written
after a terribly active period of my life—I mean, politically active,
because I was principal private secretary to the Regent of Greece
just before going to Poros. Of course poems do not appear like
an eruption by a volcano; they need preparation. And I think back
on "Thrush," I can well mark notes, lines, which I had started
writing during the previous year, that most active year. Nevertheless, I remember days when the job was killing, because I was not
a politician, I was just a servant, a public servant, and I remember
days when I started going to my office at something like eight
o'clock in the morning and returned back home the next day at
five o'clock in the morning without having had any meal or any
sleep. I mention that, of course, not in order to move you but in
order to show you that, after all, time was pressing then. But I
was also writing. Of course, there are other things which influenced my work at that time, and among other things I might
mention the fact that I returned to my country after a great
period of longing, at the end of the war.

INTERVIEWER: Do you feel that, in addition to the lines you
wrote, the poem was gestating in some significant way during this
very active period, so that when you went to Poros it could come
out as the coherent work it is in a relatively short period? A month
of vacation, wasn't it?

SEFERIS: Two months. The first long holiday I ever had during
my career—the longest one.

INTERVIEWER: And you were able to write the poem—and it
is a long poem—in effect during one sitting: the long sitting of
that two-month vacation?

SEFERIS: No. You'll find the story of my writing that poem in
the diary of this period, the period of '46 on Poros. I used to go

for a swim—no, first I would cut wood in the garden (which was a huge garden), then go to the sea, and then work up to night, up to darkness, which started at seven o'clock. And it is strange, you know, how—excuse me for talking like this—I noticed how one is cleansed progressively by such a life. For example, I noticed that cleansing in my dreams, as I mentioned in this diary which has been recently published.

INTERVIEWER: I have only one more really general topic to bring up. I wonder if you feel, as the result of your rather unique position in Greek letters now—I suppose any poet has a unique position in his country once he's won the Nobel Prize—if you feel that this in any way has affected your sense of a public role as a man of letters as distinct from your private role as a poet—any responsibility you may feel towards younger poets, for instance, towards the cultural life around you, or any position you may sense you have to maintain in relation to your country.

SEFERIS: I should from the beginning tell you quite bluntly— if I can say it in English—that the Nobel Prize is an accident, no more than an accident. It's not an appointment. And I have no feeling that I have been appointed to any sort of function. It is just an accident which one has to try and forget as soon as possible. Otherwise, if you are overdazzled by that sort of thing, you get lost and founder. At the time I won the prize, there was a sort of—how can I put it in English?—a sort of Cassandra-like critic who wrote that Seferis should be very careful because he's going to be completely dried up as far as his work is concerned and even die from various illnesses since that sort of thing happens to people who have that kind of success. He was just exaggerating the one side of it without considering, after all, what showed in the way I reacted to the prize. For example, I said in Stockholm to my judges (or whatever they are): "Gentlemen, I thank you"—this at the end of a sort of lecture I gave there— "for allowing me, after a long effort, to be *nobody,* to be unnoticed, as Homer says of Ulysses." And I was quite sincere. After all, I don't recognize the right of anybody to take you by the back of your neck and throw you into a sort of ocean of empty responsibilities. Why, that's scandalous, after all.

INTERVIEWER: Now let's move away from the issue of the Nobel Prize. Greece, being a small country, seems to me to have always had, somehow, a tradition (it's an informal tradition, unlike the British one) of an unofficial but generally recognized poet laureate—a feeling among poets and their followers that there is one spokesman for poetry in each particular generation—even if the role of spokesman is sometimes self-assumed. Sikelianos, for example, played that role. And in his day, so did Palamas.

SEFERIS: Well, yes, God bless them, but I'm sorry to say that I never felt I was the spokesman for anything or anybody. There are no credentials which appoint anybody to be a spokesman for something. Now others consider that a sort of function which must be performed; but I think that is, after all, why I have written so little. I've never felt the obligation; I have to consider only that I am not dried up as a poet and to write. I mean that has been my feeling from the very beginning. I remember when I published my first book, there were lots of people who said: "Mr. Seferis, you must now try to show us that you can do more." I answered them: "Gentlemen, you must consider that every poem published by me is the last one. I never have any feeling about its continuation." My last poem. And if I write another one, it's a great blessing. Now how much I have worked in order to produce the next poem, or how much I have not worked, is another matter—a private matter. Others think that they are the voices of the country. All right. God bless them. And sometimes they've been very good in that function.

INTERVIEWER: Joyce felt that way a bit. I'm thinking of the famous remark by Stephen Dedalus at the end of *A Portrait of the Artist as a Young Man*, "to forge in the smithy of my soul the uncreated conscience of my race."

SEFERIS: I can give you another example. In my youth there was an enormous amount of discussion about the problem of knowing, or trying to define, what is Greek and what is not Greek —praising one thing as Greek and condemning something else as un-Greek: trying, in short, to establish "the real" Greek tradition.

So I wrote, "Greekness is the sum of the authentic works which are going to be produced by Greeks." We cannot say that we have *some* works creating the conscience of Greece. We see a line, but surrounded by large margins of darkness. It isn't simple. I don't know what my voice is. If others, for the time being, consider that it is *their* conscience, so much the better. It's up to them to decide. It's not up to me to impose; because you cannot be a sort of dictator in these matters.

INTERVIEWER: Some would think yours the healthy attitude, but there are other people who feel that a Nobel Prize winner, especially when he is the only one the country has ever had, *ought* to be a spokesman and a public conscience.

SEFERIS: It might be so, but, after all, one takes the attitude which is imposed on him by his nature, or whatever you call it. At the same time, I have never forced myself to write anything which I didn't think necessary. When I say "necessary," I mean which I *had* to express or be smothered.

INTERVIEWER: Well, I've run out of questions. Since you don't have any grand advice for the younger generation, I've nothing more to ask you.

SEFERIS: I *have* advice.

INTERVIEWER: Oh you *do?* Good.

SEFERIS: I have the following advice to give to the younger Greek generation: to try to exercise themselves as much as they can in the modern Greek language. And not to write it upside down. I have to tell them that in order to write, one must believe in what one does, not seeming to believe that one is believing something. They must remember that the only job in which one cannot lie is poetry. You can't lie in poetry. If you are a liar, you'll always be discovered. Perhaps now, perhaps in five years, in ten years, but you are going to be discovered eventually if you are lying.

INTERVIEWER: When you speak of lying, you're speaking first of all about lying against your emotional . . .

SEFERIS: I don't know what I mean. Perhaps it is an emotional thing. In the reality of one's thoughts. I don't know. I mean, there is a special sound about the solid, the sound thing. You knock against it, and it renders a sort of sound which proves that it is genuine.

INTERVIEWER: Do you think every writer always knows himself whether the sound he hears is genuine or not?

SEFERIS: No. It is difficult to say. But he must somehow have an instinct—a guiding instinct—which says to him: "My dear boy, my dear chap, be careful; you are going to fall. You are exaggerating at this moment." And then, when he hears that, he should not take a drug in order to say to himself: "Why, you are all right, my dear." You are not all right, my dear, at all.

EDMUND KEELEY

8. John Steinbeck

John Steinbeck supported himself financially through his boyhood and young manhood in Salinas, California, where he was born of Irish and German stock on February 27, 1902. Although he entered Stanford University in 1919, financial necessities made it impossible for him to complete his education. In 1925 he worked his way to New York City on a cattle boat to try to get his early writing published. When this attempt failed, he worked as a newspaper reporter for a time and then returned to California, where he pursued his writing while working at such jobs as fruit picker, surveyor, chemical laboratory assistant, and caretaker.

In the two decades after the publication of his first book in 1932, Steinbeck published sixteen long works of fiction, widely different in both content and form. His first popular success was *Tortilla Flat* (1935). Other major works were *In Dubious Battle* (1936), *Of Mice and Men* (1937), *The Red Pony* (1937), *The Long Valley* (1938), *The Grapes of Wrath* (1939), *Cannery Row* (1945), *The Pearl* (1947), and *East of Eden* (1952).

After his considerable success as a novelist, he returned to journalism during World War II as a war correspondent in Italy and later in Russia. Steinbeck's writing pace slowed after 1952. He wrote *Sweet Thursday* (1954), *Once There Was a War* (1958), *The Winter of Our Discontent* (1961) and *Travels with Charley* (1962). In 1962 he was awarded the Nobel Prize. John Steinbeck died on December 20, 1968.

on a dark night suddenly created by a flash of lightning. There it was. Maybe I'll write it and put it away. But it was all there. And it was good.

I don't seem to be listening but I do listen. And sometimes I don't hear the unspoken word for a long time but usually I get to it. My mind works almost as slowly as my reading. Mentally I move my lips too.

Everyman (working title) continues to grow in my mind. It could stretch out in all directions but it must be held back and down so that the implications are inherent but not stated. My chest! it's a dramatic thing. We'll do it, too. And only throw it away after it has every chance. Now it has beginning middle and end and that's what three acts are and that's why there are three acts. The 5 act play is still three acts. And the form was imposed by the human mind, not by play wrights or critics. This doesn't mean that external reality has beginning middle and end but simply that the human brain perceives it so. This letter is growing pedagogic, isn't it?

Nede says now that he went to S.F. to get some insurance. And maybe he died. Who am I to ask?

This is the first page of this letter. There will be more before I send it. An anecdote is about to happen but I will only put it in after it happens. More later.

John Steinbeck letter

Toni Frissell

John Steinbeck

[John Steinbeck had agreed to a Paris Review interview late in his life. He had earlier been coy about it but then wanted the interview very much. He was, unfortunately, too sick to work on the project, though it was at the end often in his thoughts. With this interest of his in mind, the editors of this magazine compiled a number of comments on the art of fiction that John Steinbeck made over the years. Some come from the East of Eden diaries, published in December 1969 by The Viking Press under the title Journal of a Novel. Others are excerpted from letters, some of which have been collected under the title Steinbeck: A Life in Letters and published in October 1975 by Viking. The quotes have been organized under various topic headings rather than chronologically, as they are in the diaries and letters. Nathaniel Benchley, a close friend of the author, has provided the introduction.]

By rights this preface or introduction or whatever it is should be called "Compliments of a Friend," because I have neither the perspective nor the desire to offer up a critique of John Steinbeck's writing even if anyone would listen. Furthermore, nobody has asked me to, so we're all that much better off. I knew him, and I know a little bit of what he thought about writing, and that will be my contribution.

He once said that to write well about something you had to either love it or hate it very much, and that in a sense was a mirror of his own personality. Things were either black or white, and although he might change his basic position (as he eventually did about the Vietnam war), if you were on his side, you could do no wrong, and if you were agin him, you could do no right. It wasn't as simplistic as that may make it sound, but there were very few gray areas where he was concerned. And when he wrote, you certainly knew whose side he was on. You hoped it was yours.

Long ago, he was quoted as saying that genius was a little boy chasing a butterfly up a mountain. He later insisted that what he'd really said was that it was a butterfly chasing a little boy up a mountain (or a mountain chasing a butterfly up a little boy; I've forgotten which), and I think in some ways he was haunted by having caught his butterfly so early in the game. He never said this in so many words (to me, at any rate), but his fierce dedication to his writing, and his conviction that every word he put down was the best he could find, were signs of a man who dreaded ever having it said that he was slipping, or that he hadn't given it his best. One time, at the behest of a son of mine at Exeter, he wrote a few paragraphs for the seventy-sixth anniversary edition of The Ex-onian; he called it "In Awe of Words," and with the permission of the management I'll reproduce it here, because as usual he says these things better for himself.

A man who writes a story is forced to put into it the best of his knowledge and the best of his feeling. The discipline of the written word punishes both stupidity and dishonesty. A writer lives in awe of words for they can be cruel or kind, and they can change their meanings right in front of you. They pick up flavors and odors like butter in a refrigerator. Of course, there are dishonest writers who go on for a little while, but not for long—not for long.

A writer out of loneliness is trying to communicate like a distant star sending signals. He isn't telling or teaching or ordering. Rather he seeks to establish a relationship of meaning, of feeling, of observing. We are lonesome animals. We spend all life trying to be less lonesome. One of our ancient methods is to tell a story begging the listener to say—and to feel—

"Yes, that's the way it is, or at least that's the way I feel it. You're not as alone as you thought."

Of course a writer rearranges life, shortens time intervals, sharpens events, and devises beginnings, middles and ends. We do have curtains—in a day, morning, noon and night, in a man, birth, growth and death. These are curtain rise and curtain fall, but the story goes on and nothing finishes.

To finish is sadness to a writer—a little death. He puts the last word down and it is done. But it isn't really done. The story goes on and leaves the writer behind, for no story is ever done.

Reading through his obituaries, I found a good deal of analytical writing about his work, and one rewrite man ventured the personal note that he was considered shy, but nowhere did I see a word about one of the most glorious facets of his character, which was his humor. All good humor defies analysis (E. B. White likened it to a frog, which dies under dissection), and John's defied it more than most, because it was not gag-type humor but was the result of his wildly imaginative mind, his remarkable store of knowledge, and his precision with words. This respect for, and precision with, words led him to avoid almost every form of profanity; where most people would let their rage spill out the threadbare obscenities, he would concoct some diatribe that let off the steam and was at the same time mildly diverting. One example should suffice: At Easter about three years ago we were visiting the Steinbecks at Sag Harbor, and John and I arose before the ladies to make breakfast. He hummed and puttered about the kitchen with the air of a man who was inventing a new form of toaster, and suddenly the coffee pot boiled over, sending torrents of coffee grounds over the stove and clouds of vapor into the air. John leaped for the switch, shouting, "Nuts! No wonder I'm a failure! No wonder nobody ever asks for my hand in marriage! Nuts!" By that time both he and the coffee had simmered down, and he started a new pot. I think that this was the day he stoutly denied having a hangover, and after a moment of reflection added, "Of course, I do have a headache that starts at the base of my spine . . ." He spent the rest of the morning painting an Easter egg black, as a protest.

There was, oddly, a lot of little boy left in him, if by little boy you can mean a searching interest in anything new, a desire to do or to find or to invent some sort of diversion, a fascination with any gadget of any sort whatsoever, and the ability to be entertained by comparative trivia. He was the only adult I have ever seen who would regularly laugh at the Sunday comics; he raised absolute hell in our kitchen with an idea for making papier-mâché in the Waring blender with a combination of newspaper and water and flour; and he would conduct frequent trips to the neighborhood toy store, sometimes just to browse through the stock and sometimes to buy an item like a cap pistol as a Valentine's Day present for his wife. To be with him was to be on a constant parranda, *either actual or intellectual, and the only person bewildered by it was his children's nurse, who once said, "I don't see why Mr. Steinbeck and Mr. Benchley go out to those bars, when there's all that free liquor at home."*

And late at night, over some of the "free" liquor at home, he would sometimes read Synge's translations of Petrarch's sonnets to Laura, and then he would weep. It wasn't the liquor; it was the lilt of Synge's words and the ache in Petrarch's heart, and there was one of the sonnets that I never once heard him read through to the end.

NATHANIEL BENCHLEY

ON GETTING STARTED

It is usual that the moment you write for publication—I mean
one of course—one stiffens in exactly the same way one does
when one is being photographed. The simplest way to overcome
this is to write it *to* someone, like me. Write it as a letter aimed
at one person. This removes the vague terror of addressing the
large and faceless audience and it also, you will find, will give a
sense of freedom and a lack of self-consciousness.*

Now let me give you the benefit of my experience in facing 400
pages of blank stock—the appalling stuff that must be filled. I
know that no one really wants the benefit of anyone's experience
which is probably why it is so freely offered. But the following are
some of the things I have had to do to keep from going nuts.

1. Abandon the idea that you are ever going to finish. Lose
track of the 400 pages and write just one page for each day, it
helps. Then when it gets finished, you are always surprised.

2. Write freely and as rapidly as possible and throw the whole
thing on paper. Never correct or rewrite until the whole thing is
down. Rewrite in process is usually found to be an excuse for not
going on. It also interferes with flow and rhythm which can only
come from a kind of unconscious association with the material.

3. Forget your generalized audience. In the first place, the
nameless, faceless audience will scare you to death and in the
second place, unlike the theatre, it doesn't exist. In writing, your
audience is one single reader. I have found that sometimes it helps
to pick out one person—a real person you know, or an imagined
person and write to that one.

4. If a scene or a section gets the better of you and you still
think you want it—bypass it and go on. When you have finished
the whole you can come back to it and then you may find that
the reason it gave trouble is because it didn't belong there.

---

*From a letter to Pascal Covici, Jr., April 13, 1956

5. Beware of a scene that becomes too dear to you, dearer than the rest. It will usually be found that it is out of drawing.

6. If you are using dialogue—say it aloud as you write it. Only then will it have the sound of speech.*

ON LUCK

You know on my left hand on the pad just below the little finger, I have a dark brown spot. And on my left foot in a corresponding place I have another one almost the same. One time a Chinese, seeing the spot on my hand, became very much excited and when I told him about the one on my foot he was keenly interested. He said that in Chinese palmistry the hand spot was a sign of the greatest possible good luck and the one on my foot doubled it. These spots are nothing but a dark pigmentation. I've had them from birth. Indeed, they are what is known as birthmarks. But the reason I brought it up is this. For the last year and a half, they have been getting darker. And if I am to believe in my spots, this must mean that the luck is getting better. And sure enough I have Elaine [Mrs. John Steinbeck] and what better luck could there be. But the spots continue to darken and maybe that means that I am going to have a book, too. And that would be great good luck, too.

ON WORK HABITS

Mark Twain used to write in bed—so did our greatest poet.† But I wonder how often they wrote in bed—or whether they did it twice and the story took hold. Such things happen. Also I would like to know what things they wrote in bed and what things they wrote sitting up. All of this has to do with comfort in writing and what its value is. I should think that a comfortable body would let the mind go freely to its gathering.

---

*From a letter to Robert Wallsten, February 1962
†Mr. Benchley believes this is probably Stevenson.

You know I always smoke a pipe when I work—at least I used to and now I have taken it up again. It is strange—as soon as a pipe begins to taste good, cigarettes become tasteless. I find I smoke fewer and fewer cigarettes. Maybe I can cut them out entirely for a while. This would be a very good thing. Even with this little change, my deep-seated and perennial cigarette cough is going away. A few months without that would be a real relief.

I have dawdled away a good part of my free time now carving vaguely on a scrap of mahogany, but I guess I have been thinking too. Who knows. I sit here in a kind of a stupor and call it thought.

Now I have taken the black off my desk again, clear down to the wood, and have put a green blotter down. I am never satisfied with my writing surface.

My choice of pencils lies between the black Calculator stolen from Fox Films and this Mongol 2⅜ F which is quite black and holds its point well—much better in fact than the Fox pencils. I will get six more or maybe four more dozen of them for my pencil tray.

I have found a new kind of pencil—the best I have ever had. Of course it costs three times as much too but it is black and soft but doesn't break off. I think I will always use these. They are called Blackwings and they really glide over the paper.

In the very early dawn, I felt a fiendish desire to take my electric pencil sharpener apart. It has not been working very well and besides I have always wanted to look at the inside of it. So I did and found that certain misadjustments had been made at the factory. I corrected them, cleaned the machine, oiled it and now it works perfectly for the first time since I have it. There is one reward for not sleeping.

Today is a dawdly day. They seem to alternate. I do a whole of a day's work and then the next day, flushed with triumph, I dawdle. That's today. The crazy thing is that I get about the same number of words down either way. This morning I am clutching the pencil very tight and this is not a good thing. It means I am not relaxed. And in this book I want to be just as relaxed as possible. Maybe that is another reason I am dawdling. I want that calmness to settle on me that feels so good—almost like a robe of cashmere it feels.

It has been a good day of work with no harm in it. I have sat long over the desk and the pencil has felt good in my hand. Outside the sun is very bright and warm and the buds are swelling to a popping size. I guess it is a good thing I became a writer. Perhaps I am too lazy for anything else.

On the third finger of my right hand I have a great callus just from using a pencil for so many hours every day. It has become a big lump by now and it doesn't ever go away. Sometimes it is very rough and other times, as today, it is as shiny as glass. It is peculiar how touchy one can become about little things. Pencils must be round. A hexagonal pencil cuts my fingers after a long day. You see I hold a pencil for about six hours every day. This may seem strange but it is true. I am really a conditioned animal with a conditioned hand.

I am really dawdling today when what I want to write is in my head. It is said that many writers talk their books out and so do not write them. I think I am guilty of this to a large extent. I really talk too much about my work and to anyone who will listen. If I would limit my talk to inventions and keep my big mouth shut about work, there would probably be a good deal more work done.

The callus on my writing finger is very sore today. I may have to sandpaper it down. It is getting too big.

The silly truth is that I can take almost any amount of work but I have little tolerance for confusion.

ON INSPIRATION

I hear via a couple of attractive grapevines, that you are having trouble writing. God! I know this feeling so well. I think it is never coming back—but it does—one morning, there it is again.

About a year ago, Bob Anderson [the playwright] asked me for help in the same problem. I told him to write poetry—not for selling—not even for seeing—poetry to throw away. For poetry is the mathematics of writing and closely kin to music. And it is also the best therapy because sometimes the troubles come tumbling out.

Well, he did. For six months he did. And I have three joyous letters from him saying it worked. Just poetry—anything and not designed for a reader. It's a great and valuable privacy.

I only offer this if your dryness goes on too long and makes you too miserable. You may come out of it any day. I have. The words are fighting each other to get out.*

ON VERSE

Certain events such as love, or a national calamity, or May, bring pressure to bear on the individual, and if the pressure is strong enough, something in the form of verse is bound to be squeezed out. National calamities and loves have been few in my life, and I do not always succumb to May.

My first gem called forth quite adverse criticism, although I considered it extremely apropos at the time. It was published on a board fence, and was in the form of free verse. It ran something like this:

> *Gertie loves Tom, and*
> *Tom loves Gertie.*

This is the only one of my brain children which has attracted attention, and the attention it attracted has made me backward about publishing any of my later works.†

---

*From a letter to Robert Wallsten, February 19, 1960.
†From a letter to Professor William Herbert Carruth, Early 1920s

ON THE SHORT STORY

Although it must be a thousand years ago that I sat in your class in story writing at Stanford, I remember the experience very clearly. I was bright-eyed and bushy-brained and prepared to absorb from you the secret formula for writing good short stories, even great short stories.

You canceled this illusion very quickly. The only way to write a good short story, you said, was to write a good short story. Only after it is written can it be taken apart to see how it was done. It is a most difficult form, you told us, and the proof lies in how very few great short stories there are in the world.

The basic rule you gave us was simple and heartbreaking. A story to be effective had to convey something from writer to reader and the power of its offering was the measure of its excellence. Outside of that, you said, there were no rules. A story could be about anything and could use any means and technique at all —so long as it was effective.

As a subhead to this rule, you maintained that it seemed to be necessary for the writer to know what he wanted to say, in short, what he was talking about. As an exercise we were to try reducing the meat of a story to one sentence, for only then could we know it well enough to enlarge it to three or six or ten thousand words.

So there went the magic formula, the secret ingredient. With no more than that you set us on the desolate lonely path of the writer. And we must have turned in some abysmally bad stories. If I had expected to be discovered in a full bloom of excellence, the grades you gave my efforts quickly disillusioned me. And if I felt unjustly criticized, the judgments of editors for many years afterwards upheld your side, not mine.

It seemed unfair. I could read a fine story and could even know how it was done, thanks to your training. Why could I not do it myself? Well, I couldn't, and maybe it's because no two stories dare be alike. Over the years I have written a great many stories and I still don't know how to go about it except to write it and take my chances.

If there is a magic in story writing, and I am convinced that there is, no one has ever been able to reduce it to a recipe that can be passed from one person to another. The formula seems to lie solely in the aching urge of the writer to convey something he feels important to the reader. If the writer has that urge, he may sometimes but by no means always find the way to do it.

It is not so very hard to judge a story after it is written, but after many years, to start a story still scares me to death. I will go so far as to say that the writer who is not scared is happily unaware of the remote and tantalizing majesty of the medium.

I wonder whether you will remember one last piece of advice you gave me. It was during the exuberance of the rich and frantic twenties and I was going out into that world to try to be a writer.

You said, "It's going to take a long time, and you haven't any money. Maybe it would be better if you could go to Europe."

"Why?" I asked.

"Because in Europe poverty is a misfortune, but in America it is shameful. I wonder whether or not you can stand the shame of being poor."

It wasn't too long afterwards that the depression came down. Then everyone was poor and it was no shame any more. And so I will never know whether or not I could have stood it. But surely you were right about one thing, Edith. It took a long time—a very long time. And it is still going on and it has never got easier. You told me it wouldn't.*

ON HACK WRITING

I think the manuscript ["Murder at Full Moon"] enclosed in this package is self explanatory. For some time now, I have been unhappy. The reason is that I have a debt and it is making me miserable.

It is quite obvious that people do not want to buy the things

---

*From a letter to Edith Mirrielees, March 8, 1962

I have been writing. Therefore, to make the money I need, I must write the things they want to read. In other words, I must sacrifice artistic integrity for a little while to personal integrity. Remember this when this manuscript makes you sick. And remember that it makes me a great deal sicker than it does you.

Conrad said that only two things sold, the very best and the very worst. From my recent efforts, it has been borne to me that I am not capable of writing the very best yet. I have no doubt that I shall be able to in the future, but at present, I cannot. It remains to be seen whether I can write the very worst.

I will tell you a little bit about the enclosed ms. It was written complete in nine days. It is about sixty two or three thousand words long. It took two weeks to type. In it I have included all the cheap rackets I know of, and have tried to make it stand up by giving it a slightly burlesque tone. No one but my wife and my folks know that I have written it, and no one except you will know. I see no reason why a nom de plume should not be respected and maintained. The nom de plume I have chosen is Peter Pym.

The story holds water better than most, and I think it has a fairish amount of mystery. The burlesqued bits, which were put in mostly to keep my stomach from turning every time I sat down at the typewriter, may come out.*

ON SIZE

It has been said often that a big book is more important and has more authority than a short book. There are exceptions of course but it is very nearly always true. I have tried to find a reasonable explanation for this and at last have come up with my theory, to wit: The human mind, particularly in the present, is troubled and fogged and bee-stung with a thousand little details from taxes to war worry to the price of meat. All these usually get

---

*From a letter to Amasa Miller, December 1930

together and result in a man's fighting with his wife because that is the easiest channel of relief for inner unrest. Now—we must think of a book as a wedge driven into a man's personal life. A short book would be in and out quickly. And it is possible for such a wedge to open the mind and do its work before it is withdrawn leaving quivering nerves and cut tissue. A long book, on the other hand, drives in very slowly and if only in point of time remains for a while. Instead of cutting and leaving, it allows the mind to rearrange itself to fit around the wedge. Let's carry the analogy a little farther. When the quick wedge is withdrawn, the tendency of the mind is quickly to heal itself exactly as it was before the attack. With the long book perhaps the healing has been warped around the shape of the wedge so that when the wedge is finally withdrawn and the book set down, the mind cannot ever be quite what it was before. This is my theory and it may explain the greater importance of a long book. Living with it longer has given it greater force. If this is true a long book, even not so good, is more effective than an excellent short story.

ON CHARACTER

It is hard to open up a person and to look inside. There is even a touch of decent reluctance about privacy but writers and detectives cannot permit the luxury of privacy. In this book [*East of Eden*] I have opened lots of people and some of them are going to be a little bit angry. But I can't help that. Right now I can't think of any work which requires concentration for so long a time as a big novel.

Sometimes I have a vision of human personality as a kind of foetid jungle full of monsters and daemons and little lights. It seemed to me a dangerous place to venture, a little like those tunnels at Coney Island where "things" leap out screaming. I have been accused so often of writing about abnormal people.

It would be a great joke on the people in my book if I just left them high and dry, waiting for me. If they bully me and do what they choose I have them over a barrel. They can't move until I pick up a pencil. They are frozen, turned to ice standing one foot up and with the same smile they had yesterday when I stopped.

ON INTENT

The craft or art of writing is the clumsy attempt to find symbols for the wordlessness. In utter loneliness a writer tries to explain the inexplicable. And sometimes if he is very fortunate and if the time is right, a very little of what he is trying to do trickles through —not ever much. And if he is a writer wise enough to know it can't be done, then he is not a writer at all. A good writer always works at the impossible. There is another kind who pulls in his horizons, drops his mind as one lowers rifle sights. And giving up the impossible he gives up writing. Whether fortunate or unfortunate, this has not happened to me. The same blind effort, the straining and puffing go on in me. And always I hope that a little trickles through. This urge dies hard.

Writing is a very silly business at best. There is a certain ridiculousness about putting down a picture of life. And to add to the joke—one must withdraw for a time from life in order to set down that picture. And third one must distort one's own way of life in order in some sense to simulate the normal in other lives. Having gone through all this nonsense, what emerges may well be the palest of reflections. Oh! it's a real horse's ass business. The mountain labors and groans and strains and the tiniest of rodents come out. And the greatest foolishness of all lies in the fact that to do it at all, the writer must believe that what he is doing is the most important thing in the world. And he must hold to this illusion even when he knows it is not true. If he does not, the work is not worth even what it might otherwise have been.

All this is a preface to the fear and uncertainties which clamber over a man so that in his silly work he thinks he must be crazy because he is so alone. If what he is doing is worth doing—why don't more people do it? Such questions. But it does seem a desperately futile business and one which must be very humorous to watch. Intelligent people live their lives as nearly on a level as possible—try to be good, don't worry if they aren't, hold to such opinions as are comforting and reassuring and throw out those which are not. And in the fullness of their days they die with none of the tearing pain of failure because having tried nothing they have not failed. These people are much more intelligent than the fools who rip themselves to pieces on nonsense.

It is the fashion now in writing to have every man defeated and destroyed. And I do not believe all men are destroyed. I can name a dozen who were not and they are the ones the world lives by. It is true of the spirit as it is of battles—the defeated are forgotten, only the winners come themselves into the race. The writers of today, even I, have a tendency to celebrate the destruction of the spirit and god knows it is destroyed often enough. But the beacon thing is that sometimes it is not. And I think I can take time right now to say that. There will be great sneers from the neurosis belt of the south, from the hard-boiled writers, but I believe that the great ones, Plato, Lao Tze, Buddha, Christ, Paul, and the great Hebrew prophets are not remembered for negation or denial. Not that it is necessary to be remembered but there is one purpose in writing that I can see, beyond simply doing it interestingly. It is the duty of the writer to lift up, to extend, to encourage. If the written word has contributed anything at all to our developing species and our half developed culture, it is this: Great writing has been a staff to lean on, a mother to consult, a wisdom to pick up stumbling folly, a strength in weakness and a courage to support sick cowardice. And how any negative or despairing approach can pretend to be literature I do not know. It is true that we are weak and sick and ugly and quarrelsome but if that is all we ever were, we would millenniums ago have disappeared from the face of the earth, and a few remnants of fossilized jaw bones, a few teeth in strata of limestone would be the only mark our species would have left on the earth.

It is too bad we have not more humor about this. After all it is only a book and no worlds are made or destroyed by it. But it becomes important out of all proportion to its importance. And

I suppose that is essential. The dunghill beetle must be convinced of the essential quality in rolling his ball of dung, and a golfer will not be any good at it unless striking a little ball is the most important thing in the world. So I must be convinced that this book is a pretty rare event and I must have little humor about it. Can't afford not to have. The story has to move on and on and on and on. It is like a machine now—set to do certain things. And it is about to clank to its end.

I truly do not care about a book once it is finished. Any money or fame that results has no connection in my feeling with the book. The book dies a real death for me when I write the last word. I have a little sorrow and then go on to a new book which is alive. The rows of my books on the shelf are to me like very well embalmed corpses. They are neither alive nor mine. I have no sorrow for them because I have forgotten them, forgotten in its truest sense.

ON THE CRAFT OF WRITING

The time now comes finally to move the book. I have dawdled enough. But it has been a good thing. I don't yet know what the word rate will be. That will depend on many things. But I do think the hour rate should be fairly constant. I am about finished with these long and characteristic meanderings. It is with real fear that I go to the other. And I must forget even that I want it to be good. Such things belong only in the planning stage. Once it starts, it should not have any intention save only to be written. All is peace now. And all is quiet. What little things there are, are here and good. Posture and attitude are so very important. And since these things have to go on for a very long time, they must become almost a way of life and a habit of thought. So that no one may say, I lost by being lost. This is the last bounce on the board, the last look into the pool. The time has come for the dive. The time has really come.

I suffer as always from the fear of putting down the first line. It is amazing the terrors, the magics, the prayers, the straitening shyness that assails one. It is as though the words were not only indelible but that they spread out like dye in water and color everything around them. A strange and mystic business, writing. Almost no progress has taken place since it was invented. The Book of the Dead is as good and as highly developed as anything in the 20th century and much better than most. And yet in spite of this lack of a continuing excellence, hundreds of thousands of people are in my shoes—praying feverishly for relief from their word pangs.

I learned long ago that you cannot tell how you will end by how you start. I just glanced up this page for instance. Look at the writing at the top—ragged and angular with pencils breaking in every line, measured as a laboratory rat and torn with nerves and fear. And just half an hour later it has smoothed out and changed considerably for the better.

Now I had better get into today's work. It is full of strange and secret things, things which should strike deep into the unconscious like those experimental stories I wrote so long ago. Those too were preparation for this book and I am using the lessons I've learned in all the other writing.

I have often thought that this might be my last book. I don't really mean that because I will be writing books until I die. But I want to write this one *as though* it were my last book. Maybe I believe that every book should be written that way.

I hope I can keep all the reins in my hands and at the same time make it sound as though the book were almost accidental. That is going to be hard to do but it must be done. Also I'll have to lead into the story so gradually that my reader will not know what is happening to him until he is caught. That is the reason for the casual—even almost flippant—sound. It's like a man setting a trap for a fox and pretending with pantomime that he doesn't know there is a fox or a trap in the country.

I split myself into three people. I know what they look like. One speculates and one criticizes and the third tries to correlate. It usually turns out to be a fight but out of it comes the whole week's work. And it is carried on in my mind in dialogue. It's an odd experience. Under such circumstances it might be one of those schizophrenic symptoms but as a working technique, I do not think it is bad at all.

I do indeed seem to feel creative juices rushing toward an outlet as semen gathers from the four quarters of a man and fights its way into the vesicle. I hope something beautiful and true comes out—but this I know (and the likeness to coition still holds). Even if I knew nothing would emerge from this book I would still write it. It seems to me that different organisms must have their separate ways of symbolizing, with sound or gesture, the creative joy —the flowering. And if this is so, men also must have their separate ways—some to laugh and some to build, some to destroy and yes, some even creatively to destroy themselves. There's no explaining this. The joy thing in me has two outlets: one a fine charge of love toward the incredibly desirable body and sweetness of woman and second—mostly both—the paper and pencil or pen. And it is interesting to think what paper and pencil and the wriggling words are. They are nothing but the trigger into joy— the shout of beauty—the cacajada of the pure bliss of creation. And often the words do not even parallel the feeling except sometimes in intensity. Thus a man full of a bursting joy may write with force and vehemence of some sad picture—of the death of beauty or the destruction of a lovely town—and there is only the effectiveness to prove how great and beautiful was his feeling.

My work does not coagulate. It is as unmanageable as a raw egg on the kitchen floor. It makes me crazy. I am really going to try now and I'm afraid that the very force of the trying will take all the life out of the work. I don't know where this pest came from but I know it is not new.

We work in our own darkness a great deal with little real knowledge of what we are doing. I think I know better what I am doing than most writers but it still isn't much.

I guess I am terrified to write finish on the book for fear I myself will be finished.

Suddenly I feel lonely in a curious kind of way. I guess I am afraid. That always comes near the end of a book—the fear that you have not accomplished what you started to do. That is as natural as breathing.

In a short time that will be done and then it will not be mine any more. Other people will take it over and own it and it will drift away from me as though I had never been a part of it. I dread that time because one can never pull it back, it's like shouting good-bye to someone going off in a bus and no one can hear because of the roar of the motor.

ON COMPETITION

You know I was born without any sense of competition. This is a crippling thing in many ways. I don't gamble because it is meaningless. I used to throw the javelin far, but I never really cared whether it was farthest. For a while I was a vicious fighter but it wasn't to win. It was to get it over and get the hell out of there. And I never would have done it at all if other people hadn't put me in the ring. The only private fights I ever had were those I couldn't get away from. Consequently I have never even wondered about the comparative standing of writers. I don't understand that. Writing to me is a deeply personal, even a secret function and when the product is turned loose it is cut off from me and I have no sense of its being mine. Consequently criticism doesn't mean anything to me. As a disciplinary matter, it is too late.*

ON PUBLISHING

Although some times I have felt that I held fire in my hands and spread a page with shining—I have never lost the weight of clumsiness, of ignorance, of aching inability.

A book is like a man—clever and dull, brave and cowardly,

---

*From a letter to John O'Hara, June 8, 1949

beautiful and ugly. For every flowering thought there will be a page like a wet and mangy mongrel, and for every looping flight a tap on the wing and a reminder that wax cannot hold the feathers firm too near the sun.

Well—then the book is done. It has no virtue any more. The writer wants to cry out— "Bring it back! Let me rewrite it or better— Let me burn it. Don't let it out in the unfriendly cold in that condition."

As you know better than most, Pat, the book does not go from writer to reader. It goes first to the lions—editors, publishers, critics, copy readers, sales department. It is kicked and slashed and gouged. And its bloodied father stands attorney.

EDITOR: The book is out of balance. The reader expects one thing and you give him something else. You have written two books and stuck them together. The reader will not understand.

WRITER: No, sir. It goes together. I have written about one family and used stories about another family as—well, as counterpoint, as rest, as contrast in pace and color.

EDITOR: The reader won't understand. What you call counterpoint only slows the book.

WRITER: It has to be slowed—else how would you know when it goes fast?

EDITOR: You have stopped the book and gone into discussions of God knows what.

WRITER: Yes, I have. I don't know why. Just wanted to. Perhaps I was wrong.

SALES DEPARTMENT: The book's too long. Costs are up. We'll have to charge five dollars for it. People won't pay five dollars. They won't buy it.

WRITER: My last book was short. You said then that people won't buy a short book.

PROOFREADER: The chronology is full of holes. The grammar has no relation to English. On page so and so you have a man look in the World Almanac for steamship rates. They aren't there. I checked. You've got Chinese New Year wrong. The characters aren't consistent. You describe Liza Hamilton one way and then have her act a different way.

EDITOR: You make Cathy too black. The reader won't believe her. You make Sam Hamilton too white. The reader won't believe him. No Irishman ever talked like that.

WRITER: My grandfather did.

EDITOR: Who'll believe it.

2ND EDITOR: No children ever talked like that.

WRITER *(losing temper as a refuge from despair):* God damn it. This is my book. I'll make the children talk any way I want. My book is about good and evil. Maybe the theme got into the execution. Do you want to publish it or not?

EDITORS: Let's see if we can't fix it up. It won't be much work. You want it to be good, don't you? For instance, the ending. The reader won't understand it.

WRITER: Do you?

EDITOR: Yes, but the reader won't.

PROOFREADER: My God, how you do dangle a participle. Turn to page so and so.

There you are, Pat. You came in with a box of glory and there you stand with an arm full of damp garbage.

And from this meeting a new character has emerged. He is called The Reader.

THE READER:

He is so stupid you can't trust him with an idea.
He is so clever he will catch you in the least error.
He will not buy short books.
He will not buy long books.
He is part moron, part genius and part ogre.
There is some doubt as to whether he can read.*

---

*From a letter to Pascal Covici, 1952

ON TITLES

I have never been a title man. I don't give a damn what it is
called. I would call it [East of Eden] Valley to the Sea which is
a quotation from absolutely nothing but has two great words and
a direction. What do you think of that? And I'm not going to
think about it any more.

ON CRITICS

This morning I looked at the Saturday Review, read a few
notices of recent books, not mine, and came up with the usual
sense of horror. One should be a reviewer or better a critic, these
curious sucker fish who live with joyous vicariousness on other
men's work and discipline with dreary words the thing which
feeds them. I don't say that writers should not be disciplined, but
I could wish that the people who appoint themselves to do it were
not quite so much of a pattern both physically and mentally.

I've always tried out my material on my dogs first. You know,
with Angel, he sits there and listens and I get the feeling he
understands everything. But with Charley, I always felt he was
just waiting to get a word in edgewise. Years ago, when my red
setter chewed up the manuscript of Of Mice and Men, I said at
the time that the dog must have been an excellent literary critic.

Time is the only critic without ambition.

Give a critic an inch, he'll write a play.

ON RELAXATION

My greatest fault, at least to me, is my lack of ability for
relaxation. I do not remember ever having been relaxed in my
whole life. Even in sleep I am tight and restless and I awaken so
quickly at any change or sound. It is not a good thing. It would

be fine to relax. I think I got this through my father. I remember his restlessness. It sometimes filled the house to a howling although he did not speak often. He was a singularly silent man— first I suppose because he had few words and second because he had no one to say them to. He was strong rather than profound. Cleverness only confused him—and this is interesting—he had no ear for music whatever. Patterns of music were meaningless to him. I often wonder about him. In my struggle to be a writer, it was he who supported and backed me and explained me—not my mother. She wanted me desperately to be something decent like a banker. She would have liked me to be a successful writer like Tarkington but this she didn't believe I could do. But my father wanted me to be myself. Isn't that odd. He admired anyone who laid down his line and followed it undeflected to the end. I think this was because he abandoned his star in little duties and let his head go under in the swirl of family and money and responsibility. To be anything pure requires an arrogance he did not have, and a selfishness he could not bring himself to assume. He was a man intensely disappointed in himself. And I think he liked the complete ruthlessness of my design to be a writer in spite of mother and hell. Anyway he was the encourager. Mother always thought I would get over it and come to my senses.

ON HAVING A WRITER IN THE FAMILY

This is sad news, but I can't think of a thing you can do about it. I can remember the horror which came over my parents when they became convinced that it was so with me—and properly so. What you have and they had to look forward to is life made intolerable by a mean, cantankerous, opinionated, moody, quarrelsome, unreasonable, nervous, flighty, irresponsible son. You will get no loyalty, little consideration and desperately little attention from him. In fact you will want to kill him. I'm sure my father and mother often must have considered poisoning me. There will be no ease for you or for him. He won't even have the decency to be successful or if he is, he will pick at it as though it were failure for it is one of the traits of this profession that it always fails if the writer is any good. And Dennis [Dennis Murphy] is not only a writer but I am dreadfully afraid a very good one.

I hasten to offer Marie and you my sympathy but I must also warn you that you are helpless. Your function as a father from now on will be to get him out of jail, to nurture him just short of starvation, to watch in despair while he seems to be irrational— and your reward for all this will be to be ignored at best and insulted and vilified at worst. Don't expect to understand him, because he doesn't understand himself. Don't for God's sake, judge him by ordinary rules of human virtue or vice or failings. Every man has his price but the price of a writer, a real one, is very hard to find and almost impossible to implement. My best advice to you is to stand aside, to roll with the punch and particularly to protect your belly. If you are contemplating killing him, you had better do it soon or it will be too late. I can see no peace for him and little for you. You can deny relationship. There are lots of Murphys.*

ON HONORS

I think of a number of pieces which should be done but that I as a novelist can't or should not do. One would be on the ridiculous preoccupation of my great contemporaries, and I mean Faulkner and Hemingway, with their own immortality. It is almost as though they were fighting for billing on the tombstone.

Another thing I could not write and you can is about the Nobel Prize. I should be scared to death to receive it, I don't care how coveted it is. But I can't say that because I have not received it. But it has seemed to me that the receivers never do a good nor courageous piece of work afterwards. It kind of retires them. I don't know whether this is because their work was over anyway

---

*From a letter to John Murphy, February 21, 1957

or because they try to live up to the prize and lose their daring or what. But it would be a tough hazard to overcome and most of them don't. Maybe it makes them respectable and a writer can't dare to be respectable. The same thing goes for any kind of honorary degrees and decorations. A man's writing becomes less good with the numbers of his honors. It might be that fear in me that has made me refuse those L.L.D.'s that are constantly being put out by colleges. It may also be the reason why I have never been near the Academy even though I was elected to it. It may also be the reason I gave my Pulitzer money away.*

ON HEMINGWAY

The first thing we heard of Ernest Hemingway's death was a call from the London Daily Mail, asking me to comment on it. And quite privately, although something of this sort might be expected, I find it shocking. He had only one theme—only one. A man contends with the forces of the world, called fate, and meets them with courage. Surely a man has a right to remove his own life but you'll find no such possibility in any of H's heros. The sad thing is that I think he would have hated accident much more than suicide. He was an incredibly vain man. An accident while cleaning a gun would have violated everything he was vain about. To shoot yourself with a shotgun in the head is almost impossible unless it is planned. Most such deaths happen when a gun falls, and then the wound is usually in the abdomen. A practiced man does not load a gun while cleaning it. Indeed a hunting man would never have a loaded gun in the house. There are shotguns over my mantle but the shells are standing on the shelf below. The guns are cleaned when they are brought in and you have to unload a gun to clean it. H had a contempt for mugs. And only a mug would have such an accident. On the other hand, from what I've read, he seems to have undergone a personality change

---

*Six years after this extract from a 1956 letter to Pascal Covici, Jr., Steinbeck himself won the Nobel Prize.

in the last year or so. Certainly his last summer in Spain and the resulting reporting in Life were not in his old manner. Perhaps, as Paul de Kruif told me, he had had a series of strokes. That would account for the change.

But apart from all that—he has had the most profound effect on writing—more than anyone I can think of. He has not a vestige of humor. It's a strange life. Always he tried to prove something. And you only try to prove what you aren't sure of. He was the critics' darling because he never changed style, theme nor story. He made no experiments in thinking nor in emotion. A little like Capa,* he created an ideal image of himself and then tried to live it. I am saddened at his death. I never knew him well, met him a very few times and he was always pleasant and kind to me although I am told that privately he spoke very disparagingly of my efforts. But then he thought of other living writers not as contemporaries but as antagonists. He really cared about his immortality as though he weren't sure of it. And there's little doubt that he has it.

One thing interests me very much. For a number of years he has talked about a big book he was writing and then about several books written and put away for future publication. I have never believed these books exist and will be astonished if they do. A writer's first impulse is to let someone read it. Of course I may be wrong and he may be the exception. For the London Daily Express, I have two lines by a better writer than either of us. They go—

> *"He was a man, take him for all in all,*
> *I shall not look upon his like again."*

And since he was called Papa—the lines are doubly applicable.†

---

*Robert Capa, the famous *Life* photographer.
†From a letter to Pascal Covici, July 1, 1961

ON FAME

It's nice over here because every place you look is a view. Most of them ruins—you can't find who built them or when or why. It makes ambition seem a little ridiculous. I've written a lot of books and some are very nice or have some nice things in them. And it's nice to be asked how it felt to write *God's Little Acre* and *Farewell to Arms.**

Little presses write to me for manuscripts and when I write back that I haven't any, they write to ask if they can print the letter saying I haven't any.†

LAST LETTER**

Dear Elizabeth:

I have owed you this letter for a very long time—but my fingers have avoided the pencil as though it were an old and poisoned tool.

Edited by GEORGE PLIMPTON *and* FRANK CROWTHER

---

*From a letter to Elia Kazan, Nice, France, November 22 1961
†From a letter to Elizabeth Otis, July 1939
**To Elizabeth Otis, his agent—found long after his death under the blotter on his work table by his wife, Elaine Steinbeck.

9. Christopher Isherwood

Christopher Isherwood was born in Cheshire, England, on August 26, 1904. He briefly attended Cambridge (1924–25) and just as briefly studied medicine (1927–28, University of London), before settling down to writing. His first novel, *All the Conspirators,* was published in 1928, and his second, *The Memorial,* in 1932. During the 1930s, he collaborated with W. H. Auden on three plays—*The Dog Beneath the Skin* (1935), *The Ascent of F6* (1936), and *On the Frontier* (1938)— and on a travel book, *Journey to a War* (1939). But Isherwood spent most of the decade out of England. His four years in Berlin during Hitler's rise to power produced two more novels: *Mr. Norris Changes Trains* (1937) and *Goodbye to Berlin* (1939), from which the successful plays (and movies) *I Am a Camera* and *Cabaret* were derived.

Isherwood came to the United States in 1939 and in 1946 became an American citizen. His works written here include the novels *Prater Violet* (1945), *The World in the Evening* (1954), *Down There on a Visit* (1962), *A Single Man* (1964), and *A Meeting By the River* (1967); a travel book, *The Condor and the Cows* (1949); a memoir of his parents, *Kathleen and Frank* (1971); several translations, including *The Intimate Journal of Charles Baudelaire* (1947); and with Swami Prabhavananda *The Bhagavad-Gita* (1944) and *How to Know God* (1953).

Since 1939 Mr. Isherwood has occasionally written scenarios for MGM., Warner Brothers, and other movie companies. He has taught at Los Angeles State College and the University of California campuses at Santa Barbara and Los Angeles. He lives in Santa Monica, California.

In my last letter I think I mentioned the ~~perist persisting~~ still-lingering in_fluence, here, of the British ? You feel its ghost rahter wistfully h∧nting the present,

now powerless to exert any direct authority and ~~look- ing down~~ regarding the scene with the reproachful air of ~~a dismissed~~ an unwanted adviser. The architecture of the older buildings is full of funny charming evocations of ~~nineteenth century~~ Victorian England. For instance, there's a gate which way leads into the grounds of the Monastery; it's ~~only a couple of hundred yards~~ just down the lane from our guest-house. Now ~~when~~ I ~~first~~ The moment set eyes on this gateway I felt a sort of confused recognition, ~~ND AFTER EXAMINIG IT~~ and after looking it over carefully a couple of times I suddenly realized what it reminded me of --- one of the back gates of ~~my~~ our college at Cambridge, over which I sometimes had to climb, when I returned from trips to ~~town~~ London, after hours ! This gateway was ~~most~~ probably built

Don Bachardy

Christopher Isherwood

Christopher Isherwood's home is in "the canyon" on the edge of Santa Monica, California—a quiet bohemian district of stucco houses inhabited mostly by people involved in the arts. It preserves much of the character it must have had thirty years ago when it first became a haven for refugees from the vast sprawl of Los Angeles. But Demon Change is just around the corner. In 1973 Santa Monica is being Miamified. Pallid apartment blocks with factitious names (Highland Glen, Sunset Towers) are rising all around, and the coastline is dominated by fat piles of concrete.

Still, the developers have not yet hit the Canyon (though they are widening the road amid clouds of dust above Isherwood's house), and you can see the ocean in the distance, a silvery blue, dotted with wet-suited surfers riding the swell like seals. The house is built into the steep side of the canyon, and you must slither down a driveway, past a garage containing two Volkswagens, side by side, to the door. Isherwood himself opens and leads the visitor into the living room. He is dressed with great neatness: navy-blue jacket, open shirt, gray, well-pressed pants. He is neatly constructed, too: short, spry ("like a jockey," said Virginia Woolf), with a lean, suntanned face. His most striking features are the bony, Celtic-looking nose and the pellucid blue eyes, which focus on you in oddly hypnotic fashion, as if observing neither dress, nor manner-isms, but Something Deeper. We agree to drink tea. "Do look around," he says, "while I make it."

The living room is high, white, a bit ascetic, but cool despite the hot July afternoon. Nearly all the paintings are modern, including several graphics of the kind that show cubes and cones suspended in space. There are many books, little furniture, and no clutter. A terrace has been added ("We eat breakfast here usually"), and vines cover it. The little houses descend below and climb the far side of the valley. This is the neighborhood lovingly described in A Single Man, by general agreement the finest of Isherwood's ten novels. There is even a gay bar, which fits exactly a favorite haunt of that book's protagonist, "down on the corner of the ocean highway, across from the beach, its `round green porthole lights shining to welcome you." But it is called The Friend Ship, not The Starboard Side.

Isherwood looks almost startled when you ask why he lives in California: "Why, it's my home. I've spent almost half my life here." Originally, he was drawn by the presence of Aldous Huxley and Gerald Heard, with whom he wanted to discuss pacifism and the impending war. There were trips to New York, lectures at universities, a journey across country by bus, and during the war, after he had registered as a conscientious objector, a spell in Phila-delphia working for a Quaker refugee hostel: "But apart from that I suppose I don't know this country awfully well. I've been an American citizen for—what, nearly thirty years; yet I still seem very British, even to myself. I've lived in eleven places in America, and all of them are within sight of this window."

In recent years, in common with many other writers and artists, Isherwood has become outspoken about the problems and advan-tages of being homosexual. He has discussed the subject in print

and on television (the Cavett show). He says, "For me as a writer,
it's never been a question of 'homosexuality,' but of otherness, of
seeing things from an oblique angle. If homosexuality were the
norm, it wouldn't be of interest to me as a writer."

Isherwood works every morning and then usually walks to the
ocean to swim. The substance of this interview was therefore re-
corded in a series of late-afternoon sessions—tea-time. Possibly the
conversation reflects something of the hour.

INTERVIEWER: You don't mind if I record this? I have a terrible
memory.

ISHERWOOD: Of course not. So do I.

INTERVIEWER: I wanted to ask first how you came to write *A
Meeting by the River.* It seems so different from your earlier
novels.

ISHERWOOD: You know of course that I've been involved with
a Hindu monk, Swami Prabhavananda, for almost the entire
length of my life in America—more than thirty years now. A few
years ago, there was a centenary of the birth of Vivekananda, who
is the chief disciple of Ramakrishna and a great inspirer of Gandhi
—he had all kinds of ideas about the future of India. So there was
a great national celebration, especially in Bengal, that year, and
they decided to have one of those congresses that they so dearly
love with speakers from foreign lands; and Swami said would I
come along. So I did. At the same time, two monks from the
Vedanta monastery here were coming out to India to take their
final vows, sannyas, and I was in close contact with their feelings
and the whole predicament of being about to take sannyas. For
a long time I'd wanted to write a confrontation story where the
representative of something meets the representative of something else, and quite suddenly it came to me that this was the way
to do it. I talked a great deal with the monks afterwards while I
was writing it and checked up immensely on the details. I had
been to the monastery once before with Don [Bachardy] in 1957,
but that was only briefly. . . . It was infinitely more comfortable
than the hotel in Calcutta! Perfectly clean, with nice simple little

rooms and a place where you washed down with a bucket of water.

INTERVIEWER: Has your involvement with Vedanta changed your life?

ISHERWOOD: It's made a very great difference, but I couldn't exactly describe to you what the difference is. I could say what, so to speak, I've got out of it. I simply became convinced, after a long period of knowing Swami Prabhavananda, that there is such a thing as mystic union or the knowledge—we get into terrible semantics here—that there is such a thing as mystical experience. That was what seemed to me extraordinary—the thing I had completely dismissed.

INTERVIEWER: There's a passage in one of your books in which you and Auden are on a train, and you're savagely attacking religion, and he says: "Be careful, my dear, if you carry on like that, one day you'll have such a conversion." Do you think of it in those terms, as a conversion?

ISHERWOOD: Yes. I rather think so. I went through all sorts of attitudes to it. There was a period when I thought I might become a monk myself.

INTERVIEWER: What would that have meant, in practice?

ISHERWOOD: It would have meant living at the Vedanta center in Los Angeles; I'd probably have spent a great deal of my time helping to translate Hindu classics and increasing my knowledge about Vedanta philosophy; and perhaps giving lectures when I got to be a Swami, which I should have been by this time if I'd stayed with it—it's about twelve years before you take the final vows. Not long after I met Swami Prabhavananda, the war began, and I went to work with the Quakers at a hostel for refugees in Philadelphia, and after 1940 and Pearl Harbor I volunteered to join a Quaker ambulance corps going to China; but they only wanted qualified doctors or automobile mechanics—it was essential to be able to repair the ambulance. Then I would have registered as a conscientious objector and gone to a forestry camp for firefighting—like the one in *Paul*—but suddenly in the midst of the war they lowered the age limit, and I wasn't liable for service. I was completely at a loose end, I'd untied all ties; and then

Prabhavananda said, "Why don't you come up to the center and help me translate the Gita," which we did. There was a general feeling that I might become a monk, but then I decided, rightly or wrongly, that I didn't have a vocation. But I've always remained in touch with Swami Prabhavananda; in fact, I see him every week.

INTERVIEWER: I've never been quite sure what people mean when they talk of a vocation.

ISHERWOOD: Well, would you say there is such a thing as having a literary vocation? Let me put it like this: You know the sort of person who goes around thinking I Wish I Were A Writer, and perhaps he does write a bit; and in the end his friends say, well, the trouble was he had no talent. Really, talent is vocation: there is such a thing as having a natural aptitude for a way of life; not everybody can become a monk.

INTERVIEWER: It's the overwhelming desire to do that thing, then.

ISHERWOOD: Yes, the desire to do that rather than anything else. In the end it would have meant giving up a whole area of my writing.

INTERVIEWER: And you would have to be celibate.

ISHERWOOD: Yes, they make a great point out of that.

INTERVIEWER: All religions do, don't they?

ISHERWOOD: One has to look at it from two angles, to hear the Hindus explain it. One is that by being celibate, you store up energy; and since there is only one life force, one kind of energy, that is what you are using, in one way or another. Even that Hindu attitude was a tremendous revelation to me. I'd been brought up in this puritanical way to think of flesh and spirit, the low and the high, the forces of lust and the forces of . . . something else. But they think it is the same thing on different levels: the Hindus have this image of what they call a serpent power, that rises through different centers—like an elevator that calls at the lust department on the bottom floor and rises to other levels. That's one aspect of it—really little more than athletes are told: to lay off while they're in training. From the other side there is the aspect of being devoted to this search, of avoiding human entanglements and devoting oneself to the love of God. And yet, of course, the Hindus are the first to agree that all love is related, and that one can go a very long way through genuine devotion to another human being. One always talks as if loving someone was simple and easy, but in fact it can be very hard work.

INTERVIEWER: The play of *A Meeting by the River* had a big success here in Los Angeles.

ISHERWOOD: I'm awfully glad. One of the most gratifying of all expressions on one's friends' faces is when they are genuinely surprised that you had it in you. It *is* far more realized than the book: it plays out the undecided duel between the two brothers more intensely, and so the nature of the comedy comes out more clearly.

INTERVIEWER: What made you choose that book to dramatize? You once described *A Meeting* as "rather a secret little book"; and the letter form seems prohibitive.

ISHERWOOD: Well, I would never have thought we could dramatize it. It was largely James Bridges, who's an old friend, who insisted that we could. Then we asked ourselves: *Is* it possible? Then it became a challenge; and then we saw that the very fact that the characters were all elsewhere—except for the two principals—imposed a technique which was fun: the people are there, and yet they're not there, just as they are in life.

INTERVIEWER: My one reservation about *A Meeting by the River* was that it seemed rather withdrawn about the ecstatic side of religious experience—a bit veiled: there were no Dostoevskian agonies and ecstasies. Do you think religious experience of this kind can be transmitted in writing?

ISHERWOOD: I think it's awfully difficult to do, but possible: Dostoevsky does it better than almost anybody. One day somebody gave Prabhavananda *The Brothers Karamazov*. Now, although he has read all kinds of books, he certainly doesn't restrict himself, he had read no novels. And he said, "But this is absolutely marvelous!" He was astounded; he adored the character of Father Zossima. He really thought that all novels must be like this. I'm afraid he was badly let down. But I think the experience of many people who take to contemplative religion is that when you first stir the thing up you get extraordinary moments of joy, a sense of excitement which tends later to disappear and only come back when you're much further on. There's no question that Prabhavananda has such moments, and then he's quite something. In *A Meeting by the River*, though, Oliver is rather dour: his temperament is such that it's rather difficult for him to feel that kind of joy. He has something of that kind of experience when he sits on the stone bench in the monastery, and he feels that Swami has been sitting beside him. This is one thing we rewrote in the play and tried to bring out more strongly, making it more like a series of ejaculations: "Yes! Yes, I saw him! He was actually *there!*"—that kind of thing. It's written now in a way that makes it easier for the actor to project that kind of ecstatic joy. It's really a terrific sense of relief: that after all the whole thing is true! You've been telling yourself that it is, but you didn't absolutely believe it, and it's only after you've had such an experience that you realize it really is: There's always a further dimension of belief which you don't think you have reached. I agree that it's rather missing from the book; I hope it isn't from the play.

INTERVIEWER: Perhaps it's a Western Christian attitude to expect these agonies: I guess what I'm saying is that the Hindu religion may be more joyous. I missed the suffering.

ISHERWOOD: No, the Hindus are not so impressed by suffering: They don't think it's something marvelous in quite the same way. It's true that Ramakrishna said that people shed buckets of tears over their families and their bank accounts, but they won't shed one tear for God. . . . The Bengalis, anyway, are so absolutely non-Nordic, very lively and bright and mercurial, and if they weep, it's not for long; much more like the Italians.

INTERVIEWER: Edward Upward once said that you became a pacifist after your journey to the war in China: Was that in fact a turning point for you?

ISHERWOOD: Well, I've always hated explanations that sound so rational. I'm quite sure that I've had a strong leaning towards pacifism throughout my life. But it was very convenient to say that, and it's not exactly a lie. It did bring things home to see what people look like after they've been killed in an air raid, to see the effects of gas gangrene on boy soldiers, to see millions of innocent civilians dragged into a war they neither wanted nor understood.

INTERVIEWER: Here's a quotation that interested me from *Down There on A Visit.* The narrator is going through a crisis of sorts about his pacifism at the start of World War II, and he says: "Suppose I have in my power an army of five million men. I can destroy it instantly by pressing an electric button. The five millionth man is Waldemar. Will I press that button? No, of course not, even if the four million, nine hundred and ninety nine thousand, nine hundred and ninety-nine others are world-destroying fiends." Is this your basic, personal reason for being a pacifist?

ISHERWOOD: Oh yes—because once you have refused to press the button on account of Waldemar, you can never press it. Because Waldemar might be absolutely anybody! And since then, I've had occasion to say this, tentatively thinking it might be regarded as a self-regarding, capricious argument—but to my surprise people said that it had convinced them more than some high-sounding reasons for being a pacifist. They thought it sensible. But really I was just trying to describe what, when you're driven into a corner, makes you react that way.

INTERVIEWER: What does Vedanta teach?

ISHERWOOD: It's quite ambivalent on the subject. The Hindus believe in one's dharma, one's duty, one's nature; they say the great need is to discover one's dharma, which, of course, is an intense mystery nowadays; in classical India you had your caste; your caste had its own duties. If you belonged to the second caste, the warriors, you either fought or became a monk . . . rather like the middle ages.

INTERVIEWER: I suppose the Christian position in justifying war is that the wicked simply profit from meekness and go on to worse evil.

ISHERWOOD: But then that's a political argument, really. It's not an argument that cuts any ice in reference to what we're talking about. . . . Above all, and this is really what made the greatest impression on me when I was young, I got into my head how loathsome older people were when they preached war, when they were well past the age when they could be sent out to die. And I always said to myself, I won't be like that when I get old. And yet you know, one of the best and noblest men I've known, Bertie Russell, got into exactly that situation. We talked about it, and he was marvelous—he said how it embarrassed him, but yet that he did believe this war—the Second World War—was different. As you know, he fearlessly opposed World War I. I said, Well, I didn't think you could only oppose some wars. Just as later I've sometimes got into arguments with people who specifically resist just Vietnam, for instance. Except that on a political level one's absolutely entitled to do that.

INTERVIEWER: Do you follow a routine when you're writing a novel? A certain number of hours a day, that sort of thing?

ISHERWOOD: I don't have any special routine. The great thing is to get after it every day, and that to my mind applies to everything one does; even the tiniest act of the will towards a thing is better than not doing it at all.

INTERVIEWER: Do you type?

ISHERWOOD: Yes. For many years I've written on a typewriter.

INTERVIEWER: How long does it take you to write a book?

ISHERWOOD: Hard to say. Eighteen months, two years for *A Single Man*. I wrote three drafts in that time. When I was young, I used to proceed like a rock climber: I had to get to a certain point, and then I considered that everything below me was conquered. But now I don't do that at all. I go through the first time in a very slapdash way, and if I get into some nonsense or digressions, I write it through to the end and come out on the other side. I'm not at all perfectionist at first. I do all the polishing in the last draft. When I was young, I was absolutely fanatical. I wrote in longhand, and I couldn't bear for there to be any erasures on the paper, and since this was before all these wonderful breakthroughs with Liquid Paper, etc., I used to scratch words out with a razor and then polish the paper with my thumbnail and write it in again. It was terrible! I wasted so much energy fussing!

INTERVIEWER: Have your books been widely translated? What countries like them?

ISHERWOOD: Everything has been done in French and Italian; a certain amount in German, Swedish, Danish, Dutch. One little thing, a story called *The Nowaks*, in Russian. A couple of Czech and Spanish translations. But I don't think they're really popular in translations. It may be a question of nuance. The French really liked the books; they've been more sympathetic than anybody. The Germans, who you might think would be interested, were not all that much. The Berlin Stories, to some extent; the play of *I Am a Camera* was performed in Germany. There are things that are very difficult to translate: half puns and concealed quotations and little things like that.

INTERVIEWER: Is there any particular aspect of your work that you dislike?

ISHERWOOD: Well, my attitude's rather like Pontius Pilate: What I have written I have written, you know; and I can't imagine—as some writers have—going through a book and producing a rewritten version. There are some gross mistakes which I should change if I could ever remember to. Wrong words in German . . . silly things like that.

INTERVIEWER: Do you rewrite much?

ISHERWOOD: Yes, a great deal. What I tend to do is not so much pick at a thing but sit down and rewrite it completely. Both for *A Single Man* and *A Meeting by the River* I wrote three entire drafts. After making notes on one draft I'd sit down and rewrite it again from the beginning. I've found that's much better than patching and amputating things. One has to rethink the thing completely.

INTERVIEWER: I noticed a remarkable number of changes in the version of "Mr. Lancaster" that originally appeared in the *London Magazine* and the final version of the book.

ISHERWOOD: You're really a student! But you're quite right. I just changed my whole attitude in certain parts of that.

INTERVIEWER: Do you work fast?

ISHERWOOD: I don't know; it seems to take me quite a time to finish a book. . . . They say D. H. Lawrence used to write second drafts and never look at the first.

INTERVIEWER: Why did you cut what seemed to me a climactic scene from "Paul" about hashish smoking?

ISHERWOOD: Simply because it didn't relate to Paul, the character. It related to me. I thought we were getting too far away from Paul.

INTERVIEWER: When I read it later in *Exhumations,* I wished you'd left it in.

ISHERWOOD: Well, we did have it in even when the book was in proof. I only cut it at the last moment. Perhaps I was wrong to do so.

INTERVIEWER: One thing that surprised me about Ambrose, from the same book *(Down There on A Visit),* was a distinct lack of enthusiasm for things Greek; you absolutely didn't partake of that special British literary worship of that part of the world.

ISHERWOOD: Well, it wasn't the best way of seeing Greece; here we were, holed up on this island, and we got rather used to it. But I remember certain things about Greece that moved me tremendously.

INTERVIEWER: Yet this Hellenic syndrome, the fetish for Greece, never shows in your writing. I'm thinking of . . . Durrell . . . lots of them from Byron onwards. Greece means to them what Italy did to Forster.

ISHERWOOD: Well, I was very prejudiced in my youth against the values of the academic world; and since then I've become prejudiced in another way because I think that Hindu philosophy is so much broader in its scope than that of, say, Plato. That's a temperamental thing, perhaps, but I'm not really knocked over by the Greeks. I can't feel that "everything started in Greece," or "had they not been there, there would be nothing." I daresay this is my ignorance, but it's how I feel. One aspect of Italy turned me on far more. I had the atypical experience of never seeing Italy when I was young. I went first in 1955 with Don; we went like two innocents, and we were duly stunned. I was, what, fifty-one?

And I was seeing all this for the first time. It was late in the year, with few people about, and the most marvelous Indian summer. We drove through Tuscany, and in Milan we met an old friend, King Vidor, who was making *War and Peace,* and took absurd home movies of that. All his best takes were ruined because the Italian extras were having such a terrific time falling off bridges and roaring with laughter. And it all culminated in a rather banal —I suppose—experience, which was also the greatest part of the trip. We went to Venice and arrived in a thick fog and occupied a vast suite in some grand hotel where the prices had been slashed to a tenth because of the season. And in the morning I went to the window and there was this wonderful Guardi sunlight, and the lagoon, and Santa Maria della Salute. It simply hit me over the head, and I burst into tears. I've never felt like that to the same extent, except perhaps when I saw Yosemite, which was rather different.

INTERVIEWER: Which of your books gave you the greatest trouble to write?

ISHERWOOD: That miserable *World in the Evening,* because it's several different books. You know, I almost hate that book. I hate her,* and her pathos, and her heart disease—which I got out of a book called *When Doctors Are Patients.* It was written by doctors who had different complaints, and one of them gave a marvelous description of what it's like to have heart disease, from which I copied several scenes, the situations, that is, her terror, and so on. I rewrote them completely, of course. But it was a remarkable book. This doctor caught the drama of the thing, and he was objective about it. In the middle of being scared, he was saying "How interesting." This I tried to catch in describing Elizabeth Rydal and her attacks.

INTERVIEWER: What went wrong with the book?

ISHERWOOD: I started to write an "I" book about working in a Quaker hospital. And then I thought that the "I" of the story

---

*Elizabeth Rydal, the Katherine Mansfield–type novelist, who is the novel's central character.

was so peculiar that I must explain how he got into a hospital at all. So I decided that he must have some sort of upset in his own life, and instead of sticking to the facts, which were far more interesting, I devised this young gentleman with a wife who is cheating on him and all that. And from then on we were in trouble. One lie leads to another, and it was all so factitious and false. In the first chapter of *The World in the Evening* there's a couple making it in an outside doll's house. This actually existed. I got to know Norma Shearer's son and went down to her beach house with him and saw this great big doll's house, big enough for children to get inside, and my first thought was, What a wonderful place to screw in. And the whole scene evolved from that idea. It'd be a nice movie. Jane, the wife, was practically the only decent character in that book. The Quaker aunt isn't too bad —perhaps a bit too holy. Stephen, the principal character, is a kind of goodie-goodie, full of false humility. I know exactly what I should have done in that book. I should have written it from the point of view of a minor character, a slightly hostile person. Then it would have been all right. It would simply have sounded then as if I was a stinker. A very good thing in a novel, to have a minor character who's hostile. Maugham did it, more or less. He was looking to see what the lie was in the lives of the other characters, and when he found it, he gloated appropriately.

INTERVIEWER: Do you have a favorite among your books?

ISHERWOOD: Oh, *A Single Man*. I think it's the only book of mine where I did more or less what I wanted to do. It didn't get out of control.

INTERVIEWER: It's also the fiercest in tone.

ISHERWOOD: Oh, do you think so? I think it's terribly restrained.

INTERVIEWER: I meant the revenge fantasies George has driving on the freeway and so on.

ISHERWOOD: Oh, yes. I wanted to show that there was something boiling underneath. But that was a very deliberately written book. It wasn't composed with "hands trembling with fury."

INTERVIEWER: Have you tried consciously to give your later

novels, those written in America, any religious or Vedantic basis?

ISHERWOOD: In a way. The first book I wrote after I'd become involved with Vedanta was very definitely an attempt to put myself back in an earlier phase of my life, and therefore I scrupulously left Vedanta out of it. There is at the end of *Prater Violet* a kind of soliloquy that's very pessimistic in tone. I made it so deliberately because I was trying to give a true account of how I felt at that time. But of course it was really conditioned by contact with Vedanta.

INTERVIEWER: Does Vedanta appear at all in *A Single Man?*

ISHERWOOD: There are touches: the image at the end of the rock pools that are separate entities while the tide is out; and then the water comes, and they are all one flood of consciousness, and you can't say that one is separate from the others. But of course it's not about someone who's religious in any sense. The man in *A Single Man* is a stoic, a very back-to-the-wall character.

INTERVIEWER: But possibly your belief in Vedanta influenced you to write about George in quite a different way than you otherwise would?

ISHERWOOD: Perhaps I felt more objective towards him. I really admire the sort of person that George is: It isn't me at all. Here is somebody who really has *nothing* to support him except a kind of gradually waning animal vitality, and yet he fights, like a badger, and goes on demanding, fighting for happiness. That attitude I think rather magnificent. If I were in George's place, I would think about killing myself because I'm less than George. George is heroic.

INTERVIEWER: But is George's life style dreadful to you, then?

ISHERWOOD: We have to be careful about what we mean by dreadful. I don't mean I'm condemning it morally. I couldn't live it without some kind of support.

INTERVIEWER: Would you write more about homosexuality if you were starting out now as a writer?

ISHERWOOD: Yes, I'd write about it a great deal. It is an exceedingly interesting subject, and I couldn't, or I thought I couldn't, go into it. It's interesting because it's so much more than just "homosexuality"; it's very precious in a way, however inconvenient it may be. You see things from a different angle, and you see how everything is changed thereby.

INTERVIEWER: Maugham's habit of writing about his male characters from a hidden gay angle gives his work a curious ambiguity.

ISHERWOOD: The book of his that seems to me most homosexual is *The Narrow Corner*. I think it's my favorite. A very romantic book. It's set on a ship. There's this beautiful boy who's wanted by everybody, including the police. There's a wonderful doctor with a Chinese assistant who smokes opium. Very glamorous. I adore that book.

INTERVIEWER: What good do you think the gay liberation movement is doing in the United States? What do you think of its tactics?

ISHERWOOD: I think it's a necessary way of doing things. It's part of an enormous uncoordinated army which is advancing on various fronts towards recognition, toleration, and the acquisition of very simple rights. I never want to knock anything people do in a movement like that unless they resort to bomb throwing or something which is completely destructive.

INTERVIEWER: How about the protests against Vice Squad tactics at the L.A. police HQ, or the disruptions at these conventions of psychiatrists who seem these days to be the arch enemies of gay people?

ISHERWOOD: They're very valuable. I welcome them enormously. What a waste of time and taxpayer's money it is to have these healthy, well-equipped policemen used on such a frivolous chore as pushing homosexuals around in bars! This extraordinary harassment that goes on because somebody or other is supposed to have made a complaint. And at the same time the police here are saying they need more men!

INTERVIEWER: Still, public attitudes are changing.

ISHERWOOD: Oh yes. But what irritates me is the bland way people go around saying, "Oh, our attitude has changed. We don't dislike these people any more." But by the strangest coinci-

dence, they haven't taken away the injustice; the laws are still on
the books. And if you ask them why that is—"Oh, it's boring; it's
difficult; how does one go about it . . ." A thing that seems to me
almost worse than hatred and active opposition is the indifference
that most people have towards minorities. Let them rot, they
don't care, they don't care a bit! Also they're hypocritical. They
pretend to be much more shocked than they are. I often feel that
worse than the most fiendish Nazis were those Germans who
went along with the persecution of the Jews not because they
really disliked them but because *it was the thing*.

INTERVIEWER: I've heard you use the phrase "Whitmanesque
homosexuality." What exactly do you mean?

ISHERWOOD: I had in mind the concept of two men going off
together, living a life that is in many ways not confined in the
sense that recognized heterosexual marriage is confined. It's a way
of life that disturbs some people—quite needlessly, in my view—
because there is at the back of their minds this illogical fear that
something will happen. Their children will leap up and follow the
Pied Piper, the whole structure of their lives will be changed—
they don't know what the threat is. They don't know because
really there is none.

INTERVIEWER: I wanted to ask your opinion of Forster's *Maurice*, which was so heavily criticized, even attacked, in the British
press when it came out last year. Everyone had a go at it.

ISHERWOOD: What I loved about it was its passion. There
Forster really spoke.

INTERVIEWER: More than elsewhere? He always spoke in a very
passionate way, wouldn't you say?

ISHERWOOD: Yes, there's a great underlying passion. But this
is the only time he spoke about homosexuality, which he felt very
strongly about. He had a burning indignation about the way
homosexuals were treated during much of his lifetime. That I
love. I love works written in passion by great writers even when
they're a bit silly. I love Tolstoy's furious essays.

INTERVIEWER: People have called *Maurice* sentimental.

ISHERWOOD: So it is, in places. But it's a daring sentimentality.

It does honor to Forster as a man. We're not afraid of what's called pornography, but we are terribly afraid of what we call sentimentality—the rash, incautious expression of feeling. And yet that sort of sentimentality is something an awful lot of us need to practice. Have you seen any of Forster's homosexual stories? They're going to be published—a man wrote to me asking if the ones I had were the same as he'd seen. There's one—it's quite late —that's a tremendous melodrama of passion and fury . . . It takes place on a liner coming back from India. It's very moving, quite beautiful.

INTERVIEWER: Yet we have people like Muggeridge saying he "can't imagine" who reads him now.

ISHERWOOD: Forster is still Forster, and he will be read. He's someone about whom I feel Thomas Hardy's lines on Meredith apply: "No matter, further and further still thro the world's vaporous vitiate air, his words wing on, as live words will." I feel that he wings on.

INTERVIEWER: Was it E. M. Forster's writing about India and Indian religion that first interested you in the subject?

ISHERWOOD: No, I wouldn't say that was an influence. He influenced me purely as a writer by the way that he wrote. I had a glimpse from him of a whole new approach to the novel. His casualness, the way he lounges so easily into his novels, is a demonstration of something that is now really taken for granted, a kind of informality; instead of solemnly approaching the novel in the great classic manner and setting the scene, he says: One may as well begin with somebody's letters. The other people who were writing then—Wells, for example—was tremendously modern in a sense, and yet there are more vestiges of the nineteenth century in his work than in Forster's. He had relaxed, and that seemed immensely valuable. Also, he said about himself that he was a comic writer: I don't think that was quite exact. I think he's more what Gerald Heard called meta-comic; a kind of comedy that goes beyond both comedy and tragedy. Both comedy and tragedy followed to the end are tiresome, sterile, empty, and unsatisfactory.

INTERVIEWER: There's a lot of mysticism in his writing, too.

ISHERWOOD: Oh certainly, he was highly serious. But it's just that whenever people are getting hifalutin' he deflates them; and yet you never feel that he is merely sneering. He is doing it because he feels they are not really having the emotion appropriate to the occasion. In that way, both from his writing and from knowing him, he taught me a tremendous lesson. He did just the same kind of thing in person. I remember during the Spanish Civil War, we were all showing off a little bit—I was supposed to be going out on some kind of delegation (actually I didn't go, we went to China instead), but I remember I decided I must make my will. Virginia Woolf was there, too. Anyway, I was showing off a bit, and somebody said: "Morgan, why don't you come to Spain." And he said: "I'd be afraid to," and this completely deflated us. It was a remark of a really sterling character.

INTERVIEWER: Did you know Virginia Woolf well?

ISHERWOOD: Not well. She was my publisher, so to speak. Hogarth Press published *The Memorial, Mr. Norris,* and *Lions and Shadows.* I was fascinated by her, though. She was one of the most beautiful women I've met in my life, really absolutely stunning, in a very strange way. Of course she was middle-aged when I knew her. She had the quality that manic-depressive people have of being up to the sky one minute, down into despair and darkness the next. She had these terrible phases, as we know now; but what one saw was her tremendous animation and fun, on a gossipy level. She loved tea-table talk. One time I was at her place with a lot of people, and something happened to me that's never again happened in my life. We had tea, and she said, "Do stay to dinner." So I did and sat there absolutely enthralled. And suddenly, with a terrible shock, at about ten in the evening, I remembered that I was supposed to be going on a very romantic trip to Paris with somebody who was in fact waiting at the airport at that moment. I had completely forgotten about it. She had that effect on people.

INTERVIEWER: What brought you out here in the first place?

ISHERWOOD: I came out here primarily because the people I

really knew in America were here. I knew Gerald Heard, and I was very anxious to talk to him about pacifism. Also I wanted very much to meet Aldous Huxley, whom I didn't know before I came here. And I'd always wanted to see the West, in a romantic sort of way; so I just took off. We came by bus, stopping at various places. It took us about a month. People said that was the way to see America; and it was, I think; better than going on the train. We started in New York, then Washington, New Orleans, El Paso, Houston, and into New Mexico.

INTERVIEWER: It sounds a bit like Humbert Humbert's trip with Lolita.

ISHERWOOD: It does, rather. I always loved the part of *Lolita*, the descriptions of the motels and that world of travel. I liked the film very much, too. I'm a great fan of Kubrick.

INTERVIEWER: Heard was a pacifist, of course?

ISHERWOOD: Yes. He was one of the most astounding people I ever met. He was a wonderful myth maker. It was something approximately like knowing Jung. He saw the great archetypes that govern life to an extraordinary extent, and he knew an immense amount about what was going on in the world, all the really important advances on different scientific fronts, and how they related to each other; and he had taken in the whole area of mysticism and reconciled that with his other areas of knowledge. And he was Irish and had that magic gift of talk. An absolute spellbinder, and yet really extraordinarily little known.

INTERVIEWER: Was that perhaps because he wrote a body of work that makes such a complex structure. You have to read all the books to comprehend the scale. . . .

ISHERWOOD: Very complex. And also he had a very meandering and involuted style. He started with great sentences that wander on and on. There's a very crude parody of the way he talks in *Down There on a Visit*, in the character of Augustus Parr. He was the sort of person who, if you asked: "What do you think about Vietnam?" would answer, "I suppose you know, of course, Holstein's great work on the soldier ant . . ." and then go into a tremendous dissertation and about fifteen minutes later you would realize that this was a very appropriate way of answering the question. By that time, however, you'd be so awfully interested in what he was saying that you'd forgotten what your question was. But if you did remember, then you saw that he did in fact answer the question. But you had to sit still for it. He gave very definite answers, yet at the same time contrived not to be dogmatic.

INTERVIEWER: What did he think of the way you portrayed him?

ISHERWOOD: I think he thought it was a bit much, a bit of a caricature. But he wasn't offended. He liked my writing quite a bit. I dedicated *A Meeting by the River* to him because he liked it so much.

INTERVIEWER: You lived close to him for several years, then?

ISHERWOOD: Very close, yes. He had an incredibly protracted death. He had a series of slight strokes and very slowly lost the faculty of speech. I think it went on for three years. And yet all the time you felt this very, very bright mind and no distress at any of it. He seemed to live more and more in a kind of meditative state and just be aware of the body lying there, obviously irreparable and soon to be abandoned, and he finally died very unobtrusively, just as he was about to drink some soup. He had a secretary who looked after him with absolutely superhuman devotion. One thing he was afraid of, as many of us are here, was of going into a hospital. The California hospitals are really something. It's not that they're not marvelous; it's just that the most awful inhuman way to die is in one of them. Michael Barrie knew this, and he looked after him day and night throughout this whole period. I don't think he would have lived much longer himself if Gerald hadn't died. He'd lost so much weight, and he was like a wisp moving about. He could hardly lift Gerald at the end. He's more or less recovered physically now. He has masses and masses of material which he'll either put into shape or give to someone.

INTERVIEWER: When Aldous Huxley died, he took LSD, I believe.

ISHERWOOD: An incredibly weak dose. His wife asked the doctor, and he said, "Sure, what does it matter?" Needless to say, rumors got around until people were talking as if she'd performed a mercy killing or something, which was idiotic. I urged her, among other people, to print it, to stop all this nonsense. People talk about him as if he were an absolute hophead, but she told me—and she knows a good deal about drugs—that in many cases the kids who are really into this thing might take more in a single week than Aldous took in his entire life. He used very, very small amounts and almost always under scientific conditions . . . because it began as a scientific thing. A scientist from Canada asked if he would submit to it as a scientific experiment. He was very much against indiscriminate use, and he believed that everybody took far too much.

INTERVIEWER: Stravinsky refers to you very affectionately in one of the books with Craft. What do you remember about him?

ISHERWOOD: I always think of Stravinsky in a very physical way. He was physically adorable; he was cuddly—he was so little, and you wanted to protect him. He was very demonstrative, a person who—I suppose it was his Russianness—was full of kisses and embraces. He had great warmth. He could be fearfully hostile and snub people and attack his critics and so forth, but personally, he was a person of immense joy and warmth. The first time I came to his house, he said to me: "Would you like to hear my Mass before we get drunk?" He was always saying things like that. He seemed to me to have a wonderful appreciation for all the arts. He spoke English fluently, but it astonished me what an appreciation he had of writing in the English language, although he was really more at home in German or French—after Russian.

INTERVIEWER: In the Craft books, he manages superbly.

ISHERWOOD: Yes, they're marvelous. When I was seeing a great deal of him, I was usually drinking a great deal, too, because he had these wonderful drinks. I recall a fatal, beautiful liquid called Marc—Marc de Bourgogne—made out of grape pits, colorless but powerful beyond belief. I used to think to myself, God-damit, I'm drunk again, and here's Igor saying these marvelous things, and I won't remember one of them in the morning. And along came Craft's books years later, and I recognized that this was the very essence of what he'd been saying.

INTERVIEWER: He accuses you of falling asleep on one occasion during some of his music.

ISHERWOOD: Oh yes, I'm sure I did. When I think of those days, I really seem to have behaved very oddly. I remember once I'd actually passed out on the floor, and, looking up, I saw at an immense altitude above me, Aldous Huxley, who was very tall, standing up and talking French to Stravinsky, who never seemed to get overcome, however much he drank. And Aldous, who I think was very fond of me, was looking at me rather curiously, as much as to say, "Aren't you going a little far?" It's not like me to behave like that, or so I imagine. Perhaps it is. But I suddenly realized how relaxed I felt, how completely at home. It didn't matter if I blotted my copy book.

INTERVIEWER: The Marc was at work?

ISHERWOOD: Well, you can get drunk in many ways, but the Stravinskys projected the most astounding coziness. Because Vera Stravinsky was a part of it, she had enormous charm and style, and she's very amusing. Going out with them was always an experience. We drove up once to the Sequoia forest, and I remember Stravinsky, so tiny, looking up at this enormous giant Sequoia and standing there for a long time in meditation and then turning to me and saying: "That's serious."

INTERVIEWER: Are you musical?

ISHERWOOD: No, not at all. In the first place I'm very conventional. I don't consider that you really have a feeling about an art unless you react to its most modern manifestations. In the graphic arts I'm much more flexible and interested in all kinds of painting. But with the best will in the world, I just don't dig a lot of modern music. I like Beethoven and so on.

INTERVIEWER: But you like Stravinsky's music.

ISHERWOOD: Yes. But even with Stravinsky it took me an awfully long time.

INTERVIEWER: W. H. Auden has also worked with Stravinsky. You first knew Auden at school, didn't you?

ISHERWOOD: Yes, at my first boarding school, but he was three years younger than I. He showed absolutely no interest in poetry in those days. He was a very scientific little boy—the son of a doctor—interested in metallurgy, geology, mining. He knew a great deal about the different mines in England, and he loved going on hikes in the North Country to visit them. He had a mystique, a tremendously strong myth world, that he carried with him from early childhood. Then I met him again when he was eighteen and I was twenty-one, and he showed me all the poems he had written—not at all the kind of thing he's known for now. It was imitative, but brilliantly so; it sounded a bit like Hardy or Frost, or Edward Thomas.

INTERVIEWER: How did you work with Auden on your collaborations?

ISHERWOOD: He was constantly showing me his work, and we'd discuss it. Then one day—it was in the winter of 1934–35—he sent me a play called *The Chase*, and I made suggestions that would fill it out. There were parts that I could write and things that only he could write; and in this way we began to put together this enormous, loosely constructed thing called *The Dog Beneath the Skin*. It's never been performed in its entirety; it's too long. We were truly astonished at how well it was received at a London theater, so we thought, well, we must do this again. And we consciously thought of a subject, the study of a leader like Lawrence of Arabia but translated into terms of mountain climbing —*The Ascent of F6*. We wanted to contrast mountain climbing for climbing's sake and mountain climbing used for political ends, just as Lawrence went into the desert first because he loved it and ended up being used politically. Auden was the composer, the poet, and my function was to write the prose and lay out general lines. Later, Auden took over some of the prose, but I didn't write a line of poetry, apart from one scrap of doggerel. By the time we reached *On the Frontier*, Auden was writing more than I, although it was still definitely a collaboration. The first play we wrote more or less by correspondence, sending each other pages. But on the second and third play we worked together, in Portugal and elsewhere. Auden, who loves to be indoors, would work inside the house, and I'd be working out in the garden. He got through his stint—including some of his finest poetry—with amazing speed. We did very little polishing; and off it went to the publishers.

INTERVIEWER: Did you see him often, or correspond?

ISHERWOOD: Oh yes, we were very close friends, but the circumstances of our lives kept us apart. Very occasionally he came here and stayed with us, and sometimes we saw him in New York or England. He detested California, you know, it's too hot or bright or something. He moved to Austria, where it rains a lot; he loved that. And England, too, of course.

INTERVIEWER: Do you show your work to others much? Do you ask advice on it?

ISHERWOOD: Yes, I've shown work to people on many occasions. Sometimes I've profited from it a lot. The good suggestions were usually about structure. And sometimes people have objected very strongly to something, and I've taken it out.

INTERVIEWER: You don't find any difficulty in talking about what you're working on?

ISHERWOOD: No, except that you're opening such a can of beans, you have to talk for an hour to explain what you're doing. But I've often found that simply talking about one's problems ends in you yourself coming up with the answer.

INTERVIEWER: Have you any superstitions about writing?

ISHERWOOD: I do have a sense of auspicious days. I like to celebrate some significant day by starting a new piece of work.

INTERVIEWER: Are you superstitious, period?

ISHERWOOD: Jungians say there's no such thing as an Old Wives' Tale: in other words, if people say it's bad luck to walk under ladders, there must be a reason for it. I'm negatively superstitious—which means, of course, that I respect the superstition, I don't disbelieve in it: I walk under ladders, find the number thirteen favorable, invariably refuse to send chain letters on because I feel there's something wrong in submitting to the evil magic of a chain letter. One has to rise above it.

INTERVIEWER: You spoke earlier of sexual abstinence and the resulting storing up of energy: Is this a practice you've consciously tried in your writing?

ISHERWOOD: No, that's seen more as a means towards spiritual concentration than artistic concentration; although some artists do say that during periods of intense creativity they find the sex drive has been . . . I hate the word sublimated . . . redirected. I'm quite open to the argument that it would work with anything. But in my case it was concerned with the period when I was trying to live a monastic life at the Vedanta Center in Los Angeles.

INTERVIEWER: Was there a moment when you knew that you would be a writer?

ISHERWOOD: I feel I always wanted to be a writer. My father, without, I think, realizing what he was doing, made me think of writing as play rather than work. He was always telling me stories, encouraging me, taking an interest in my toy theater, and so on. And it seems to me that writing has been a game that I have gone on playing ever since. I am inclined to think of writers who bore me as being "workers."

INTERVIEWER: Both your parents wrote well, didn't they? Your father's letters in *Kathleen and Frank* are very observant.

ISHERWOOD: That's partly because he was quite a good artist. I've never known an artist who couldn't write better than average. Their eye for detail and power of describing people is remarkable. I see this in Don Bachardy and all my friends who are artists. They write letters that are full of understanding and observation. My father had that to a great extent. In one of his letters from South Africa during the Boer War there's a beautiful passage about the deep blue light which is reflected from the roofs of corrugated iron out on the Veldt, and how ridiculous it is to call corrugated iron ugly. He looked at a thing and asked himself, "What does it look like?" not "What is the popular preconception?" One of my earliest memories is that once, when I was trying to paint, imitating him, he asked me: "What color is that tree?" I said it was green, of course: Trees as a genus are green. "No it isn't," he said. And in that light, when I *looked*, the tree was blue.

INTERVIEWER: Are you a constant observer, consciously look-ing for things you can use as a writer?

ISHERWOOD: I think I'm a very unobservant person, one who goes straight to concepts about people and ignores evidence to the contrary and the bric-a-brac surrounding that person. Stephen Spender said an amusing thing about Yeats—that he went for days on end without noticing anything, but then, about once a month, he would look out of a window and suddenly be aware of a swan or something, and it gave him such a stunning shock that he'd write a marvelous poem about it. That's more the kind of way I operate: suddenly something pierces the reverie and self-absorption that fill my days, and I see with a tremendous flash the extraordinariness of that person or object or situation.

INTERVIEWER: Can you say something about the process of turning a real person into a fictional character?

ISHERWOOD: It happens through the process of thinking of them in their eternal, magic, symbolic aspects: It's rather the way you feel when you fall in love with somebody and that person ceases to be just another face in the crowd. The difference is that in art, almost by definition, everybody is quite extraordinary if only you can see them as such. When you're writing a book, you ask yourself: What is it that so intrigues me about this person— be it good or bad, that's neither here nor there, art knows nothing of such words. Having discovered what it is you really consider to be the essence of the interest you feel in this person, you then set about heightening it. The individuals themselves aren't quite up to this vision you have of them. Therefore you start trying to create a fiction-character that is quintessentially what you see as interesting in the individual, without all the contradictions that are inseparable from a human being, aspects that don't seem exciting or marvelous or beautiful. The last thing you're trying to do is get an overall picture of somebody, since then you'd end up with nothing.

INTERVIEWER: Is writing pleasurable?

ISHERWOOD: It's almost beyond the question of pleasure, isn't it? Is it pleasurable to work out at the gym? It is, and it isn't, but you have the feeling while you're doing it that it's something on the plus side. You're very absorbed in writing, and you don't ask yourself if it's pleasurable or distasteful. Making yourself write can be painful, and wonderful when you do. The will has asserted itself, and you feel good again.

INTERVIEWER: If you had to advise a young writer, what sort of pitfalls would you warn him against?

ISHERWOOD: Hard to say. It depends much more on your character than your talent. Some pursuits could be dangerous for a writer without much stamina. But I think, if you have enough drive and strength, there's very little that's going to hurt you. Many remarkable writers not only survive immense amounts of hack work, they gain know-how from it. Writers who've been in the newspaper business, for example—instead of moaning and regarding themselves as slaves and prostitutes, they've in fact learnt how to write more concisely. George Borrow, who wrote the most mountainous works of sheer plodding involving an enormous output of energy, was still able to write *Lavengro* and *The Romany Rye*, which to me are two of the most fascinating books ever written.

INTERVIEWER: Well, do you think writers who settle down in California, in the entertainment industry, compromise themselves in some way, or is that a fiction?

ISHERWOOD: I'll bet Shakespeare compromised himself a lot; anybody who's in the entertainment industry does to some extent. But are you going to sink or swim? There's a most awful daintiness in the idea that everything you write should be just so—perfection —and all the rest carefully destroyed so that it won't hurt your image. Often this is a dangerous kind of vanity. Goodness knows, I've written lots of stuff that I hate, but there it is, flapping around in the vaults of various motion-picture studios; and sometimes I've done good work for the cinema. If you want the money, and you want to live that way, you've just got to take it. I suppose, under ideal circumstances, I would say, have some other profession and keep your writing for yourself. That amazing man Henry Yorke, who writes under the name of Henry Green, has found time during most of his adult life to run a big business, and yet every day he puts in a stint of work on one of his novels. You can survive anything if you've got the stamina.

INTERVIEWER: What's your favorite novel about the entertainment industry?

ISHERWOOD: I'm very fond of Fitzgerald's unfinished last novel, *The Last Tycoon.* I never met him, but I don't think Fitzgerald was too worried about "compromise": He wrote a lot of stuff for magazines and so forth that wasn't up to his standards.

INTERVIEWER: Did you ever consciously change or adopt a way of life or accept friendships that you felt would help you as a writer?

ISHERWOOD: No. I didn't, for example, go to Germany because I thought it was a marvelous untilled field to cultivate. I personally believe that there is a part of one's subconscious will that directs one's life, that there is a part of me that is carrying out long-range schemes. I believe that this part of my will also knows when I shall die, and how much time I've got and everything else. I believe it has schemes which often, in my ignorance, I frustrate— schemes which are not always necessarily for the best. But I'm quite willing to suppose that it was this part of my will that caused me to go to Germany, or to California. . . . I see certain places as symbols in one's consciousness. I found the notion of the Far West infinitely romantic. I used to be thrilled by the expression *l'extrème Orient.* If you tell me that Bray Head is the westernmost point in Europe, I immediately experience a slight desire to go there. But no conscious voice said it would be a smart thing to go to Germany or California. It might be a good thing for a writer to go to prison or be sentenced to death and reprieved at the last moment, like Dostoevsky; I daresay it did wonders for his writing; and maybe this unconscious director steered him along those paths. Who can tell?

INTERVIEWER: Have you ever been completely stuck on a book?

ISHERWOOD: Oh yes.

INTERVIEWER: And how'd you get unstuck?

ISHERWOOD: Patience. Persistence. Putting it away and then coming back to it. Never allowing myself to get frantic. Repeating to myself, "There's no deadline; it'll be finished when it's finished." Sometimes, I can get a helpful idea from the unconscious by irritating it—deliberately writing nonsense until it intervenes, as it were, saying, "All right, idiot, let me fix this."

INTERVIEWER: Did you like the film of *Cabaret?*

ISHERWOOD: Oh, a bit . . .

INTERVIEWER: Do you have a work in progress?

ISHERWOOD: What I'm writing now is simply a reconstruction of some diaries which I failed to keep. I have a fairly continuous narrative of the years 1939 to '44. I not only kept a diary, I wrote fill-in passages to explain things that were missing. More or less at the time. Then again, from about 1955 on to the present day I kept a diary on and off, at least a couple of entries a month. But there's a very bald patch in between from '45 to '53, and that I'm trying to fill out. I have this one thing to clue me in, which is that aside from trying to keep a journal, I keep a day-to-day diary in which I say things like who came to the house where we had supper, if we saw a movie or a play. It's very convenient for remembering names and when things happened. And out of these diaries, I'm trying to reconstruct what happened all those years ago. In those days I wasn't as careful as I am now. I'm horrified to find, as I look at these diaries of twenty-five years ago or more, that I don't remember who the people were. "Bill and Tony were constantly in and out. We went to La Jolla"—or something. I haven't the bluest idea who they were! That requires quite a lot of research—I spent some time at UCLA the other day looking up things. It's a lot of fun, but whether it will amuse anyone else is another matter. I'm doing it entirely for myself. This diary writing is tremendously useful. I've quarried into it—the other diaries—for a lot of my books.

INTERVIEWER: Would you think of publishing what you're working on now in your lifetime?

ISHERWOOD: No, it couldn't be in my lifetime. In writing these diaries, I've got into the whole sex thing: I became interested in thinking why one does certain things, why one's attracted to certain people—one's type, as they used to say, one's ideal. Is that really true? Does one really have a "type"? What do people represent as archetypes, so to speak? It's been my experience, and I'm sure lots of people's, there is an ideal person who you imagine is your, ah, *dream;* but if you examine your life, you seem to find that if in fact you did meet someone who resembled that person, you didn't have any relationship with him at all, or only a very unsatisfactory one, and the really important relationships occurred with quite other people. So the question arises: Why is that? I've been going into all this, using for my text any actual relationships I had during this period. But I've got rather carried away by the subject, and I've gone back to earlier experiences to fill it out. It's perhaps the kind of thing you can only do in your old age. Sometimes you find an encounter with someone who is so stunningly what you think you want that the whole encounter becomes purely symbolic—it doesn't really mean anything at all. Like a restaurant: it's good because it's Chasen's. You don't really ask yourself if it's good; you just say, "Wow . . . I got to eat at the Four Seasons," or whatever it is. But it's just about whatever happened to happen in those years. In general, I've been rather discreet otherwise in my diaries.

INTERVIEWER: You spoke somewhere of a project called the "Autobiography of my Books."

ISHERWOOD: Yes. I even gave some lectures about it at Berkeley, about 1959. I thought I would describe the principal subjects in my books and point out that every writer has certain subjects that they write about again and again, and that most people's books are just variations on certain themes. I thought I'd like to write a book about this. And then I realized that I didn't know nearly enough about my principal themes, which were my father and mother, and the home place, and one's longing to get away from it, and what that's represented by: the other place. So I started studying my parents' letters and diaries, and I got into writing *Kathleen and Frank.* The other project was abandoned, but if anybody ever wanted to know where a lot of stuff in my books comes from, they would find the answers in *Kathleen and Frank*.

INTERVIEWER: Is there a book you would like to write but haven't?

ISHERWOOD: I'm interested in writing something about now. Old age. I've never read anything except Gide's *The Chips Are Down*, which seemed satisfactory, a marvelous book about old age.

INTERVIEWER: It isn't a subject people like very much.

ISHERWOOD: No, exactly, it's one of those subjects that people think are an absolute bore.

INTERVIEWER: You never seem too oppressed by what so many Europeans moan about here—vulgarity, crassness, all the rest of it.

ISHERWOOD: I think I'd been prepared for it. I was shocked, in 1939, by what I saw of the segregation in traveling across the United States. I could never understand that it applied to *me*, personally. I caused great distress once by sitting in the wrong section of a train. I was hot and tired and in a hurry and jumped into a coach and slowly became aware that the coach was for black people. And I thought, well, this is California now, we're not segregated officially. But I soon saw that I was really causing great uneasiness; everyone wanted me to leave. I didn't understand all these ramifications.

INTERVIEWER: Do you have a special liking for the Southern Californian way of living?

ISHERWOOD: Well, there are certain things you have to get used to like driving on the freeways, which some people find shattering, and a certain kind of ugliness, which is only ugliness in the eye of the beholder. There is enormous beauty here; the coastline is still magnificent. But to me it means an ideal place to work. It's my home now. I've lived here half my life, much longer than anywhere else. I traveled about so much when I was young, I never had a home before. This place seems to fit me like a glove. And beyond that there's a tremendous kind of vitality.

INTERVIEWER: You sometimes seem very defensive in your

books about America. There's the scene in *A Single Man*, for instance, in which George assails a woman who is vaunting the naturalness of Mexico above the United States . . .

ISHERWOOD: I used to hear a lot against America when I went back to England. People took such very superior attitudes. They don't understand a bit what the feeling is here, what it's all about. I feel it's so easy to condemn this country; but they don't understand that this is where the mistakes are being made—and made first, so that we're going to get the answers first. I feel that very strongly. I feel it's marvelous the way we talk about our failings. You know, there's an odd quotation in one of Edward Upward's novels: something like "We shall not perish, because we are not afraid to speak of our failings, and thus we shall learn to overcome our failings." It's a quotation from Stalin! Really! But it could be said here. We really do, in spite of our failings, in spite of everything, really air things here. Quite brutally. It's a violent country, and this, at least historically, is one of the more violent states. It's no place for people who want to sleep quietly in their beds.

W. I. SCOBIE

10. W. H. Auden

W. H. Auden was born in York, England, on February 21, 1907, and was educated at Gresham's School, Holt, and Christ Church, Oxford. In the 1930s he collaborated with Christopher Isherwood, an old school companion, on the plays *The Dog Beneath the Skin* (1935), *The Ascent of F6* (1936), and *On the Frontier* (1938), as well as on *Journey to a War*, a prose record of his 1938 travels in China. Auden's early volumes of poetry include *Poems* (1930), *The Orators* (1932), *Look, Stranger!* (1936), and *On This Island* (1937). Also in 1937, he published *Letters from Iceland*, a travel book of prose and poetry on which he collaborated with Louis MacNeice.

In 1938 Auden left England for America; he became a U.S. citizen in 1946. In addition to teaching at many American universities, he edited the *Oxford Book of Light Verse* (1938) and continued to publish more poetry, including *Another Time* (1940); *For the Time Being* (1944); and *The Age of Anxiety* (1947), for which he won the Pulitzer Prize. These were followed by *Nones* (1951); *The Shield of Achilles* (1955), for which he won the National Book Award; *About the House* (1965); *City Without Walls* (1969); *Epistle to a Godson and Other Poems* (1972); and *Thank You, Fog* (1974).

Auden was also the author of a great deal of occasional prose, including *The Enchafèd Flood* (1950); *Making, Knowing and Judging*, his inaugural lecture as Professor of Poetry at Oxford (1956); and *The Dyer's Hand* (1962). In addition, in collaboration with Chester Kallman, he wrote libretti for operas by Stravinsky, Hans Werner Henze, and other composers.

Dr. Auden received many honors, among them two Guggenheim Fellowships; the Award of Merit from the American Academy of Arts and Letters (1945), the Bollingen Prize (1954), the Feltrinelli Prize (1957), the Alexander Droutzkoy Memorial Award (1959), the Guinness Poetry Award (1959), and the National Medal for Literature (1967). Dr. Auden died in Vienna on September 28, 1973.

Last night, sucked giddy down

The funnel of my dream,

I saw myself within

A buried engine-room.

Dynamos, boilers, lay

In tickling silence, I,

Gripping an oily rail,

Talked feverishly ~~with an~~ to me

~~Hare~~-lipped philosopher,

Who spluttered "Is that all?",

And winked a lecher's eye,

"Puella defututa"

And laughed himself away.

Professional listener

Who ~~of tutors~~ proclaims month and hour

In ecstasy of pain

I know, ~~old boy~~ I know / I know,

And reached his hand for mine.

W.H. Auden manuscript, page 2 of *Poem II* ("I chose this lean country") from *Poems 1928*. From the Henry W. and Albert A. Berg Collection, The New York Public Library, Astor, Lenox and Tilden Foundations

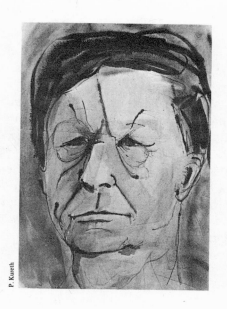

P. Kureth

W. H. Auden

AUDEN: *What's that again?*

INTERVIEWER: *I wondered which living writer you would say has served as the prime protector of the integrity of our English tongue . . . ?*

AUDEN: *Why me, of course!*

Conversation, Autumn 1972

He was sitting beneath two direct white lights of a plywood portico, drinking a large cup of strong breakfast coffee, chain-smoking cigarettes and doing the crossword puzzle which appears on the daily book review page of The New York Times—*which, as it happened, this day contained, along with his photo, a review of his most recent volume of poetry.*

When he had completed the puzzle, he unfolded the paper, glanced at the obits, and went to make toast.

Asked if he had read the review, Auden replied: "Of course not.

245

Obviously these things are not meant for me . . ."

His singular perspectives, priorities and tastes, were strongly manifest in the décor of his New York apartment, which he used in the winter. Its three large high-ceilinged main rooms were painted dark gray, pale green, and purple. On the wall hung drawings of friends—Elizabeth Bishop, E. M. Forster, Paul Valéry, Chester Kallman—framed simply in gold. There was also an original Blake watercolor, The Act of Creation, *in the dining room, as well as several line drawings of male nudes. On the floor of his bedroom, a portrait of himself, unframed, faced the wall.*

The cavernous front living room, piled high with books, was left dark except during his brief excursions into its many boxes of manuscripts or for consultations with the Oxford English Dictionary.

Auden's kitchen was long and narrow, with many pots and pans hanging on the wall. He preferred such delicacies as tongue, tripe, brains, and Polish sausage, ascribing the eating of beefsteak to the lower orders (it's madly non-U!"). He drank Smirnoff martinis, red wine, and cognac, shunned pot, and confessed to having, under a doctor's supervision, tried LSD: "Nothing much happened, but I did get the distinct impression that some birds were trying to communicate with me."

His conversation was droll, intelligent, and courtly, a sort of humanistic global gossip, disinterested in the machinations of ambition, less interested in concrete poetry, absolutely exclusive of electronic influence.

As he once put it: "I just got back from Canada, where I had a run-in with McLuhan. I won."

INTERVIEWER: You've insisted we do this conversation without a tape recorder. Why?

AUDEN: Because I think if there's anything worth retaining, the reporter ought to be able to remember it. Truman Capote tells the story of the reporter whose machine broke down halfway into an interview. Truman waited while the man tried in vain to fix it and finally asked if he could continue. The reporter said not to bother—he wasn't used to listening to what his subjects said!

INTERVIEWER: I thought your objection might have been to the instrument itself. You have written a new poem condemning the camera as an infernal machine.

AUDEN: Yes, it creates sorrow. Normally, when one passes someone on the street who is in pain, one either tries to help him, or one simply looks the other way. With a photo there's no human decision; you're not there; you can't turn away; you simply gape. It's a form of voyeurism. And I think close-ups are rude.

INTERVIEWER: Was there anything that you were particularly afraid of as a child? The dark, spiders, and so forth.

AUDEN: No, I wasn't very scared. Spiders, certainly—but that's different, a personal phobia which persists through life. Spiders and octopi. I was certainly never afraid of the dark.

INTERVIEWER: Were you a talkative child? I remember your describing somewhere the autistic quality of your private world.

AUDEN: Yes, I was talkative. Of course there were things in my private world that I couldn't share with others. But I always had a few good friends.

INTERVIEWER: When did you start writing poetry?

AUDEN: I think my own case may be rather odd. I was going to be a mining engineer or a geologist. Between the ages of six and twelve, I spent many hours of my time constructing a highly elaborate private world of my own based on, first of all, a land-scape, the limestone moors of the Pennines; and secondly, an industry—lead mining. Now I found in doing this, I had to make certain rules for myself. I could choose between two machines necessary to do a job, but they had to be real ones I could find in catalogues. I could decide between two ways of draining a mine, but I wasn't allowed to use magical means. Then there came a day which later on, looking back, seems very important. I was planning my idea of the concentrating mill—you know, the platonic idea of what it should be. There were two kinds of machinery for separating the slime, one I thought more beautiful than the other, but the other one I knew to be more efficient. I felt myself faced with what I can only call a moral choice—it was my duty to take the second and more efficient one. Later, I realized, in constructing this world which was only inhabited by me, I was already beginning to learn how poetry is written. Then, my final decision, which seemed to be fairly fortuitous at the time, took place in 1922, in March when I was walking across a field with a friend of mine from school who later became a painter. He asked me, "Do you ever write poetry?" and I said, "No"—I'd never thought of doing so. He said: "Why don't you?"—and at that point I decided that's what I would do. Looking back, I conceived how the ground had been prepared.

INTERVIEWER: Do you think of your reading as being an influence in your decision?

AUDEN: Well, up until then the only poetry I had read, as a child, were certain books of sick jokes—Belloc's *Cautionary Tales, Struwwelpeter* by Hoffmann, and Harry Graham's *Ruthless Rhymes for Heartless Homes*. I had a favorite, which went like this:

> *Into the drinking well*
> *The plumber built her*
> *Aunt Maria fell;*
> *We must buy a filter.*

Of course I read a good deal about geology and lead mining. Sopwith's *A Visit to Alston Moore* was one, *Underground Life* was another. I can't remember who wrote it. I read all the books of Beatrix Potter and also Lewis Carroll. Andersen's "The Snow Queen" I loved, and also Haggard's *King Solomon's Mines*. And I got my start reading detective stories with Sherlock Holmes.

INTERVIEWER: Did you read much of Housman?

AUDEN: Yes, and later I knew him quite well. He told me a very funny story about Clarence Darrow. It seems that Darrow had written him a very laudatory letter, claiming to have saved several clients from the chair with quotes from Housman's poetry. Shortly afterwards, Housman had a chance to meet Darrow. They had a very nice meeting, and Darrow produced the trial transcripts he had alluded to. "Sure enough," Housman told me, "there were two of my poems—both misquoted!" These are the minor headaches a writer must live with. My pet peeve is people who send for autographs but omit putting in stamps.

INTERVIEWER: Did you meet Christopher Isherwood at school?

AUDEN: Yes, I've known him since I was eight and he was ten, because we were both in boarding school together at St. Edmund's School, Hindhead, Surrey. We've known each other ever since. I always remember the first time I ever heard a remark which I decided was witty. I was walking with Mr. Isherwood on a Sunday walk—this was in Surrey—and Christopher said, "I think God must have been tired when He made this country." That's the first time I heard a remark that I thought was witty.

INTERVIEWER: Did you have good teachers?

AUDEN: Except in mathematics, I had the good luck to have excellent teachers, especially in science. When I went up for my *viva*, Julian Huxley showed me a bone and asked me to tell him what it was. "The pelvis of a bird," I said, which happened to be the right answer. He said: "Some people have said it was the skull of an extinct reptile."

INTERVIEWER: Have you ever taught writing?

AUDEN: No, I never have. If I had to "teach poetry," which, thank God, I don't, I would concentrate on prosody, rhetoric, philology, and learning poems by heart. I may be quite wrong, but I don't see what can be learned except purely technical things— what a sonnet is, something about prosody. If you did have a poetic academy, the subjects should be quite different—natural history, history, theology, all kinds of other things. When I've been at colleges, I've always insisted on giving ordinary academic courses—on the eighteenth century, or Romanticism. True, it's wonderful what the colleges have done as patrons of the artists. But the artists should agree not to have anything to do with contemporary literature. If they take academic positions, they should do academic work, and the further they get away from the kind of thing that directly affects what they're writing, the better. They should teach the eighteenth century or something that won't interfere with their work and yet earn them a living. To teach creative writing—I think that's dangerous. The only possibility I can conceive of is an apprentice system like those they had in the Renaissance—where a poet who was very busy got students to finish his poems for him. Then you'd *really* be teaching, and you'd be responsible, of course, since the results would go out under the poet's name.

INTERVIEWER: I noticed that in your early works, there seems to be a fierceness towards England. There's a sense of being at war with where you are—and that this is lacking in poems you've written here in the United States: that you seem more at home.

AUDEN: Yes, quite. I'm sure it's partly a matter of age. You know, everybody changes. It's frightfully important for a writer to be his age, not to be younger or older than he is. One might ask, "What should I write at the age of sixty-four," but never, "What should I write in 1940." It's always a problem, I think.

INTERVIEWER: Is there a certain age when a writer is at the height of his powers?

AUDEN: Some poets, like Wordsworth, peter out fairly early. Some, like Yeats, have done their best work late in life. Nothing is calculable. Aging has its problems, but they must be accepted without fuss.

INTERVIEWER: What made you choose the U.S. as a home?

AUDEN: Well, the difficulty about England is the cultural life —it *was* certainly dim, and I suspect it still is. In a sense it's the same difficulty one faces with some kinds of family life. I love my family very dearly, but I don't want to live with them.

INTERVIEWER: Do you see any demarcation between the language you have used since you came to America, and the language you used in England?

AUDEN: No, not really. Obviously you see little things, particularly when writing prose: very minor things. There are certain rhymes which could not be accepted in England. You would rhyme "clerk" and "work" here, which you can't in England. But these are minor—saying "twenty of" instead of "twenty to" or "aside from" instead of "apart from."

INTERVIEWER: How long have you lived here, and where in

America were you before taking this apartment?

AUDEN: I've been here since '52. I came to America in '39. I lived first in Brooklyn Heights, then taught for a while in Ann Arbor, then at Swarthmore. I did a stint in the army, with the *U.S. Strategic Bombing Survey.* The army didn't like our report at all because we proved that, in spite of all of our bombing of Germany, their weapons production didn't go down until after they had lost the war. It's the same in North Vietnam—the bombing does no good. But you know how army people are. They don't like to hear things that run contrary to what they've thought.

INTERVIEWER: Have you had much contact with men in politics and government?

AUDEN: I have had very little contact with such men. I knew some undergraduates, of course, while I was at Oxford, who eventually made it—Hugh Gaitskell, Crossman, and so forth. I think we should do very well without politicians. Our leaders should be elected by lot. The people could vote their conscience, and the computers could take care of the rest.

INTERVIEWER: How about writers as leaders? Yeats, for instance, held office.

AUDEN: And he was terrible! Writers seldom make good leaders. They're self-employed, for one thing, and they have very little contact with their customers. It's very easy for a writer to be unrealistic. I have not lost my interest in politics, but I have come to realize that, in cases of social or political injustice, only two things are effective: political action and straight journalistic reportage of the facts. The arts can do nothing. The social and political history of Europe would be what it has been if Dante, Shakespeare, Michelangelo, Mozart, et al., had never lived. A poet, *qua* poet, has only one political duty, namely, in his own writing to set an example of the correct use of his mother tongue which is always being corrupted. When words lose their meaning, physical force takes over. By all means, let a poet, if he wants to, write what is now called an *'engagé'* poem, so long as he realizes that it is mainly himself who will benefit from it. It will enhance his literary reputation among those who feel the same as he does.

INTERVIEWER: Does this current deterioration and corruption of language, imprecision of thought, and so forth scare you—or is it just a decadent phase?

AUDEN: It terrifies me. I try by my personal example to fight it; as I say, it's a poet's role to maintain the sacredness of language.

INTERVIEWER: Do you think the present condition of our civilization will be seen by the future, if there is one, as a prewar decadence?

AUDEN: No, I don't think it has anything to do with the fact of another war. But in the old days people knew what the words meant, whatever the range of their vocabulary. Now people hear and repeat a radio and TV vocabulary thirty per cent larger than they know the meaning of. The most outrageous use of words I've ever experienced was once when I was a guest on the David Susskind TV program. During a break he had to do a plug for some sort of investment firm, and he announced that these people were "integrity-ridden!" I could not believe my ears!

INTERVIEWER: You have said bad art is bad in a very contemporary way.

AUDEN: Yes. Of course one can be wrong about what is good or bad. Taste and judgment can differ. But one has to be loyal to oneself and trust one's own taste. I can, for instance, enjoy a good tear-jerking movie, where, oh, an old mother is put away in a home—even though I know it's terrible, the tears will run down my cheeks. I don't think good work ever makes one cry. Housman said he got a curious physical sensation with good poetry—I never got any. If one sees *King Lear,* one doesn't cry. One doesn't have to.

INTERVIEWER: You have said that the story of your patron Saint Wystan was rather Hamlet-like. Are you a Hamlet-poet?

AUDEN: No, I couldn't be less. For myself I find that Shakespeare's greatest influence has been his use of a large vocabulary. One thing that makes English so marvelous for poetry is its great range and the fact that it is an uninflected language. One can turn verbs into nouns and vice versa, as Shakespeare did. One cannot do this with inflected languages such as German, French, Italian.

INTERVIEWER: In the early thirties, did you write for an audience that you wanted to jolt into awareness?

AUDEN: No, I just try to put the thing out and hope somebody will read it. Someone says: "Whom do you write for?" I reply: "Do you read me?" If they say, "Yes," I say, "Do you like it?" If they say, "No," then I say, "I don't write for you."

INTERVIEWER: Well, then, do you think of a particular audience when writing certain poems?

AUDEN: Well, you know it's impossible to tell. If you have someone in mind . . . well, most of them are probably dead. You wonder whether they'll approve or not, and then you hope—that somebody will even read you after you're dead *yourself.*

INTERVIEWER: You have always been a formalist. Today's poets seem to prefer free verse. Do you think that's an aversion to discipline?

AUDEN: Unfortunately that's too often the case. But I can't understand—strictly from a hedonistic point of view—how one can enjoy writing with no form at all. If one plays a game, one needs rules, otherwise there is no fun. The wildest poem has to have a firm basis in common sense, and this, I think, is the advantage of formal verse. Aside from the obvious corrective advantages, formal verse frees one from the fetters of one's ego. Here I like to quote Valéry, who said a person is a poet if his imagination is stimulated by the difficulties inherent in his art and *not* if his imagination is dulled by them. I think very few people can manage free verse—you need an infallible ear, like D. H. Lawrence, to determine where the lines should end.

INTERVIEWER: Are there any poets you've read who have seemed to you to be kindred spirits? I'm thinking of Campion here, with whom you share a great fascination with metrics.

AUDEN: Yes, I do have several pets, and Campion is certainly among them. Also George Herbert and William Barnes, and yes, all shared a certain interest in metrics. These are the poets I should have liked to have had as friends. As great a poet as Dante might have been, I wouldn't have had the slightest wish to have known him personally. He was a terrible prima donna.

INTERVIEWER: Can you say something about the genesis of a poem? What comes first?

AUDEN: At any given time, I have two things on my mind: a theme that interests me and a problem of verbal form, meter, diction, etc. The theme looks for the right form: the form looks for the right theme. When the two come together, I am able to start writing.

INTERVIEWER: Do you start your poems at the beginning?

AUDEN: Usually, of course, one starts at the beginning and works through to the end. Sometimes, though, one starts with a certain line in mind, perhaps a last line. One starts, I think, with a certain idea of thematic organization, but this usually alters during the process of writing.

INTERVIEWER: Do you have any aids for inspiration?

AUDEN: I never write when I'm drunk. Why should one need aids? The Muse is a high-spirited girl who doesn't like to be brutally or coarsely wooed. And she doesn't like slavish devotion —then she lies.

INTERVIEWER: And comes up with "moon-faced Nonsense, that erudite forger," as you said in one of your "Bucolics."

AUDEN: Quite. Poetry is not self-expression. Each of us, of course, has a unique perspective which we hope to communicate. We hope that someone reading it will say, "Of course, I knew that all the time but never realized it before." On the whole I agree here with Chesterton, who said, "The artistic temperament is a disease that affects amateurs."

INTERVIEWER: Many poets are night workers, manic, irregular in their habits.

AUDEN: Sorry, my dear, one mustn't be bohemian!

INTERVIEWER: Why do you disapprove of the recent publication of Eliot's *Waste Land* drafts?

AUDEN: Because there's not a line he left out which makes one wish he'd kept it. I think this sort of thing encourages amateurs to think, "Oh, look—I could have done as well." I think it shameful that people will spend more for a draft than for a completed poem. Valerie Eliot didn't like having to publish the drafts, but once they were discovered, she knew they would have to come out eventually—so she did it herself to insure that it was done as well as possible.

INTERVIEWER: But isn't there some truth to be had from the knowledge that a poet does quite literally start in the "foul rag and bone shop of the heart?"

AUDEN: It may be necessary for him to start there, but there is no reason for others to pay it a visit. Here I like the quote of Valéry, which says that when people don't know anything else they take their clothes off.

INTERVIEWER: In your *Commonplace Book* you've written: Behaviorism works—so does torture.

AUDEN: It does work. But I'm sure if I were given Professor B. F. Skinner and supplied with the proper drugs and appliances, I could have him in a week reciting the Athanasian Code—in public. The problem with the behavioralists is that they always manage to exclude themselves from their theories. If all our acts are conditioned behavior, surely our theories are, too.

INTERVIEWER: Do you see any spirituality in all those hippies out on St. Marks Place? You've lived among them for some time now.

AUDEN: I don't know any of them, so how could I tell? What I do like about them is that they have tried to revive the spirit of "Carnival," something which has been conspicuously lacking in our culture. But I'm afraid that when they renounce work entirely, the fun turns ugly.

INTERVIEWER: Your new poem "Circe" deals with this subject, particularly:

> She does not brutalise her victims (beasts could
> bite or bolt). She simplifies them to flowers,
> sessile fatalists, who don't mind and only
>   can talk to themselves.

Obviously you know that generation better than you admit.

AUDEN: I must say that I do admire the ones who won't compete in the rat race, who renounce money and worldy goods. I couldn't do that, I'm far too worldy.

INTERVIEWER: Do you own any credit cards?

AUDEN: One. I never use it if I can help it. I've used it only once, in Israel, to pay a hotel bill. I was brought up believing that you should not buy anything you cannot pay cash for. The idea of debt appalls me. I suppose our whole economy would collapse if everyone had been brought up like me.

INTERVIEWER: Are you a good businessman—do you drive a hard bargain, and so forth?

AUDEN: No. That's not a subject I care to think about.

INTERVIEWER: But you do get what you can for your poetry. I was surprised the other day to see a poem of yours in *Poetry*—which only pays fifty cents a line.

AUDEN: Of course I get what I can—who wouldn't? I think I got my check from them the other day and used it up before I noticed I'd gotten it.

INTERVIEWER: Are you a gourmet?

AUDEN: I'm very fond of my food. I'm lucky when I'm in Austria because my friend Mr. Kallman is an expert chef, so I'm rather spoiled in the summer. It's different here where I live alone. Sometimes when one is cooking for oneself, one gets a craze for something. Once I had a craze for turnips. But with solitary eating one doesn't like to spend much time and simply gobbles it up fast. Certainly I like good wine, but I don't make a thing of it. There's a red table wine, Valpolicella, which I like to drink both when I'm in Austria and when I'm here. It travels much better than Chianti, which, when you drink it here, always tastes like red ink.

INTERVIEWER: Do you ever miss a meal while in the process of writing?

AUDEN: No. I live by my watch. I wouldn't know to be hungry if I didn't have my watch on!

INTERVIEWER: What are the worst lines you know—preferably by a great poet?

AUDEN: I think they occur in Thomas Hardy's *The Dynasts*, in which Napoleon tries to escape from Elba. There's a quatrain which goes like this:

> *Should the corvette arrive*
> *With the aging Scotch colonel,*
> *Escape would be frustrate,*
> *Retention eternal.*

That's pretty hard to beat!

INTERVIEWER: How about Yeats'

> *Had de Valera eaten Parnell's heart*

or Eliot's

> *Why should the aged eagle stretch its wings?*

AUDEN: Those aren't bad, really, just unintentionally comic. Both would have made wonderful captions for a Thurber cartoon. As an undergraduate at Oxford I came up with one:

> *Isobel with her leaping breasts*
> *Pursued me through a summer . . .*

Think what a marvelous cartoon Thurber could have done to that! Whoops! Whoops! Whoops!

INTERVIEWER: What's your least favorite Auden poem?

AUDEN: "September 1, 1939." And I'm afraid it's gotten into a lot of anthologies.

INTERVIEWER: Of which poem are you proudest?

AUDEN: It occurs in my commentary on Shakespeare's *Tempest*, a poem written in prose, a pastiche of the late Henry James —"Caliban's Speech to the Audience."

INTERVIEWER: Have you ever finished a book you've hated?

AUDEN: No, I've skipped . . . actually I did, once. I read the whole of *Mein Kampf* because it was necessary to know what he thought. But it was not a pleasure.

INTERVIEWER: Have you reviewed a book you've hated?

AUDEN: Very rarely. Unless one is a regular reviewer, or one is reviewing a book of reference where the facts are wrong—then it's one's duty to inform the public, as one would warn them of watered milk. Writing nasty reviews can be fun, but I don't think the practice is very good for the character.

INTERVIEWER: What's the nicest poetic compliment you've ever received?

AUDEN: It came in a most unusual way. A friend of mine, Dorothy Day, had been put in the women's prison at 6th Avenue and 8th Street for her part in a protest. Well, once a week at this place, on a Saturday, the girls were marched down for a shower. A group were being ushered in when one, a whore, loudly proclaimed:

> *Hundreds have lived without love,*
> *But none without water . . .*

A line from a poem of mine which had just appeared in *The New Yorker*. When I heard this, I knew I hadn't written in vain!

INTERVIEWER: Have you read any books on Women's Lib?

AUDEN: I'm a bit puzzled by it. Certainly they ought to complain about the ad things, like ladies' underwear, and so forth.

INTERVIEWER: Are there any essential differences between male and female poetry?

AUDEN: Men and women have opposite difficulties to contend with. The difficulty for a man is to avoid being an aesthete—to avoid saying things not because they are true, but because they are poetically effective. The difficulty for a woman is in getting sufficient distance from the emotions. No woman is an aesthete. No woman ever wrote nonsense verse. Men are playboys, women realists. If you tell a funny story—only a woman will ever ask: "Did it really happen?" I think if men knew what women said to each other about them, the human race would die out.

INTERVIEWER: Do you think it would be better if women ran the human race?

AUDEN: I think foreign policy should definitely be taken out of men's hands. Men should continue making machines, but women ought to decide which machines ought to be made. Women have far better sense. They would never have introduced the internal combustion engine or any of the evil machines. Most kitchen machines, for example, are good; they don't obliterate other skills. Or other people. With our leaders it is all too often a case of one's little boy saying to another, "My father can lick your father." By now, the toys have gotten far too dangerous.

INTERVIEWER: Have you known any madmen?

AUDEN: Well, of course, I've known people who went off their heads. We all have. People who go into the bin and out again. I've known several people who were manic-depressives. I've often thought a lot of good could be done for them if they would organize a manic-depressives anonymous. They could get together and do each other some good.

INTERVIEWER: I don't think it would work.

AUDEN: Well, everybody has their ups and downs!

INTERVIEWER: If you were to go mad, what do you think your madness would be?

AUDEN: I couldn't imagine going mad. It's simply something my imagination cannot take. One can be dotty—but that's different! There's a very funny book called *The Three Christs of Ypsilanti*, about a hospital in which there are three gents, all of whom believe themselves to be the Lord. Which is common enough, except in the case of one—who had actually found a disciple!

INTERVIEWER: What about collaboration? Did you ever go through your poems with T. S. Eliot?

AUDEN: No, one can't expect other people to do such things. He was very good to me; he encouraged me. He wasn't jealous of other writers. I had met him just before I left Oxford. I'd sent him some poems, and he asked me to come to see him. He published the first thing of mine that was published—it was "Paid on Both Sides"—which came out in *The Criterion* in '28 or '29.

INTERVIEWER: Was Isherwood helpful at this time?

AUDEN: Oh, enormously. Of course one depends at that age on one's friends; one reads one's work, and they criticize it. That's the same in every generation.

INTERVIEWER: Did you collaborate with him at this point, at Oxford?

AUDEN: The first time I collaborated with Isherwood must have been in '33 or '34—*The Dog Beneath the Skin*. I've always enjoyed collaborating very much. It's exciting. Of course, you can't collaborate on a particular poem. You can collaborate on a translation, or a libretto, or a drama, and I like working that way, though you can only do it with people whose basic ideas you share —each can then sort of excite the other. When a collaboration works, the two people concerned become a third person, who is different from either of them in isolation. I have observed that when critics attempt to say who wrote what they often get it wrong. Of course, any performed work is bound to be a collaboration, anyway, because you're going to have performers and producers and God knows what.

INTERVIEWER: How do you look back now on the early plays you wrote with Isherwood?

AUDEN: None of them will quite do, I think. I have a private weakness for *Dogskin*, which I think, if properly done, is fun, except that you have to cut all the choruses. There is some quite nice poetry in there, but dramatically it won't do. This was something that was just selfish on my part, wanting to write some poetry which had nothing to do, really, with drama.

INTERVIEWER: Do you feel that the state of the theater today is conducive to poetic drama?

AUDEN: The difficulty, I think, is that the tradition of actors and verse has been so lost. In opera, for example, the whole tradition of singing has never stopped. The trouble with people who write official poetic drama—drama written in verse—is that they can default so easily either by writing something which is so nearly prose that it might just as well *be* prose—or something which is not theatrical. Actually, Mr. Kallman and I had a very interesting experience. We'd done a translation of *The Magic*

Flute for NBC television, and we decided to put the spoken interludes into couplets. Nearly everybody in the cast, of course, were singers . . . who had never spoken verse before; there was only one part played by a professional actor. With the singers, we could teach them immediately how to speak verse. The singers, who had never spoken verse before, could get it in ten minutes because they knew what a beat was. But we had awful trouble with the professional actor.

INTERVIEWER: Do you feel that the conventions of acting in the American theater destroy this ability to speak a line even more?

AUDEN: They won't keep still, of course. It's like a football match. Poetry is very unnaturalistic. One of the great things about opera singing is that you cannot pretend it's naturalistic.

INTERVIEWER: Do you feel an opera libretto is limiting—that it requires sacrifices . . . ?

AUDEN: Well, yes. Of course, you have to forget all about what you ordinarily mean by writing poetry when you're writing poetry to be read or spoken or sung. It's a completely different art. Naturally, one's subordinate to the composer. And one's judged, really, by how much one stimulates him. But that's half the fun of it: being limited. Something you think of, which in cold blood would be absolute trash, suddenly, when it is sung, becomes interesting. And vice versa.

INTERVIEWER: Which harks back to Addison's remark about Italian opera in London at the turn of the eighteenth century— that whatever is too stupid to say can be sung.

AUDEN: Well, it's not quite true—particularly these days when composers are much more dependent on the quality of the libretto than they were. It has been true ever since Strauss and Hofmannsthal that the librettist isn't a pure flunky.

INTERVIEWER: How did the collaboration of *The Rake's Progress* proceed?

AUDEN: Mr. Kallman and I prepared the libretto beforehand, though I talked to Mr. Stravinsky first, and we got some idea of the kind of thing he wanted to do. What had excited him was an idea that he felt would be an interesting subject for an opera. It was the last Hogarth scene in Bedlam where there was a blond man with a sort of broken fiddle. Now, actually Stravinsky never used this, but intuitively he thought, "Now this is an interesting idea." In the end it wasn't used at all.

INTERVIEWER: Could you characterize your working relationship with Stravinsky.

AUDEN: He was always completely professional. He took what I sent him and set it to music. He always took enormous trouble to find out what the rhythmic values were, which must have been difficult for him, since prior to my working with him he had never set in English.

INTERVIEWER: Did you correspond as did Strauss and Hofmannsthal?

AUDEN: No. The funny thing about their correspondence— which we're very fortunate to have—was that they chose to work through the mails because they couldn't stand one another!

INTERVIEWER: Did you and Stravinsky discuss the work over the phone?

AUDEN: No, I don't like the phone very much and never stay on long if I can help it. You get some people who simply will not get off the line! I remember the story of the man who answered the phone and was kept prisoner for what seemed an age. The lady talked and talked. Finally, in desperation, he told her, "Really, I must go. I hear the phone ringing!"

INTERVIEWER: What is your Hans Werner Henze opera about?

AUDEN: It's about the early twentieth-century sort of artist-genius who, in order to get his work done, must exploit other people. A sort of real monster. A poet. It is set in an Austrian mountain inn in the year 1910. There was an amusing mix-up about its title, *Elegy for Young Lovers,* which appeared on a lawyer's power-of-attorney document as *Allergy for Young Lovers.*

INTERVIEWER: Did you involve yourself in its production?

AUDEN: Naturally. As much as I was allowed to, which with modern stage directors is not always easy.

INTERVIEWER: Do you enjoy all the ruckus?

AUDEN: Yes, I do. I'm terribly short-tempered.

INTERVIEWER: Does poetry contain music?

AUDEN: One can speak of verbal "music" so long as one remembers that the sound of words is inseparable from their meaning. The notes in music do not denote anything.

INTERVIEWER: What is the difference in your aims when you write a piece of verse which is to be set to music? Is there a difference in your method?

AUDEN: In writing words to be set to music, one has to remember that, probably, only one word in three will be heard. So, one must avoid complicated imagery. Suitable are verbs of motion, interjections, lists, and nouns like Moon, Sea, Love, Death.

INTERVIEWER: You wrote the U.N. anthem to be set by Casals. What were your aims and methods there?

AUDEN: The problem in writing the U.N. theme, in which one must not offend anybody's conception of Man, Nature, the world, was how to avoid the most dreary clichés. I decided that the only thing to do was to make all the imagery musical, for music, unlike language, is international. Casals and I corresponded, and he was extremely generous about altering his music if, as once or twice, I felt he had accented syllables wrongly.

INTERVIEWER: Where did you pick up your interest in the Icelandic Sagas?

AUDEN: My father brought me up on them. His family originated in an area which once served as headquarters for the Viking army. The name *Auden* is common in the Sagas, usually spelled *Audun.* But we have no family trees or anything like that. My mother came from Normandy—which means that she was half Nordic, as the Normans were. I had an ancestor named Birch, who married Constable. The family, I understand, was furious that she had married a painter. I've seen some of his portraits of her—she must have been quite beautiful. I've another relative who's married to a Hindu. This goes along better, I think, with the family line, which says that either one marries an Englishman —or one marries a Brahmin!

INTERVIEWER: And your father was a doctor?

AUDEN: Yes, he was. But at the time my mother married him, medicine was not considered one of the respectable professions. One of her aunts told her shortly before the wedding, "Well, marry him if you must, but no one will call on you!"

INTERVIEWER: You believe in class distinctions, then, social forms and formats?

AUDEN: To a degree, yes; one talks to people one has something to say to—it keeps things running a bit more smoothly. And I think the first prerequisite to civilization is an ability to make polite conversation.

INTERVIEWER: Many artists and writers either join the media or use its techniques in composing or editing their work.

AUDEN: It certainly has never tempted me. I suppose with some people like Norman Mailer it works out all right. Personally, I don't see how any civilized person can watch TV, far less own a set. I prefer detective stories, especially Father Brown. I also don't particularly care for science fiction. I read some Jules Verne in my youth, but I'm not very interested in other planets. I like them where they are, in the sky.

INTERVIEWER: Are there any media which to you are strictly taboo?

AUDEN: Yes: TV, all movies except the comic ones—Charlie Chaplin and the Marx Brothers were quite funny—and rock and roll all are taboo for me.

INTERVIEWER: Newspapers?

AUDEN: They're painful, but one has to read them to know whatever is happening. I try to get through them as soon as possible. It's never very pleasant in the morning to open *The New York Times*.

INTERVIEWER: Have you read, or tried to read, *Finnegans Wake?*

AUDEN: I'm not very good on Joyce. Obviously he's a very great genius—but his work is simply too long. Joyce said himself that he wanted people to spend their life on his work. For me life is too short, and too precious. I feel the same way about *Ulysses*. Also, *Finnegans Wake* can't be read the way one reads ordinarily.

You can dip in, but I don't think anyone could read it straight through and remember what happened. It's different in small doses. I remember when *Anna Livia Plurabelle* came out, published separately, I was able to get through it and enjoy it. On the whole I like novels to be short, and funny. There are a few exceptions, of course; one knows with Proust, for instance, that it couldn't have been any shorter. I suppose my favorite modern novelists are Ronald Firbank and P. G. Wodehouse—because both deal with Eden.

INTERVIEWER: Are you aware, by the way, that you are mentioned on page 279 of *Finnegans Wake?*

AUDEN: That I know. I could not have given you the page number—but I have seen the footnote.

INTERVIEWER: Would you care to comment on Yeats?

AUDEN: I find it very difficult to be fair to Yeats because he had a bad influence on me. He tempted me into a rhetoric which was, for me, oversimplified. Needless to say, the fault was mine, not his. He was, of course, a very great poet. But he and Rilke had a bad effect on me, so it's difficult for me to judge either fairly.

INTERVIEWER: What about Eliot's influence?

AUDEN: Eliot can have very little direct stylistic influence on other poets, actually. What I mean is that it is very rare that one comes across a poem and can say, "Ah, he's been reading Eliot." One can with Yeats or Rilke, but not with Eliot. He's a very idiosyncratic poet and not imitatable. My work is much easier to use as a stylistic model. And I don't say this about Eliot in any pejorative sense at all. It's the same with Gerard Manley Hopkins —both are extremely idiosyncratic and cannot readily be adapted to one's own sensibility. When it's attempted, what you end up with is simply Hopkins-and-water.

INTERVIEWER: Do you think "Gerontion" is Eliot's greatest poem?

AUDEN: Again, this idea of choosing. Why should one? Obviously, one wants a lot of them.

INTERVIEWER: Well, then, do you think "Gerontion" is a very mystical poem?

AUDEN: I'm not sure if "mystical" is quite the right word. Certainly a part of his work is based on a rather peculiar vision he's had. That's part of why he's so idiosyncratic. Probably something in his early youth. Here I think a comment he made about Dante's Beatrice is very revealing. Although Dante claimed to have been nine when he met her, Eliot was sure they must have met at a still earlier age. I think that's very revealing about Eliot. And all those images of children swinging from apple trees . . . must refer to some very powerful early vision. But he wasn't a confessional poet, so we don't know who it was.

INTERVIEWER: Eliot was purportedly influenced in that direction by the poetry of St. John of the Cross, which we can safely say is mystical. Do you read him much?

AUDEN: His poetry is very remarkable, but not exactly my cup of tea. Essentially because I don't think the mystical experience can be verbalized. When the ego disappears, so does power over language. I must say that he was extremely daring—he uses the most daring metaphors for orgasm. This probably has to do with the fact that in both cases, orgasm and mystical union, the ego is forgotten.

INTERVIEWER: Do you spend much time on affairs of the Church?

AUDEN: No—apart from going on Sundays.

INTERVIEWER: But you do have a reputation in theological circles; you've had some doings with The Guild of Episcopal Scholars.

AUDEN: Oh, that just had to do with some advice they wanted on the revision of the Psalms. Actually, I'm passionately anti-liturgical-reform, and would have The Book of Common Prayer kept in Latin. Rite is the link between the dead and the unborn and needs a timeless language, which in practice means a dead language. I'm curious to know what problems they are having in Israel, where they speak what was long an unspoken language.

INTERVIEWER: Do you speak Hebrew?

AUDEN: No, I wish I knew it. Obviously it's a marvelous language. Something else I wish we had in my Church is the Seder.

I've been to one or two and was enormously impressed. We don't have anything like that. The Last Supper is a communal thing, but not a family thing.

INTERVIEWER: What about the rites of marriage?

AUDEN: Well, I'm perfectly congenial to the idea of weddings, but what I think ruins so many marriages, though, is this romantic idea of falling in love. It happens, of course, I suppose to some people who are possessed of unusually fertile imaginations. Undoubtedly it is a mystical experience which occurs. But with most people who think they are in love I think the situation can be described far more simply, and, I'm afraid, brutally. The trouble with all this love business is one or the other partner ends up feeling bad or guilty because they don't have it the way they've read it. I'm afraid things went off a lot more happily when marriages were arranged by parents. I do think it is absolutely essential that both partners share a sense of humor and an outlook on life. And, with Goethe, I think marriages should be celebrated more quietly and humbly, because they are the beginning of something. Loud celebrations should be saved for successful conclusions.

INTERVIEWER: What is that big book over there?

AUDEN: It's Goethe's autobiography. It's amazing. If I were asked to do an autobiography of my first twenty-six years, I don't think I could fill up sixty pages. And here Goethe fills up eight hundred! Personally I'm interested in history, but not in the past. I'm interested in the present and in the next twenty-four hours.

INTERVIEWER: What's the name of your cat?

AUDEN: I haven't got any now.

INTERVIEWER: What about Mosé?

AUDEN: Mosé was a dog.

INTERVIEWER: Who was Rolfi Strobl?

AUDEN: Our housekeeper's dog, an Alsatian. There must have been a bitch in the neighborhood because the poor thing ran out on the Autobahn one day and was run over. We had a very funny experience with Mosé one time. We had gone to Venice for the opening of *The Rake's Progress*, which was being broadcast over the radio. Mosé was staying with some friends at the time, who were listening in. The minute my voice came over the airwaves, Mosé's ears perked up, and he ran over to the speaker—just like His Master's Voice!

INTERVIEWER: What happened to your cats?

AUDEN: They had to be put away because our housekeeper died. They, too, were named from opera, Rudimace and Leonora. Cats can be very funny, too, and have the oddest ways of showing they're glad to see you. Rudimace always peed in our shoes.

INTERVIEWER: And then there's your new poem, "Talking to Mice." Have you any favorite mythological mice?

AUDEN: Mythological! What on earth could you be referring to? Are there any, aside from Mickey Mouse? You must mean fictional mice!

INTERVIEWER: I must.

AUDEN: Oh yes, there's the mice of Beatrix Potter, of which I'm quite fond.

INTERVIEWER: How about Mickey?

AUDEN: He's all right.

INTERVIEWER: Do you believe in the Devil?

AUDEN: Yes.

INTERVIEWER: In Austria you live on Audenstrasse. Do your neighbors know who you are?

AUDEN: My neighbors there know I'm a poet. The village I live in was the home of a famous Austrian poet, Joseph Weinheber, so they're used to having a poet around the place. He committed suicide in '45.

INTERVIEWER: How about your neighbors here?

AUDEN: I don't know. My stock went up last year, I know. There was a feature on me in the *Daily News*—which everyone here seems to read. After that they figured I must be somebody. It was very nice to get all that attention.

INTERVIEWER: Do you think writers receive more respect abroad than here?

AUDEN: I wouldn't say so. I've told people I'm a medieval historian when asked what I do. It freezes conversation. If one tells them one's a poet, one gets these odd looks which seem to say, "Well, what's he living off?" In the old days a man was proud to have in his passport, Occupation: Gentleman. Lord Antrim's passport simply said, Occupation: Peer—which I felt was correct. I've had a lucky life. I had a happy home, and my parents provided me with a good education. And my father was both a physician and a scholar, so I never got the idea that art and science were opposing cultures—both were entertained equally in my home. I cannot complain. I've never had to do anything I really disliked. Certainly I've had to do various jobs I would not have taken on if I'd had the money; but I've always considered myself a worker, not a laborer. So many people have jobs they don't like at all. I haven't, and I'm grateful for that.

MICHAEL NEWMAN

11. Eudora Welty

Eudora Welty has lived almost all of her life in Jackson, Mississippi, where she was born in 1909. She attended Mississippi State College for Women for two years and received her A.B. from the University of Wisconsin in 1929. After a year at the Columbia School of Advertising, she returned to Jackson in 1932 to pursue her writing. Since then she has departed only for a rare visit to Europe, an annual trip to New York, and an occasional reading at a college.

The short story has always been her forte, although she has written a number of novels: *The Robber Bridegroom* (1942), *Delta Wedding* (1946), *The Ponder Heart* (1954), *Losing Battles* (1970), and *The Optimist's Daughter* (1972).

Her first published story, "Death of a Traveling Salesman," appeared in 1936 in *Manuscript,* an obscure quarterly. During the next five years she was published in many distinguished periodicals, most frequently in *The Southern Review.* Her first collection of stories, *A Curtain of Green,* did not appear until 1941. It was followed by three more collections: *The Wide Net* (1943), *The Golden Apples* (1949), and *The Bride of Innisfallen* (1955). She has also written a children's book, *The Shoe Bird* (1964), and published a collection of photographs, *One Time, One Place* (1971). In all her work, her scene has been the South.

Miss Welty was recipient of the Creative Arts Medal for Fiction at Brandeis University, 1966. She is a member of the National Institute of Arts and Letters and has since 1958 been an honorary consultant in American letters of the Library of Congress.

"Bywy River, my father killed his last bear. Blessed old

    Dragged her home,

sow / Laid her across ~~the~~ doorstep."

 "Granny! Did you ever have a <u>father</u>? And <u>mother</u>?" cried.

Elvie.

 "Mama said, 'Take that back where you found it, Mr. Blaikie.

You're nothing but bragging now,'" said Granny.

 ~~"When? When, Granny, where, Elvie pleaded.~~

 ~~"~~ ~~was~~ ~~for~~ ~~true?~~ ~~Elvie~~ ~~begged~~ ~~to~~ ~~know.~~ ~~"~~

 "Was you <u>born</u>?" Elvie pleaded to know. "Granny!

Like Lady May?"

 "Granny'd like <u>her</u> picture taken!" Aunt Beck divined. "Ninety

today!"

 "With all of us!" cried Aunt Birdie. "A picture with Granny

in the middle. Haul her out here in the broil, see what you can

get, Sister Cleo!"

 Miss Beulah was summoned, and stood at center back, the ~~Beechams~~

Beecham   (The men squatted or reclined on the ground.

~~bank~~ wives lined up at her sides.) Granny sat composed in the cen-

ter, and for the only time that day drew the pipe from her pocket,

in order to pose with it cocked in her mouth. ~~Then~~ The aunts as

one dropped their hands before them, as if called to the door in

their aprons. ~~But~~ ~~an~~ ~~Aunt~~ ~~Nannie's~~ ~~jaw~~ ~~gaunt~~ ~~became~~ ~~was~~ like

~~sleeved~~ ~~arms~~ ~~were~~ ~~folded~~ ~~across~~ ~~in~~ ~~front.~~

Has Cleo a
Herself, or was
they any picture?

Jill Krementz

Eudora Welty

*During Eudora Welty's brief stay in New York, we met in her room
at the Algonquin Hotel an hour or so after her train had arrived
in Penn Station. She had given me the wrong room number, so I
first saw her peering out of her door as the elevator opened. A tall,
large-boned, gray-haired woman greeted me apologetically. She
was admittedly nervous about being interviewed, particularly on a
tape recorder. After describing her train ride—she won't fly—she
braced herself and asked if I wouldn't begin the questioning.*

Once the interview (which appeared in the 1972 Fall issue of
The Paris Review) *got under way, she grew more at ease. As she
herself might say, she was not* unforthcoming. *She speaks with a
Deep Southern drawl, deliberately, measuring her words, listening,
so it seems, to her own voice. She is extremely private and won't
answer anything personal about herself or about friends.*

273

INTERVIEWER: You wrote somewhere that we should still tolerate Jane Austen's kind of family novel. Is Austen a kindred spirit?

WELTY: *Tolerate?* I should just think so! I love and admire all she does, and profoundly, but I don't read her or anyone else for "kindredness." The piece you're referring to was written on assignment for *Brief Lives,* an anthology Louis Kronenberger was editing. He did offer me either Jane Austen or Chekhov, and Chekhov I do dare to think is more "kindred." I feel closer to him in spirit, but I couldn't read Russian, which I felt whoever wrote about him should be able to do. Chekhov is one of us—so close to today's world, to my mind, and very close to the South—which Stark Young pointed out a long time ago.

INTERVIEWER: Why is Chekhov close to today's South?

WELTY: He loved the singularity in people, the individuality. He took for granted the sense of family. He had the sense of fate overtaking a way of life, and his Russian humor seems to me kin to the humor of a Southerner. It's the kind that lies mostly in character. You know, in *Uncle Vanya* and *The Cherry Orchard,* how people are always gathered together and talking and talking, no one's really listening. Yet there's a great love and understanding that prevails through it, and a knowledge and acceptance of each other's idiosyncracies, a tolerance of them, and also an acute enjoyment of the dramatic. Like in *The Three Sisters,* when the fire is going on, how they talk right on through their exhaustion, and Vershinin says, "I feel a strange excitement in the air," and laughs and sings and talks about the future. That kind of responsiveness to the world, to whatever happens, out of their own deeps of character seems very Southern to me. Anyway, I took a temperamental delight in Chekhov, and gradually the connection was borne in upon me.

INTERVIEWER: Do you ever return to Virginia Woolf?

WELTY: Yes. She was the one who opened the door. When I read *To the Lighthouse,* I felt, Heavens, *what is this?* I was so excited by the experience I couldn't sleep or eat. I've read it many times since, though more often these days I go back to her diary. Any day you open it to will be tragic, and yet all the marvelous things she says about her work, about working, leave you filled with joy that's stronger than your misery for her. Remember— "I'm not very far along, but I think I have my statues against the sky"? Isn't that beautiful?

INTERVIEWER: About your own work, are you surprised that *Losing Battles* was on the best-seller list—a first for you, I believe?

WELTY: It occurred to me right at first it must be a fluke—that whoever had that place on the best-seller list had just got up and given me his seat—let the lady sit down, she's tottering. Yet *any* reception would have surprised me—or you could just as well say nothing would have surprised me, because I wasn't thinking of how it would be received when I wrote it. I thought about the opinion of a handful of friends I would love to have love that book, but not about the public.

INTERVIEWER: Do you write for your friends?

WELTY: At the time of writing, I don't write for my friends or myself, either; I write for *it*, for the pleasure of *it*. I believe if I stopped to wonder what So-and-so would think, or what I'd feel like if this were read by a stranger, I would be paralyzed. I care what my friends think, very deeply—and it's only after they've read the finished thing that I really can rest, deep down. But in the writing, I have to just keep going straight through with only the *thing* in mind and what it dictates.

It's so much an inward thing that reading the proofs later can be a real shock. When I received them for my first book—no, I guess it was for *Delta Wedding*—I thought, *I* didn't write this. It was a page of dialogue—I might as well have never seen it before. I wrote to my editor, John Woodburn, and told him something had happened to that page in the typesetting. He was kind, not even surprised—maybe this happens to all writers. He called me up and read me from the manuscript—word for word what the proofs said. Proofs don't shock me any longer, yet there's still a strange moment with every book when I move from the position of writer to the position of reader, and I suddenly see my words with the eyes of the cold public. It gives me a terrible sense of exposure, as if I'd gotten sunburned.

INTERVIEWER: Do you make changes in galleys?

WELTY: I correct or change words, but I can't rewrite a scene or make a major change because there's a sense then of someone looking over my shoulder. It's necessary, anyway, to trust that moment when you were sure at last you had done all you could, done your best for that time. When it's finally in print, you're delivered—you don't ever have to look at it again. It's too late to worry about its failings. I'll have to apply any lessons this book has taught me toward writing the next one.

INTERVIEWER: Is *Losing Battles* a departure from your previous fiction?

WELTY: I wanted to see if I could do something that was new for me: translating every thought and feeling into action and speech, speech being another form of action—to bring the whole life of it off through the completed gesture, so to speak. I felt that I'd been writing too much by way of description, of introspection on the part of my characters. I tried to see if I could make everything shown, brought forth, without benefit of the author's telling any more about what was going on inside the characters' minds and hearts. For me, this makes almost certainly for comedy —which I love to write best of all. Now I see it might be a transition toward writing a play.

INTERVIEWER: Did you know what you were going to write before you put it on paper?

WELTY: Yes, it was there in my head, but events proliferated as I went along. For instance, I thought all the action in the novel would be contained in one day and night, but a folder started to fill up with things marked "Next A.M." I didn't foresee the stories that grew out of the stories—that was one of the joys of working the novel out. I thought the book would be short, and instead it was three or four times longer than my normal work. There's no way of estimating its original length because I had great chunks of things in paper clips which weren't numbered until they went to the printer. And I must have thrown away at least as much as I kept in the book.

INTERVIEWER: Did you learn anything new about writing dialogue?

WELTY: I believe so. In its beginning, dialogue's the easiest thing in the world to write when you have a good ear, which I think I have. But as it goes on, it's the most difficult, because it has so many ways to function. Sometimes I needed to make a speech do three or four or five things at once—reveal what the character said but also what he thought he said, what he hid, what others were going to think he meant, and what they misunderstood, and so forth—all in his single speech. And the speech would have to keep the essence of this one character, his whole particular outlook in concentrated form. This isn't to say I succeeded. But I guess it explains why dialogue gives me my greatest pleasure in writing. I used to laugh out loud sometimes when I wrote it—the way P. G. Wodehouse is said to do. I'd think of some things my characters would say, and even if I couldn't use it, I would write the scene out just to let them loose on something —my private show.

INTERVIEWER: Where does the dialogue come from?

WELTY: Familiarity. Memory of the way things get said. Once you have heard certain expressions, sentences, you almost never forget them. It's like sending a bucket down the well and it always comes up full. You don't know you've remembered, but you have. And you listen for the right word, in the present, and you hear it. Once you're into a story everything seems to apply—what you overhear on a city bus is exactly what your character would say on the page you're writing. Wherever you go, you meet part of your story. I guess you're tuned in for it, and the right things are sort of magnetized—if you can think of your ears as magnets. I could hear someone saying—and I had to cut this out—"What, you never ate goat?" And someone answering, "Goat! Please don't say you serve *goat* at this reunion. I wasn't told it was *goat* I was served. I thought—" and so on, and then the recipe, and then it ended up with—I can't remember exactly now—it ended with, "You can do a whole lot of things with vinegar." Well, all these things I would just laugh about and think about for so long and put them in. And then I'd think, that's just plain indulgence. Take it out! And I'd take it out.

INTERVIEWER: Are you an eavesdropper?

WELTY: I'm not as much as I used to be, or would like to be, because I don't hear as well as I used to, or there's too much other noise everywhere. But I've heard some wonderful remarks. Well, in the South, everybody stays busy talking all the time—they're not sorry for you to overhear their tales. I don't feel in helping myself I ever did anything underhanded. I was *helping out.*

INTERVIEWER: Do you think this oral tradition, so to speak, accounts for your vigorous use of dialogue?

WELTY: I think it accounts for the pleasure people take in a story told. It's a treasure I helped myself to. I took it for my ways and means, and that's proper and justified: Our people talk that way. They learn and teach and think and enjoy that way. Southerners do have, they've inherited, a narrative sense of human destiny. This may or may not come out in *Losing Battles.* A reunion is everybody remembering together—remembering and relating when their people were born and what happened in their lives, what that made happen to their children, and how it was that they died. There's someone to remember a man's whole life, every bit of the way along. I think that's a marvelous thing, and I'm glad I got to know something of it. In New York you may have the greatest and most congenial friends, but it's extraordinary if you ever know anything about them except that little wedge of their life that you meet with the little wedge of your life. You don't get that sense of a continuous narrative line. You never see the full circle. But in the South, where people don't move about as much, even now, and where they once hardly ever moved away at all, the pattern of life was always right there.

INTERVIEWER: Would you say that Southerners—Deep Southerners—are more open than Northerners?

WELTY: I think we have a sort of language we all understand and speak—a shorthand of some kind, based on familiarity—but I'm not sure we're more open. We may not tell as much as we think we do, and we may not hide as much as we think we do. We're just more used to talking—as you can see—and the subject doesn't especially cut us down.

INTERVIEWER: And that profoundly affects your fiction?

WELTY: I think that's what gives a pattern to it, and a sense of its shape to me. I do want to say that I'm only speaking for myself when I speak of Southern qualities, because I don't know how other people work. It may be entirely different, especially with a genius like William Faulkner, who had such a comprehensive sense of the whole deep, deep past and more far-reaching, bred-in country knowledge than I have, which is so valuable, besides all the rest of his equipment that I don't need to tell you about.

INTERVIEWER: Did you know Faulkner?

WELTY: Slightly and over a long period of time, but not well. I liked him ever so much. We met at a dinner party in Oxford, just old friends of his and old friends of mine, which was the right way for it to happen, and it was just grand. We sang hymns, and we sang some old ballads—and the next day he invited me to go sailing. If we ever met in New York, we just talked about being in Oxford. *He* didn't bring up writing, and if he didn't, you know *I* wasn't going to bring it up! But when he was working in Hollywood, he once wrote me a two-line letter—this was long before we met—and told me he liked a little book of mine called *The Robber Bridegroom* and said would I let him know if he could ever do anything for me. It was on a little piece of notebook paper, written in that fine, neat, sort of unreadable hand, in pencil—and I've lost it.

INTERVIEWER: Did you feel at all influenced by his presence?

WELTY: I don't honestly think so. It is hard to be sure about such things. I was naturally in the deepest awe and reverence of him. But that's no help in your own writing. Nobody can help you but yourself. So often I'm asked how I could have written a word with William Faulkner living in Mississippi, and this question amazes me. It was like living near a big mountain, something majestic—it made me happy to know it was there, all that work of his life. But it wasn't a helping or hindering presence. Its magnitude, all by itself, made it something remote in my own working life. When I thought of Faulkner it was when I *read*.

On the other hand, he didn't seem remote to everybody in being our great writer. I know a story about him, though he never knew anybody knew of it, I'd bet. Mississippi is full of writers, and I heard this from the person it was told to. A lady had decided she'd write a novel and got along fine till she came to the love scene. "So," she told my friend, "I thought, there's William Faulkner, sitting right up there in Oxford. Why not send it to William Faulkner and ask him?" So she sent it to him, and time went by, and she didn't ever hear from him, and so she called him up. Because there he was. She said, "Mr. Faulkner, did you ever get that love scene I sent you?" He said yes, he had got it. And she said, "Well, what did you think of it?" And he said, "Well, honey, it's not the way I'd do it—but you go *right ahead.*" Now, wasn't that gentle of him?

INTERVIEWER: Do people give you unpublished manuscripts to read? I mean, women especially tend to write voluminous historical novels, and I wonder if any of them are in Jackson.

WELTY: I wouldn't be surprised. I don't think there's any neck of the woods they're not in. Yes, I get sent manuscripts, but those historical and Gothic novels are really a subject on which I know nothing, and I say so. There is, in point of fact, a good deal of writing talent in general around our state now—a lot of good young ones, serious ones.

INTERVIEWER: Did you ever feel part of a literary community, along with people like Flannery O'Connor, Carson McCullers, Katherine Anne Porter, or Caroline Gordon?

WELTY: I'm not sure there's any dotted line connecting us up, though all of us knew about each other, and all of us, I think, respected and read each other's work and understood it. And some of us are friends of long standing. I don't think there was any passing about of influences, but there's a lot of pleasure in thinking in whose lifetimes your own lifetime has happened to come along. Of course, Katherine Anne Porter was wonderfully generous to me from the beginning. At the time I began sending my first stories to *The Southern Review,* she read them and wrote to me from Baton Rouge inviting me to come down to see her. It took me, I suppose, six months or a year to fully get up my nerve. Twice I got as far as Natchez and turned around and came back. But I finally did get there, and Katherine Anne couldn't have been more welcoming. Later on, she wrote the introduction to my first book of stories, and I owe her very much for that. We've been friends all these years.

INTERVIEWER: How would you feel about a biography about yourself?

WELTY: Shy, and discouraged at the very thought, because to me a writer's work should be everything. A writer's whole feeling, the force of his whole life, can go into a story—but what he's worked for is to get an objective piece down on paper. That should be read instead of some account of his life, with that understanding—here is something which now exists and was made by the hands of this person. Read it for what it is. It doesn't even matter too much whose hands they were. Well, of course, it does—I was just exaggerating to prove my point. But your private life should be kept private. My own I don't think would particularly interest anybody, for that matter. But I'd guard it; I feel strongly about that. They'd have a hard time trying to find something about me. I think I'd better burn everything up. It's best to burn letters, but at least I've never kept diaries or journals. All my manuscripts I've given to the Department of Archives and History in Jackson as they came out because that's my hometown and the director is a lifelong friend. But I don't give them everything. I must have a trunk full of stuff that I didn't give because I didn't think it was anybody's else's concern, or that anybody would even care to see my mistakes and false turns. Like about eating goat and all the million things that I left out.

INTERVIEWER: Why do *Losing Battles* and *Delta Wedding* take place back in the 1920s and 1930s?

WELTY: It was a matter of setting the stage and confining the story. These are both family stories, and I didn't want them inhibited by outward events I couldn't control. In the case of *Delta Wedding,* I remember I made a careful investigation to find the year in which nothing very terrible had happened in the Delta by way of floods or fires or wars which would have taken the men away. I settled it by the almanac. It was a little inconvenient for me because I myself was only a little girl during the era I was writing about—that's why I let a little girl be the observer of part of it. In the case of *Losing Battles,* I wanted to write about a family who had *nothing.* A bare stage. I chose the time that was the very hardest, when people had the least and the stage could be the barest—and that was the Depression, of course.

INTERVIEWER: Do you prefer working with a bare stage?

WELTY: In this case, it was in order to overcrowd it with people. I start with ideas about character and situation, and the technique grows out of these as I grow into the work. It's different, of course, for every story. In *Losing Battles* I wanted to write about people who had nothing at all and yet had all the resources of their own character and situation to do what they could about their lives.

INTERVIEWER: Were you familiar with plantation life when you wrote *Delta Wedding?*

WELTY: No, but I had some friends who came from there, and I used to hear their stories, and I'd be taken on picnics and visits there. Family visits. The Delta is very rich and visually striking, but completely flat. I would find it maddening after days with nothing but the horizon. Just before you reach it, there are high bluffs, and to get in you plunge down a deep hill, and from then on there's nothing but flatness. Some of the things I saw and heard began to stick. Some family tales and sayings are right in the book, though by now I can't remember which are true and which are made up.

INTERVIEWER: John Crowe Ransom wrote in a review that *Delta Wedding* might well be "one of the last novels in the tradition of the Old South."

WELTY: I revere Mr. Ransom, but his meaning here is not quite clear to me. I wasn't trying to write a novel of the Old

South. I don't think of myself as writing out of any special tradition, and I'd hesitate to accept that sanction for *Delta Wedding*. I'd hesitate still more today because the term itself, "Old South," has a connotation of something unreal and not quite straightforward.

INTERVIEWER: Your parents weren't from the Deep South originally. Do you think that contributed to your ironic perspective?

WELTY: It may have given me balance. But other factors mattered more. My father's father owned a farm in Southern Ohio, and my mother's father was a country lawyer and farmer in West Virginia, and both my mother's parents came from Virginia families made up mostly of teachers and preachers. Some of these wrote for newspapers or kept journals, though none wrote fiction. But the family influence I felt came from the important fact that they all loved to read and that I was brought up with books. Yet my parents would have been the people they were, people of character, no matter where they were from, and I would have been their child wherever I was born. I'm a native Southerner, but as a writer I think background matters most in how well it teaches you to look around and see clearly what's there and in how deeply it nourishes your imagination.

INTERVIEWER: "Where is the Voice Coming From?" is about the Medgar Evers assassination and must be your only topical story.

WELTY: I'm certain it is. It pushed up through something else I was working on. I had been having a feeling of uneasiness over the things being written about the South at that time because most of them were done in other parts of the country, and I thought most were synthetic. They were perfectly well-intentioned stories but generalities written from a distance to illustrate generalities. When that murder was committed, it suddenly crossed my consciousness that I knew what was in that man's mind because I'd lived all my life where it happened. It was the strangest feeling of horror and compulsion all in one. I tried to write from the interior of my own South, and that's why I dared to put it in the first person. The title isn't very good; I'd like to get a better one. At the time I wrote it—it was overnight—no one knew who the murderer was, and I just meant by the title that whoever was speaking, I—the writer—knew, was in a position to know, what the murderer must be saying and why.

INTERVIEWER: Do real events hinder you in writing?

WELTY: Well, if you write about an actual event, you can't shape it the way you can an imaginary one. In "The Voice" I was writing about the real thing, and at the point of its happening. I was like a real-life detective trying to discover who did it. I don't mean the name of the murderer but his *nature*. That's not really a short-story writer's prerogative, or is it? Anyway, as events went to prove, I think I came close to pinpointing the mind, but I went a bit wide of the mark in placing the social background of the person arrested for it. As a friend of mine said, "You thought it was a Snopes, and it was a Compson." However, in some ways, that isn't a very lasting distinction any more.

INTERVIEWER: Do you see a difference between your early stories in *A Curtain of Green* and *The Wide Net* where you deal more with the grotesque and grim than you do in *The Bride of the Innisfallen?*

WELTY: It's a difference not really in subject matter so much as in the ways I approached it. In those early stories I'm sure I needed the device of what you call the "grotesque." That is, I hoped to differentiate characters by their physical qualities as a way of showing what they were like inside—it seemed to me then the most direct way to do it. This is an afterthought, though. I don't suppose I did it as consciously as all that, and I didn't know it was the easiest way. But it is easier to show somebody as lonely if you make him deaf and dumb than if you go feeling your way into his mind. And there was another reason for making the boy in "First Love" a deaf character: one of the other characters—Aaron Burr—was a real person. I couldn't invent conversation for him as I could for an imaginary character, so I had him speak in front of a deaf boy who could report and interpret him in his own way—that is, to suit the story. It's instinctive for a writer to show acute feeling or intense states of emotion by translating it into something visible—red hair, if nothing else. But it's not necessary. I believe I'm writing about the same inward things now without resorting to such obvious devices. But all devices—and the use of symbols is another—must come about organically, out of the story. I feel emphatic about that.

INTERVIEWER: Are you also talking here about other early stories like "Lily Daw and the Three Ladies" and "Petrified Man"?

WELTY: Well, when I wrote my first stories, I wrote much faster, and it failed to occur to me that I could write them any other way, and perhaps better the second time. They show all the weaknesses of the headlong. I never rewrote, I just wrote. The plots in these stories are weak because I didn't know enough to worry about plots. In the dialogue stories, they came into being exactly as the dialogue led them along. I didn't realize their real weakness until I began reading stories in public—and my ear told me. They could have been made stronger so easily. Sometimes I fixed them up a little for my readings—cut, transposed—small things, just to see the difference.

INTERVIEWER: What inspired "Powerhouse"?

WELTY: I wrote it in one night after I'd been to a concert and dance in Jackson where Fats Waller played. I tried to write my idea of the life of the traveling artist and performer—not Fats Waller himself, but any artist—in the alien world and tried to put it in the words and plot suggested by the music I'd been listening to. It was a daring attempt for a writer like me—as daring as it was to write about the murderer of Medgar Evers on *that* night —and I'm not qualified to write about music or performers. But trying it pleased me then, and it still does please me.

INTERVIEWER: Are there problems with ending a story?

WELTY: Not so far, but I could have made mistakes without knowing it yet. It's really part of plotting to know the exact moment you're through. I go by my ear, and this may trick me. When I read, I hear what's on the page. I don't know whose voice it is, but some voice is reading to me, and when I write my own stories, I hear it, too. I have a visual mind, and I *see* everything

I write, but I have to hear the words when they're put down. Oh, that sounds absurd. This is not the same as working with dialogue, which of course is another, specialized, kind of hearing.

INTERVIEWER: Your first stories were about Paris.

WELTY: It's not worth remembering. That was when I was a college freshman, sixteen years old. Oh, you know, I was writing about the great world, of which I only knew Jackson, Mississippi. But part of it stemmed from my sense of mystery in people and places, and that's legitimate and lifelong. As for Paris, I remember a sentence I opened one story with, to show you how bad I was: "Monsieur Boule inserted a delicate dagger in Mademoiselle's left side and departed with a poised immediacy." I like to think I didn't take myself seriously then, but I did.

INTERVIEWER: When you sent out "Death of a Traveling Salesman," how did you know you had ended your apprenticeship?

WELTY: I was just beginning it! I was thrilled to find that out. I hadn't conceived of a story's actually being taken. A boy up the street, an old friend, Hubert Creekmore, who's dead now, knew all about sending stories out. He was a writer who started before I did and published many good novels and poems. I wouldn't let him read anything I wrote but just asked him, "Hubert, do you know where I can send this?"—and he said to John Rood of *Manuscript*. So I sent it off, and John Rood took it, and of course I was flabbergasted. So was Hubert! I believe I've always been lucky—my work has always landed safely and among friends.

INTERVIEWER: You were lucky to escape the novel-first requirement that publishers seem to impose upon young writers. They're wary of short story collections.

WELTY: I owe that to John Woodburn, my first editor, who was then at Doubleday, and to Diarmuid Russell, my agent and friend of many years now. I owe it to my nature, too, because I never wrote anything that didn't spring naturally to mind and engage my imagination.

INTERVIEWER: Compared to your stories, I see your novels as

looser, freer, happier works which enjoy reconciliations and a final sense of communion.

WELTY: My natural temperament is one of positive feelings, and I really do work for resolution in a story. I don't think we often see life resolving itself, not in any sort of perfect way, but I like the fiction writer's feeling of being able to confront an experience and resolve it as art, however imperfectly and briefly —to give it a form and try to embody it—to hold it and express it in a story's terms. You have more chance to try it in a novel. A short story is confined to one mood, to which everything in the story pertains. Characters, setting, time, events, are all subject to the mood. And you can try more ephemeral, more fleeting things in a story—you can work more by suggestion—than in a novel. Less is resolved, more is suggested, perhaps.

INTERVIEWER: You reserve the short story for the ephemeral and the novel for the resolution?

WELTY: I can only say such things after the fact. If I'd known I was going to finish *Losing Battles* as a long novel, I don't know that I'd have begun it. I'm a short-story writer who writes novels the hard way, and by accident. You see, all my work grows out of the work itself. It seems to set its form from the idea, which is complete from the start, and a sense of the form is like a vase into which you pour something and fill it up. I have that completely in mind from the beginning, and I don't realize how far I can wander and yet come back. The flexibility and freedom are exciting to me, not being used to them, and they are hard to come by. But no one could have enjoyed more learning those lessons than I did. There's no end to what can be tried, is there? So better luck next time.

INTERVIEWER: Do you think critics have made too much of you as a regional writer, taking off from your own essays on the subject?

WELTY: I don't mind being called a regional writer. It's the critic's job to place and judge. But the critic can't really have a say in what a writer chooses to write about—that's the writer's lone responsibility. I just think of myself as writing about human beings, and I happen to live in a region, as do we all, so I write about what I know—it's the same case for any writer living anywhere. I also happen to love my particular region. If this shows, I don't mind.

INTERVIEWER: Is place your source of inspiration?

WELTY: Not only that, it's my source of knowledge. It tells me the important things. It steers me and keeps me going straight, because place is a definer and a confiner of what I'm doing. It helps me to identify, to recognize and explain. It does so much for you of itself. It saves me. Why, you couldn't write a story that happened nowhere. *I* couldn't, anyway. I couldn't write anything that abstract. I wouldn't be interested in anything that abstract.

INTERVIEWER: How about the function of place in "No Place for You, My Love"?

WELTY: That story is the one that place did the most for. It really wrote the story. I saw that setting only one time—the Delta of the Mississippi River itself, down below New Orleans where it winds toward the Gulf—one time only. Which smote me. It started the story and made it for me—and *was* the story, really. At its very least, place is essential, though. Time and place make the framework that any story's built on. To my mind, a fiction writer's honesty begins right there, in being true to those two facts of time and place. From there, imagination can take him anywhere at all.

You can equally well be true, I feel, to an *impression* of place. A new place seen in a flash may have an impact almost as strong as the place you've grown up in, one you're familiar with down to the bone and know what it's like without having to think. I've written about place from either one extreme or the other but not from partial familiarity or guessing—there's no solidity there.

INTERVIEWER: "Music from Spain" takes place in San Francisco.

WELTY: That's using impression of place. I was in San Francisco for only three or four months—that's seeing it in a flash. That story was all a response to a place, an act of love at first sight.

It's written from the point of view of the stranger, of course—the only way to write about a strange place. On the other hand, I couldn't write a story laid in New York, where I've come so many times—because it's both familiar and unfamiliar, a no man's land.

INTERVIEWER: Where is Morgana, in *The Golden Apples?*

WELTY: It's a made-up Delta town. I was drawn to the name because I always loved the conception of *Fata Morgana*—the illusory shape, the mirage that comes over the sea. All Delta places have names after people, so it was suitable to call it Morgana after some Morgans. My population might not have known there was such a thing as *Fata Morgana*, but illusions weren't unknown to them, all the same—coming in over the cottonfields.

INTERVIEWER: Do you see a similarity between Miss Eckhart in *The Golden Apples* and Julia Mortimer in *Losing Battles*, both being schoolteachers who were civilizing agents and therefore outsiders?

WELTY: It doesn't have to be "therefore"—though mine were indeed outsiders. I suppose they are kin, but teachers like those are all over the South and maybe everywhere else, too—dedicated, and losing their battles, but not losing them every time. I went all through grammar school in Jackson under a principal all of us who went there still remember and talk about—Miss Lorena Duling. This isn't to say I based my character on her, but she gave me insight into what it meant to be a great teacher. And so was my mother one. All her teaching was done by the time I came along, but she told me stories about it. She taught in the little mountain schools in West Virginia, riding to her school on horseback and crossing the river in a boat, teaching children older than she was—she started at fifteen. I think it was my mother who made seventeen silver dollars the first month she taught, and after that they never could quite come up to that high a standard—which also happened to Miss Julia Mortimer. The shaping influence of teachers like that stays real for a lifetime.

INTERVIEWER: I see another group of characters forming a pattern in your work. Virgie Rainey, in *The Golden Apples*, is an individualist and outsider and similar in that respect to Robbie Reid of *Delta Wedding* and Gloria Short of *Losing Battles.*

WELTY: In looking back I can see the pattern. It's funny—when I'm writing, I never see a repeat I make in large or small degree. I learn about it later. In Jackson they were recently doing a play of *The Ponder Heart* when I had just finished writing *Losing Battles.* The new novel was so fresh in my mind, whereas I hadn't thought of *The Ponder Heart* for years. But when I sat in at rehearsals, I kept seeing bits and pieces come up that I thought I had invented for *Losing Battles,* and there they were in another version in *Ponder Heart.* So I thought, it's sort of dismaying, but there it is. Your mind works that way. Yet they occur to me as new every time.

INTERVIEWER: Do you write when you're away from home?

WELTY: I've found it possible to write almost anywhere I've happened to try. I like it at home better because it's much more convenient for an early riser, which I am. And it's the only place where you can really promise yourself time and keep out interruptions. My ideal way to write a short story is to write the whole first draft through in one sitting, then work as long as it takes on revisions, and then write the final version all in one, so that in the end the whole thing amounts to one long sustained effort. That's not possible anywhere, but it comes nearest to being possible in your own home.

INTERVIEWER: Do you typewrite?

WELTY: Yes, and that's useful—it helps give me the feeling of making my work objective. I can correct better if I see it in typescript. After that, I revise with scissors and pins. Pasting is too slow, and you can't undo it, but with pins you can move things from anywhere to anywhere, and that's what I really love doing —putting things in their best and proper place, revealing things at the time when they matter most. Often I shift things from the very beginning to the very end. Small things—one fact, one word —but things important to me. It's possible I have a reverse mind and do things backwards, being a broken left-hander. Just so I've caught on to my weakness.

INTERVIEWER: You rewrite considerably?

WELTY: Yes, I do. Some things I let alone from first to last—the kernel of the story. You know enough not to touch something if it's right. The hardest thing for me is getting people in and out of rooms—the mechanics of a story. A simple act of putting on clothes is almost impossible for me to describe without many false starts. You have to be quick and specific in conveying that sort of action or fact, and also as neat and quiet about it as possible so that it doesn't obtrude. And I find that very challenging, especially to describe an action that I don't do very well myself, like sewing. I made Aunt Lexie in *Losing Battles* a poor sewer so that I wouldn't have to describe it too well. The easiest things to write about are emotions.

INTERVIEWER: And yet the most difficult thing would seem to be the hidden reaches of the human heart, the mystery, those impalpable emotions.

WELTY: For a writer those things are what you start with. You wouldn't have started a story without that awareness—that's what made you begin. That's what makes a character, projects the plot. Because you write from the inside. You can't start with how people look and speak and behave and come to know how they feel. You must know exactly what's in their hearts and minds before they ever set visible foot on the stage. You must know all, then not tell it all, or not tell too much at once: simply the right thing at the right moment. And the same character would be written about entirely differently in a novel as opposed to a short story. In a story you don't go into a character in order to develop him. He was born full grown, and he's present there to perform his part in the story. He's subservient to his function, and he doesn't exist outside it. But in a novel, he may. So you may have to allow for his growth and maybe hold him down and not tell everything you know, or else let him have his full sway—make room for a hero, even, in more spacious premises.

INTERVIEWER: Can you talk objectively about your language, perhaps about your use of metaphor?

WELTY: I don't know how to because I think of the actual

writing as having existence only in the story. When I think of something, I put it into a narrative form, not in analytical form, and so anything I say would be artificial. Which reminds me of an Armenian friend of mine, an artist, who told me that his dreams all happened in the same place. When he went to bed, he'd imagine himself on a sled going down a steep hill; at the foot of the hill was a little town, and by the time he reached it, he was asleep, and his dreams happened right there. He didn't know why or how. And to go to the ridiculous and yet the sublime, there's W. C. Fields, who read an analysis of how he juggled. He couldn't juggle for six years afterwards. He'd never known that was how it was done. He'd just thrown up the balls and juggled.

LINDA KUEHL

12. John Berryman

Born in McAlester, Oklahoma, on October 25, 1914, John Berryman received degrees from Columbia in 1936 and Clare College, Cambridge, in 1938. He taught at Wayne State University, Harvard, Princeton, the University of Washington, the University of Cincinnati, and the University of Minnesota, where from 1955 until his death in 1972 he was Regents Professor of Humanities.

Berryman's articles appeared in many academic journals, and he was the author of a biography, *Stephen Crane* (1950), but he is primarily known as a poet. His first collection, *Poems*, appeared in 1942. This was followed by *The Dispossessed* (1948) and *Homage to Mistress Bradstreet* (1956), which established his reputation. His major work, however, has been considered the Dream Songs, which he began in 1955: *77 Dream Songs* (1964) won the Pulitzer Prize in 1965, and *His Toy, His Dream, His Rest: 308 Dream Songs* (1968) received the National Book Award in 1969. The complete *Dream Songs* was published in 1969. His other later books include *Berryman's Sonnets* (1967), *Short Poems* (1967), and a novel, *Recovery* (1973).

Berryman received many honors, among them the Guarantors and Levinson prizes from *Poetry* magazine (1948), the Shelley Memorial Award (1949), the American Academy Award (1950), the Harriet Monroe Poetry Prize from the University of Chicago (1957), and the Academy of American Poets Fellowship (1966).

John Berryman took his own life on January 7, 1972.

I heard, could be, a Hey there from the wing,
and I wort on: Miss Bessie soundin good
that one, that night of all,
I feelin fair mysef, taxes & things
seem to be back in line, like everybody should
and nobody in the snow on call

so, as I say, the house is givin hell
to Yellow Dog, I blowin like it too
and Bessie always do
when she make a very big sound--after, well,
no sound--I see she totterin--I cross which stage
even at Henry's age

in 2-3 seconds: then we wait and see.
I hear strange horns, Pinetop he hit some chords,
Charley start Empty Bed,
they all come hangin Christmas on some tree
after all trees was thrown out--for the birds, *white*
back to the birds instead.

re/

rel.|rel.|

black

hospital's

*Is there a Negro
slang term?*

John Berryman's "68th Dream Song"

Rollie McKenna

John Berryman

On a Sunday afternoon in late July 1970, John Berryman gave a reading of his poems in a small "people's park" in Minneapolis near the west bank campus of the University of Minnesota. Following the reading, I introduced myself—we hadn't seen each other since I was his student, eight years earlier—and we spent the afternoon in conversation at his house. He had had a very bad winter, he explained, and had spent much of the spring in the extended-care ward at St. Mary's Hospital. I asked him about doing an interview. He agreed, and we set up an appointment for late October.

Berryman spent a week in Mexico at the end of the summer—and had "a marvelous time." A trip to upstate New York for a reading followed, and by early October he was back at St. Mary's. It was there that the interview was conducted, during visiting hours on the twenty-seventh and twenty-ninth of October.

He looked much better than he had during the summer, was

heavier and more steady on his feet. He again smoked, and drank coffee almost continually. The room was spacious, and Berryman was quite at home in it. In addition to the single bed, it contained a tray-table that extended over the bed, a chair, and two night-stands, one of which held a large AM-FM radio and the usual hospital accoutrements. Books and papers covered the other night-stand, the table, and the broad window sill.

Berryman was usually slow to get going on an answer, as he made false starts looking for just the right words. Once he started talking, he would continue until he had exhausted the subject—thus some of his answers are very long. This method left unasked questions, and the most important of these were mailed to him later for written answers. In contrast to the taped answers, the written answers turned out to be brief, flat, and even dull. (These have been discarded.) By way of apology, he explained that he was again devoting his energies almost entirely to writing poetry.

An edited typescript of the interview was sent him in January 1971. He returned it in March, having made very few changes. He did supply some annotations, and these have been left as he put them.

INTERVIEWER: Mr. Berryman, recognition came to you late in comparison with writers like Robert Lowell and Delmore Schwartz. What effect do you think fame has on a poet? Can this sort of success ruin a writer?

BERRYMAN: I don't think there are any generalizations at all. If a writer gets hot early, then his work ought to become known early. If it doesn't, he is in danger of feeling neglected. We take it that all young writers overestimate their work. It's impossible not to—I mean if you recognized what shit you were writing, you wouldn't write it. You have to believe in your stuff—every day has to be the new day on which the new poem may be *it*. Well, fame supports that feeling. It gives self-confidence, it gives a sense of an actual, contemporary audience, and so on. On the other hand, unless it is sustained, it can cause trouble—and it is very seldom sustained. If your first book is a smash, your second book gets kicked in the face, and your third book, and lots of people, like Delmore, can't survive that disappointment. From that point of view, early fame is very dangerous indeed, and my situation, which was so painful to me for many years, was really in a way beneficial.

I overestimated myself, as it turned out, and felt bitter, bitterly neglected; but I had certain admirers, certain high judges on my side from the beginning, so that I had a certain amount of support. Moreover, I had a kind of indifference on my side—much as Joseph Conrad did. A reporter asked him once about reviews, and he said, "I don't read my reviews. I measure them." Now, until I was about thirty-five years old, I not only didn't read my reviews, I didn't measure them, I never even looked at them. That is so peculiar that close friends of mine wouldn't believe me when I told them. I thought that was indifference, but now I'm convinced that it was just that I had no skin on—you know, I was afraid of being killed by some remark. Oversensitivity. But there was an *element* of indifference in it, and so the public indifference to my work was countered with a certain amount of genuine indifference on my part, which has been very helpful since I became a celebrity. Auden once said that the best situation for a poet is to be taken up early and held for a considerable time and then dropped after he has reached the level of indifference.

Something else is in my head; a remark of Father Hopkins to Bridges. Two completely unknown poets in their thirties—fully mature—Hopkins, one of the great poets of the century, and Bridges, awfully good. Hopkins with no audience and Bridges with thirty readers. He says, "Fame in itself is nothing. The only thing that matters is virtue. Jesus Christ is the only true literary critic. But," he said, "from any lesser level or standard than that, we must recognize that fame is the true and appointed setting of men of genius." That seems to me appropriate. This business about geniuses in neglected garrets is for the birds. The idea that a man is somehow no good just because he becomes very popular, like Frost, is nonsense, also. There are exceptions, Chatterton, Hopkins, of course, Rimbaud, you can think of various cases, but on the whole, men of genius were judged by their contemporaries very much as posterity judges them. So if I were talking to a young writer, I would recommend the cultivation of extreme indifference to both praise and blame because praise will lead you to vanity, and blame will lead you to self-pity, and both are bad for writers.

INTERVIEWER: What is your reaction to such comments as: "If Berryman is not America's finest living poet, then he is surely running a close second to Lowell"?

BERRYMAN: Well, I don't know. I don't get any *frisson* of excitement back here, and my bank account remains the same, and my view of my work remains the same, and in general I can say that everything is much the same after that is over.

INTERVIEWER: It seems that you, along with Frost and several other American writers, were appreciated earlier in England than in America.

BERRYMAN That's true. More in Frost's case. Stephen Crane is another.

INTERVIEWER: Why do you think this is true?

BERRYMAN: I wonder. The literary cultures are still very different. Right this minute, for example, the two best reviewers of poetry in English, and perhaps the only two to whom I have paid the slightest attention, are both Englishmen—Kermode and Alvarez. Of course, that's just a special case—ten years ago it was different, but our people have died or stopped practicing criticism. We couldn't put out a thing like the *Times Literary Supplement.* We just don't have it. Education at the elite level is better in England, humanistic education—never mind technical education, where we are superior or at least equal—but Cambridge, Oxford, London, and now the red-brick universities provide a much higher percentage of intelligent readers in the population —the kind of people who listen to the Third Programme and read the *Times Literary Supplement.* They are rather compact and form a body of opinion from which the reviewers, both good and mediocre, don't have to stand out very far. In our culture, we also, of course, have good readers, but not as high a percentage—and they are incredibly dispersed geographically. It makes a big difference.

INTERVIEWER: You, along with Lowell, Sylvia Plath, and several others, have been called a confessional poet. How do you react to that label?

BERRYMAN: With rage and contempt! Next question.

INTERVIEWER: Are the sonnets "confessional"?

BERRYMAN: Well, they're about her and me. I don't know. The word doesn't mean anything. I understand the confessional to be a place where you go and talk with a priest. I personally haven't been to confession since I was twelve years old.

INTERVIEWER: You once said: "I masquerade as a writer. Actually I am a scholar." At another time you pointed out that your passport gives your occupation as "Author" and not "Teacher." How do your roles as teacher and scholar affect your role as poet?

BERRYMAN: Very, very hard question. Housman is one of my heroes and always has been. He was a detestable and miserable man. Arrogant, unspeakably lonely, cruel, and so on, but an absolutely marvelous minor poet, I think, and a great scholar. And I'm about *equally* interested in those two activities. In him they are perfectly distinct. You are dealing with an absolute schizophrenic. In me they seem closer together, but I just don't know. Schwartz once asked me why it was that all my Shakespearean study had never showed up anywhere in my poetry, and I couldn't answer the question. It was a piercing question because his early poems are really very much influenced by Shakespeare's early plays. I seem to have been sort of untouched by Shakespeare, although I have had him in my mind since I was twenty years old.

INTERVIEWER: I don't agree with that. One of the dream songs, one of those written to the memory of Delmore Schwartz—let me see if I can find it. Here, number 147. These lines:

Henry's mind grew blacker the more he thought.
He looked onto the world like the act of an aged whore.
Delmore Delmore.
He flung to pieces and they hit the floor.

That sounds very Shakespearean to me.

BERRYMAN: That sounds like *Troilus and Cressida,* doesn't it? One of my very favorite plays. I would call that Shakespearean. Not to praise it, though, only in description. I was half hysterical writing that song. It just burst onto the page. It took only as long to compose as it takes to write it down.

INTERVIEWER: Well, that covers scholarship. How about teaching? Does teaching only get in the way of your work as a poet?

BERRYMAN: It depends on the kind of teaching you do. If you teach creative writing, you get absolutely nothing out of it. Or English—what are you teaching? People you read twenty years ago. Maybe you pick up a little if you keep on preparing, but very few people keep on preparing. Everybody is lazy, and poets, in addition to being lazy, have another activity which is very demanding, so they tend to slight their teaching. But I give courses in the history of civilization, and when I first began teaching here I nearly went crazy. I was teaching Christian origins and the Middle Ages, and I had certain weak spots. I was O.K. with *The Divine Comedy* and certain other things, but I had an awful time of it. I worked it out once, and it took me nine hours to prepare a fifty-minute lecture. I have learned much more from giving these lecture courses than I ever learned at Columbia or Cambridge. It has forced me out into areas where I wouldn't otherwise have been, and since I am a scholar, these things are connected. I make myself acquainted with the scholarship. Suppose I'm lecturing on Augustine. My Latin is very rusty, but I'll pay a certain amount of attention to the Latin text in the Loeb edition, with the English across the page. Then I'll visit the library and consult five or six old and recent works on St. Augustine, who is a particular interest of mine, anyway. Now all that becomes part of your equipment for poetry, even for lyric poetry. The Bradstreet poem is a very learned poem. There is a lot of theology in it, there is a lot of theology in *The Dream Songs*. Anything is useful to a poet. Take observation of nature, of which I have absolutely none. It makes possible a world of moral observation for Frost, or Hopkins. So scholarship and teaching are directly useful to my activity as a writer.

INTERVIEWER: But not the teaching of creative writing. You don't think there is any value in that for you as a poet.

BERRYMAN: I enjoy it. Sometimes your kids prove awfully good. Snodgrass is well known now, and Bill Merwin—my students— and others, and it's delightful to be of service to somebody. But most of them have very little talent, and you can't overencourage them; that's impossible. Many of my friends teach creative writing. I'm not putting it down, and it certainly is an honest way of earning a living, but I wouldn't recommend it to a poet. It is better to teach history or classics or philosophy or the kind of work I do here in Humanities.

INTERVIEWER: You have given Yeats and Auden as early influences on your poetry. What did you learn from them?

BERRYMAN: Practically everything I could then manipulate. On the other hand, they didn't take me very far because by the time I was writing really well, in 1948—that's the beginning of the Bradstreet poem and the last poems in the collection called *The Dispossessed*—there was no Yeats around and no Auden. Some influence from Rilke, some influence from a poet whom I now consider very bad, Louis Aragon, in a book called *Crèvecoeur* —he conned me. He took all his best stuff from Apollinaire, whom I hadn't then read, and swept me off my feet. I wrote a poem called "Narcissus Moving," which is as much like Aragon as possible, and maybe it's just as bad. I don't know. Then the Bradstreet poem—it is not easy to see the literary ancestry of that poem. Who has been named? Hopkins. I don't see that. Of course there are certain verbal practices, but on the whole, not. The stanza has been supposed to be derived from the stanza of "The Wreck of the Deutschland." I don't see that. I have never read

"The Wreck of the Deutschland," to tell you the truth, except the first stanza. Wonderful first stanza. But I really just couldn't get onto it. It's a set piece, and I don't like set pieces. I'll bet it's no good—well, you know, not comparable with the great short poems. Then Lowell has been named. I see the influence of *Lord Weary's Castle* in some of the later poems in *The Dispossessed*. There's no doubt about it. In the Bradstreet poem, as I seized inspiration from *Augie March*, I sort of seized inspiration, I think, from Lowell, rather than imitated him. I can't think, offhand— I haven't read it in many years—of a single passage in the Bradstreet poem which distinctly sounds like Lowell. However, I may be quite wrong about this since people have named him. Other people? I don't think so.

INTERVIEWER: How about Eliot? You must have had to reckon with Eliot in one way or another, positively or negatively.

BERRYMAN: My relationship with Eliot was highly ambiguous. In the first place, I refused to meet him on three occasions in England, and I think I mentioned this in one of the poems I wrote last spring. I had to fight shy of Eliot. There was a certain amount of hostility in it, too. I only began to appreciate Eliot much later, after I was secure in my own style. I now rate him very high. I think he is one of the greatest poets who ever lived. Only sporadically good. What he would do—he would collect himself and write a masterpiece, then relax for several years writing prose, earning a living, and so forth; then he'd collect himself and write another masterpiece, very different from the first, and so on. He did this about five times, and after the *Four Quartets* he lived on for twenty years. Wrote absolutely nothing. It's a very strange career. Very—a pure system of spasms. My career is like that. It is horribly like that. But I feel deep sympathy, admiration, and even love for Eliot over all the recent decades.

INTERVIEWER: You knew Dylan Thomas pretty well, didn't you?

BERRYMAN: Pretty well, pretty well. We weren't close friends.

INTERVIEWER: Any influence there?

BERRYMAN: No. And that's surprising, very surprising, because we used to knock around in Cambridge and London. We didn't discuss our poetry much. He was far ahead of me. Occasionally he'd show me a poem, or I'd show him a poem. He was very fond of making suggestions. He didn't like a line in a poem of mine, later published by Robert Penn Warren in *The Southern Review,* called "Night and the City"—a very bad poem modeled on a poem by John Peale Bishop called "The Return." Well, Dylan didn't like one line, and so he proposed this line: "A bare octagonal ballet for penance." Now, my poem was rather incoherent, but couldn't contain—you know, in the military sense—it couldn't contain that! I was very fond of him. I loved him, and I thought he was a master. I was wrong about that. He was not a master; he became a master only much later on. What he was then is a great rhetorician. Terrific. But the really great poems only came towards the end of World War II, I think. There was no influence.

INTERVIEWER: Do you think he had an impulse towards self-destruction?

BERRYMAN: Oh, absolutely. He was doomed already when I first knew him. Everybody warned him for many years.

INTERVIEWER: Can one generalize on that? So many of the poets of your generation have encountered at least personal tragedy—flirting with suicide, and so on.

BERRYMAN: I don't know. The record is very bad. Vachel Lindsay killed himself. Hart Crane killed himself, more important. Sara Teasdale—quite a good poet at the end, killed herself. Then Miss Plath recently. Randall—it's not admitted, but apparently he did kill himself—and Roethke and Delmore might just as well have died of alcoholism. They died of heart attacks, but that's one of the main ways to die from alcoholism. And Dylan died in an alcoholic coma. Well, the actual cause of death was bronchitis. But he went into shock in the Chelsea, where I was staying also, and they got him to the hospital in an ambulance, where he was wrongly treated. They gave him morphine, which is contra-indicated in cases of alcoholic shock. He wouldn't have lived, anyway, but they killed him. He lay in a coma for five days.

INTERVIEWER: You were there, weren't you?

BERRYMAN: I was in the corridor, ten feet away.

INTERVIEWER: What was it like to take high tea with William Butler Yeats?

BERRYMAN: All I can say is that my mouth was dry and my heart was in my mouth. Thomas had very nearly succeeded in getting me drunk earlier in the day. He was full of scorn for Yeats, as he was for Eliot, Pound, Auden. He thought my admiration for Yeats was the funniest thing in that part of London. It wasn't until about three o'clock that I realized that he and I were drinking more than usual. I didn't drink much at that time; Thomas drank much more than I did. I had the sense to leave. I went back to my chambers, Cartwright Gardens, took a cold bath, and just made it for the appointment. I remember the taxi ride over. The taxi was left over from the First World War, and when we arrived in Pall Mall—we could see the Atheneum—the driver said he didn't feel he could get in. Finally I decided to abandon ship and take off on my own. So I went in and asked for Mr. Yeats. Very much like asking, "Is Mr. Ben Jonson here?" And he came down. He was much taller than I expected, and haggard. Big, though, big head, rather wonderful looking in a sort of a blunt, patrician kind of way, but there was something shrunken also. He told me he was just recovering from an illness. He was very courteous, and we went in to tea. At a certain point, I had a cigarette, and I asked him if he would like one. To my great surprise he said yes. So I gave him a Craven-A and then lit it for him, and I thought, Immortality is mine! From now on it's just a question of reaping the fruits of my effort. He did most of the talking. I asked him a few questions. He did not ask me any questions about myself, although he was extremely courteous and very kind. At one point he said, "I have reached the age when my daughter can beat me at croquet," and I thought, Hurrah, he's human! I made notes on the interview afterwards, which I have probably lost. One comment in particular I remember. He said, "I never revise now"— you know how much he revised his stuff—"but in the interests of a more passionate syntax." Now that struck me as a very good remark. I have no idea what it meant and still don't know, but the longer I think about it, the better I like it. He recommended various books to me by his friend, the liar, Gogarty, and I forget who else. The main thing was just the presence and existence of my hero.

INTERVIEWER: William Faulkner once ventured to rate himself among contemporary novelists. He rated Thomas Wolfe first, himself second, Dos Passos third, Hemingway fourth, and Steinbeck fifth.

BERRYMAN: Oh, no! Really? That's deluded! The list is abominable. I think what must have happened is this. There are two ways to rank writers: in terms of gift and in terms of achievement. He was ranking Wolfe in terms of gift. Wolfe had a colossal gift. His achievement, though—to rank him first and Hemingway fourth is openly grotesque.

INTERVIEWER: Would you be interested in doing this, in ranking yourself among contemporary American poets?

BERRYMAN: I don't think I could do it. I'll tell you why. First, most of these characters are personal friends of mine, and you just don't sit around ranking your friends. After I published *The Dispossessed* in '48, I quit reviewing poetry. By that time I knew most of the people writing verse, and how can you deliver a fair judgment of the man you had dinner with the night before? Preposterous! It's supposed to be easy, but actually it's impossible. My love of such poets as Schwartz, *In Dreams Begin Responsibilities*, Roethke, and Lowell, *Lord Weary's Castle*, is very great. I would love to be in their company, and I feel convinced that I am, but I don't want to do any ranking. It's just not a sweat.

INTERVIEWER: In *The Dream Songs* there is a passage about assistant professors becoming associate professors by working on your poems. How do you feel about being cannon fodder for aspiring young critics and graduate students?

BERRYMAN: As for the graduate students, some of the work they do is damned interesting. A woman somewhere in the South did an eighty-page thesis investigating the three little epigraphs to the *77 Dream Songs* and their bearing on the first three books of the poem. I must say that her study was exhaustive—very little left to be found out on that subject! But it's good, careful work. I take a pleased interest in these things, though there is ineptness and naïveté, and they get all kinds of things wrong and impute to me amazing motives. Another woman thought I was influenced by Hebrew elegiac meter. Now my Hebrew is primitive, and I don't even know what Hebrew elegiac meter is—and, moreover, neither does she. It's a harmless industry. It gets people degrees. I don't feel against it, and I don't feel for it. I sympathize with the students.

The professional critics, those who know what the literary, historical, philosophical, and theological score is, have not really gone to work yet, and may not do so for a long time yet. I did have a letter once from a guy who said: "Dear Mr. Berryman, Frankly I hope to be promoted from assistant professor to associate professor by writing a book about you. Are you willing to join me in this unworthy endeavor?" So I joined him. I answered all his questions. I practically flew out to pour out his drinks while he typed.

INTERVIEWER: I would like to change the subject now and talk about your work. Let's start with *The Dream Songs*. As you know, there is some controversy over the structure of the work—why it was first published in two volumes, why it consists of seven sections of varying lengths, and so on. What structural notion did you have in mind in writing it?

BERRYMAN: Several people have written books about *The Dream Songs*, not published, and one of them, a woman, sees it as a series of three odysseys, psychological and moral, on the part of Henry, corresponding vaguely to Freud's differentiation of the personality into superego or conscience, ego or façade or self, and id or unconscious. Each has a starting point and a terminus and so forth. I don't know whether she is right or not, but if so, I did not begin with that full-fledged conception when I wrote the first dream song.

I don't know what I had in mind. In *Homage to Mistress Bradstreet* my model was *The Waste Land*, and *Homage to Mis-*

tress Bradstreet is as unlike *The Waste Land* as it is possible for me to be. I think the model in *The Dream Songs* was the other greatest American poem—I am very ambitious—"Song of My-, self"—a very long poem, about sixty pages. It also has a hero, a personality, himself. Henry is accused of being me and I am accused of being Henry and I deny it and nobody believes me. Various other things entered into it, but that is where I started.

The narrative, such as it is, developed as I went along, partly out of my gropings into and around Henry and his environment and associates, partly out of my readings in theology and that sort of thing, taking place during thirteen years—awful long time— and third, out of certain partly preconceived and partly developing as I went along, sometimes rigid and sometimes plastic, structural notions. That is why the work is divided into seven books, each book of which is rather well unified, as a matter of fact. Finally I left the poem open to the circumstances of my personal life. For example, obviously if I hadn't got a Guggenheim and decided to spend it in Dublin, most of Book VII wouldn't exist. I have a personality and a plan, a metrical plan—which is original, as in *Homage to Mistress Bradstreet.* I don't use other people as metrical models. I don't put down people who do—I just don't feel satisfied with them.

I had a personality and a plan and all kinds of philosophical and theological notions. This woman thinks the basic philosophical notion is Hegelian, and it's true that at one time I was deeply interested in Hegel. She also thinks, and so do some other people, that the work is influenced by the later work of Freud, especially *Civilization and Its Discontents,* and that is very likely. For years I lectured on the book every year here at Minnesota, so I am very, very familiar with it—almost know it word by word. But at the same time I was what you might call open-ended. That is to say, Henry to some extent was in the situation that we are all in in actual life—namely, he didn't know and I didn't know what the bloody fucking hell was going to happen next. Whatever it was he had to confront it and get through. For example, he dies in Book IV and is dead throughout the book, but at the end of the

poem he is still alive, and in fairly good condition, after having
died himself *again.*

The poem does not go as far as "Song of Myself." What I mean
by that is this: Whitman denies that "Song of Myself" is a long
poem. He has a passage saying that he had long thought that there
was no such thing as a long poem and that when he read Poe he
found that Poe summed up the problem for him. But here it is,
sixty pages. What's the notion? He doesn't regard it as a literary
work at all, in my opinion—he doesn't quite say so. It proposes
a new religion—it is what is called in Old Testament criticism a
wisdom work, a work on the meaning of life and how to conduct
it. Now I don't go that far—*The Dream Songs* is a literary composition, it's a long poem—but I buy a little of it. I think Whitman
is right with regard to "Song of Myself." I'm prepared to submit
to his opinion. He was crazy, and I don't contradict madmen.
When William Blake says something, I say thank you, even
though he has uttered the most hopeless fallacy that you can
imagine. I'm willing to be their loving audience. I'm just hoping
to hear something marvelous from time to time, marvelous and
true. Of course *The Dream Songs* does not propose a new system;
that is not the point. In that way it is unlike "Song of Myself."
It remains a literary work.

INTERVIEWER: Christopher Ricks has called *The Dream Songs*
a theodicy. Did you have any such intention in writing the poem?

BERRYMAN: It is a tough question. The idea of a theodicy has
been in my mind at least since 1938. There is a passage in
Delmore's first book, *In Dreams Begin Responsibilities*, which
goes: "The theodicy I wrote in my high school days / Restored
all life from infancy." Beautiful! He is the most underrated poet
of the twentieth century. His later work is *absolutely* no good, but
his first book is a masterpiece. It will come back—no problem. So
that notion's always been with me. I can't answer the question.
I simply don't know. I put my stuff, in as good condition as I can
make it, on the table, and if people want to form opinions, good,
I'm interested in the opinions. I don't set up as a critic of my own
work. And I'm not kidding about that.

INTERVIEWER: You once said that, among other things, a long poem demands "the construction of a world rather than the reliance upon one already existent." Does the world of *The Dream Songs* differ from the existent world?

BERRYMAN: This is connected with your previous question. I said that *The Dream Songs* in my opinion—only in my opinion —does not propose a new system, like Whitman. But as to the creation of a world: It's a hard question to answer. Suppose I take this business of the relation of Henry to me, which has interested so many people, and which is categorically denied by me in one of the forewords. Henry both is and is not me, obviously. We touch at certain points. But I am an actual human being; he is nothing but a series of conceptions—my conceptions. I brush my teeth; unless I say so somewhere in the poem—I forget whether I do or not—he doesn't brush his teeth. He only does what I make him do. If I have succeeded in making him believable, he performs all kinds of other actions besides those named in the poem, but the reader has to make them up. That's the world. But it's not a religious or philosophical system.

INTERVIEWER: Where did you get the name Henry?

BERRYMAN: Ah, big sweat about that, too. Did I get it from *The Red Badge of Courage* or *A Farewell to Arms* or what? O.K., I'll tell you where it came from. My second wife, Ann, and I were walking down Hennepin Avenue one momentous night. Everything seemed quite as usual, but it was going to puzzle literary critics on two continents many years later. Anyway, we were joking on our way to a bar to have a beer, and I decided that I hated the name Mabel more than any other female name, though I could mention half a dozen others that I didn't like, either. We had passed from names we liked to names we disliked, and she decided that Henry was the name that she found completely unbearable. So from then on, for a long time, in the most cozy and affectionate lover kind of talk—we hadn't been married very long at this time—she was Mabel and I was Henry in our scene. So I started the poem. The poem began with a song that I killed. I've never printed it. It set the prosodic pattern, but for various reasons I killed it. It had not only a hero but a heroine. It was mostly about Henry, but it also had Mabel in it. It began:

> *The jolly old man is a silly old dumb*
> *with a mean face, humped, who kills dead.*
> *There is a tall who loves only him.*
> *She has sworn "Blue to you forever,*
> *grey to the little rat, go to bed."*
> *I fink it's bads all over.*

It winds up:

> *Henry and Mabel ought to but can't.*
> *Childness let's have us honey—*

Then, for reasons which I don't remember, I wiped Mabel out and never printed that song. For a long time after that, every now and then Ann would complain that Mabel didn't seem to be taking any part in the poem, but I couldn't find myself able to put her back in the poem, so it has no heroine. There are groups of heroines, but no individual heroine. By the way, that first song sounds quite good. Maybe I ought to pull it out.

INTERVIEWER: You once said in speaking of *Homage to Mistress Bradstreet* that you started out thinking you would write a fifty-line poem and ended up with fifty-seven stanzas. When you started *The Dream Songs*, did you know how long it was going to be, or how far you were going to go?

BERRYMAN: No, I didn't. But I was aware that I was embarked on an epic. In the case of the Bradstreet poem, I didn't know. The situation with that poem was this. I invented the stanza in '48 and wrote the first stanza and the first three lines of the second stanza, and then I stuck. I had in mind a poem roughly the same length as another of mine, "The Statue"—about seven or eight stanzas of eight lines each. Then I stuck. I read and read and read and thought and collected notes and sketched for five years until, although I was still in the second stanza, I had a mountain of notes and draftings—no whole stanzas, but passages as long as five lines. The whole poem was written in about two months, after which I was a ruin for two years. When I finally got going, I had this incredible mass of stuff and a very good idea of the shape of the poem, with the exception of one crucial point, which was this. I'll tell you in a minute why and how I got going. The great exception was this; it did not occur to me to have a dialogue between them—to insert bodily Henry into the poem . . . *Me*, to insert me, in my own person, John Berryman, *I*, into the poem . . .

INTERVIEWER: Was that a Freudian slip?

BERRYMAN: I don't know. Probably. Nothing is accidental except physics. Modern physics is entirely accidental. I did not have the idea of putting him in as a demon lover. How he emerged was this. The idea was not to take Anne Bradstreet as a poetess—I was not interested in that. I was interested in her as a pioneer heroine, a sort of mother to the artists and intellectuals who would follow her and play a large role in the development of the nation. People like Jefferson, Poe, and me.* Well, her life was very hard in many, many ways. The idea was to make it even harder than it had been in history. There is a lot of history in the poem. It is a historical poem, but a lot of it is invented, too. I decided to tempt her. She was unbelievably devoted to her husband. Her few really touching passages, both in verse and in prose, are about her love for her husband, who was indeed a remarkable man—and she was a remarkable woman, and she loved him, with a passion that can hardly be described, through their whole life together, from the age of sixteen on. I decided to tempt her. I could only do this in a fantasy; the problem was to make the fantasy believable, and some people think I have completely failed with that. It is not for me to judge. I am deeply satisfied. I only do the best I can—I think I succeeded, and some other people do, too.

So, with the exception of the dialogue in the middle—that's the middle third of the poem—all the rest was one whole plan, but it took a series of shocks to get it going. What happened. My

---

*Get the delusion (J. B., March 1971).

wife and I were living in Princeton, had been for a year. She was
in the hospital in New York for an operation, what they call a
woman's operation, a kind of parody of childbirth. Both she and
I were feeling very bitter about this since we very much wanted
a child and had not had one. So I had very, very strong emotions
and solitude. Second, at this point Saul Bellow had almost
finished *Augie March*, his first important novel and one of the
great American novels, I think. His later novels are far more
important still, but *Augie March* is a landmark. He had almost
finished that and wanted me to see it. We didn't know each other
very well—since then he has become perhaps my best friend—
but he was living just a few blocks away. I remember sitting in
my chair, drinking as usual, reading the typescript. It was very
long, about nine hundred pages. I was amazed. The word "breakthrough" has become kind of a cliché. Every two minutes somebody in *Life, Time,* or *Fortune* has a breakthrough. But the term
does describe something that actually happens. A renaissance.
Suddenly, where there was pure stasis, the place is exploding. For
example, the twelfth century—suddenly Europe was blazing with
intelligence and power and insight, fresh authority, all the things
that had been missing for centuries. I recognized in *Augie March*
a breakthrough—namely, the wiping out of the negative personality that had created and inhabited his earlier work. Some critics
like those novels, but in my opinion they're shit. They're well
written, and if you look closely, you can see a genius coming, but
the genius is absolutely not there—he is in a straitjacket. In *Augie*
he's there.

My plans for the Bradstreet poem had got very ambitious by
that time. I no longer had any idea of a fifty-line poem. That was
five years before. My idea was now very ambitious. The Bradstreet
poem is just as ambitious as *The Dream Songs*. Saul once said to
me that it is the equivalent of a five-hundred page psychological
novel. That is exactly my opinion, also—in spite of the fact that
it is short, the poem is highly concentrated. So I was exhilarated.
One of my pals had made a major attempt. You know, these

things don't happen very often. Most even very fine artists don't
try to put up the Parthenon, you know, and most of those who
do turn out to be impostors. Merely grandiose, like Benjamin
Haydon, Keats's friend. A very good, very minor painter who
thought he was Michelangelo, then killed himself. It's hard to
take the risk of joining that terrible, frightful company. Con-
temptible, pathetic, they move your heart, but they draw you to
scorn. Saul had decided to make a big attempt, so my idea of my
poem improved.

And the third thing was that I had recently reread, for the first
time in many years, *Anna Karenina*, which I think is the best
portrait of a woman in world literature. You just can't mention
any other attempt at a woman, except perhaps *Madame Bovary*.
I recently reread it for a seminar I am giving, and I have a very
high regard for it. It's a beauty. It deserves its reputation, which
is saying a lot. But *Anna Karenina* is even greater. The only
woman in American literature is Hester Prynne, and she is very
good. I have great respect for her and the book, but *Mistress
Bradstreet* is much more ambitious. It is very unlikely that it is
better, but it attempts more.* So again my notion of my poem
expanded. The fourth thing that got me going was this. I had
been in group therapy. The analyst who had been treating me
individually for several years set up a group. There were two
lawyers, a chemist, an alcoholic housewife, a psychiatric social
worker, and me. I tried to run the group, of course, and they all
killed me. I would leave, and come back, and so on, but it was
a shattering business—I mean, emotionally shattering—much
more so than individual therapy had been. That had been kind
of cozy. Well, I got fed up and left the group forever, and this
left me blazing with hostility and feelings of gigantism, defeated
gigantism. So these four things—the deep wound of Eileen's
tragic operation, Saul's wonderful daring, Tolstoy's commanding
achievement, and the emotional shock of my experience with the

---

*Delusion (J. B., March 1971).

group—swung me into action, and suddenly I was on fire every second.

INTERVIEWER: What was your method of composition on that poem? You must have worked very hard to finish it in two months.

BERRYMAN: I started out writing three stanzas a day, but that was too much, so I developed a more orderly method. I got one of those things that have a piece of glassine over a piece of paper, and you can put something in between and see it but not touch it. I would draft my stanza and put it in there. Then I would sit and study it. I would make notes, but I wouldn't touch the manuscript until I thought I was in business—usually not for hours. Then I'd take it out, make the corrections, put it back in, and study it some more. When I was finally satisfied, I'd take it out and type it. At that point I was done—I never touched any stanza afterward. I limited myself to one a day. If I finished at eleven in the morning, I still did not look at the next stanza until the next morning. I had a terrible time filling the hours—whiskey was helpful, but it was hard.

INTERVIEWER: Do you consider your latest book, *Love & Fame*, a long poem?

BERRYMAN: *Love & Fame* is very shapely and thematically unified, and in that it resembles a long poem. But it is absolutely and utterly not a long poem at all; it's a collection of lyrics. The last eleven all happen to be prayers, but even there each poem is on its own. This is even more true in the earlier sections. It is unified through style and, because most of the poems are autobiographical, based on the historical personality of the poet. By historical I mean existing in time and space, occupying quanta.

INTERVIEWER: How does the composition of *Love & Fame* compare with that of your earlier work? Did you write these poems more quickly than the long poems?

BERRYMAN: The composition was like that of the Bradstreet poem, and to some extent like that of *The Dream Songs*, many of which were also written in volcanic bursts. Not all. I worked daily over a period of years, but sometimes I would write fifty in a burst and then not write any for months. The Bradstreet poem, as I say, took two months. *Love & Fame* took about three months.

INTERVIEWER: What made you turn back to the short form after having written two long poems?

BERRYMAN: When I finished *The Dream Songs* two years ago, I was very tired. I didn't know whether I would ever write any more poems. As I told you, it took me two years to get over the Bradstreet poem before I started *The Dream Songs.* Your idea of yourself and your relation to your art has a great deal to do with what actually happens. What happened in this case was something that contradicted my ideas, as follows. I saw myself only as an epic poet. The idea of writing any more short poems hadn't been in my mind for many years. The question after *The Dream Songs* was whether I would ever again attempt a long poem, and I thought it improbable, so I didn't expect to write any more verse.

But suddenly one day last winter I wrote down a line; "I fell in love with a girl." I looked at it, and I couldn't find anything wrong with it. I thought, "God damn it, that is a *fact.*" I felt, as a friend of mine says: "I feel comfortable with that." And I looked at it until I thought of a second line, and then a third line, and then a fourth line, and that was a stanza. Unrhymed. And the more I looked at it, the better I liked it, so I wrote a second stanza. And then I wrote some more stanzas, and you know what? I had a lyric poem, and a very good one. I didn't know I had it in me! Well, the next day I knocked out a stanza, changed various lines, this and that, but pretty soon it looked classical. As classical as one of the *Rubáiyát* poems—without the necessities of rhyme and meter, but with its own necessities. I thought it was as good as any of my early poems, and some of them are quite good; most of them are not, but some are. Moreover, it didn't resemble any verse I had ever written in my entire life, and moreover, the subject was entirely new, solely and simply myself. Nothing else.

A subject on which I am an expert. Nobody can contradict me.*
I believe strongly in the authority of learning. The reason Milton
is the greatest English poet except for Shakespeare is because of
the authority of his learning. I am a scholar in certain fields, but
the subject on which I am a real authority is me, so I wiped out
all the disguises and went to work. In about five or six weeks I had
what was obviously a book called *Love & Fame*.

I had forty-two poems and was ready to print them, but
they were so weird, so unlike all my previous work that I was
a little worried. I had encouragement from one or two friends,
but still I didn't know what to do. I had previously sent the
first poem to Arthur Crook at the *Times Literary Supplement*.
He was delighted with it and sent me proof. I, in turn, was
delighted that he liked the poem, so I corrected the proof and
sent him five more—I didn't want the poem to appear alone.
So he printed the six, which made up a whole page—very
nice typographically—and this was further encouragement.
But I still wasn't sure. Meanwhile, I was in hospital. I was a
nervous wreck. I had lost nineteen pounds in five weeks and
had been drinking heavily—a quart a day. So I had my publisher in New York, Giroux, xerox a dozen copies, which I
sent out to friends of mine around the country for opinions. It
is a weird thing to do—I've never heard of anybody else doing
it—but I did it, looking for reassurance, confirmation, wanting
criticism, and so on, and I got some very good criticism. Dick
Wilbur took "Shirley & Auden," one of the most important
lyrics in Part I—some of the poems are quite slight, and others are very ambitious—and gave it hell. And I agreed—I
adopted almost every suggestion.

I also got some confirmation and reassurance, but there were
other opinions as well. Edmund Wilson, for whose opinion I have
a high regard, found the book hopeless. He said there were some
fine lines and striking passages. How do you like that? It is like
saying to a beautiful woman, "I like your left small toenail; that's

---

*Delusion (J. B., March 1971).

very nice indeed," while she's standing there stark naked looking like Venus. I was deeply hurt by that letter. And then other responses were very strange. Mark Van Doren, my teacher, an old, old friend and a wonderful judge of poetry, also wrote. I forget exactly what he said, but he was very heavy on it. He said things like "original," and "will be influential," and "will be popular," and so on, but "will also be feared and hated." What a surprising letter! It took me days to get used to it, and it took me days even to see what he meant. But now I see what he means. Some of the poems are threatening, very threatening to some readers, no doubt about it. Just as some people find me threatening—to be in a room with me drives them crazy. And then there is a good deal of obscenity in the poems, too. And there is a grave piety in the last poems, which is going to trouble a lot of people. You know, the country is full of atheists, and they really are going to find themselves threatened by those poems. *The Saturday Review* printed five of them, and I had a lot of mail about them—again expressing a wide variety of opinion. Some people were just purely grateful for my having told them how to put what they'd felt for years. Then there are others who detest them—they don't call them insincere, but they just can't believe it.

INTERVIEWER: There has always been a religious element in your poems, but why did you turn so directly to religious subject matter in these poems?

BERRYMAN: They are the result of a religious conversion which took place on my second Tuesday in treatment here last spring. I lost my faith several years ago, but I came back—by force, by necessity, because of a rescue action—into the notion of a God who, at certain moments, definitely and personally intervenes in individual lives, one of which is mine. The poems grow out of that sense, which not all Christians share.

INTERVIEWER: Could you say something more about this rescue action? Just what happened?

BERRYMAN: Yes. This happened during the strike which hit campus last May, after the Cambodian invasion and the events at Kent State. I was teaching a large class—seventy-five students

—Tuesday and Thursday afternoons, commuting from the hospital, and I was supposed to lecture on the Fourth Gospel. My kids were in a state of crisis—only twenty-five had shown up the previous Thursday, campus was in chaos, there were no guidelines from the administration—and besides lecturing, I felt I had to calm them, tell them what to do. The whole thing would have taken no more than two hours—taxi over, lecture, taxi back. I had been given permission to go by my psychiatrist. But at the beginning of group therapy that morning at ten, my counselor, who is an Episcopalian priest, told me that he had talked with my psychiatrist, and that the permission to leave had been rescinded. Well, I was shocked and defiant.

I said, "You and Dr. So-and-So have no authority over me. I will call a cab and go over and teach my class. My students need me."

He made various remarks, such as "You're shaking."

I replied, "I don't shake when I lecture."

He said, "Well, you can't walk, and we are afraid you will fall down."

I said, "I can walk," and I could. You see, I had had physical permission from my physician the day before.

Then the whole group hit me, including a high official of the university, who was also in treatment here. I appealed to him, and even he advised me to submit. Well, it went on for almost two hours, and at last I submitted—at around eleven-thirty. Then I was in real despair. I couldn't just ring up the secretary and have her dismiss my class—it would be grotesque. Here it was, eleven-thirty, and class met at one-fifteen. I didn't even know if I could get my chairman on the phone to find somebody to meet them. And even if I could, who could he have found that would have been qualified? We have no divinity school here. Well, all kinds of consolations and suggestions came from the group, and suddenly my counselor said, "Well, I'm trained in divinity. I'll give your lecture for you."

And I said, "You're kidding!" He and I had had some very sharp exchanges. I had called him sarcastic, arrogant, tyrannical, incompetent, theatrical, judgmental, and so on.

He said, "Yes, I'll teach it if I have to teach it in Greek!"
I said, "I can't believe it. Are you serious?"
He said, "Yes, I'm serious."
And I said, "I could kiss you."
He said, "Do." There was only one man between us, so I leaned over and we embraced. Then I briefed him and gave him my notes, and he went over and gave the lecture. Well, when I thought it over in the afternoon, I suddenly recalled what has been for many years one of my favorite conceptions. I got it from Augustine and Pascal. It's found in many other people, too, but especially in those heroes of mine. Namely, the idea of a God of rescue. He saves men from their situations, off and on during life's pilgrimage, and in the end. I completely bought it, and that's been my position since.

INTERVIEWER: What about the role of religion in your earlier works? I remember that when the *Sonnets* came out, one critic, writing in *The New York Review of Books,* spoke of "the absence of thematic substance" in your poems generally. Another critic, writing in *The Minnesota Review,* picked this up and disagreed with it, pointing out what he felt was a firm religious basis in the sonnets—the question of guilt and atonement, etc. What would you say about the role of religion generally in your poetry?

BERRYMAN: It's awfully hard for me to judge. I had a strict Catholic training. I went to a Catholic school and I adored my priest, Father Boniface. I began serving Mass under him at the age of five, and I used to serve six days a week. Often there would be nobody in the church except him and me. Then all that went to pieces at my father's death, when I was twelve. Later, I went to a High Church Episcopalian school in Connecticut, called South Kent, and I was very fond of the Chaplain there. His name was Father Kemmis, and although I didn't feel about him as I had about Father Boniface as a child, I still felt very keen and was a rapt Episcopalian for several years. Then, when I went to Columbia, all that sort of dropped out. I never lost the sense of God in the two roles of creator and sustainer—of the mind of man and all its operations, as a source of inspiration to great scientists, great artists, saints, great statesmen. But my experience last spring gave me a third sense, a sense of a God of rescue, and I've been operating with that since. Now the point is, I have been interested not only in religion but in theology all my life. I don't know how much these personal beliefs, together with the interest in theology and the history of the Church, enter into particular works up to those addresses to the Lord in *Love & Fame*. I really think it is up to others—critics, scholars—to answer your question. By the way, those addresses to the Lord are not Christian poems. I am deeply interested in Christ, but I never pray to him.* I don't know whether he was in any special sense the son of God, and I think it is quite impossible to know.† He certainly was the most remarkable *man* who ever lived. But I don't consider myself a Christian. I do consider myself a Catholic, but I'd just as soon go to an Episcopalian church as a Catholic church. I do go to Mass every Sunday.

INTERVIEWER: Let's turn to new directions. What has happened to the poem about heaven set in China, titled "Scholars at the Orchard Pavilion," which you were working on a couple of years ago? Are you still working on that?

BERRYMAN: I intended that to be rather a long poem. As with the Bradstreet poem, I invented the stanza—it's a very beautiful, sort of hovering, seven-line stanza, unrhymed—and wrote the first stanza and stuck. I then accumulated notes on Chinese art history in most of the major forms. Chinese art is much more complicated than ours—they have many forms. I have a whole library on Chinese art and early Chinese philosophy, Chinese history, Chinese folk tales, ghost stories, all kinds of Chinese stuff. I even tried to learn classical Chinese one time, but I decided after a few days that it was not for me.

Anyway, I finally decided that I was nowhere, that all this accumulation of knowledge was fascinating and valuable to me,

---

*Situation altered; see "Ecce Homo," poem to be published in *The New Yorker* (J. B., March 1971).
†Delusion (J. B., March 1971).

but that I was personally not destined to write a Chinese epic. So at that point I felt fine, and I wrote a second stanza, and a third stanza, and a fourth stanza. They're not as good as the first stanza, but they are all pretty good. And then I put some asterisks, and that's what I'll publish sooner or later. I may say, "Scholars at the Orchard Pavilion: A Fragment."

INTERVIEWER: Where do you go from here?

BERRYMAN: I have written another book of poetry called *Delusions*. It won't be out for some time yet, however. We're doing a volume of my prose, probably spring or fall of '72. After that —I am very much interested in the question, or will be when I get my breath back from the composition of the last nine months. I've written over a hundred poems in the last six months. I'm a complete wreck. I'm hopelessly underweight and the despair of about four competent doctors. When I get my breath back—it may be next spring—maybe I'll begin to think. I don't know whether I'll ever write any more verse at all. The main question is whether I will ever again undertake a long poem, and I just can form no idea.

There are certain subjects that have interested me for a long time, but nothing commanding and obsessive, as both the Bradstreet poem and *Dream Songs* were. What is involved in the composition of a long poem, at least by my experience, is five to ten years. I don't know how long I'll live. Probably I wouldn't be able to begin it for—well it took me two years to get over the Bradstreet poem. I finished *The Dream Songs* only two years ago, and I've written two more books since, besides a lot of other literary work. I've been working on a play, an anthology, and revising the volume of my criticism. I probably wouldn't get to it for at least three to five years. That makes me getting on to sixty. Taking on a new long poem at the age of sixty is really something. I have no idea whether I would still have the vigor and ambition, need, that sort of thing, to do it.

I have a tiny little secret hope that, after a decent period of silence and prose, I will find myself in some almost impossible life situation and will respond to this with outcries of rage, rage and love, such as the world has never heard before. Like Yeats's great outburst at the end of his life. This comes out of a feeling that endowment is a very small part of achievement. I would rate it about fifteen or twenty per cent. Then you have historical luck, personal luck, health, things like that, then you have hard work, sweat. And you have ambition. The incredible difference between the achievement of A and the achievement of B is that B *wanted* it, so he made all kinds of sacrifices. A could have had it, but he didn't give a damn. The idea that everybody wants to be President of the United States or have a million dollars is simply not the case. Most people want to go down to the corner and have a glass of beer. They're very happy. In *Henderson the Rain King*, the hero keeps on saying, "I want. I want." Well, I'm that kind of character. I don't know whether that is exhausted in me or not, I can't tell.

But what I was going on to say is that I do strongly feel that among the greatest pieces of luck for high achievement is ordeal. Certain great artists can make out without it, Titian and others, but mostly you need ordeal. My idea is this: The artist is extremely lucky who is presented with the worst possible ordeal which will not actually kill him. At that point, he's in business. Beethoven's deafness, Goya's deafness, Milton's blindness, that kind of thing. And I think that what happens in my poetic work in the future will probably largely depend not on my sitting calmly on my ass as I think, "Hmm, hmm, a long poem again? Hmm," but on being knocked in the face, and thrown flat, and given cancer, and all kinds of other things short of senile dementia. At that point, I'm out, but short of that, I don't know. I hope to be nearly crucified.

INTERVIEWER: You're not knocking on wood.

BERRYMAN: I'm scared, but I'm willing. I'm sure this is a preposterous attitude, but I'm not ashamed of it.*

PETER A. STITT

---

*Delusion (J. B., March 1971).

13. Anthony Burgess

John Anthony Burgess Wilson was born in Manchester, England, on February 25, 1917. Raised a Roman Catholic, he attended local parochial schools and graduated with honors in English literature from Manchester University in 1940. He served in the Army Education Corps from 1940 to 1946, attaining the rank of sergeant-major; for three years he was stationed on Gibraltar, where his first novel, *A Vision of Battlements* (not published until 1965) is set.

After the war Burgess held several teaching posts, including that of Colonial Education Officer in Malaya and Borneo from 1954 to 1959. During this period he wrote his Malayan trilogy, *The Long Way Wanes* (1956–59). When illness forced his repatriation in 1959, he became a professional writer and one of London's leading critics. His other novels include *The Right to an Answer* (1960), *The Doctor Is Sick* (1960) *The Worm and the Ring* (1961), *Devil of a State* (1961), *A Clockwork Orange* (1962), *Honey for the Bears* (1963), *Nothing Like the Sun* (1964), *The Eve of Saint Venus* (1964), *Tremor of Intent* (1966), *Enderby* (1968), *MF* (1971), and *Napoleon Symphony* (1974). *One Hand Clapping* (1961) was published under the pen name Joseph Kell. Burgess has also written *Re: Joyce* (1965), a critical study, and *Shakespeare* (1970), a biography, besides editing *A Shorter Finnegans Wake* (1966). *The Novel Now*, a critical survey, appeared in 1967, followed by a collection of essays and reviews called *Urgent Copy* (1968).

In his spare moments Burgess returns to composing, his first love. One of his symphonies has been performed and he has written the incidental music for a production of his own new translation of *Cyrano de Bergerac*.

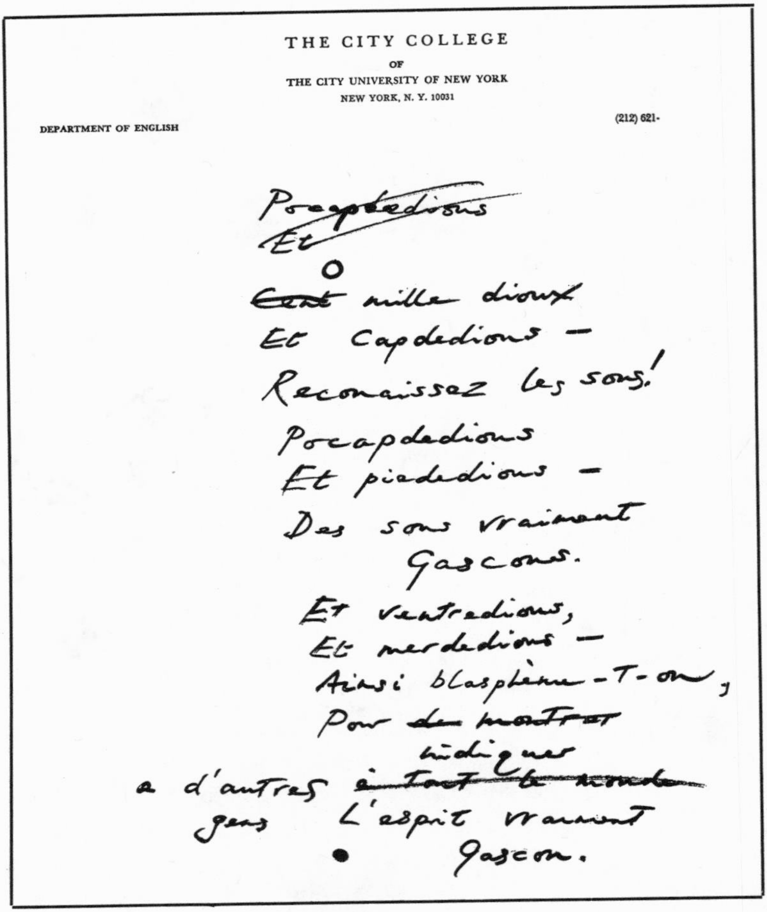

THE CITY COLLEGE
OF
THE CITY UNIVERSITY OF NEW YORK
NEW YORK, N. Y. 10031

DEPARTMENT OF ENGLISH

(212) 621-

~~Pocapdedious~~
~~Et~~
O
~~Cent~~ mille dioux
Et Capdedious —
Reconaissez les sons!
Pocapdedious
Et piadedious —
Des sons vraiment
Gascons.
Et ventredious,
Et merdedious —
Ainsi blasphème-t-on,
Pour ~~de montrer~~ indiquer
a d'autres ~~à tout le monde~~ gens
L'esprit vraiment
Gascon.

Anthony Burgess manuscript page

Anthony Burgess

Much of the interview was conducted through an exchange of letters from June 1971 until the summer of 1972. On December 2, 1972, a portion of the interview was taped at the Center for Twentieth Century Studies of the University of Wisconsin. Burgess's schedule during his two-day visit had been backbreaking; there was scarcely a break in the round of class visits, Joyce readings, and interviews. Tired as he appeared after that routine, Burgess showed no tendency to curb the flow of his responses; and his spoken portions, when spliced with the previous exchanges, seem as polished as a written draft.

INTERVIEWER: Are you at all bothered by the charges that you are too prolific or that your novels are too allusive?

BURGESS: It has been a sin to be prolific only since the Bloomsbury group—particularly Forster—made it a point of good manners to produce, as it were, costively. I've been annoyed less by sneers at my alleged overproduction than by the imputation that to write much means to write badly. I've always written with great care and even some slowness. I've just put in rather more hours a day at the task than some writers seem able to. As for allusiveness—meaning, I suppose, literary allusiveness—that's surely in the tradition. Any book has behind it all the other books that have been written. The author's aware of them; the reader ought to be aware, too.

INTERVIEWER: At what time of day do you usually work?

BURGESS: I don't think it matters much; I work in the morning, but I think the afternoon is a good time to work. Most people sleep in the afternoon. I've always found it a good time, especially if one doesn't have much lunch. It's a quiet time. It's a time when one's body is not at its sharpest, not at its most receptive—the body is quiescent, somnolent; but the brain can be quite sharp. I think, also, at the same time that the unconscious mind has a habit of asserting itself in the afternoon. The morning is the conscious time, but the afternoon is a time in which we should deal much more with the hinterland of the consciousness.

INTERVIEWER: That's very interesting. Thomas Mann, on the other hand, wrote religiously virtually every day from nine to one, as though he were punching a time clock.

BURGESS: Yes. One can work from nine to one, I think it's ideal; but I find that the afternoon must be used. The afternoon has always been a good time for me. I think it began in Malaya when I was writing. I was working all morning. Most of us slept in the afternoon; it was very quiet. Even the servants were sleeping, even the dogs were asleep. One could work quietly away under the sun until dusk fell, and one was ready for the events of the evening. I do most of my work in the afternoon.

INTERVIEWER: Do you imagine an ideal reader for your books?

BURGESS: The ideal reader of my novels is a lapsed Catholic and failed musician, short-sighted, color-blind, auditorily biased, who has read the books that I have read. He should also be about my age.

INTERVIEWER: A very special reader indeed. Are you writing,

then, for a limited, highly educated audience?

BURGESS: Where would Shakespeare have got if he had thought only of a specialized audience? What he did was to attempt to appeal on all levels, with something for the most rarefied intellectuals (who had read Montaigne) and very much more for those who could appreciate only sex and blood. I like to devise a plot that can have a moderately wide appeal. But take Eliot's *The Waste Land*, very erudite, which, probably through its more popular elements and its basic rhetorical appeal, appealed to those who did not at first understand it but made themselves understand it: The poem, a terminus of Eliot's polymathic travels, became a starting point for other people's erudition. I think every author wants to *make* his audience. But it's in his own image, and his primary audience is a mirror.

INTERVIEWER: Do you care about what the critics think?

BURGESS: I get angry at the stupidity of critics who willfully refuse to see what my books are really about. I'm aware of malevolence, especially in England. A bad review by a man I admire hurts terribly.

INTERVIEWER: Would you ever change the drift of a book—or any literary project—because of a critic's comments?

BURGESS: I don't think—with the exception of the excision of that whole final chapter of *A Clockwork Orange*—I've ever been asked to make any changes in what I've written. I do feel that the author has to know best about what he's writing—from the viewpoint of structure, intention, and so on. The critic has the job of explaining deep-level elements which the author couldn't know about. As for saying where—technically, in matters of taste and so on—a writer is going wrong, the critic rarely says what the author doesn't know already.

INTERVIEWER: You've mentioned the possibility of working with Stanley Kubrick on a film version of Napoleon's life. Can you remain completely independent in devising the novel you're currently writing about Napoleon?

BURGESS: The Napoleon project, which began with Kubrick, has now got beyond Kubrick. I found myself interested in the subject in a way that didn't suggest a film adaptation and am now working on something Kubrick couldn't use. It's a pity about the money and so on, but otherwise I'm glad to feel free, nobody looking over my shoulder.

INTERVIEWER: Has working as a professional reviewer either helped or hindered the writing of your novels?

BURGESS: It did no harm. It didn't stop me writing novels. It gave facility. It forced me into areas that I wouldn't have voluntarily entered. It paid the bills, which novels rarely do.

INTERVIEWER: Did it bring you involuntarily to any new subjects or books that have become important to you?

BURGESS: It's good for a writer to review books he is not supposed to know anything about or be interested in. Doing reviewing for magazines like *Country Life* (which smells more of horses than of calfskin bindings) means doing a fine heterogeneous batch which often does open up areas of some value in one's creative work. For instance, I had to review books on stable management, embroidery, car engines—very useful solid stuff, the very stuff of novels. Reviewing Lévi-Strauss's little lecture on anthropology (which nobody else wanted to review) was the beginning of the process which led me to write the novel *MF*.

INTERVIEWER: You've stressed the importance of punctuality to a good reviewer. Do you find that a creative writer need stick to a strict work schedule, too?

BURGESS: The practice of being on time with commissioned work is an aspect of politeness. I don't like being late for appointments; I don't like craving indulgence from editors in the matter of missed deadlines. Good journalistic manners tend to lead to a kind of self-discipline in creative work. It's important that a novel be approached with some urgency. Spend too long on it, or have great gaps between writing sessions, and the unity of the work tends to be lost. This is one of the troubles with *Ulysses*. The ending is different from the beginning. Technique changes halfway through. Joyce spent too long on the book.

INTERVIEWER: Are you suggesting that Molly Bloom's soliloquy is an inappropriate ending because it's technically different from the opening three chapters devoted to Stephen Dedalus?

BURGESS: I don't mean the very end of *Ulysses*. I mean that from the Cyclops episode on, Joyce decides to lengthen his chapters to make the reading time correspond with the imagined time of enactment. In that sense the book is technically not so much a unity as people like to think. Compare the Aeolus episode with the Oxen of the Sun and you'll see what I mean.

INTERVIEWER: Considering the length of time that Proust spent on his novel and that Mann devoted to *Joseph and His Brothers*, is seven years really so long for a work as great as *Ulysses?* What, then, about the seventeen years Joyce frittered away on *Finnegans Wake?*

BURGESS: Time spent on a book is perhaps no concern of the reader's really. (*Madame Bovary*, a comparatively short book, took longer to write, surely, than the *Joseph* sequence.) The whole question is whether the writer can be the same person, with the same aims and approach to technique, over a long stretch of time. *Ulysses*, being innovative, had to go on being more and more innovative as it was written, and this makes it a sort of disunity. *Finnegans Wake*, though it took much longer, got its essential technique established pretty early.

INTERVIEWER: Your new book, *Joysprick*, is coming out soon, I understand. How does it differ in emphasis from *Re: Joyce?*

BURGESS: It covers a little of the same ground but not very much. It's an attempt to examine the nature of Joyce's language, not from a strictly linguistic point of view but from a point of view which may be said to be exactly halfway between literary criticism and linguistics; it doesn't use many technical terms. It makes a phonetic analysis of Joyce's language; there aren't many linguists who can do this nowadays. Phonetics is rather old hat. But it does examine the dialects of *Ulysses*, the importance of establishing a pronunciation in *Finnegans Wake*, an analysis of the way Joyce constructs a sentence. It is not a profound book; it is meant to be a beginner's guide to the language of Joyce, and the real work of probing into Joyce's linguistic method must be left to a more scholarly person than myself.

INTERVIEWER: You say that you are taking what you call an old-fashioned phonetic approach to Joyce's language; and yet in *MF* you make use of Lévi-Strauss's structuralism. Are you at all interested in considering Joyce from the point of view of structural linguistics?

BURGESS: I don't think that's my line; I think this has to be left to a scholar. I think somebody has to be in a university, has to be not engaged as I am in the production of books and teaching and lecturing and living a pretty varied "show-biz" life; this is a job for a cool scholar. I don't think I qualify to do it. I'm interested in what sounds Joyce is hearing when he is writing down the speech of Molly Bloom and Leopold Bloom and the minor characters. It's a matter of great literary import, I would suggest, because the final monologue of Molly Bloom inclines a particular way of speech which is not consonant with her declared background. Here in Joyce there is something very implausible about the fact that Molly Bloom is the daughter of a major, brought up in the Gibraltar garrison, coming to Dublin speaking and thinking like any low Dublin fishwife. This seems to be totally inconsistent, and the point has not even been made before. I know Gibraltar better than Joyce did and better than most Joyce scholars. I'm trying to examine this.

INTERVIEWER: If Molly's monologue is too elegant, isn't it one of Joyce's points to have the poetic emerge from the demotic?

BURGESS: It's not elegant enough. I mean the fact that she uses Irish locutions like "Pshaw." She would not use any such term, she would not.

INTERVIEWER: There's a geographical thing.

BURGESS: There's a pattern implied. There's a social thing. In a very small garrison town like Gibraltar with this man, Major Tweedy, whose previous wife is Spanish, his half-Spanish daughter would speak either Spanish as a first language (and not with the usual grammar) or English as a first language—but certainly both languages, in the first instance in an Andalusian way, and in the second instance in a totally class-conscious, pseudo-patrician way. She would not come back to Dublin and suddenly start speaking like a Dublin fishwife.

INTERVIEWER: So Molly's language is probably closer in terms of social background to that of Nora Barnacle.

BURGESS: It is indeed; this final image is an image of Nora Barnacle and not of Molly at all. And as we know from Nora's letters, Joyce must have studied the letters and learned from them how to set down this warm womanly pattern of speech. Nora wrote the letters totally without punctuation, and sometimes it is hard to distinguish between a chunk of one of Nora's letters and a chunk of Molly's final monologue.

INTERVIEWER: I'm looking forward to this book. Have you thought of writing a long, expansive novel?

BURGESS: I have in mind two long novels—one on a theatrical family from the middle ages till today, the other on a great British composer. The projects are so big that I'm scared of starting on them.

INTERVIEWER: Could you begin with a few excerpts in the form of short stories?

BURGESS: I can't write short stories, not easily, anyway, and I'd rather keep my novel dark until it's ready for the light. I made the mistake once of publishing a chapter of an emergent novel in the *Transatlantic Review* and the sight of the extract in cold print turned me against the project. This is my one unfinished novel.

INTERVIEWER: Do you still hope to write a novel about Theseus' encounter with the Minotaur, or has Rawcliffe's scenario in *Enderby* disposed of that project?

BURGESS: As for the Minotaur idea, I have thought of publishing a volume of all Enderby's poems, and they would include *The Pet Beast* (which has become, incidentally, the title of the Italian version of *Enderby—La Dolce Bestia*). I can see the sense of pretending that someone else has written your book for you, especially your book of poems. It frees you of responsibility— "Look, I know this is bad, but I didn't write it—one of my characters wrote it." *Don Quixote, Lolita, Ada*—it's an old and still lively tradition. I don't get writing blocks except from the stationer, but I do feel so sickened by what I write that I don't want to go on.

INTERVIEWER: Do you write the big scenes first, as Joyce Cary did?

BURGESS: I start at the beginning, go on to the end, then stop.

INTERVIEWER: Is each book charted completely in advance?

BURGESS: I chart a little first—list of names, rough synopsis of chapters, and so on. But one daren't overplan; so many things are generated by the sheer act of writing.

INTERVIEWER: Do you write nonfiction any differently?

BURGESS: The process is the same.

INTERVIEWER: Is the finished product much influenced by the fact that you do the first draft on the typewriter?

BURGESS: I don't write drafts. I do page one many, many times and move on to page two. I pile up sheet after sheet, each in its final state, and at length I have a novel that doesn't—in my view —need any revision.

INTERVIEWER: Then you don't revise at all?

BURGESS: Revising, as I said, is done with each page, not with each chapter or the whole book. Rewriting a whole book would bore me.

INTERVIEWER: Why did you decide to continue *Inside Mr. Enderby,* the first half of *Enderby,* after several years?

BURGESS: I planned the work as the long book that came out in America, but—since I was approaching the end of the one year that the doctors had given me to live—I was not able to do more than the first half in 1959–60. Unwillingness of the publishers to publish *Inside Mr. Enderby*—as Part I was called in England— made me delay the writing of Part II. But I had it all in my mind right at the start.

INTERVIEWER: After the doctors had diagnosed a brain tumor following your collapse in a Brunei classroom, why did you choose to write during that "terminal year" rather than travel, say? Were you confined in semi-invalid status?

BURGESS: I was no semi-invalid. I was very fit and active. (This made me doubt the truth of the diagnosis.) But to travel the world one needs money, and this I didn't have. It's only in fiction that "terminal year" men have something tucked away. The fact is that my wife and I needed to eat, and so on, and the only job I could do (who would employ me?) was writing. I wrote much because I was paid little. I had no great desire to leave a literary name behind me.

INTERVIEWER: Did your style change at all during that year, possibly as a result of your feeling under sentence?

BURGESS: I don't think so. I was old enough to have established some kind of narrative style; but the real business of working on style, of course, came later. The novels written in this so-called quasi-terminal year—pseudo-terminal year—were not written with, you know, excessive speed; it was just a matter of working hard every day, working very hard every day—and *all* day—including the evenings. A good deal of care went into the works, and what people look for in what seems an excessive amount of production is evidence of carelessness. There may be a little of that; but it's not because of the speed or apparent speed but because of flaws in my own makeup. I don't think it is possible to say that a particular work is obviously written during the terminal year. I don't think there is any qualitative difference between the various novels; and certainly I was not aware of any influence on style, on way of writing, caused by this knowledge.

INTERVIEWER: Several of your novels contain poetry written by various characters. Have you thought of writing poetry again seriously?

BURGESS: I've seen produced my version of *Cyrano de Bergerac.* This is in rhyme, and it worked well, as I expected it to. But I don't plan volumes of verse—too naked, too personal. I plan further stage translations—*Peer Gynt,* Chekhov's *Chaika*—and I'm working on a musical of *Ulysses.* I'm much more likely to return to music. I've been asked to write a clarinet concerto, and my music to *Cyrano* has gone down well enough.

INTERVIEWER: Do you ever use musical forms in designing your novels?

BURGESS: Ah yes, one can learn a lot from musical forms, I'm planning a novel in the style of a classical symphony—minuet and all. The motivations will be purely formal, so that a development section in which sexual fantasies are enacted can follow a realistic exposition with neither explanation nor transitional device, returning to it (now as recapitulation) with a similar lack of psychological justification or formal trickery.

INTERVIEWER: Composers traffic heavily in transitions. Isn't this particular instance of literary composition by musical analogy an example of "formal trickery," best understood by the reader who is at least an amateur musician?

BURGESS: I think that music does teach practitioners in other arts useful formal devices, but the reader doesn't have to know their provenance. Here's an example. A composer modulates from one key to another by the use of the "punning" chord, the augmented sixth (punning because it is also a dominant seventh). You can change, in a novel, from one scene to another by using a phrase or statement common to both—this is quite common. If the phrase or statement means different things in the different contexts, so much the more musical.

INTERVIEWER: One notices that the form of *A Vision of Battlements* is meant to be similar to that of Ennis's passacaglia, but can any but the most tenuously analogous relation be established between literature and music generally?

BURGESS: I agree that the musico-literary analogies can be pretty tenuous, but in the widest possible formal sense—sonata form, opera, and so on—we've hardly begun to explore the possibilities. The Napoleon novel I'm writing apes the *Eroica* formally—irritable, quick, swiftly transitional in the first movement (up to Napoleon's coronation); slow, very leisurely, with a binding beat suggesting a funeral march for the second. This isn't pure fancy: It's an attempt to unify a mass of historical material in the comparatively brief space of about 150,000 words. As for the reader having to know about music—it doesn't really matter much. In one novel I wrote, "The orchestra lunged into a loud chord of twelve notes, all of them different." Musicians hear the discord, nonmusicians don't, but there's nothing there to baffle them and prevent them reading on. I don't understand baseball terms, but I can still enjoy Malamud's *The Natural*. I don't play bridge, but I find the bridge game in Fleming's *Moonraker* absorbing—it's the emotions conveyed that matter, not what the players are doing with their hands.

INTERVIEWER: What about film technique as an influence on your writing?

BURGESS: I've been much more influenced by the stage than by the film. I write in scenes too long for unbroken cinematic representation. But I like to run a scene through in my mind before writing it down, seeing everything happen, hearing some of the dialogue. I've written for both television and cinema, but not very successfully. Too literary, or something. I get called in by makers of historical films to revise the dialogue, which they then restore to its original form.

INTERVIEWER: What happened to the proposed film versions of *Enderby* and *Nothing Like the Sun?*

BURGESS: The filming of *Enderby* fell through because the producer dropped dead at the Cannes film festival. The Shakespeare project came almost when Warner Brothers was being sold, and all existing enterprises were scrapped when the new regime started. It may, however, yet be fulfilled. Film people are very conservative about dialogue: They honestly believe that the immediate grasp of lexical meaning is more important than the impact of rhythm and emotionally charged sound. It's regarded as cleverer to pretend that the people of the past would have spoken like us if they'd been lucky enough to know how to do so, delighted with the opportunity to view themselves and their times from our angle. *The Lion in Winter* is thought to be a triumphant solution of the medieval dialogue problem, but of course it's just cheap.

INTERVIEWER: Does your novel in progress pose any special linguistic problems that may create obstacles for Stanley Kubrick as well?

BURGESS: The Napoleon novel is difficult from the dialogue

angle, but my instinct tells me to use rhythms and vocabulary not much different from our own. After all, Byron's *Don Juan* could almost have been written today. I imagine the soldiers speaking as today's soldiers speak.

They're speaking in French, anyway. As for the Napoleon film, Kubrick must go his own way, and he'll find it a difficult way.

INTERVIEWER: Do you expect to write any more historical novels?

BURGESS: I'm working on a novel intended to express the feel of England in Edward III's time, using Dos Passos' devices. I believe there's great scope in the historical novel, so long as it isn't by Mary Renault or Georgette Heyer. The fourteenth century of my novel will be mainly evoked in terms of smell and visceral feelings, and it will carry an undertone of general disgust rather than hey-nonny nostalgia.

INTERVIEWER: Which of Dos Passos' techniques will you use?

BURGESS: The novel I have in mind, and for which I've done a ninety-page plan, is about the Black Prince. I thought it might be amusing blatantly to steal the Camera Eye and the Newsreel devices from Dos Passos just to see how they might work, especially with the Black Death and Crécy and the Spanish campaign. The effect might be of the fourteenth century going on in another galaxy where language and literature had somehow got themselves into the twentieth century. The technique might make the historical characters look remote and rather comic—which is what I want.

INTERVIEWER: Are Mary Renault's retellings of Greek myths as bad as all that?

BURGESS: Oh, they're not unsatisfactory, far from it. Rattling good reads if you like that sort of thing. They just don't excite me, that's all. It's undoubtedly my fault.

INTERVIEWER: Do you expect to write another novel of the future, like *A Clockwork Orange* or *The Wanting Seed?*

BURGESS: I don't plan a novel about the future except for a mad novella in which England has become a mere showplace run by America.

INTERVIEWER: Is England going to become simply an oversized tourist boutique—or the fifty-first state?

BURGESS: I used to think that England might become just a place that liked to be visited—like that island in J. M. Barrie's *Mary Rose*—but now I see that so many of the things worth seeing—old things—are disappearing so that England can become a huge Los Angeles, all motorways, getting about more important than actually getting anywhere. England is now going into Europe, not—as I had once expected and even hoped—America, and I think it will now have Europe's faults without its virtues. The decimal coinage is a monstrosity, and soon there'll be liters of beer, as in *Nineteen Eighty-Four*, and no cheap wine or caporal tobacco. Absorption, anyway, since England either has to absorb or be absorbed. Napoleon has won.

INTERVIEWER: You mentioned that *A Clockwork Orange* has a concluding chapter in the British edition that isn't available in the American ones. Does this bother you?

BURGESS: Yes, I hate having two different versions of the same book. The U.S. edition has a chapter short, and hence the arithmological plan is messed up. Also, the implied view of juvenile violence as something to go through and then grow out of is missing in the American edition; and this reduces the book to a mere parable, whereas it was intended to be a novel.

INTERVIEWER: What happens in that twenty-first chapter?

BURGESS: In Chapter 21 Alex grows up and realizes that ultraviolence is a bit of a bore, and it's time he had a wife and a malenky googoogooing malchickiwick to call him dadada. This was meant to be a mature conclusion, but nobody in America has ever liked the idea.

INTERVIEWER: Did Stanley Kubrick consider filming the Heinemann version?

BURGESS: Kubrick discovered the existence of this final chapter when he was halfway through the film, but it was too late to think of altering the concept. Anyway, he, too, an American, thought it too milk-and-watery. I don't know what to think now. After all, it's twelve years since I wrote the thing.

INTERVIEWER: Did you attempt to get the complete novel published here?

BURGESS: Yes—well, I was very dubious about the book itself. When I wrote the book, my agent was not willing to present it to a publisher, which is rather unusual; and the sort of publishers in England were very dubious about the book. So when the American publisher made this objection to the final chapter, I didn't feel myself to be in a very strong position. I was a little hesitant to judge the book; I was a little too close to it. I thought: Well, they may be right. Because authors do tend to be (especially after the completion of a book) very uncertain about the value of the book; and perhaps I gave in a little too weakly, but my concern was partly a financial one. I wanted it to be published in America, and I wanted some money out of it. So I said, "Yes." Whether I'd say "Yes" now, I don't know; but I've been persuaded by so many critics that the book is better in its American form that I say, "All right, they know best."

INTERVIEWER: Would it be possible for an American press to put out a limited, hard-bound edition which includes the excluded chapter as a sort of appendix?

BURGESS: I think this should be possible. The best way of doing it is to bring out an annotated edition of the book with this final chapter—an idea which is being resisted by my publishers for some reason, I don't know why. I would be very interested in the comments of the average, say, American student on the differences between the two versions. Because I'm not able to judge myself very clearly now as to whether I was right or wrong. What is *your* opinion, what do you feel about that?

INTERVIEWER: I find the last chapter problematical in that while it creates an entirely different context for the work, it seems anticlimactic after the neat resurrection of the old Alex in the twentieth chapter.

BURGESS: Yes.

INTERVIEWER: Still it should remain, because your meaning is altered by the cutting off of the context.

BURGESS: Well, the worst example I know of unjustified translation is to be found in Ford Madox Ford's *Parade's End*, where in the British edition, under the imprint of Bodley Head, Graham Greene has taken upon himself to present *Parade's End* as a trilogy, saying he doesn't think the final novel, *The Last Post*, works, and he feels perhaps Ford would have agreed with him; and therefore he has taken the liberty of getting rid of the final book. I think Greene is wrong; I think that whatever Ford said, the work is a tetralogy, and the thing is severely maimed with the loss of his final book. An author is not to be trusted in his judgment of this sort of thing. Authors very frequently try to be indifferent to their books. Certainly they are so sick of their books that they don't want to make any serious judgment on them. The problem comes up, you see, when one reads Evelyn Waugh's *A Handful of Dust*, because this frightful ending (where Tony Last spends all his time reading Dickens to this half-breed in the jungle), appeared previously as a short story; and knowing the short story one has a strange attitude to the book. Which makes us feel that here is a deliberate pasting together, where this giant figure at the end that turns up does not spring automatically out of the book but is just taken arbitrarily from another work. Perhaps one shouldn't know too much about these things. Of course, one can't avoid it. These two versions of Samuel Butler's *Way of All Flesh*—this raises the problem. Which version would we like better, which is the right version? It's better to know only one thing, to be fairly ignorant of what was going on. You know, behind the version we know.

INTERVIEWER: Isn't this an argument against publishing a complete *A Clockwork Orange*, since a twenty-chapter version is embedded in everyone's mind?

BURGESS: I don't know; they're both relevant. They seem to me to express in a sense the difference between the British approach to life and the American approach to life. There may be something very profound to say about this difference in these different presentations of the novel. I don't know; I'm not able to judge.

INTERVIEWER: In *A Clockwork Orange* and *Enderby* especially there's a persistent strain of mockery toward youth culture and its music. Is there anything good about them?

BURGESS: I despise whatever is obviously ephemeral and yet is shown as possessing some kind of ultimate value. The Beatles, for instance. Most youth culture, especially music, is based on so little knowledge of tradition, and it often elevates ignorance into a virtue. Think of the musically illiterate who set themselves up as "arrangers." And youth is so conformist, so little concerned with maverick values, so proud of being rather than making, so bloody sure that it and it alone *knows*.

INTERVIEWER: You used to play in a jazz band. Is there any hope that their interest in rock music may lead youth to jazz— or even to classical music?

BURGESS: I still play jazz, chiefly on a four-octave electric organ, and I prefer this to listening to it. I don't think jazz is for listening but for playing. I'd like to write a novel about a jazz pianist, or, better, about a pub pianist—which I once was, like my father before me. I don't think rock leads on to a liking for jazz. The kids are depressingly static in their tastes. They do so want *words*, and jazz gets along very nicely without words.

INTERVIEWER: In two of your novels the wordsmiths Shakespeare and Enderby are inspired by the Muse. But you've said as well that you like to regard your books as "works of craftsmanship for sale."

BURGESS: The Muse in *Nothing Like the Sun* was not a real muse—only syphilis. The girl in *Enderby* is really sex, which, like syphilis, has something to do with the creative process. I mean, you can't be a genius and sexually impotent. I still think that inspiration comes out of the act of making an artifact, a work of craft.

INTERVIEWER: Are works of art the products of strong libido?

BURGESS: Yes, I think art is sublimated libido. You can't be a eunuch priest, and you can't be a eunuch artist. I became interested in syphilis when I worked for a time at a mental hospital full of GPI cases. I discovered there was a correlation between the spirochete and mad talent. The tubercle also produces a lyrical drive. Keats had both.

INTERVIEWER: Has your interest in Mann's *Doctor Faustus* influenced the use of syphilis and other diseases in your own work?

BURGESS: I've been much influenced by the thesis of Mann's *Doctor Faustus,* but I wouldn't want to have syphilis myself in order to be Wagner or Shakespeare or Henry VIII. Some prices are too high to pay. Oh, you'll want examples of these GPI talents. There was one man who'd turned himself into a kind of Scriabin, another who could give you the day of the week for any date in history, another who wrote poems like Christopher Smart. Many patients were orators or grandiose liars. It was like being imprisoned in a history of European art. Politics as well.

INTERVIEWER: Have you used in your novels any of the GPI cases that you encountered?

BURGESS: I did have the intention at one time of writing a long novel—a kind of *Magic Mountain,* I suppose—about life in a mental hospital; and perhaps I may yet get down to it. Of course, the trouble is it would take on a kind of political significance. People might think of works like *Cancer Ward;* it might be thought as presenting a clearly marked division between the patients and the hospital staff. One would be trading in a sort of political allegory; it's so easy to do that. Yet what interests me about a mental hospital that specializes in General Paralysis of the Insane is this relationship between disease and talent. Some of the tremendous skills that these patients show—these tremendous mad abilities—all stem out of the spirochete. I have pursued this in a couple of novels (or at least in one novel), but to do it on a larger scale would require a kind of rationale which I haven't yet worked out. I don't think it should be done purely as a documentary novel, as a naturalistic presentation of what life is like in such hospitals; but it does suggest to me that it's tied up with symbols of some kind—tied up with an interior, deeper meaning. Of course one never knows what this meaning will be, but *The Magic Mountain* has its deeper meanings beneath the naturalistic surface. I wouldn't want to imitate that. One has to wait, I'm afraid—a long time sometimes—for the experience one's had to present itself in workable form, as a form that can be shaped into something like a work of art.

INTERVIEWER: Do you see any contradiction in choosing a craftsman like Joyce as one of your literary models while classifying yourself as a "Grub Street writer" at the same time?

BURGESS: Why contradiction? But I've never really regarded Joyce as a literary model. Joyce can't be imitated, and there's no imitation Joyce in my work. All you can learn from Joyce is the exact use of language. "Grub Street writer" means Dr. Johnson as well as our wretched columnists, and Johnson was an exact user of language.

INTERVIEWER: You've certainly studied Joyce very thoroughly. Does knowing what he has done open more doors than it closes?

BURGESS: Joyce opened doors only to his own narrow world; his experiments were for himself only. But all novels are experimental, and *Finnegans Wake* is no more spectacular an experiment than, say, *Prancing Nigger* or *His Monkey Wife*. It looks spectacular because of the language. *MF,* believe it or not, is a completely original experiment.

INTERVIEWER: Isn't Joyce's attempt to devote virtually an entire novel to the Unconscious more than a purely linguistic experiment?

BURGESS: Yes, of course. The wakeworld is only narrow in that it's asleep, fixed on one set of impulses only, has too few characters.

INTERVIEWER: Can't contemporary writers use some of Joyce's techniques without being mere imitators?

BURGESS: You can't use Joyce's techniques without being Joyce. Technique and material are one. You can't write like Beethoven without writing Beethoven, unless you're Beethoven.

INTERVIEWER: Has Nabokov influenced your work at all? You've praised *Lolita* highly.

BURGESS: Reading *Lolita* meant that I enjoyed using lists of things in *The Right to an Answer.* I've not been much influenced by Nabokov, nor do I intend to be. I was writing the way I write before I knew he existed. But I've not been impressed so much by another writer in the last decade or so.

INTERVIEWER: Yet you've been called an "English Nabokov," probably because of the cosmopolitan strain and verbal ingenuity in your writing.

BURGESS: No influence. He's a Russian, I'm English. I meet him halfway in certain temperamental endowments. He's very artificial, though.

INTERVIEWER: In what way?

BURGESS: Nabokov is a natural dandy on the grand international scale. I'm still a provincial boy scared of being too nattily dressed. All writing is artificial, and Nabokov's artifacts are only contrived in the *récit* part. His dialogue is always natural and masterly (when he wants it to be). *Pale Fire* is only termed a novel because there's no other term for it. It's a masterly literary artifact which is poem, commentary, casebook, allegory, sheer structure. But I note that most people go back to reading the poem, not what surrounds the poem. It's a fine poem, of course. Where Nabokov goes wrong, I think, is in sometimes *sounding* old-fashioned—a matter of rhythm, as though Huysmans is to him a sound and modern writer whose tradition is worthy to be worked in. John Updike sounds old-fashioned sometimes in the same way —glorious vocabulary and imagery but a lack of muscle in the rhythm.

INTERVIEWER: Does Nabokov rank at the top with Joyce?

BURGESS: He won't go down in history as one of the greatest names. He's unworthy to unlatch Joyce's shoe.

INTERVIEWER: Have any new writers appeared of late that you think are destined for greatness?

BURGESS: I can't think of any in England. The trouble with American writers is that they die before becoming great—Nathanael West, Scott Fitzgerald, etc. Mailer will become a great autobiographer. Ellison will be great if only he'll write more. Too many *homines unius libri* like Heller.

INTERVIEWER: American writers certainly tend to burn themselves out early, at least. Do you think it takes more than one book for a writer to earn the label "great"?

BURGESS: A man can write one book that can be great, but this doesn't make him a great writer—just the writer of a great book. Samuel Butler's *Way of All Flesh* is a great novel, but nobody calls Butler a great novelist. I think a writer has to extend very widely, as well as plunge very deep, to be a great novelist.

INTERVIEWER: Did Fitzgerald write a great novel?

BURGESS: I don't think Fitzgerald's books great—style too derivatively romantic, far less of that curious freshness of vision than you find in Hemingway—Hemingway is a great novelist, I think, but he never wrote a great novel (a great novella, yes). I think America likes its artists to die young, in atonement for materialist America's sins. The English leave the dying young to Celts like Dylan Thomas and Behan. But I can't understand the American literary block—as in Ellison or Salinger—unless it means that the blocked man isn't forced economically to write (as the English writer, lacking campuses and grants, usually is) and hence can afford the luxury of fearing the critics' pounce on a new work not as good as the last (or the first). American writers drink a lot when they're "blocked" and drunkenness—being a kind of substitute for art—makes the block worse. I've found it best, especially since my first wife, who drank less than I, died of cirrhosis, to drink little. But I smoke much, and that's probably worse than five martinis a day.

INTERVIEWER: You've spoken highly of Defoe as a novelist and practical journalist, and you also admire Sterne as a writer. What special appeal do these eighteenth-century writers have for you?

BURGESS: I admire Defoe because he worked hard. I admire Sterne because he did everything the French are trying so unhandily to do now. Eighteenth-century prose has a tremendous vitality and scope. Not Fielding, though. Sentimental, too much given to contrivances. Sterne and Swift (who, Joyce said, should have exchanged names) are men one can learn technically from all the time.

INTERVIEWER: Speaking of the French—your playful novels of ideas tend to be more in the French literary tradition, perhaps, than any other. Has this kept them from becoming better known in England and America?

BURGESS: The novels I've written are really medieval Catholic in their thinking, and people don't want that today. God forbid they should be "French." If they're not read, it's because the vocabulary is too big, and people don't like using dictionaries when they're reading mere novels. I don't give a damn, anyway.

INTERVIEWER: This Catholic emphasis accounts in part for the frequent comparisons made between your novels and Evelyn Waugh's, and yet you've said you don't find Waugh's aristocratic idea of Catholicism attractive. What do you like about his work?

BURGESS: Waugh is funny, Waugh is elegant, Waugh is economical. His Catholicism, which I despise as all cradle Catholics despise converts, is the thing in him which means least to me. Indeed, it injures his *Sword of Honour.*

INTERVIEWER: This charge has often been made—along with that of sentimentality—against *Brideshead Revisited,* but *Sword of Honour* is often called the best novel in English about World War II. How does Waugh's (or Guy Crouchback's) Catholicism weaken it?

BURGESS: Crouchback's Catholicism weakens *Sword of Honour* in the sense that it sectarianizes the book—I mean, we have Crouchback's moral view of the war, and this is not enough: We need something that lies beneath religion. In our age it's a weakness to make Catholic theology the basis of a novel since it means everything's cut and dried and the author doesn't have to rethink things out. The weakness of Greene's *Heart of the Matter* is derived from its author's fascination with theology: the sufferings of the hero are theological sufferings, invalid outside the narrow field of Catholicism. When I taught Waugh and Greene to Muslim students in Malaya, they used to laugh. Why can't this man have two wives if he wants them, they would say. What's wrong with eating the bit of bread the priest gives you when you've been sleeping with a woman not your wife, and so on. They never laughed at the tragic heroes of the Greeks and Elizabethans.

INTERVIEWER: Does the difference between cradle and convert Catholicism influence an author's work in such an essential way that you tend to prefer a novelist like François Mauriac to Graham Greene?

BURGESS: English converts to Catholicism tend to be bemused by its glamor and even look for more glamor in it than is actually there—like Waugh, dreaming of an old English Catholic aristocracy, or Greene, fascinated by sin in a very cold-blooded way. I wished I liked Mauriac more as a writer. The fact is that I prefer the converted Catholics because they happen to be better novelists. I do try to forget that Greene is a Catholic when I read him. He, too, is now, I think, trying to forget. *The Comedians* was a kind of philosophical turning point. *Travels with My Aunt* is deliciously free of morality of any kind, except a very delightful kind of inverted morality.

INTERVIEWER: In an essay on Waugh you mentioned "the Puritan that lurks in every English Catholic." Do you see this residue of Puritanism lurking in your own writing at all?

BURGESS: Of course it's in me. We English take our Catholicism seriously, which the Italians and French don't, and that makes us earnest and obsessed about sin. We really absorbed hell—perhaps a very Nordic notion—and think about it when committing adultery. I'm so Puritanical that I can't describe a kiss without blushing.

INTERVIEWER: Are there any limits that you think an author should observe in the language he uses to present controversial subject matter?

BURGESS: My aversion to describing amorous details in my work is probably that I treasure physical love so highly I don't want to let strangers in on it. For, after all, when we describe copulation we're describing our own experiences. I like privacy. I think that other writers should do what they can do, and if they can spend—as one of my American girl students did—ten pages on the act of fellatio without embarrassing themselves, very good luck to them. But I think there's more artistic pleasure to be gained from the ingenious circumvention of a taboo than from what is called total permissiveness. When I wrote my first Enderby novel, I had to make my hero say "For cough," since "Fuck off" was not then acceptable. With the second book the climate had changed, and Enderby was at liberty to say "Fuck off." I wasn't happy. It was too easy. He still said "For cough," while others responded with "Fuck off." A compromise. Literature, however, thrives on taboos, just as all art thrives on technical difficulties.

INTERVIEWER: Several years ago you wrote, "I believe the wrong God is temporarily ruling the world and that the true God has gone under," and added that the novelist's vocation predisposes him to this Manichaean view. Do you still believe this?

BURGESS: I still hold this belief.

INTERVIEWER: Why do you think that the novelist is predisposed to regard the world in terms of "essential opposition"? Unlike the Manichaeans you seem to maintain a traditional Christian belief in original sin.

BURGESS: Novels are about conflicts. The novelist's world is one of essential oppositions of character, aspiration, and so on. I'm only a Manichee in the widest sense of believing that duality is the ultimate reality; the original-sin bit is not really a contradiction, though it does lead one on to depressingly French heresies, like Graham Greene's own Jansenism, as well as Albigensianism (Joan of Arc's religion), Catharism, and so on. I'm entitled to an eclectic theology as a novelist, if not as a human being.

INTERVIEWER: In planning your novels, have you ever considered separating them, as Simenon does, into "commercial" and "uncommercial" works or, like Greene, into "novels" and "entertainments"?

BURGESS: All my novels belong to the one category—intended to be, as it were, serious entertainment, no moral aim, no solemnity. I want to please.

INTERVIEWER: Aren't you divorcing morality from aesthetics? This view is certainly consistent with your dismissal in *Shakespeare* of the Anglo-Saxon notion that a great artist must have a great moral sensibility.

BURGESS: I don't divorce morals and aesthetics. I merely believe that a man's literary greatness is no index of his personal

ethics. I don't, true, think that the job of literature is to teach us
how to behave, but I think it can make clearer the whole business
of moral choice by showing what the nature of life's problems is.
It's after truth, which is not goodness.

INTERVIEWER: You've said that the novel gets an implied set
of values derived from religion but that other arts, such as music
and architecture, are, unlike fiction, "neutral." Does this make
them more or less attractive at this point?

BURGESS: I enjoy writing music precisely because one is divorced from "human" considerations like belief, conduct. Pure
form, nothing more. But then I tend to despise music just because
it is so *mindless*. I've been writing a string quartet based on a
musical theme that Shakespeare throws at us, in sol-fa notation,
in *Love's Labour's Lost* (the theme is CDGAEF), and it's been
pure, bliss. I've been thoroughly absorbed by it, on planes, in hotel
bedrooms, anywhere where I had nothing else to do and there was
no bloody musak playing. (Don't the musak purveyors ever think
of the people who actually have to write music?) Now I'm a little
ashamed that the music engages nothing but purely formal problems. So I oscillate between a hankering after pure form and a
realization that literature is probably valuable because it *says
things*.

INTERVIEWER: How does political neutrality figure in all this?
In your novels the neutrals, such as Mr. Theodorescu in *Tremor
of Intent*, are usually villains.

BURGESS: If art should be neutral, if it can, life should be
committed, if it can. There's no connection between political and
religious neutrality and that blessed *achieved* neutrality of, say,
music. Art is, so to speak, the church triumphant, but the rest of
life is in the church militant. I believe that good and evil exist,
though they have nothing to do with art, and that evil has to be
resisted. There's no inconsistency in holding an aesthetic so different from such an ethic.

INTERVIEWER: Several of your recent novels have exotic foreign settings, even though you remarked a few years ago that the
artist should exhaust the resources of the "here and now" as a

true test of his art. Have you changed your mind?

BURGESS: Yes, I changed my mind. I'm limited by temperament, I now discover, to being moved or excited by any place in the world so long as it's not England. This means that all my settings must be "exotic."

INTERVIEWER: Why do you consider England so dull a subject?

BURGESS: Dull for me if not for others. I like societies where there's a dynamism of conflict. In other words, I think novels should be about the whole of a society—by implication if nothing else—and not just a little pocket inside. English fiction tends to be about these pockets—love affairs in Hampstead, Powell's bohemian aristocracy, Snow's men of power. Dickens gave you the lot, like Balzac. Much modern American fiction gives you the lot. You could reconstruct the whole of modern America from even a little mad fantasy like Phil Roth's *The Breast*. But I may have a personal thing about England—a sense of exclusion, and so on. It may even be so simple a matter as liking extreme climates, fights in bars, exotic waterfronts, fish soup, a lot of garlic. I find it easier to imagine a surrealistic version of New Jersey than of old England, though I could see some American genius making a whole strange world of Mr. Heath's inheritance. Probably (as Thomas Pynchon never went to Valletta or Kafka to America) it's best to imagine your own foreign country. I wrote a very good account of Paris before I ever went there. Better than the real thing.

INTERVIEWER: Was this in *The Worm and the Ring?*

BURGESS: Yes. Paris was a town I always tried to avoid: But I've been more and more in it recently and find that the account of Paris I wrote (although it smells of maps and tourist guides) is not unlike the reality. This is true also with Joyce's Gibraltar in *Ulysses;* one has no need to visit the country to write about the country.

INTERVIEWER: And yet you draw a good picture of Leningrad in *Honey for the Bears.*

BURGESS: Oh, I knew Leningrad. Yes, that's right. But not too well; for if one gets to know a town too well, then the sharpness of the impression is blunted, and one is not interested in writing about it. Anyway, the interesting point is that one first meets a town through its smells; this is especially true in Europe. Leningrad has a peculiar smell of its own, and you become habituated to these smells in time, and you forget what they are; and you're not able to approach it in those highly sensuous terms when writing about it if you know a place too well. If you're in a town for about a month somewhere, you can't retain a sensuous impression. As with Paris, you smell the Gauloise when you arrive; but you cease to smell the Gauloise in time. You get so used to it.

INTERVIEWER: You've said that Leningrad resembles Manchester. How are they alike?

BURGESS: I think it was just the sense of the architecture, the rather broken-down architecture of Leningrad, the sense of large numbers of the working class, rather shabbily dressed. And I suppose in some ways the *smell* of Manchester—I always associated Manchester with the smell of tanneries, very pungent smells, as you know. I got this same smell out of Leningrad. It's a small thing, but these small things have a curious habit of becoming important. You try to fix a place in your mind. I don't know what the smell of Milwaukee is, I don't think the American cities have any smell. That's probably why they are rather unmemorable. Smell is most elusive of the senses. To a novelist it is somehow the most important of the senses.

INTERVIEWER: You've also said that the serious novelist should be prepared to stay in one place and really get to know it. Do you hope to do this with Italy now?

BURGESS: Again, I seem to have changed my mind. I think I shall want to invent places more than merely reproduce them, and don't please put this down to the influence of *Ada*. The next four novels will be set, respectively, in medieval England, modern New Jersey, Italy in the last fifty years, Jane Austen's England.

INTERVIEWER: Have your travels given you a special sense of the variety of human types, such as Forster's Prof. Godbole?

BURGESS: Fundamentally people are all the same, and I've lived among enough different races long enough to be dogmatic about this. Godbole in *A Passage to India* is an eccentric mystic of the type that any culture can throw up.

INTERVIEWER: At this point do you regard yourself as an expatriate Englishman or as an exile?

BURGESS: A verbal quibble. I've voluntarily exiled myself, but not forever. Nevertheless, I can't think of any good reason for going back to England except on a holiday. But one is, as Simone Weil said, faithful to the cuisine one was brought up on, and that probably constitutes patriotism. I am sometimes mentally and physically ill for Lancashire food—hot pot, lobscowse, and so on —and I have to have these things. I'm loyal to Lancashire, I suppose, but not strongly enough to wish to go back and live there.

INTERVIEWER: What are "hot pot" and "lobscowse"?

BURGESS: Hot pot, or Lancashire hot pot, is made in this way. An earthenware dish, a layer of trimmed lamb chops, a layer of sliced onions, a layer of sliced potatoes, then continue the layers till you reach the top. Add seasoned stock. On top put mushrooms or more potato slices to brown. Add oysters or kidneys as well if you wish. Bake in a moderate oven for a long time. Eat with pickled cabbage. Lobscowse is a sailor's dish from Liverpool (Liverpudlians are called "scousers" or "scowsers") and is very simple. Dice potatoes and onions and cook in a pan of seasoned water. When they're nearly done, get rid of excess liquid and add a can or two of cubed (or diced) corned beef. Heat gently. Eat with mixed pickles. I love cooking these dishes, and, once known, everybody loves them. They're honest and simple. Lancashire has a great cuisine, including a notable shop cuisine—meaning you can buy great delicacies in shops. Lancashire women traditionally work in the cotton mills and cook dinner only at weekends. Hence the things you can get in cooked food shops—fish and chips, Bury puddings, Eccles cakes, tripe, cowheel, meat pies (hot, with gravy poured into a hole from a jug), and so on. Fish and chips is now, I think, internationally accepted. Meat and potato pie is perhaps the greatest of the Lancashire dishes—a "drier" hot pot with a fine flaky crust.

INTERVIEWER: I'm tempted to visit Manchester. Lawrence

Durrell, another expatriate English writer, has said that since
America and Russia are going to determine our future, one is
obliged to stop traveling and start thinking when one is in either
country. It's different, he says, from going to Italy—a pure pleasure. Do you agree?

BURGESS: Durrell has never yet said anything I could agree
with. He reminds me of that TV show woman in America, Virginia Graham. I just don't know what the hell he can mean by
that. In America and Russia I meet people, get drunk, eat, just
as I do in Italy. I see no signs of purely metaphysical import.
Those are left to governments, and governments are what I try
to ignore. All governments are evil, including that of Italy.

INTERVIEWER: That sounds vaguely anarchic, or at least un-
American. Did you have an undergraduate Marxist period, like
Victor Crabbe in *The Long Day Wanes?*

BURGESS: I was never a Marxist, though I was always, even as
an undergraduate, ready to play the Marxist game—analyzing
Shakespeare in Marxist terms, and so on. I always loved dialectical
materialism. But it was a structuralist love from the start. To take
socialism seriously, as opposed to minimal socialization (what
America needs so desperately), is ridiculous.

INTERVIEWER: Doesn't "minimal socialization" require an in-
crease in the size and power of central government? Only the
American federal government can fund the equivalent of the
English or Scandinavian health plans; the need for inexpensive
medical treatment is acute here.

BURGESS: I loathe the State but concede that socialized medicine is a priority in any civilized country today. In England it
saved me from bankruptcy during my wife's final illness (though
perhaps a private insurance policy might have taken care of it.
You can't opt out of the state scheme, however). Socialized medicine—which in England was a liberal idea, anyway—doesn't have
to mean out and out socialism with everything nationalized. If
America gets it, it will be only the doctors and dentists who will
try not to make it work, but, as in England, there's no reason why
a private practice shouldn't coexist with a national health one.

You go to a dentist in England, and he says "Private or National Health?" The difference in treatment is hardly noticeable, but the State materials (tooth fillings, spectacles, and so on) are inferior to what you buy as a private patient.

INTERVIEWER: Do these views make you a political conservative, then? You've said you would reluctantly vote conservative in England.

BURGESS: I think I'm a Jacobite, meaning that I'm traditionally Catholic, support the Stuart monarchy and want to see it restored, and distrust imposed change even when it seems to be for the better. I honestly believe that America should become monarchist (preferably Stuart) because with a limited monarchy you have no president, and a president is one more corruptible element in government. I hate all republics. I suppose my conservatism, since the ideal of a Catholic Jacobite imperial monarch isn't practicable, is really a kind of anarchism.

INTERVIEWER: Many Americans believe their presidency has evolved into a form of monarchy, with unhappy results. Do you see anarchy as a viable political alternative?

BURGESS: The U.S. presidency is a Tudor monarchy plus telephones. Your alternative is either a return to the limited monarchy of the British Commonwealth—a constitutional monarch is at least out of politics and can't get dirty or corrupt—or devolution into unfederated states with a loose cooperative framework for large development schemes. Anarchy is a man's own thing, and I think it's too late in the day to think of it as a viable system or nonsystem in a country as large as America. It was all right for Blake or for Thoreau, both of whom I admire immensely, but we'll never get it so full-blooded again. All we can do is keep pricking our government all the time, disobeying all we dare (after all, we have livings to earn), asking why, maintaining a habit of distrust.

INTERVIEWER: You've urged fellow artists to seek depth by "digging for the mythical." Are you more interested in creating new myths or in re-examining old ones, as you did with the *Aeneid* in *A Vision of Battlements?*

BURGESS: At present I'm interested in what structuralism can teach us about myth. I don't think I can invent my own myths, and I still think there's a great deal of fictional revivification possible with regard to such myths as the Jason/Golden Fleece one (on which I plan a novel, incidentally). Existing myths carry useful depth, a profundity of meaning which saves the novelist a lot of inventive trouble.

INTERVIEWER: How does Jason's pursuit of the Golden Fleece apply to our time?

BURGESS: My Jason novel, if I ever write it, will just use the Argonaut story as a framework for picaresque adventures. No deeper significance.

INTERVIEWER: Have you considered basing a novel on myths associated with Oriental religions, as Mann did in *The Transposed Heads?*

BURGESS: Strangely, I've been contemplating making a musical play out of Mann's *The Transposed Heads*—very charming, but only a game despite the claims of psychological profundity sometimes made for it. I've six years in the East but am not greatly drawn to Eastern myths, except that of the endless Javanese shadow-play, which is like *Finnegans Wake*, anyway. But I've thought of a novel based on Munshi Abdullah's *Hikayat.* That German hunger for the East—Hesse as well as Mann—is very curious. They might not have seen it as so romantic if they'd been colonial officers. Perhaps that's what they really wanted to be.

INTERVIEWER: Structuralism plays a big part in *MF.* How important is it to you as a novelist of ideas?

BURGESS: Structuralism is the scientific confirmation of a certain theological conviction—that life is binary, that this is a duoverse and so on. What I mean is that the notion of essential opposition—not God/Devil but just x/y—is the fundamental one, and this is a kind of purely structuralist view. We end up with form as more important than content, with speech and art as phatic processes, with the big moral imponderables as mere hot air. Marshall McLuhan has been limping along this track independently of Lévi-Strauss. How marvelous that the essential bifurcation which is man is expressed in trousers that carry Lévi-Strauss's name.

INTERVIEWER: Along with establishing a firm connection between language and myth, you've also indicated about the future of the novel that "only through the exploration of language can the personality be coaxed into yielding a few more of its secrets." Would you expand on that?

BURGESS: By extension of vocabulary, by careful distortion of syntax, by exploitation of various prosodic devices traditionally monopolized by poetry, surely certain indefinite or complex areas of the mind can more competently be rendered than in the style of, say, Irving Stone or Wallace.

INTERVIEWER: Are you ever tempted to lavish complex prose on a simple protagonist, as Flaubert did in *A Simple Heart?*

BURGESS: Try and make your language fit your concept of the subject more than the subject itself. "Here's this stupid man who's written a most highly wrought work about a housemaid called Félicité." But Flaubert was concerned, surely, with the nobility of that heart and lavished his prose riches upon it. Style is less a preoccupation than a perennial problem. Finding the right style for the subject, I mean. This must mean that the subject comes first and the style after.

INTERVIEWER: You've referred to yourself as a "serious novelist who is attempting to extend the range of subject matter available to fiction." How have you tried to do this?

BURGESS: I've written about the dying British empire, lavatories, structuralism, and so on, but I don't really think that that kind of subject matter is what I had in mind when I made that statement. I meant the modification of the sensibility of the British novel, which I may have achieved a little, a very little. The new areas are more technical than thematic.

INTERVIEWER: In *The Novel Now* you said that the novel is the only important literary form we have left. Why do you think this is true?

BURGESS: Yes, the novel is the only *big* literary form we have left. It is capable of enclosing the other, lesser, literary forms, from the play to the lyric poem. Poets are doing well enough, especially in America, but they can't achieve the architectonic skill which once lay behind the epic (for which the novel is now a substitute). The short, sharp burst—in music as well as poetry —is not enough. The novel has the monopoly of *form* today.

INTERVIEWER: Granted this limited primacy of the novel, it's disturbing that novel sales in general are declining and that public attention is focused more on nonfiction. Are you tempted to turn more to biography, for example, in the future?

BURGESS: I shall carry on with novelizing and hope for some little reward on the side. Biography is very hard work, no room for invention. But if I were a young man now, I wouldn't dream of trying to become a professional novelist. But some day, perhaps soon, the old realization will come back—that reading about imaginary characters and their adventures is the greatest pleasure in the world. Or the second greatest.

INTERVIEWER: What is the first?

BURGESS: That depends upon your own tastes.

INTERVIEWER: Why do you regret becoming a professional novelist?

BURGESS: I think that the mental strain, the worry, you know, the self-doubt, are hardly worth the candle; the agonies of creation and the sense of responsibility to one's muse—all these various things become more than one can live with.

INTERVIEWER: Are the odds much longer today against anyone's sustaining himself by quality fiction writing?

BURGESS: I don't know. I know that the older I get the more I want to live and the less opportunity I have. I don't think I wanted to become chained to an art form; establishing one's identity through an art form, one is a kind of Frankenstein creating a monster, so to speak. I wish I could live easier; I wish I didn't have the sense of responsibility to the arts. More than anything, I wish I didn't have the prospect of having to write certain novels, which must be written because nobody else will write them. I wish I were freer, I like freedom; and I think I would have been much happier living as a colonial officer writing the odd novel in my spare time. Then I would have been happier than as a sort of professional man of letters, making a living out of words.

INTERVIEWER: Do film versions help or hinder novels?

BURGESS: Films help the novels they're based on, which I both resent and am grateful for. My *Clockwork Orange* paperback has sold over a million in America, thanks to dear Stanley. But I don't like being beholden to a mere film maker. I want to prevail through pure literature. Impossible, of course.

INTERVIEWER: You've referred to *A Vision of Battlements,* your first novel, "like all my stories since, as a slow and cruel stripping off of illusion," yet you are often called a comic writer. Is comedy by nature so cruel, or do you consider yourself more as a satirist?

BURGESS: Comedy is concerned with truth quite as much as tragedy; and the two, as Plato recognized, have something fundamental in common. They're both stripping processes; they both tear off externals and show man as a poor forked animal. Satire is a *particular* kind of comedy, limiting itself to particular areas of behavior, not to the general human condition. I don't think I'm a satirist.

INTERVIEWER: Are you a black humorist as well—or are all these categories too confining?

BURGESS: I think I'm a comic writer, *malgré moi.* My Napoleon is turning out comic, and I certainly didn't intend that. I don't think I know what black humor is. Satirist? Satire is a difficult medium, ephemeral unless there's tremendous vitality in the form itself—like *Absalom and Achitophel, Tale of a Tub, Animal Farm:* I mean, the work has to subsist as story or poetry even when the objects of the satire are forgotten. Satire is now an element in some other form, not a form in itself. I like to be called just a novelist.

INTERVIEWER: About ten years ago you wrote that you considered yourself a pessimist but believed that "the world has much solace to offer—love, food, music, the immense variety of race and language, literature, the pleasure of artistic creation." Would you make up the same list of saving graces today?

BURGESS: Yes, no change.

INTERVIEWER: Georges Simenon, another professional, has said that "writing is not a profession but a vocation of unhappiness. I don't think an artist can ever be happy." Do you think this is true?

BURGESS: Yes, Simenon's right. My eight-year-old son said the other day: "Dad, why don't you write for *fun?*" Even he divined that the process as I practice it is prone to irritability and despair. I suppose, apart from my marriage, I was happiest when I was doing a teaching job and had nothing much to think about in the vacations. The anxiety involved is intolerable. And—I differ here from Simenon—the financial rewards just don't make up for the expenditure of energy, the damage to health caused by stimulants and narcotics, the fear that one's work isn't good enough. I think, if I had enough money, I'd give up writing tomorrow.

JOHN CULLINAN

14. Jack Kerouac

Jack Kerouac was born of French-Canadian parents on March 12, 1922, in Lowell, Massachusetts. He attended Columbia College, where he met Lucien Carr, William Burroughs, John Clellon Holmes, and Allen Ginsberg, and was introduced by Ginsberg to Neal Cassady. Kerouac and these friends formed the core of the "beat" movement of the early 1950s. From 1946 to 1948 Kerouac wrote *The Town and the City*, published in 1950. Kerouac and Cassady embarked on a cross-country trip in 1947, the first of a series of wild journeys that continued unabated for the next three years. In 1951 he wrote the teletype-role manuscript of *On the Road* in three weeks in New York, though he was unable to find a publisher for six years. Kerouac spent that time, as he said, "writing whatever came into my head, hopping freights, hitch-hiking, and working as a railroad brakeman, deckhand and scullion on merchant ships, government fire lookout, and hundreds of assorted jobs." During those years he wrote *Visions of Cody, Doctor Sax, Book of Dreams, The Subterraneans, Mexico City Blues,* and others. With the publication of *On the Road* in 1957, he achieved immediate fame, and his other books found their way into print shortly thereafter.

In the early 1960s he finished *Desolation Angels,* and wrote *Dharma Bums* and *Big Sur.* In the last three years of his life, he pulled away from his former friends, moved back to Lowell (where he wrote *Vanity of Duluoz* in 1967), and married Stella Sampas, an old friend. Kerouac lived in Lowell with his mother and Stella until 1969, when his mother's poor health brought about a move to St. Petersburg, Florida, where he died of abdominal hemorrhaging on October 21, 1969.

Jack Kerouac manuscript page

J. Oliver Mitchell

Jack Kerouac

Jack Kerouac is now forty-five years old. His thirteenth novel,
Vanity of Duluoz, *was published earlier this year (1967). He lives*
with his wife of one year, Stella, and his invalid mother in a brick
ranch-style house in a residential district of Lowell, Massachusetts,
the city in which he spent all of his childhood. The Kerouacs have
no telephone. Ted Berrigan had contacted Kerouac some months
earlier and persuaded him to do the interview. When he felt the
time had come for their meeting to take place, he simply showed
up at the Kerouacs' house. Two friends, poets Aram Saroyan and
Duncan McNaughton, accompanied him. Kerouac answered his
ring; Berrigan quickly told him his name and the visit's purpose.
Kerouac welcomed the poets, but before he could show them in,
his wife, a very determined woman, seized him from behind and
told the group to leave at once.

"Jack and I began talking simultaneously, saying 'Paris Review'!
'Interview!' etc.," Berrigan recalls, "while Duncan and Aram be-

*gan to slink back toward the car. All seemed lost, but I kept talking
in what I hoped was a civilized, reasonable, calming and friendly
tone of voice, and soon Mrs. Kerouac agreed to let us in for twenty
minutes, on the condition that there be no drinking.*

*"Once inside, as it became evident that we actually were in
pursuit of a serious purpose, Mrs. Kerouac became more friendly,
and we were able to commence the interview. It seems that people
still show up constantly at the Kerouacs' looking for the author of*
On the Road *and stay for days, drinking all the liquor and diverting
Jack from his serious occupations.*

*"As the evening progressed the atmosphere changed considerably, and Mrs. Kerouac, Stella, proved a gracious and charming
hostess. The most amazing thing about Jack Kerouac is his magic
voice, which sounds exactly like his works, and is capable of the
most astounding and disconcerting changes in no time flat. It
dictates everything, including this interview.*

*"After the interview, Kerouac, who had been sitting throughout
the interview in a President Kennedy-type rocker, moved over to a
big poppa chair, and said, 'So you boys are poets, hey? Well, let's
hear some of your poetry'. We stayed for about an hour longer, and
Aram and I read some of our things. Finally, he gave each of us
a signed broadside of a recent poem of his, and we left."*

*Some portions of this interview have been filled out with Kerouac's written replies to questions put to him subsequent to the
interview. It was felt these additions would add substance to the
portrait of the author and his métier.*

INTERVIEWER: Could we put the footstool over here to put this
on?

STELLA: Yes.

KEROUAC: God, you're so inadequate there, Berrigan.

INTERVIEWER: Well, I'm no tape-recorder man, Jack. I'm just
a big talker, like you. O.K., we're off.

KEROUAC: O.K.? *(Whistles)* O.K.?

INTERVIEWER: Actually I'd like to start . . . the first book I ever
read by you, oddly enough, since most people first read *On the*

Road . . . the first one I read was *The Town and the City* . . .

KEROUAC: Gee!

INTERVIEWER: I checked it out of the library . . .

KEROUAC: Gee! . . . Did you read *Dr. Sax?* . . . *Tristessa?* . . .

INTERVIEWER: You better believe it. I even read *Rimbaud.* I have a copy of *Visions of Cody* that Ron Padgett bought in Tulsa, Oklahoma.

KEROUAC: Screw Ron Padgett! You know why? He started a little magazine called *White Dove Review* in Kansas City, was it? Tulsa? Oklahoma . . . yes. He wrote, Start our magazine off by sending us a great big poem. So I sent him the "Thrashing Doves." And then I sent him another one and he rejected the second one because his magazine was already started. That's to show you how punks try to make their way by scratching down on a man's back. Aw, he's no poet. You know who's a great poet? I know who the great poets are.

INTERVIEWER: Who?

KEROUAC: Let's see, is it . . . William Bissette of Vancouver. An Indian boy. Bill Bissette, or Bissonnette.

SAROYAN: Let's talk about Jack Kerouac.

KEROUAC: He's not better than Bill Bissette, but he's very original.

INTERVIEWER: Why don't we begin with editors. How do you . . .

KEROUAC: O.K. All my editors since Malcolm Cowley have had instructions to leave my prose exactly as I wrote it. In the days of Malcolm Cowley, with *On the Road* and *The Dharma Bums,* I had no power to stand by my style for better or for worse. When Malcolm Cowley made endless revisions and inserted thousands of needless commas like, say, Cheyenne, Wyoming (why not just say Cheyenne Wyoming and let it go at that, for instance), why, I spent $500 making the complete restitution of the *Bums* manuscript and got a bill from Viking Press called "Revisions." Ha ho ho. And so you asked about how do I work with an editor . . . well, nowadays I am just grateful to him for his assistance in proofreading the manuscript and in discovering logical errors, such as dates,

names of places. For instance in my last book I wrote Firth of
Forth then looked it up, on the suggestion of my editor, and
found that I'd really sailed off the Firth of Clyde. Things like that.
Or I spelled Aleister Crowley "Alisteir," or he discovered little
mistakes about the yardage in football games . . . and so forth. By
not revising what you've already written you simply give the
reader the actual workings of your mind during the writing itself:
you confess your thoughts about events in your own unchangeable
way . . . well, look, did you ever hear a guy telling a long wild tale
to a bunch of men in a bar and all are listening and smiling, did
you ever hear that guy stop to revise himself, go back to a previous
sentence to improve it, to defray its rhythmic thought impact
. . . If he pauses to blow his nose, isn't he planning his next
sentence? and when he lets that next sentence loose, isn't it once
and for all the way he wanted to say it? Doesn't he depart the
thought of that sentence and, as Shakespeare says, "forever holds
his tongue" on the subject, since he's passed over it like a part of
the river flows over a rock once and for all and never returns and
can never flow any other way in time? Incidentally, as for my bug
against periods, that was for the prose in *October in the Railroad
Earth*, very experimental, intended to clack along all the way like
a steam engine pulling a 100-car freight with a talky caboose at
the end, that was my way at the time, and it still can be done if
the thinking during the swift writing is confessional and pure and
all excited with the life of it. And be sure of this, I spent my entire
youth writing slowly with revisions and endless re-hashing specu-
lation and deleting and got so I was writing one sentence a day
and the sentence had no FEELING. Goddamn it, FEELING is
what I like in art, not CRAFTINESS and the hiding of feelings.

INTERVIEWER: What encouraged you to use the "spontaneous" style of *On the Road?*

KEROUAC: I got the idea for the spontaneous style of *On the
Road* from seeing how good old Neal Cassady wrote his letters
to me, all first person, fast, mad, confessional, completely serious,
all detailed, with real names in his case however (being letters).
I remembered also Goethe's admonition, well Goethe's prophecy

that the future literature of the West would be confessional in nature; also Dostoevsky prophesied as much and might have started in on that if he'd lived long enough to do his projected masterwork, *The Great Sinner*. Cassady also began his early youthful writing with attempts at slow, painstaking, and-all-that-crap craft business, but got sick of it like I did, seeing it wasn't getting out his guts and heart the way it *felt* coming out. But I got the flash from his style. It's a cruel lie for those West Coast punks to say that I got the idea of *On the Road* from him. All his letters to me were about his younger days before I met him, a child with his father, et cetera, and about his later teenage experiences. The letter he sent me is erroneously reported to be a 13,000 word letter . . . no, the 13,000 word piece was his novel *The First Third*, which he kept in his possession. The letter, the main letter I mean, was 40,000 words long, mind you, a whole short novel. It was the greatest piece of writing I ever saw, bet-ter'n anybody in America, or at least enough to make Melville, Twain, Dreiser, Wolfe, I dunno who, spin in their graves. Allen Ginsberg asked me to lend him this vast letter so he could read it. He read it, then loaned it to a guy called Gerd Stern who lived on a houseboat in Sausalito California, in 1955, and this fellow lost the letter: overboard I presume. Neal and I called it, for convenience, the *Joan Anderson Letter* . . . all about a Christmas weekend in the poolhalls, hotel rooms, and jails of Denver, with hilarious events throughout and tragic too, even a drawing of a window, with measurements to make the reader understand, all that. Now listen: this letter would have been printed under Neal's copyright, if we could find it, but as you know, it was my property as a letter to me, so Allen shouldn't have been so careless with it, nor the guy on the houseboat. If we can unearth this entire 40,000 word letter Neal shall be justified. We also did so much fast talking between the two of us, on tape recorders, way back in 1952, and listened to them so much, we both got the secret of LINGO in telling a tale and figured that was the only way to express the speed and tension and ecstatic tomfoolery of the age. . . . Is that enough?

INTERVIEWER: How do you think this style has changed since *On the Road?*

KEROUAC: What style? Oh, the style of *On the Road.* Well as I say, Cowley riddled the original style of the manuscript there, without my power to complain, and since then my books are all published as written, as I say, and the style has varied from the highly experimental speedwriting of *Railroad Earth* to the in-grown-toenail-packed mystical style of *Tristessa,* the *Notes from the Underground* (by Dostoevsky) confessional madness of *The Subterraneans,* the perfection of the three as one in *Big Sur,* I'd say, which tells a plain tale in a smooth buttery literate run, to *Satori in Paris* which is really the first book I wrote with drink at my side (cognac and malt liquor) . . . and not to overlook *Book of Dreams,* the style of a person half awake from sleep and ripping it out in pencil by the bed . . . yes, pencil . . . what a job! bleary eyes, insaned mind bemused and mystified by sleep, details that pop out even as you write them you don't know what they mean, till you wake up, have coffee, look at it, and see the logic of dreams in dream language itself, see? . . . and finally I decided in my tired middle age to slow down and did *Vanity of Duluoz* in a more moderate style so that, having been so esoteric all these years, some earlier readers would come back and see what ten years had done to my life and thinking . . . which is after all the only thing I've got to offer, the true story of what I saw and how I saw it.

INTERVIEWER: You dictated sections of *Visions of Cody.* Have you used this method since?

KEROUAC: I didn't dictate sections of *Visions of Cody.* I typed up a segment of taped conversation with Neal Cassady, or Cody, talking about his early adventures in L.A. It's four chapters. I haven't used this method since; it really doesn't come out right, well, with Neal and with myself, when all written down and with all the Ahs and the Ohs and the Ahums and the fearful fact that the damn thing is turning and you're *forced* not to waste electricity or tape. . . . Then again, I don't know, I might have to resort to that eventually; I'm getting tired and going blind. This question stumps me. At any rate, everybody's doing it, I hear, but I'm still scribbling. . . . McLuhan says we're getting more oral so I guess we'll all learn to talk into the machine better and better.

INTERVIEWER: What is that state of "Yeatsian semi-trance" which provides the ideal atmosphere for spontaneous writing?

KEROUAC: Well, there it is, how can you be in a trance with your mouth yapping away . . . writing at least is a silent meditation even though you're going 100 miles an hour. Remember that scene in *La Dolce Vita* where the old priest is mad because a mob of maniacs have shown up to see the tree where the kids saw the Virgin Mary? He says, "Visions are not available in all this frenetic foolishness and yelling and pushing; visions are only obtainable in silence and meditation." Thar. Yup.

INTERVIEWER: You have said that haiku is not written spontaneously but is reworked and revised. Is this true of all your poetry? Why must the method for writing poetry differ from that of prose?

KEROUAC: No, first; haiku is best reworked and revised. I know, I tried. It has to be completely economical, no foliage and flowers and language rhythm, it has to be a simple little picture in three little lines. At least that's the way the old masters did it, spending months on three little lines and coming up, say, with:

> *In the abandoned boat,*
> *The hail*
> *Bounces about.*

That's Shiki.

But as for my regular English verse, I knocked it off fast like the prose, using, get this, the size of the notebook page for the form and length of the poem, just as a musician has to get out, a jazz musician, his statement within a certain number of bars, within one chorus, which spills over into the next, but he has to stop where the chorus page *stops*. And finally, too, in poetry you can be completely free to say anything you want, you don't have to tell a story, you can use secret puns, that's why I always say, when writing prose, "No time for poetry now, get your plain tale." *(Drinks are served.)*

INTERVIEWER: How do you write haiku?

KEROUAC: Haiku? You want to hear Haiku? You see you got to compress into three short lines a great big story. First you start with a haiku situation—so you see a leaf, as I told her the other night, falling on the back of a sparrow during a great big October wind storm. A big leaf falls on the back of a little sparrow. How you going to compress that into three lines? Now in Japanese you got to compress it into seventeen syllables. We don't have to do that in American—or English—because we don't have the same syllabic bullshit that your Japanese language has. So you say: Little sparrow—you don't have to say little—everybody knows a sparrow is little . . . because they fall . . . so you say

> *Sparrow*
> *with big leaf on its back—*
> *Windstorm*

No good, don't work, I reject it.

> *A little sparrow*
> *when an autumn leaf suddenly sticks to its back*
> *from the wind.*

Hah, that does it. No, it's a little bit too long. See? It's already a little bit too long, Berrigan, you know what I mean?

INTERVIEWER: Seems like there's an extra word or something, like "when." How about leaving out "when?" Say:

> *A sparrow*
> *an autumn leaf suddenly sticks to its back—*
> *From the wind!*

KEROUAC: Hey, that's all right. I think "when" was the extra word. You got the right idea there, O'Hara! A sparrow, an autumn leaf suddenly—we don't have to say "suddenly" do we?

> *A sparrow*
> *an autumn leaf sticks to its back—*
> *From the wind!*

(Kerouac writes final version into spiral notebook.)

INTERVIEWER: "Suddenly" is absolutely the kind of word we don't need there. When you publish that will you give me a footnote saying you asked me a couple of questions?

KEROUAC *(writes)*: Berrigan noticed. Right?

INTERVIEWER: Do you write poetry very much? Do you write other poetry besides haiku?

KEROUAC: It's hard to write haiku. I write long silly Indian poems. You want to hear my long silly Indian Poem?

INTERVIEWER: What kind of Indian?

KEROUAC: Iroquois. As you know from looking at me. *(Reads from notebook)*

> *On the lawn on the way to the store*
> *44 years old for the neighbors to hear*
> *hey, looka, Ma I hurt myself. Especially*
> *with that squirt.*

What's that mean?

INTERVIEWER: Say it again.

KEROUAC: Hey, looka, Ma, I hurt myself, while on the way to the store I hurt myself I fell on the lawn I yell to my mother hey looka, Ma, I hurt myself. I add, especially with that squirt.

INTERVIEWER: You fell over a sprinkler?

KEROUAC: No, my father's squirt into my ma.

INTERVIEWER: From that distance?

KEROUAC: Oh, I quit. No, I know you wouldn't get that one. I had to explain it. *(Opens notebook again and reads)*

> *Goy means Joy.*

INTERVIEWER: Send that one to Ginsberg.

KEROUAC *(reads)*:

> Happy people so called are hypocrites—it means
> the happiness wavelength can't work without
> necessary deceit, without certain scheming and lies and
> hiding. Hypocrisy and deceit, no Indians. No smiling.

INTERVIEWER: No Indians?

KEROUAC: The reason you really have a hidden hostility towards me, Berrigan, is because of the French and Indian War.

INTERVIEWER: That could be.

SAROYAN: I saw a football picture of you in the cellar of Horace Mann. You were pretty fat in those days.

STELLA: Tuffy! Here Tuffy! Come on, kitty . . .

KEROUAC: Stella, let's have another bottle or two. Yeah, I'm going to murder everybody if they let me go. I did. Hot fudge sundaes! Boom! I used to have two or three hot fudge sundaes before every game. Lou Little . . .

INTERVIEWER: He was your coach at Columbia?

KEROUAC: Lou Little was my coach at Columbia. My father went up to him and said you sneaky long-nosed finagler. . . . He says why don't you let my son, Ti Jean, Jack, start in the Army game so he can get back at his great enemy from Lowell? And Lou Little says because he's not ready. Who says he's not ready? I say he's not ready. My father says why you long nose banana nose big crook, get out of my sight! And he comes stomping out of the office smoking a big cigar. Come out of here Jack, let's get out of here. So we left Columbia together. And also when I was in the United States Navy during the war—1942—right in front of the Admirals, he walked in and says Jack, you are right! The Germans should not be our enemies. They should be our allies, as it will be proven in time. And the Admirals were all there with their mouths open, and my father would take no shit from nobody —my father didn't have nothing but a big belly about this big *(gestures with arms out in front of him)* and he would go POOM! *(Kerouac gets up and demonstrates, by puffing his belly out in front of him with explosive force and saying POOM!)* One time he was walking down the street with my mother, arm in arm, down the lower East Side. In the old days, you know, the 1940s. And here comes a whole bunch of rabbis walking arm in arm . . . teedah–teedah-teedah . . . and they wouldn't part for this Christian man and his wife. So my father went POOM! and he knocked a rabbi right in the gutter. Then he took my mother and walked on through.

Now, if you don't like that, Berrigan, that's the history of my family. They don't take no shit from nobody. In due time I ain't going to take no shit from nobody. You can record that.

Is this my wine?

INTERVIEWER: Was *The Town and the City* written under spontaneous composition principles?

KEROUAC: Some of it, sire. I also wrote another version that's hidden under the floorboards, with Burroughs.

INTERVIEWER: Yes, I've heard rumors of that book. Everybody wants to get at that book.

KEROUAC: It's called *And the Hippos Were Boiled in Their Tanks*. The hippos. Because Burroughs and I were sitting in a bar one night and we heard a newscaster saying . . . "and so the Egyptians attacked blah blah . . . and meanwhile there was a great fire in the zoo in London and the fire raced across the fields and the hippos were boiled in their tanks! Goodnight everyone!" That's Bill, he noticed that. Because he notices them kind of things.

INTERVIEWER: You really did type up his *Naked Lunch* manuscript for him in Tangiers?

KEROUAC: No . . . the first part. The first two chapters. I went to bed, and I had nightmares . . . of great long balonies coming out of my mouth. I had nightmares typing up that manuscript . . . I said, "Bill!" He said, "Keep typing it." He said, "I bought you a goddamn kerosene stove here in North Africa, you know." Among the Arabs . . . it's hard to get a kerosene stove. I'd light up the kerosene stove, and take some bedding and a little pot, or kif as we called it there . . . or maybe sometimes hasheesh . . . there by the way it's legal . . . and I'd go toktoktoktoktoktok and when I went to bed at night, these things kept coming out of my mouth. So finally these other guys showed up like Alan Ansen and Allen Ginsberg, and they spoiled the whole manuscript because they didn't type it up the way he wrote it.

INTERVIEWER: Grove Press has been issuing his Olympia Press books with lots of changes and things added.

KEROUAC: Well, in my opinion Burroughs hasn't given us anything that would interest our breaking hearts since he wrote like he did in *Naked Lunch*. Now all he does is that break-up stuff it's called . . . where you write a page of prose, you write another page of prose . . . then you fold it over and you cut it up and you put it together . . . and shit like that . . .

INTERVIEWER: What about *Junkie*, though?

KEROUAC: It's a classic. It's better than Hemingway—it's just like Hemingway but even a little better too. It says: Danny comes into my pad one night and says, Hey, Bill, can I borrow your sap. Your sap—do you know what a sap is?

SAROYAN: A blackjack?

KEROUAC: It's a blackjack. Bill says, I pulled out my underneath drawer, and underneath some nice shirts I pulled out my blackjack. I gave it to Danny and said, Now don't lose it Danny—Danny says, Don't worry I won't lose it. He goes off and loses it.

Sap . . . blackjack . . . that's me. Sap . . . . . . blackjack.

INTERVIEWER: That's a Haiku: sap, blackjack, that's me. You better write that down.

KEROUAC: No.

INTERVIEWER: Maybe I'll write that down. Do you mind if I use that one?

KEROUAC: Up your ass with Mobil gas!

INTERVIEWER: You don't believe in collaborations? Have you ever done any collaborations, other than with publishers?

KEROUAC: I did a couple of collaborations in bed with Bill Cannastra in lofts. With blondes.

INTERVIEWER: Was he the guy that tried to climb off the subway train at Astor Place, in Holmes' *Go?*

KEROUAC: Yes. Yeah, well he says let's take all our clothes off and run around the block . . . it was raining you know. Sixteenth Street off Seventh Avenue. I said, well, I'll keep my shorts on—he says no, no shorts. I said I'm going to keep my shorts on. He said all right, but I'm not going to wear mine. And we trot trottrot

trot down the block. Sixteenth to Seventeenth . . . and we come
back and run up the stairs—nobody saw us.

INTERVIEWER: What time of day?

KEROUAC: But he was absolutely naked . . . about 3 or 4 A.M.
It rained. And everybody was there. He was dancing on broken
glass and playing Bach. Bill was the guy who used to teeter off his
roof—six flights up you know? He'd go—"you want me to fall?"
—we'd say no, Bill, no. He was an Italian. Italians are wild you
know.

INTERVIEWER: Did he write? What did he do?

KEROUAC: He says, "Jack, come with me and look down
through this peephole." We looked down through the peephole,
we saw a lot of things . . . into his toilet.

I said, "I'm not interested in that, Bill." He said, "You're not
interested in anything." Auden would come the next day, the
next afternoon, for cocktails. Maybe with Chester Kallman.
Tennessee Williams.

INTERVIEWER: Was Neal Cassady around in those days? Did
you already know Neal Cassady when you were involved with Bill
Cannastra?

KEROUAC: Oh yes, yes, ahem . . . he had a great big pack of pot.
He always was a pot happy man.

INTERVIEWER: Why do you think Neal doesn't write?

KEROUAC: He has written . . . beautifully! He has written better
than I have. Neal's a very funny guy. He's a real Californian. We
had more fun than 5000 Socony Gasoline Station attendants can
have. In my opinion he's the most intelligent man I've ever met
in my life. Neal Cassady. He's a Jesuit by the way. He used to sing
in the choir. He was a choir boy in the Catholic churches of
Denver. And he taught me everything that I now do believe about
anything that there may be to be believed about divinity.

INTERVIEWER: About Edgar Cayce?

KEROUAC: No, before he found out about Edgar Cayce he told
me all these things in the section of the life he led when he was
on the road with me—he said, We know God, don't we Jack? I
said, Yessir boy. He said, Don't we know that nothing's going to

happen wrong? Yessir. And we're going to go on and on . . . and hmmmmm ja-bmmmmmmm. . . . He was perfect. And he's always perfect. Everytime he comes to see me I can't get a word in edgewise.

INTERVIEWER: You wrote about Neal playing football, in *Visions of Cody.*

KEROUAC: Yes, he was a very good football player. He picked up two beatniks that time in blue jeans in North Beach Frisco. He said I got to go, bang bang, do I got to go? He's working on the railroad . . . had his watch out . . . 2:15, boy I got to be there by *2:20.* I tell you boys drive me over down there so I be on time with my train . . . So I can get my train on down to—what's the name of that place—San Jose? They say sure kid and Neal says here's the pot. So—"We maybe look like great bleat beatniks with great beards . . . but we are cops. And we are arresting you."

So, a guy went to the jailhouse and interviewed him from the New York Post and he said tell that Kerouac if he still believes in me to send me a typewriter. So I sent Allen Ginsberg one hundred dollars to get a typewriter for Neal. And Neal got the typewriter. And he wrote notes on it, but they wouldn't let him take the notes out. I don't know where the typewriter is. Genet wrote all of *Our Lady of the Flowers* in the shithouse . . . the jailhouse. There's a great writer, Jean Genet. He kept writing and kept writing until he got to a point where he was going to come by writing about it . . . until he came into his bed—in the can. The French can. The French jail. Prison. And that was the end of the chapter. Every chapter is Genet coming off. Which I must admit Sartre noticed.

INTERVIEWER: You think that's a different kind of spontaneous writing?

KEROUAC: Well, I could go to jail and I could write every night a chapter about Magee, Magoo, and Molly. It's beautiful. Genet is really *the* most honest writer we've had since Kerouac and Burroughs. But he came before us. He's older. Well, he's the same age as Burroughs. But I don't think I've been dishonest. Man, I've had a good time! God, man, I rode around this country free as a bee. But Genet is a very tragic and beautiful writer. And I give them the crown. And the laurel wreath. I don't give the laurel wreath to Richard Wilbur! *Or* Robert Lowell. Give it to Jean Genet and William Seward Burroughs. *And* to Allen Ginsberg and to Gregory Corso, especially.

INTERVIEWER: Jack, how about Peter Orlovsky's writings. Do you like Peter's things?

KEROUAC: Peter Orlovsky is an idiot!! He's a Russian idiot. Not even Russian, he's Polish.

INTERVIEWER: He's written some fine poems.

KEROUAC: Oh yeah. My . . . what poems?

INTERVIEWER: He has a beautiful poem called "Second Poem."

KEROUAC: "My brother pisses in the bed . . . and I go in the subway and I see two people kissing . . ."

INTERVIEWER: No, the poem that says "it's more creative to paint the floor than to sweep it."

KEROUAC: That's a lot of shit! That is the kind of poetry that was written by another Polish idiot who was a Polish nut called Apollinaire. Apollinaire is not his real name, you know.

There are some fellows in San Francisco that told me that Peter was an idiot. But I like idiots, and I enjoy his poetry. Think about that, Berrigan. But for my taste, it's Gregory.

Give me one of those.

INTERVIEWER: One of these pills?

KEROUAC: Yeah. What are they? Forked clarinets?

INTERVIEWER: They're called Obetrol. Neal is the one that told me about them.

KEROUAC: Overtones?

INTERVIEWER: Overtones? No, overcoats.

SAROYAN: What was that you said . . . at the back of the Grove anthology . . . that you let the line go a little longer to fill it up with secret images that come at the end of the sentence.

KEROUAC: He's a real Armenian! Sediment. Delta. Mud. It's where you start a poem . . .

> *As I was walking down the street one day*
> *I saw a lake where people were cutting off my rear,*
> *17,000 priests singing like George Burns*

and then you go on . . .

> *And I'm making jokes about me*
> *and breaking my bones in the earth*
> *and here I am the great John Armenian*
> *coming back to earth*

now you remember where you were in the beginning and you say . . .

> *Ahaha! Tatatatadooda . . . Screw Turkey!*

See? You remembered the line at the end . . . you lose your mind in the middle.

SAROYAN: Right.

KEROUAC: That applies to prose as well as poetry.

INTERVIEWER: But in prose you are telling a story . . .

KEROUAC: In prose you make the paragraph. Every paragraph is a poem.

INTERVIEWER: Is that how you write a paragraph?

KEROUAC: When I was running downtown there, and I was going to do this, and I was laying there, with that girl there, and a guy took out his scissors, and I took him inside there, he showed me some dirty pictures. And I went out and fell downstairs with the potato bags.

INTERVIEWER: Did you ever like Gertrude Stein's work?

KEROUAC: Never interested me too much. I liked *Melanctha* a little bit.

I should really go to school and teach these kids. I could make two thousand bucks a week. You can't learn these things. You know why? Because you have to be born with tragic fathers.

INTERVIEWER: You can only do that if you are born in New England.

KEROUAC: Incidentally, my father said your father wasn't tragic.

SAROYAN: I don't think my father is tragic.

KEROUAC: My father said that Saroyan . . . William Saroyan ain't tragic at all . . . he's fulla shit. And I had a big argument with him. *The Daring Young Man on the Flying Trapeze* is pretty tragic, I would say.

SAROYAN: He was just a young man then, you know.

KEROUAC: Yeah, but he was hungry, and he was on Times Square. Flying. A young man on the flying trapeze. That was a beautiful story. It killed me when I was a kid.

INTERVIEWER: Do you remember a story by William Saroyan about the Indian who came to town and bought a car and got the little kid to drive it for him?

STELLA: A Cadillac.

KEROUAC: What town was that?

SAROYAN: Fresno. That was Fresno.

KEROUAC: Well, you remember the night I was taking a big nap and you came up outside my window on a white horse . . .

SAROYAN: *The Summer of the Beautiful White Horse.*

KEROUAC: And I looked out the window and said what is this? You said, "My name is Aram. And I'm on a white horse."

SAROYAN: Moorad.

KEROUAC: My name is Moorad, excuse me. No, my name is . . . I was Aram, you were Moorad. You said, "Wake up!" I didn't want to wake up. I wanted to sleep. *My Name is Aram* is the name of the book. You stole a white horse from a farmer and you woke up me, Aram, to go riding with you.

SAROYAN: Moorad was the crazy one who stole the horse.

KEROUAC: Hey, what's that you gave me there?

INTERVIEWER: Obetrol.

KEROUAC: Oh, obies.

INTERVIEWER: What about jazz and bop as influences rather

than . . . Saroyan, Hemingway and Wolfe?

KEROUAC: Yes, jazz and bop, in the sense of a, say, a tenor man drawing a breath and blowing a phrase on his saxophone, till he runs out of breath, and when he does, his sentence, his statement's been made . . . that's how I therefore separate my sentences, as breath separations of the mind . . . I formulated the theory of breath as measure, in prose and verse, never mind what Olson, Charles Olson says, I formulated that theory in 1953 at the request of Burroughs and Ginsberg. Then there's the raciness and freedom and humor of jazz instead of all that dreary analysis and things like "James entered the room, and lit a cigarette. He thought Jane might have thought this too vague a gesture . . ." You know the stuff. As for Saroyan, yes I loved him as a teenager, he really got me out of the 19th century rut I was trying to study, not only his funny tone but his neat Armenian poetic I don't know what . . . he just got me . . . Hemingway was fascinating, the pearls of words on a white page giving you an exact picture . . . but Wolfe was a torrent of American heaven and hell that opened my eyes to America as a subject in itself.

INTERVIEWER: How about the movies?

KEROUAC: Yes, we've all been influenced by movies. Malcolm Cowley incidentally mentioned this many times. He's very perceptive sometimes: he mentioned that *Doctor Sax* continually mentions urine, and quite naturally it does because I had no other place to write it but on a closed toilet seat in a little tile toilet in Mexico City so as to get away from the guests inside the apartment. There incidentally is a style truly hallucinated as I wrote it all on pot. No pun intended. Ho ho.

INTERVIEWER: How has Zen influenced your work?

KEROUAC: What's really influenced my work is the Mahayana Buddhism, the original Buddhism of Gotama Sakyamuni, the Buddha himself, of the India of old . . . Zen is what's left of his Buddhism, or Bodhi, after its passing into China and then into Japan. The part of Zen that's influenced my writing is the Zen contained in the haiku, like I said, the three line, seventeen syllable poems written hundreds of years ago by guys like Basho,

Issa, Shiki, and there've been recent masters. A sentence that's short and sweet with a sudden jump of thought in it is a kind of haiku, and there's a lot of freedom and fun in surprising yourself with that, let the mind willy-nilly jump from the branch to the bird. But my serious Buddhism, that of ancient India, has influenced that part in my writing that you might call religious, or fervent, or pious, almost as much as Catholicism has. Original Buddhism referred to continual conscious compassion, brotherhood, the *dana paramita* meaning the perfection of charity, don't step on the bug, all that, humility, mendicancy, the sweet sorrowful face of the Buddha (who was of Aryan origin by the way, I mean of Persian warrior caste, and not Oriental as pictured) . . . in original Buddhism no young kid coming to a monastery was warned that "here we bury them alive." He was simply given soft encouragement to meditate and be kind. The beginning of Zen was when Buddha, however, assembled all the monks together to announce a sermon and choose the first patriarch of the Mahayana church: instead of speaking, he simply held up a flower. Everybody was flabbergasted except Kasyapa, who smiled. Kasyapa was appointed the first patriarch. This idea appealed to the Chinese like the Sixth Patriarch Hui-Neng who said, "From the beginning nothing ever was" and wanted to tear up the records of Buddha's sayings as kept in the sutras; sutras are "threads of discourse." In a way, then, Zen is a gentle but goofy form of heresy, though there must be some real kindly old monks somewhere and we've heard about the nutty ones. I haven't been to Japan. Your Maha roshi yoshi is simply a disciple of all this and not the founder of anything new at all, of course. On the Johnny Carson show he didn't even mention Buddha's name. Maybe his Buddha is Mia.

INTERVIEWER: How come you've never written about Jesus? You've written about Buddha. Wasn't Jesus a great guy too?

KEROUAC: I've never written about Jesus? In other words, you're an insane phony who comes to my house . . . and . . . all I *write about* is Jesus. I am Everhard Mercurian, General of the Jesuit Army.

SAROYAN: What's the difference between Jesus and Buddha?

KEROUAC: That's a very good question. There is no difference.

SAROYAN: No difference?

KEROUAC: But there is a difference between the original Buddha of India, and the Buddha of Vietnam who just shaves his hair and puts on a yellow robe and is a Communist agitating agent. The original Buddha wouldn't even walk on young grass so that he wouldn't destroy it. He was born in Gorakpur, the son of the Consul of the invading Persian hordes. And he was called Sage of the Warriors, and he had 17,000 broads dancing for him all night, holding out flowers, saying you want to smell it, my Lord? He says git outta here you whore. He laid a lot of them you know. But by the time he was thirty-one years old he got sick and tired . . . his father was protecting him from what was going on outside the town. And so he went out on a horse, against his father's orders and he saw a woman dying—a man being burnt on a ghat. And he said, What is all this death and decay? The servant said that is the way things go on. Your father was hiding you from the way things go on.

He says, What? My father!!—Get my horse, saddle my horse! Ride me into the forest! They ride into the forest; he says, Now take the saddle off the horse. Put it on your horse, hang it on . . . take my horse by the rein and ride back to the castle and tell my father I'll never see him again! And the servant, Kandaka, cried, he said, I'll never see you again. I don't care! Go on! Shoosh! get away!!

He spent seven years in the forest. Biting his teeth together. Nothing happened. Tormenting himself with starvation. He said, I will keep my teeth bit together until I find the cause of death. Then one day he was stumbling across the Rapti river, and he fainted in the river. And a young girl came by with a bowl of milk and said, My lord, a bowl of milk. *(Slurpppp)* He said, That gives me great energy, thank you my dear. Then he went and sat under the Bo tree. Figuerosa. The fig tree. He said, Now . . . *(demonstrates posture)* . . . I will cross my legs . . . and grit my teeth until I find the cause of death. Two o'clock in the morning, 100,000 phantoms assailed him. He didn't move. Three o'clock in the morning, the great blue ghosts!! Arrghhh!!! All *accosted* him. (You see I am really Scottish.) Four o'clock in the morning the mad maniacs of hell . . . came out of manhole covers . . . in New York City. You know Wall Street where the steam comes out? You know Wall Street, where the manhole covers . . . steam comes up? You take off them covers—yaaaaaahhh!!!!! Six o'clock, everything was peaceful—the birds started to trill, and he said, "Aha! . . . the cause of death . . . the cause of death is birth."

Simple? So he started walking down the road to Benares in India . . . with long hair, like you, see.

So, three guys. One says hey, here comes Buddha there who uh starved with us in the forest. When he sits down here on that bucket, don't wash his feet. So Buddha sits down on the bucket . . . the guy rushes up and washes his feet. Why dost thou wash his feet? Buddha says, "Because I go to Benares to beat the drum of life." And what is that? "That the cause of death is birth." "What do you mean?" "I'll show you."

A woman comes up with a dead baby in her arms. Says, Bring my child back to life if you are the Lord. He says, Sure I'll do that anytime. Just go and find one family in Sravasti that ain't had a death in the last five years. Get a mustard seed from them and bring it to me. And I'll bring your child back to life. She went all over town, man, two million people, Sravasti the town was, a bigger town than Benares by the way, and she came back and said, I can't find no such family. They've all had deaths within five years. He said, "Then, bury your baby."

Then, his jealous cousin, Devadatta, (that's Ginsberg you see . . . I am Buddha and Ginsberg is Devadatta) gets this elephant drunk . . . great big bull elephant drunk on whiskey. The elephant goes up!!!! *(trumpets like elephant going up)*—with a big trunk, and Buddha comes up in the road and gets the elephant and goes like this *(kneels)*. And the elephant kneels down. "You are buried in sorrow's mud! Quiet your trunk! Stay there!" . . . He's an elephant trainer. Then Devadatta rolled a big boulder over a cliff. And it almost hit Buddha's head. Just missed. Boooom! He says,

That's Devadatta again. Then Buddha went like this *(paces back and forth)* in front of his boys, you see. Behind him was his cousin that loved him . . . Ananda . . . which means love in Sanskrit. *(Keeps pacing)* This is what you do in jail to keep in shape.

I know a lot of stories about Buddha, but I don't know exactly what he said every time. But I know what he said about the guy who spit at him. He said, "Since I can't use your abuse you may have it back." He was great. *(Kerouac plays piano. Drinks are served.)*

SAROYAN: There's something there.

INTERVIEWER: My mother used to play that. I'm not sure how we can transcribe those notes onto a page. We may have to include a record of you playing the piano. Will you play that piece again for the record, Mr. Paderewski? Can you play "Alouette?"

KEROUAC: No. Only Afro-Germanic music. After all, I'm a square head. I wonder what whiskey will do to those obies.

INTERVIEWER: What about ritual and superstition? Do you have any about yourself when you get down to work?

KEROUAC: I had a ritual once of lighting a candle and writing by its light and blowing it out when I was done for the night . . . also kneeling and praying before starting (I got that from a French movie about George Frederick Handel) . . . but now I simply hate to write. My superstition? I'm beginning to suspect that full moon. Also I'm hung up on the number 9 though I'm told a Piscean like myself should stick to number 7; but I try to do 9 touchdowns a day, that is, I stand on my head in the bathroom, on a slipper, and touch the floor 9 times with my toe tips, while balanced. This is incidentally more than Yoga, it's an athletic feat, I mean imagine calling me "unbalanced" after that. Frankly I do feel that my mind is going. So another "ritual" as you call it, is to pray to Jesus to preserve my sanity and my energy so I can help my family: that being my paralyzed mother, and my wife, and the ever-present kitties. Okay?

INTERVIEWER: You typed out *On the Road* in three weeks, *The Subterraneans* . . . in three days and nights. Do you still produce at this fantastic rate? Can you say something of the genesis of a work before you sit down and begin that terrific typing—how much of it is set in your mind, for example?

KEROUAC: You think out what actually happened, you tell friends long stories about it, you mull it over in your mind, you connect it together at leisure, then when the time comes to pay the rent again you force yourself to sit at the typewriter, or at the writing notebook, and get it over with as fast as you can . . . and there's no harm in that because you've got the whole story lined up. Now how that's done depends on what kind of steeltrap you've got up in that little old head. This sounds boastful but a girl once told me I had a steeltrap brain, meaning I'd catch her with a statement she'd made an hour ago even though our talk had rambled a million lightyears away from that point . . . you know what I mean, like a lawyer's mind, say. All of it is in my mind, naturally, except that language that is used at the time that it is used. . . . And as for *On the Road* and *The Subterraneans,* no I can't write that fast any more. . . . Writing the Subs in three nights was really a fantastic athletic feat as well as mental, you shoulda seen me after I was done . . . I was pale as a sheet and had lost fifteen pounds and looked strange in the mirror. What I do now is write something like an average of 8,000 words a sitting, in the middle of the night, and another about a week later, resting and sighing in between. I really hate to write. I get no fun out of it because I can't get up and say I'm working, close my door, have coffee brought to me, and sit there camping like a "man of letters" "doing his eight hour day of work" and thereby incidentally filling the printing world with a lot of dreary self-imposed cant and bombast . . . bombast is Scottish word for stuffing for a pillow. Haven't you heard a politician use 1500 words to say something he could have said in exactly three words? So I get it out of the way so as not to bore myself either.

SAROYAN: Do you usually try to see everything clearly and not think of any words—just to see everything as clear as possible and then write out of the feeling. With *Tristessa,* for example.

KEROUAC: You sound like a writing seminar at Indiana University.

SAROYAN: I know but . . .

KEROUAC: All I did was suffer with that poor girl and then when she fell on her head and almost killed herself . . . remember when she fell on her head? . . . and she was all busted up and everything. She was the most gorgeous little Indian chick you ever saw. I say Indian, pure Indian. Esperanza Villanueva. Villanueva is a Spanish name from I don't know where—Castile. But she's Indian. So she's half Indian, half Spanish . . . beauty. Absolute beauty. She had bones, man, just bones, skin and bones. And I didn't write in the book how I finally nailed her. You know? I did. I finally nailed her. She said, "Shhhhhhhhhh! Don't let the landlord hear." She said, "Remember, I'm very weak and sick." I said, "I know, I've been writing a book about how you're weak and sick."

INTERVIEWER: How come you didn't put that part in the book?

KEROUAC: Because Claude's wife told me not to put it in. She said it would spoil the book.

But it was not a conquest. She was out like a light. On M. M., that's Morphine. And in fact I made a big run for her from way uptown to downtown to the slum district . . . and I said, here's your stuff. She said, "Shhhhhh!" She gave herself a shot . . . and I said, Ah . . . now's the time. And I got my little nogood piece. But . . . it was certainly justification of Mexico!

STELLA: Here kitty! He's gone out again.

KEROUAC: She was nice, you would have liked her. Her real name was Esperanza. You know what that means?

INTERVIEWER: No.

KEROUAC: In Spanish, hope. Tristessa means in Spanish, sadness, but her real name was Hope. And she's now married to the Police Chief of Mexico City.

STELLA: Not quite.

KEROUAC: Well, you're not Esperanza—I'll tell you that.

STELLA: No, I know that, dear.

KEROUAC: She was the skinniest . . . and shy . . . as a rail.

STELLA: She's married to one of the lieutenants, you told me, not to the Chief.

KEROUAC: She's all right. One of these days I'm going to go see her again.

STELLA: Over my dead body.

INTERVIEWER: Were you really writing *Tristessa* while you were there in Mexico? You didn't write it later?

KEROUAC: First part written in Mexico, second part written in . . . Mexico. That's right. '55 first part, '56 second part. What's the importance about that? I'm not Charles Olson, the great artist!

INTERVIEWER: We're just getting the facts.

KEROUAC: Charles Olson gives you all the dates. You know. Everything about how he found the hound dog on the beach in Gloucester. Found somebody jacking-off on the beach at . . . what do they call it? Vancouver Beach? Dig Dog River? . . . Dogtown. That's what they call it, "Dogtown." Well this is Shit-town on the Merrimac. Lowell is called Shit-town on the Merrimac. I'm not going to write a poem called Shit-town and insult my town. But if I was six foot six I could write anything, couldn't I?

INTERVIEWER: How do you get along now with other writers? Do you correspond with them?

KEROUAC: I correspond with John Clellon Holmes but less and less each year, I'm getting lazy. I can't answer my fan mail because I haven't got a secretary to take dictation, do the typing, get the stamps, envelopes, all that . . . and I have nothing to answer. I ain't gonna spend the rest of my life smiling and shaking hands and sending and receiving platitudes, like a candidate for political office, because I'm a writer—I've got to let my mind alone, like Greta Garbo. Yet when I go out, or receive sudden guests, we all have more fun than a barrel of monkeys.

INTERVIEWER: What are the work-destroyers?

KEROUAC: Work-destroyers . . . work-destroyers. Time-killers? I'd say mainly the attentions which are tendered to a writer of "notoriety" (notice I don't say "fame") by secretly ambitious would-be writers, who come around, or write, or call, for the sake of the services which are properly the services of a bloody literary agent. When I was an unknown struggling young writer, as saying goes, I did my own footwork, I hotfooted up and down Madison Avenue for years, publisher to publisher, agent to agent, and never once in my life wrote a letter to a published famous author asking for advice, or help, or, in Heaven above, have the nerve to actually *mail* my manuscripts to some poor author who then has to hustle to mail it back before he's accused of stealing my ideas. My advice to young writers is to get themselves an agent on their own, maybe through their college professors (as I got my first publishers through my prof Mark Van Doren) and do their own footwork, or "thing" as the slang goes . . . So the work-destroyers are nothing but certain *people*.

The work-preservers are the solitudes of night, "when the whole wide world is fast asleep."

INTERVIEWER: What do you find the best time and place for writing?

KEROUAC: The desk in the room, near the bed, with a good light, midnight till dawn, a drink when you get tired, preferably at home, but if you have no home, make a home out of your hotel room or motel room or pad: peace. *(Picks up harmonica and plays)* Boy, can I play!

INTERVIEWER: What about writing under the influence of drugs?

KEROUAC: Poem 230 from *Mexico City Blues* is a poem written purely on morphine. Every line in this poem was written within an hour of one another . . . high on a big dose of M. *(Finds volume and reads)*

> *Love's multitudinous boneyard of decay*
An hour later:
> *The spilled milk of heroes*
And hour later:
> *Destruction of silk kerchiefs by dust storm,*
An hour later:
> *Caress of heroes blindfolded to posts,*
An hour later:
> *Murder victims admitted to this life,*

An hour later:

Skeletons bartering fingers and joints,

An hour later:

The quivering meat of the elephants of kindness being torn apart by vultures

(See where Ginsberg stole that from me?)An hour later: *Conceptions of delicate kneecaps.*

Say that, Saroyan.

SAROYAN: Conceptions of delicate kneecaps.

KEROUAC: Very good. *Fear of rats dripping with bacteria.* An hour later: *Golgotha Cold Hope for Gold Hope.* Say that.

SAROYAN: Golgotha Cold Hope for Cold Hope.

KEROUAC: That's pretty cold. An hour later: *Damp leaves of Autumn against the wood of boats,* An hour later: *Seahorse's delicate imagery of glue . . .*

Ever see a little seahorse in the ocean? They're built of glue . . . did you ever sniff a seahorse? No, say that.

SAROYAN: Seahorse's delicate imagery of glue.

KEROUAC: You'll do, Saroyan. *Death by long exposure to defilement.*

SAROYAN: Death by long exposure to defilement.

KEROUAC: *Frightening ravishing mysterious beings concealing their sex.*

SAROYAN: Frightening ravishing mysterious beings concealing their sex.

KEROUAC: *Pieces of the Buddha-material frozen and sliced microscopically*

In Morgues of the North

SAROYAN: Hey, I can't say that. Pieces of the Buddha-material frozen and sliced microscopically in Morgues of the North.

KEROUAC: *Penis apples going to seed.*

SAROYAN: Penis apples going to seed.

KEROUAC: *The severed gullets more numerous than sands.*

SAROYAN: The severed gullets more numerous than sands.

KEROUAC: *Like kissing my kitten in the belly*

SAROYAN: Like kissing my kitten in the belly

KEROUAC: *The softness of our reward*

SAROYAN: The softness of our reward.

KEROUAC: Is he really William Saroyan's son? That's wonderful! Would you mind repeating that?

INTERVIEWER: We should be asking you a lot of very straight serious questions. When did you meet Allen Ginsberg?

KEROUAC: First I met Claude.* And then I met Allen and then I met Burroughs. Claude came in through the fire escape . . . there were gunshots down in the alley—Pow! Pow! and it was raining, and my wife says, here comes Claude. And here comes this blond guy through the fire escape, all wet. I said, "What's this all about, what the hell is this?" He says, "They're chasing me." Next day in walks Allen Ginsberg carrying books. Sixteen years old with his ears sticking out. He says, "Well, discretion is the better part of valor!" I said, "Aw shutup. You little twitch." Then the next day here comes Burroughs wearing a seersucker suit, followed by the other guy.

INTERVIEWER: What other guy?

KEROUAC: It was the guy who wound up in the river. This was this guy from New Orleans that Claude killed and threw in the river. Stabbed him twelve times in the heart with a Boy Scout knife.

When Claude was fourteen he was the most beautiful blond boy in New Orleans. And he joined the Boy Scout troop . . . and the Boy Scout Master was a big redheaded fairy who went to school at St. Louis University, I think it was.

And he had already been in love with a guy who looked just like Claude in Paris. And this guy chased Claude all over the country; this guy had him thrown out of Baldwin, Tulane, and Andover Prep. . . . It's a queer tale, but Claude isn't a queer.

INTERVIEWER: What about the influence of Ginsberg and Burroughs? Did you ever have any sense then of the mark the three of you would have on American writing?

---

*"Claude," a pseudonym, is also used in Vanity of Duluoz.

KEROUAC: I was determined to be a "great writer," in quotes, like Thomas Wolfe, see . . . Allen was always reading and writing poetry . . . Burroughs read a lot and walked around looking at things. . . . The influence we exerted on one another has been written about over and over again . . . We were just three interested characters, in the interesting big city of New York, around campuses, libraries, cafeterias. A lot of the details you'll find in *Vanity* . . . in *On the Road* where Burroughs is Bull Lee and Ginsberg is Carlo Marx . . . in *Subterraneans,* where they're Frank Carmody and Adam Moorad respectively, elsewhere. In other words, though I don't want to be rude to you for this honor, I am so busy interviewing myself in my novels, and have been so busy writing down these self-interviews, that I don't see why I should draw breath in pain every year of the last ten years to repeat and repeat to everybody who interviews me what I've already explained in the books themselves. . . . (Hundreds of journalists, thousands of students.) It beggars sense. And it's not that important. It's our work that counts, if anything at all, and I'm not proud of mine or theirs or anybody's since Thoreau and others like that, maybe because it's still too close to home for comfort. Notoriety and public confession in literary form is a frazzler of the heart you were born with, believe me.

INTERVIEWER: Allen said once that he learned how to read Shakespeare, that he never did understand Shakespeare until he heard you read Shakespeare to him.

KEROUAC: Because in a previous lifetime that's who I was.

> *How like a Winter hath my absence been from thee?*
> *The pleasure of the fleeting year . . . what freezings*
> *have I felt? What dark days seen? Yet Summer with his*
> *lord surcease hath laid a big turd in my orchard*
> *And one hog after another comes to eat*
> *and break my broken mountain trap, and my mousetrap*
> *too! And here to end the sonnet, you must make sure*
> *to say, tara-tara-tara . . . . . . !!!!!!*

INTERVIEWER: Is that spontaneous composition?

KEROUAC: Well, the first part was Shakespeare . . . and the second part was . . .

INTERVIEWER: Have you ever written any sonnets?

KEROUAC: I'll give you a spontaneous sonnet. It has to be what, now?

INTERVIEWER: Fourteen lines.

KEROUAC: That's twelve lines with two dragging lines. That's where you bring up your heavy artillery.

> *Here the fish of Scotland seen your eye*
> *and all my nets did creak . . .*

Does it have to rhyme?

INTERVIEWER: No.

KEROUAC:

> *My poor chapped hands fall awry*
> *and seen the Pope, his devilled eye.*
> *And maniacs with wild hair hanging about my room*
> *and listening to my tomb*
> *which does not rhyme.*

Seven lines?

INTERVIEWER: That was eight lines.

KEROUAC:

> *And all the orgones of the earth will crawl*
> *like dogs across the graves of Peru*
> *and Scotland too.*

That's ten.

> *Yet do not worry, sweet angel of mine*
> *That hast thine inheritance*
> *imbedded in mine.*

INTERVIEWER: That's pretty good, Jack. How did you do that?

KEROUAC: Without studying dactyls . . . like Ginsberg . . . I met

Ginsberg . . . I'd hitchhiked all the way back from Mexico City to Berkeley, and that's a long way baby, a long way. Mexico City across Durango . . . Chihuahua . . . Texas. I go back to Ginsberg, I go to his cottage, I say, "Hah, we're gonna play the music" . . . he says, "You know what I'm going to do tomorrow? I'm going to throw on Mark Schorer's desk a new theory of prosody! About the dactylic arrangements of Ovid!" *(Laughter)*

I said, "Quit, man. Sit under a tree and forget it and drink wine with me . . . and Phil Whalen and Gary Snyder and all the bums of San Francisco. Don't you try to be a big Berkeley teacher. Just be a poet under the trees . . . and we'll wrestle and we'll break holds." And he did take my advice. He remembered that. He said, "What are you going to teach . . . you have parched lips!" I said, "Naturally, I just came from Chihuahua. It's very hot down there, phew! you go out and little pigs rub against your legs. Phew!"

So here comes Snyder with a bottle of wine . . . and here comes Whalen, and here comes what's his name . . . Rexroth . . . and everybody . . . and we had the poetry renaissance of San Francisco.

INTERVIEWER: What about Allen getting kicked out of Columbia? Didn't you have something to do with that?

KEROUAC: Oh, no . . . he let me sleep in his room. He was not kicked out of Columbia for that. The first time he let me sleep in his room, and the guy that slept in our room with us was Lancaster who was descended from the White Roses or Red Roses of England. But a guy came in . . . the guy that ran the floor and he thought that I was trying to make Allen, and Allen had already written in the paper that I wasn't sleeping there because I was trying to make him, but he was trying to make me. But we were just actually sleeping. Then after that he got a pad . . . he got some stolen goods in there . . . and he got some thieves up there, Vicky and Huncke. And they were all busted for stolen goods, and a car turned over, and Allen's glasses broke, it's all in John Holmes' *Go.*

Allen Ginsberg asked me when he was nineteen years old, should I change my name to Allen Renard? You change your name to Allen Renard I'll kick you right in the balls! Stick to Ginsberg . . . and he did. That's one thing I like about Allen. Allen *Renard!!!*

INTERVIEWER: What was it that brought all of you together in the 50's? What was it that seemed to unify the "Beat Generation?"

KEROUAC: Oh the beat generation was just a phrase I used in the 1951 written manuscript of *On the Road* to describe guys like Moriarty who run around the country in cars looking for odd jobs, girlfriends, kicks. It was thereafter picked up by West Coast leftist groups and turned into a meaning like "beat mutiny" and "beat insurrection" and all that nonsense; they just wanted some youth movement to grab onto for their own political and social purposes. I had nothing to do with any of that. I was a football player, a scholarship college student, a merchant seaman, a railroad brakeman on road freights, a script synopsizer, a secretary . . . And Moriarty-Cassady was an actual cowboy on Dave Uhl's ranch in New Raymer Colorado . . . What kind of beatnik is that?

INTERVIEWER: Was there any sense of "community" among the Beat crowd?

KEROUAC: That community feeling was largely inspired by the same characters I mentioned, like Ferlinghetti, Ginsberg; they are very socialistically minded and want everybody to live in some kind of frenetic kibbutz, solidarity and all that. I was a loner. Snyder is not like Whalen, Whalen is not like McClure, I am not like McClure, McClure is not like Ferlinghetti, Ginsberg is not like Ferlinghetti, but we all had fun over wine anyway. We knew thousands of poets and painters and jazz musicians. There's no "beat crowd" like you say . . . what about Scott Fitzgerald and his "lost crowd," does that sound right? Or Goethe and his "Wilhelm Meister crowd?" The subject is such a bore. Pass me that glass.

INTERVIEWER: Well, why did they split in the early 60's?

KEROUAC: Ginsberg got interested in left wing politics . . . like Joyce I say, as Joyce said to Ezra Pound in the 1920's, "Don't bother me with politics, the only thing that interests me is style."

Besides I'm bored with the new avant-garde and the skyrocketing sensationalism. I'm reading Blaise Pascal and taking notes on religion. I like to hang around now with nonintellectuals, as you might call them, and not have my mind proselytized, ad infinitum. They've even started crucifying chickens in happenings, what's the next step? An actual crucifixion of a man . . . The beat group dispersed as you say in the early 60's, all went their own way, and this is my way: home life, as in the beginning, with a little toot once in a while in local bars.

INTERVIEWER: What do you think of what they're up to now? Allen's radical political involvement? Burrough's cut-up methods?

KEROUAC: I'm pro-American and the radical political involvements seem to tend elsewhere . . . The country gave my Canadian family a good break, more or less, and we see no reason to demean said country. As for Burroughs' cut-up method, I wish he'd get back to those awfully funny stories of his he used to write and those marvelously dry vignettes in *Naked Lunch*. Cut-up is nothing new, in fact that steeltrap brain of mine does a lot of cutting up as it goes along . . . as does everyone's brain while talking or thinking or writing . . . It's just an old Dada trick, and a kind of literary collage. He comes out with some great effects though. I like him to be elegant and logical and that's why I don't like the cut-up which is supposed to teach us that the mind is cracked. Sure the mind's cracked, as anybody can see in a hallucinated high, but how about an explanation of the crackedness that can be understood in a workaday moment?

INTERVIEWER: What do you think about the hippies and the LSD scene?

KEROUAC: They're already changing, I shouldn't be able to make a judgment. And they're not all of the same mind. The Diggers are different . . . I don't know one hippie anyhow . . . I think they think I'm a truckdriver. And I am. As for LSD, it's bad for people with incidence of heart disease in the family. *(Knocks microphone off footstool . . . recovers it)*

Is there any reason why you can see anything good in this yere mortality?

INTERVIEWER: Excuse me, would you mind repeating that?

KEROUAC: You said you had a little white beard in your belly. Why is there a little white beard in your mortality belly?

INTERVIEWER: Let me think about it. Actually it's a little white pill.

KEROUAC: A little white pill?

INTERVIEWER: It's good.

KEROUAC: Give me.

INTERVIEWER: We should wait till the scene cools a little.

KEROUAC: Right. This little white pill is a little white beard in your mortality which advises you and ad-vertises to you that you will be growing long fingernails in the graves of Peru.

SAROYAN: Do you feel middle-aged?

KEROUAC: No. Listen, we're coming to the end of the tape. I want to add something on. Ask me what Kerouac means.

INTERVIEWER: Jack, tell me again what Kerouac means.

KEROUAC: Now, Kairn. K(or C)A-I-R-N. What is a kairn? It's a heap of stones. Now Cornwall, kairn-wall. Now, right, kern, also K-E-R-N, means the same thing as Kairn, Kern, Kairn. Ouac means language of. So, Kernuac means the language of Cornwall. Kerr, which is like Deborah Kerr . . . ouack means language of the water. Because Kerr, Carr, etc., means water. And Kairn means heap of stones. There is no language in a heap of stones. Kerouac. Ker-water, ouac-language of. And it's related to the old Irish name, Kerwick, which is a corruption. And it's a Cornish name, which in itself means Kairnish. And according to Sherlock Holmes, it's all Persian. Of course you know he's not Persian. Don't you remember in Sherlock Holmes when he went down with Dr. Watson and solved the case down in old Cornwall and he solved the case and then he said, "Watson, the needle! Watson, the needle . . ." He said, "I've solved this case here in Cornwall. Now I have the liberty to sit around here and decide and read books, which will prove to me . . . why the Cornish people, otherwise known as the Kernuaks, or Kerouacs, are of Persian origin. The enterprise which I am about to embark upon," he then said, after he got his shot, "is fraught with eminent peril, and not fit for a lady of your tender years." Remember that?

MC NAUGHTON: I remember that.

KEROUAC: McNaughton remembers that. McNaughton. You think I would forget the name of a Scotsman?

TED BERRIGAN

15. Anne Sexton

Born on November 9, 1928, Anne Sexton was brought up in Wellesley, Massachusetts, attended Garland Junior College, and at twenty married a salesman. She became a fashion model in Boston and had two daughters. When her second child was born, she suffered a mental breakdown and twice tried to commit suicide. For a number of years she was in and out of mental hospitals.

At the age of thirty, as a means of recovery, Anne Sexton started writing. With the publication of each book, grants and awards followed. *To Bedlam and Part Way Back* (1960) led to admittance to Radcliffe's Institute for Independent Study. *All My Pretty Ones* (1962) brought her the first traveling fellowship offered by the American Academy of Arts and Letters (1963–64), a Ford Foundation grant in playwriting (1964–65), and the first literary-magazine travel grant from the Congress for Cultural Freedom (1965). In 1965 her *Selected Poems* appeared in England, and she was elected a Fellow of the Royal Society of Literature in London. Her third book, *Live or Die* (1966), won the Pulitzer Prize and the Shelley Award from the Poetry Society of America. Five more books followed: *Love Poems* (1969), *Transformations* (1971), *The Book of Folly* (1972), *The Death Notebooks* (1974), and *An Awful Rowing Towards God* (1975).

In 1972 she served as Cranshaw Professor of Literature at Colgate University and was a Professor of Creative Writing at Boston University from 1970 to 1974. She took her own life on October 4, 1974.

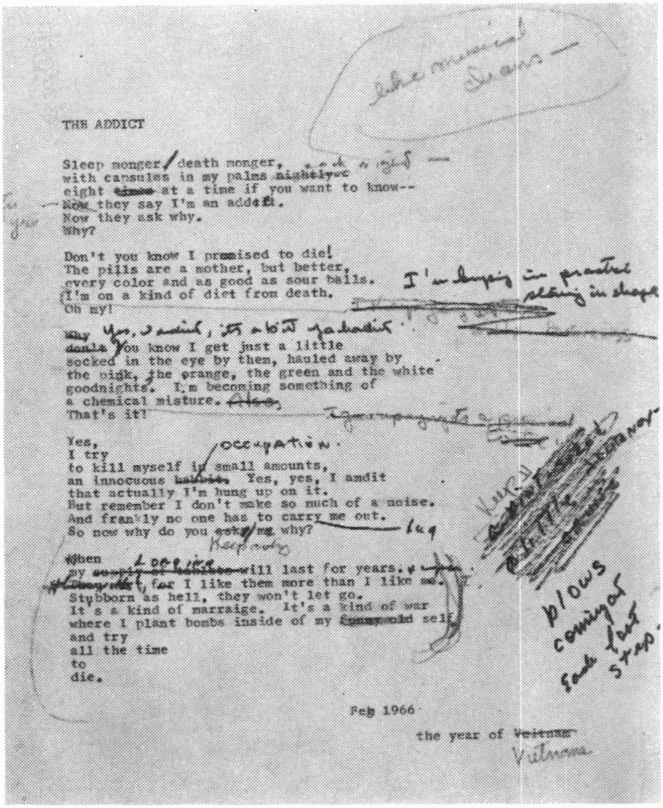

THE ADDICT

Sleep monger / death monger,
with capsules in my palms nightly,
eight times at a time if you want to know--
Now they say I'm an addict.
Now they ask why.
Why?

Don't you know I promised to die!
The pills are a mother, but better,
every color and as good as sour balls.
I'm on a kind of diet from death.
Oh my!

dont You know I get just a little
socked in the eye by them, hauled away by
the pink, the orange, the green and the white
goodnights. I'm becoming something of
a chemical mixture. Also,
That's it!

Yes,
I try
to kill myself in small amounts,
an innocuous Yes, yes, I admit
that actually I'm hung up on it.
But remember I don't make so much of a noise.
And frankly no one has to carry me out.
So now why do you asking me why?

When will last for years.
for I like them more than I like me.
Stubborn as hell, they won't let go.
It's a kind of marraige. It's a kind of war
where I plant bombs inside of my self
and try
all the time
to
die.

                                    Feb 1966

                              the year of Vietnam

handwritten annotations in margins, partially legible:
"like musical scales"
"I'm adding in practice, staying in shape"
"OCCUPATION."
"Keep only"
"blows coming but fends off, stop."
"Vietnam"

Rollie McKenna

Anne Sexton

*The interview took place over three days in the middle of August
1968. When asked about dates of publications or other events,
Anne Sexton kept saying, "Let me think, I want this to be accurate," and she'd use the births of her children as reference dates
to chronicle the event in question. Sometimes her distinctions
between real and imagined life blurred, as in scenes from Piran-
dello. Often, her answers sounded like incantations, repetitious
chants that, if pared down, would lose something of their implications, and so, for the most part, they are preserved in their entirety.
Even when replying from written notes, she read with all the
inflections and intonations of—as she describes her readings—"an
actress in her own autobiographical play."*

INTERVIEWER: You were almost thirty before you began writing poetry. Why?

SEXTON: Until I was twenty-eight I had a kind of buried self who didn't know she could do anything but make white sauce and diaper babies. I didn't know I had any creative depths. I was a victim of the American Dream, the bourgeois, middle-class dream. All I wanted was a little piece of life, to be married, to have children. I thought the nightmares, the visions, the demons would go away if there was enough love to put them down. I was trying my damndest to lead a conventional life, for that was how I was brought up, and it was what my husband wanted of me. But one can't build little white picket fences to keep nightmares out. The surface cracked when I was about twenty-eight. I had a psychotic break and tried to kill myself.

INTERVIEWER: And you began to write after the nervous breakdown?

SEXTON: It isn't quite as simple as all that. I said to my doctor at the beginning, "I'm no good; I can't do anything; I'm dumb." He suggested I try educating myself by listening to Boston's educational TV station. He said I had a perfectly good mind. As a matter of fact, after he gave me a Rorschach test, he said I had creative talent that I wasn't using. I protested, but I followed his suggestion. One night I saw I. A. Richards on educational television reading a sonnet and explaining its form. I thought to myself, "I could do that, maybe; I could try." So I sat down and wrote a sonnet. The next day I wrote another one, and so forth. My doctor encouraged me to write more. "Don't kill yourself," he said. "Your poems might mean something to someone else someday." That gave me a feeling of purpose, a little cause, something to *do* with my life, no matter how rotten I was.

INTERVIEWER: Hadn't you written limericks before that?

SEXTON: I did write some light verse—for birthdays, for anniversaries, sometimes thank-you notes for weekends. Long before, I wrote some serious stuff in high school; however, I hadn't been exposed to any of the major poets, not even the minor ones. No one taught poetry at that school. I read nothing but Sara Teasdale. I might have read other poets, but my mother said as I graduated from high school that I had plagiarized Sara Teasdale.

Something about that statement of hers . . . I had been writing a poem a day for three months, but when she said that, I stopped.

INTERVIEWER: Didn't anyone encourage you?

SEXTON: It wouldn't have mattered. My mother was top billing in our house.

INTERVIEWER: In the beginning, what was the relationship between your poetry and your therapy?

SEXTON: Sometimes, my doctors tell me that I understand something in a poem that I haven't integrated into my life. In fact, I may be concealing it from myself, while I was revealing it to the readers. The poetry is often more advanced, in terms of my unconscious, than I am. Poetry, after all, milks the unconscious. The unconscious is there to feed it little images, little symbols, the answers, the insights I know not of. In therapy, one seeks to hide sometimes. I'll give you a rather intimate example of this. About three or four years ago my analyst asked me what I thought of my parents having intercourse when I was young. I couldn't talk. I knew there was suddenly a poem there, and I selfishly guarded it from him. Two days later, I had a poem, entitled, "In the Beach House," which describes overhearing the primal scene. In it I say, "Inside my prison of pine and bedspring,/over my window sill, under my knob,/it is plain they are at/the royal strapping." The point of this little story is the image, "the royal strapping." My analyst was quite impressed with that image, and so was I, although I don't remember going any further with it then. About three weeks ago, he said to me, "Were you ever beaten as a child?" I told him that I had been when I was about nine. I had torn up a five-dollar bill that my father gave to my sister; my father took me into his bedroom, laid me down on his bed, pulled off my pants, and beat me with a riding crop. As I related this to my doctor, he said, "See, that was quite a royal strapping," thus revealing to me, by way of my own image, the intensity of that moment, the sexuality of that beating, the little masochistic seizure—it's so classic, it's almost corny. Perhaps it's too intimate an example, but then both poetry and therapy are intimate.

INTERVIEWER: Are your poems still closely connected to your therapy as in the past?

SEXTON: No. The subject of therapy was an early theme—the process itself as in "Said the Poet to the Analyst," the people of my past, admitting what my parents were really like, the whole Gothic New England story. I've had about eight doctors, but only two that count. I've written a poem for each of the two—"You, Doctor Martin" and "Cripples and Other Stories." And that will do. Those poems are about the two men as well as the strange process. One can say that my new poems, the love poems, come about as a result of new attitudes, an awareness of the possibly good as well as the possibly rotten. Inherent in the process is a rebirth of a sense of self, each time stripping away a dead self.

INTERVIEWER: Some critics admire your ability to write about the terror of childhood guilts, parental deaths, breakdowns, suicides. Do you feel that writing about the dark parts of the human psyche takes a special act of courage?

SEXTON: Of course, but I'm tired of explaining it. It seems to be self-evident. There are warnings all along the way. "Go—children—slow." "It's dangerous in there." The appalling horror that awaits you in the answer.

INTERVIEWER: People speak of you as a primitive. Was it so natural for you to dig so deeply into the painful experiences of your life?

SEXTON: There was a part of me that was horrified, but the gutsy part of me drove on. Still, part of me was appalled by what I was doing. On the one hand I was digging up shit, with the other hand, I was covering it with sand. Nevertheless, I went on ahead. I didn't know any better. Sometimes, I felt like a reporter researching himself. Yes, it took a certain courage, but as a writer one has to take the chance on being a fool . . . yes, to be a fool, that perhaps requires the greatest courage.

INTERVIEWER: Once you began writing, did you attend any formal classes to bone up on technique?

SEXTON: After I'd been writing about three months, I dared to go into the poetry class at the Boston Center for Adult Education taught by John Holmes. I started in the middle of the term, very shy, writing very bad poems, solemnly handing them in for the eighteen others in the class to hear. The most important aspect of that class was that I felt I belonged somewhere. When I first got sick and became a displaced person, I thought I was quite alone, but when I went into the mental hospital, I found I wasn't, that there were other people like me. It made me feel better— more real, sane. I felt, "These are my people." Well, at the John Holmes class that I attended for two years, I found I belonged to the poets, that I was *real* there, and I had another, "These are my people." I met Maxine Kumin, the poet and novelist, at that class. She is my closest friend. She is part superego, part sister, as well as pal of my desk. It's strange because we're quite different. She is reserved, while I tend to be flamboyant. She is an intellectual, and I seem to be a primitive. That is true about our poetry as well.

INTERVIEWER: You once told me, "I call Maxine Kumin every other line." Is that a slight exaggeration?

SEXTON: Yes. But often, I call her draft by draft. However, a lot of poems I did without her. The year I was writing my first book, I didn't know her well enough to call that often. Later, when she didn't approve of such poems as "Flee on Your Donkey"—that one took four years to complete—I was on my own. Yet once, she totally saved a poem, "Cripples and other Stories."

INTERVIEWER: In the early days, how did your relatives react to the jangling of family skeletons?

SEXTON: I tried not to show my relatives any of the poems. I do know that my mother snuck into my desk one time and read "The Double Image" before it was printed. She told me just before she died that she liked the poem, and that saved me from some added guilt. My husband liked that poem, too. Ordinarily, if I show him a poem, something I try not to do, he says, "I don't think that's too hotsy-totsy," which puts me off. I try not to do it too often. My in-laws don't approve of the poems at all. My children do—with a little pain, they do.

INTERVIEWER: In your poems, several family skeletons come out of the camphor balls—your father's alcoholic tendencies, your mother's inability to deal with your suicide attempt, your great-aunt in a straitjacket. Is there any rule you follow as to which skeletons you reveal and which you don't?

SEXTON: I don't reveal skeletons that would hurt anyone. They may hurt the dead, but the dead belong to me. Only once in a while do they talk back. For instance, I don't write about my husband or his family, although there are some amazing stories there.

INTERVIEWER: How about Holmes or the poets in your class, what did they say?

SEXTON: During the years of that class, John Holmes saw me as something evil and warned Maxine to stay away from me. He told me I shouldn't write such personal poems about the madhouse. He said, "That isn't a fit subject for poetry." I knew no one who thought it was; even my doctor clammed up at that time. I was on my own. I tried to mind them. I tried to write the way the others, especially Maxine, wrote, but it didn't work. I always ended up sounding like myself.

INTERVIEWER: You have said, "If anything influenced me, it was W. D. Snodgrass's 'Heart's Needle.' " Would you comment on that?

SEXTON: If he had the courage, then I had the courage. That poem about losing his daughter brought me to face some of the facts about my own life. I had lost a daughter, lost her because I was too sick to keep her. After I read the poem, "Heart's Needle," I ran up to my mother-in-law's house and brought my daughter home. That's what a poem should do—move people to action. True, I didn't keep my daughter at the time—I wasn't ready. But I was beginning to be ready. I wrote a disguised poem about it, "Unknown Girl in the Maternity Ward." The pain of the loss . . .

INTERVIEWER: Did you ever meet Snodgrass?

SEXTON: Yes. I'd read "Heart's Needle" in *The New Poets of England and America*. I'd written about three quarters of *To*

Bedlam and Part Way Back at the time, and I made a pilgrimage to Antioch Writer's Conference to meet and to learn from Snodgrass. He was a surprising person, surprisingly humble. He encouraged me, he liked what I was doing. He was the first established poet to like my work, and so I was driven to write harder and to allow myself, to dare myself to tell the whole story. He also suggested that I study with Robert Lowell. So I sent Mr. Lowell some of my poems and asked if he would take me into the class. By then I'd had poems published in *The New Yorker* and around a bit. At any rate, the poems seemed good enough for Lowell, and I joined the class.

INTERVIEWER: Which poems did you submit to Lowell?

SEXTON: As far as I can remember, the poems about madness —"You, Doctor Martin," "Music Swims Back to Me" . . . about ten or fifteen poems from the book.

INTERVIEWER: Was this before or after Lowell published *Life Studies?*

SEXTON: Before. I sent him the poems in the summer; the following spring *Life Studies* came out. Everyone says I was influenced by Robert Lowell's revelation of madness in that book, but I was writing *To Bedlam and Part Way Back*, the story of my madness, before *Life Studies* was published. I showed my poems to Mr. Lowell as he was working on his book. Perhaps I even influenced him. I have never asked him. But stranger things have happened.

INTERVIEWER: And when was your first book, *To Bedlam and Part Way Back*, published?

SEXTON: It was accepted that January; it wasn't published for a year and a half after that, I think.

INTERVIEWER: Where was Lowell teaching then?

SEXTON: The class met at Boston University on Tuesdays from two to four in a dismal room. It consisted of some twenty students. Seventeen graduates, two other housewives who were graduates or something, and a boy who had snuck over from M.I.T. I was the only one in that room who hadn't read *Lord Weary's Castle*.

INTERVIEWER: And Lowell, how did he strike you?

SEXTON: He was formal in a rather awkward New England sense. His voice was soft and slow as he read the students' poems. At first I felt the impatient desire to interrupt his slow, line by line readings. He would read the first line, stop, and then discuss it at length. I wanted to go through the whole poem quickly and then go back. I couldn't see any merit in dragging through it until you almost hated the damned thing, even your own poems, especially your own. At that point, I wrote to Snodgrass about my impatience, and his reply went this way, "Frankly, I used to nod my head at his every statement, and he taught me more than a whole gang of scholars could." So I kept my mouth shut, and Snodgrass was right. Robert Lowell's method of teaching is intuitive and open. After he had read a student's poem, he would read another evoked by it. Comparison was often painful. He worked with a cold chisel, with no more mercy than a dentist. He got out the decay, but if he was never kind to the poem, he was kind to the poet.

INTERVIEWER: Did you consult Robert Lowell on your manuscript of *To Bedlam and Part Way Back* before you submitted it to a publisher?

SEXTON: Yes. I gave him a manuscript to see if he thought it was a book. He was enthusiastic on the whole, but suggested that I throw out about half of it and write another fifteen or so poems that were better. He pointed out the weak ones, and I nodded and took them out. It sounds simple to say that I merely, as he once said, "jumped the hurdles that he had put up," but it makes a difference who puts up the hurdles. He defined the course, and acted as though, good race horse that I was, I would just naturally run it.

INTERVIEWER: Ultimately, what can a teacher give a writer in a creative-writing class?

SEXTON: Courage, of course. That's the most important ingredient. Then, in a rather plain way, Lowell helped me to distrust the easy musical phrase and to look for the frankness of ordinary speech. Lowell is never impressed with a display of images or sounds—those things that a poet is born with anyhow. If you have enough natural imagery, he can show you how to chain it in. He didn't teach me what to put into a poem, but what to leave out. What he taught me was taste—perhaps that's the only thing a poet can be taught.

INTERVIEWER: Sylvia Plath was a member of Lowell's class also, wasn't she?

SEXTON: Yes. She and George Starbuck heard that I was auditing Lowell's class. They kind of joined me there for the second term. After the class, we would pile in the front seat of my old Ford, and I would drive quickly through the traffic to the Ritz. I would always park illegally in a "Loading Only Zone," telling them gaily, "It's O.K., we're only going to get loaded." Off we'd go, each on George's arm, into the Ritz to drink three or four martinis. George even has a line about this in his first book of poems, *Bone Thoughts.* After the Ritz, we would spend our last pennies at the Waldorf Cafeteria—a dinner for seventy cents— George was in no hurry. He was separated from his wife; Sylvia's Ted [Hughes] was busy with his own work, and I had to stay in the city for a seven P.M. appointment with my psychiatrist . . . a funny three.

INTERVIEWER: In Sylvia Plath's last book, written just before her suicide, she was submerged by the theme of death, as you are in your book, *Live or Die.* Did you ever get around to talking about death or your suicides at the Ritz?

SEXTON: Often, very often. Sylvia and I would talk at length about our first suicide, in detail and in depth—between the free potato chips. Suicide is, after all, the opposite of the poem. Sylvia and I often talked opposites. We talked death with burned-up intensity, both of us drawn to it like moths to an electric light bulb, sucking on it. She told the story of her first suicide in sweet and loving detail, and her description in *The Bell Jar* is just that same story. It is a wonder we didn't depress George with our egocentricity; instead, I think, we three were stimulated by it— even George—as if death made each of us a little more real at the moment.

INTERVIEWER: In a BBC interview, Sylvia Plath said, "I've been very excited by what I feel is the new breakthrough that came with, say, Robert Lowell's *Life Studies* . . . This intense breakthrough into very serious, very personal emotional experience, which I feel has been partly taboo . . . I think particularly of the poetess Anne Sexton, who writes also about her experiences as a mother; as a mother who's had a nervous breakdown, as an extremely emotional and feeling young woman. And her poems are wonderfully craftsmanlike poems, and yet they have a kind of emotional psychological depth, which I think is something perhaps quite new and exciting." Do you agree that you influenced her?

SEXTON: Maybe. I did give her a sort of daring, but that's all she should have said. I remember writing to Sylvia in England after her first book, *The Colossus,* came out and saying something like, "If you're not careful, Sylvia, you will out-Roethke Roethke." She replied that I had guessed accurately. But maybe she buried her so-called influences deeper than that, deeper than any one of us would think to look, and if she did, I say, "Good luck to her!" Her poems do their own work. I don't need to sniff them for distant relatives: I'm against it.

INTERVIEWER: Did Sylvia Plath influence your writing?

SEXTON: Her first book didn't interest me at all. I was doing my own thing. But after her death, with the appearance of *Ariel,* I think I was influenced, and I don't mind saying it. In a special sort of way, it was daring again. She had dared to do something quite different. She had dared to write hate poems, the one thing I had never dared to write. I'd always been afraid, even in my life, to express anger. I think the poem, "Cripples and Other Stories," is evidence of a hate poem somehow, though no one could ever write a poem to compare to her "Daddy." There was a kind of insolence in them, saying, "Daddy, you bastard, I'm through." I think the poem, "The Addict," has some of her speech rhythms in it. She had very open speech rhythms, something that I didn't always have.

INTERVIEWER: You have said, "I think the second book lacks

some of the impact and honesty of the first, which I wrote when I was so raw that I didn't know any better." Would you describe your development from the second book to the third and from your third to the fourth?

SEXTON: Well, in the first book, I was giving the experience of madness; in the second book, the causes of madness; and in the third book, finally, I find that I was deciding whether to live or to die. In the third I was daring to be a fool again—raw, "uncooked," as Lowell calls it, with a little camouflage. In the fourth book, I not only have lived, come on to the scene, but loved, that sometime miracle.

INTERVIEWER: What would you say about the technical development from book to book?

SEXTON: In *Bedlam,* I used very tight form in most cases, feeling that I could express myself better. I take a kind of pleasure, even now, but more especially in *Bedlam,* in forming a stanza, a verse, making it an entity, and then coming to a little conclusion at the end of it, of a little shock, a little double rhyme shock. In my second book, *All My Pretty Ones,* I loosened up and in the last section didn't use any form at all. I found myself to be surprisingly free without the form which had worked as a kind of superego for me. The third book I used less form. In *Love Poems,* I had one long poem, eighteen sections, that is in form, and I enjoyed doing it in that way. With the exception of that and a few other poems, all of the book is in free verse, and I feel at this point comfortable to use either, depending on what the poem requires.

INTERVIEWER: Is there any particular subject which you'd rather deal with in form than in free verse?

SEXTON: Probably madness. I've noticed that Robert Lowell felt freer to write about madness in free verse, whereas it was the opposite for me. Only after I had set up large structures that were almost impossible to deal with did I think I was free to allow myself to express what had really happened. However in *Live or Die,* I wrote "Flee on Your Donkey" without that form and found that I could do it just as easily in free verse. That's perhaps something to do with my development as a human being and understanding of myself, besides as a poet.

INTERVIEWER: In *Live or Die*, the whole book has a marvelous structured tension—simply by the sequence of the poems which pits the wish to live against the death instinct. Did you plan the book this way? Lois Ames speaks of you as wishing to write more "live" poems because the "die" poems outnumbered them.

SEXTON: I didn't plan the book any way. In January of 1962, I started collecting new poems the way you do when a book is over. I didn't know where they would go or that they would go anywhere, even into a book. Then at some point, as I was collecting these poems, I was rereading *Henderson the Rain King* by Saul Bellow. I had met Saul Bellow at a cocktail party about a year before, and I had been carrying *Henderson the Rain King* around in my suitcase everywhere I traveled. Suddenly there I was meeting Saul Bellow, and I was overenthusiastic. I said, "Oh, oh, you're Saul Bellow, I've wanted to meet you," and he ran from the room. Very afraid. I was quite ashamed of my exuberance, and then sometime, a year later, reading *Henderson the Rain King* over again, at three in the morning, I wrote Saul Bellow a fan letter about Henderson, saying that he was a monster of despair, that I understood his position because Henderson was the one who had ruined life, who had blown up the frogs, made a mess out of everything. I drove to the mail box then and there! The next morning I wrote him a letter of apology.

Saul Bellow wrote me back on the back of a manuscript. He said to me, "Luckily, I have a message to you from the book I am writing [which was *Herzog*]. I have both your letters—the good one which was written that night at three A.M. and then the contrite one, the next day. One's best things are always followed by apoplectic, apologetic seizure. Monster of despair could be *Henderson*'s subtitle." The message that he had encircled went this way, "With one long breath caught and held in his chest, he fought his sadness over his solitary life. Don't cry you idiot, live or die, but don't poison everything." And in circling that and in sending it to me, Saul Bellow had given me a message about my whole life. That I didn't want to poison the world, that I didn't want to be the killer; I wanted to be the one who gave birth, who encouraged things to grow and to flower, not the poisoner. So I stuck that message up over my desk and it was a kind of hidden message. You don't know what these messages mean to you, yet you stick them up over your desk or remember them or write them down and put them in your wallet. One day I was reading a quote from Rimbaud that said, "Anne, Anne, flee on your donkey," and I typed it out because it had my name in it and because I wanted to flee. I put it in my wallet, went to see my doctor, and at that point was committed to a hospital for about the seventh or eighth time. In the hospital, I started to write the poem, "Flee on Your Donkey," as though the message had come to me at just the right moment. Well, this was true with Bellow's quote from his book. I kept it over my desk, and when I went to Europe, I pasted it in the front of my manuscript. I kept it there as a quotation with which to preface my book. It must have just hit me one day that *Live or Die* was a damn good title for the book I was working on. And that's what it was all about, what all those poems were about. You say there's a tension there and a structure, but it was an unconscious tension and an unconscious structure that I didn't know was going on when I was doing it.

INTERVIEWER: Once you knew the title of the book, did you count up the "live" poems and count up the "die" poems and then write any more poems because of an imbalance?

SEXTON: No, no, that's far too rigid. You can't write a poem because of an imbalance. After that I wrote "Little Girl, My Stringbean, My Lovely Woman." Then I wrote a play, then "A Little Uncomplicated Hymn" and other poems. Some were negative, and some were positive. At this time I knew that I was trying to get a book together. I had more than enough for a book, but I knew I hadn't written out the live or die question. I hadn't written the poem "Live." This was bothering me because it wasn't coming to me. Instead of that, "Cripples and Other Stories" and "The Addict" were appearing, and I knew that I wasn't finishing the book, that I hadn't come to the cycle, I hadn't given a reason. There's nothing I could do about this and then suddenly, our dog was pregnant. I was supposed to kill all the puppies when they came; instead, I let them live, and I realized that if I let *them* live, that I could let *me* live, too, that after all I wasn't a killer, that the poison just didn't take.

INTERVIEWER: Although you received a European traveling fellowship from the American Academy of Arts and Letters, there are, to date, very few poems published about your European experience. Why?

SEXTON: First of all poems aren't post cards to send home. Secondly I went to Europe with a purpose as well as with a grant. My great-aunt, who was really my best childhood friend, had sent letters home from Europe the three years that she lived there. I had written about this in a poem called "Some Foreign Letters." I had her letters with me as I left for Europe, and I was going to walk her walks and go to her places, live her life over again, and write letters back to her. The two poems that I did write about Europe mention the letters. In "Crossing the Atlantic," I mention that I have read my grandmother's letters and my mother's letters. I had swallowed their words like Dickens, thinking of Dickens' journals in America. The second poem, "Walking in Paris," was written about my great-aunt, how she used to walk fourteen or fifteen miles a day in Paris, and I call her Nana. Some critics have thought I meant Zola's Nana, but I didn't any more than I meant the Nana in Peter Pan. However the letters were stolen from my car in Belgium. When I lost the letters in Brussels, that was the end of that kind of poem that I had gone over there to write.

INTERVIEWER: You were to go abroad for a year, but you only stayed two months. Do you want to comment on that?

SEXTON: Two and a half months. I got sick over there; I lost my sense of self. I had, as my psychiatrist said, "a leaky ego" and I had to come home. I was in the hospital for a while, and then I returned to my normal life. I had to come home because I need my husband and my therapist and my children to tell me who I am. I remember, I was talking with Elizabeth Hardwick on the phone and saying, "Oh, I feel so guilty. I couldn't get along without my husband. It's a terrible thing, really, a modern woman should be able to do it." Although I may be misquoting her, I may have remembered it the way I needed to hear it, she said to me, "If I were in Paris without my husband, I'd hide in a hotel room all day." And I said, "Well, think of Mary McCarthy." And Elizabeth Hardwick said, "Mary McCarthy, she's never been without a man for a day in her life."

INTERVIEWER: From 1964 to 1965, you held a Ford Foundation Grant in playwriting and worked at Boston's Charles Street Playhouse. How did you feel writing something that had to be staged?

SEXTON: I felt great! I used to pace up and down the living room shouting out the lines, and what do they call it . . . for walking around the stage . . . *blocking* out the play as I would go along.

INTERVIEWER: Was the play [*Mercy Street*] ever performed?*

SEXTON: There were little working performances at the Charles Playhouse when we had time. It was pretty busy there. Now and then they would play out a scene for me, and then I would rewrite it and send it in to the director special delivery. He would call me up the next morning and say, "It's not right," and then I would work on it again, send it to him that evening, and then the next morning, he'd call, and so on it went. I found that I had one whole character in the play who was unnecessary because, as they acted it, the director had that person be quiet and say nothing. I realized that that dialogue was totally unnecessary, so I cut out that character.

INTERVIEWER: Did you find that the themes in your poetry overlapped into your play? Was your play an extension of your poetry?

SEXTON: Yes. Completely. The play was about a girl shuffling between her psychiatrist and a priest. It was the priest I cut out,

---

*Editor's Note: *Mercy Street* was eventually produced at New York's American Place Theater in 1969.

realizing that she really wasn't having a dialogue with him at all. The play was about all the subjects that my poems are about— my mother, my great-aunt, my father, and the girl who wants to kill herself. A little bit about her husband, but not much. The play is really a morality play. The second act takes place after death.

INTERVIEWER: Many of your poems are dramatic narratives. Because you're accustomed to handling a plot, was it easy for you to switch from verse to scene writing?

SEXTON: I don't see the difference. In both cases, the character is confronting himself and his destiny. I didn't know I was writing scenes; I thought I was writing about people. In another context —helping Maxine Kumin with her novel—I gave her a bit of advice. I told her, "Fuck structure and grab your characters by the time balls." Each one of us sits in our time; we're born, live and die. She was thinking this and that, and I was telling her to get inside her characters' lives—which she finally did.

INTERVIEWER: What were your feelings when you received the Pulitzer Prize for Poetry for *Live or Die* in 1967?

SEXTON: Of course, I was delighted. It had been a bad time for me. I had a broken hip, and I was just starting to get well, still crippled, but functioning a little bit. After I received the prize, it gave me added incentive to write more. In the months following, I managed to write a poem, "Eighteen Days Without You," in fourteen days—an eighteen-section poem. I was inspired by the recognition that the Pulitzer gave me, even though I was aware that it didn't mean all that much. After all, they have to give a Pulitzer Prize every year, and I was just one in a long line.

INTERVIEWER: Do you write a spate of poems at one time, or are you disciplined by a writing schedule?

SEXTON: Well, I'm very dissatisfied with the amount I write. My first book—although it took three years to complete—was really written in one year. Sometimes ten poems were written in two weeks. When I was going at that rate, I found that I could really work well. Now I tend to become dissatisfied with the fact that I write poems so slowly, that they come to me so slowly. When they come, I write them; when they don't come, I don't.

There's certainly no disciplined writing schedule except for the fact that when a poem comes a person must be disciplined and ready, flexing his muscles. That is, they burst forth, and you must put everything else aside. Ideally it doesn't matter what it is unless your husband has double pneumonia, or the child breaks his leg. Otherwise, you don't tear yourself away from the typewriter until you must sleep.

INTERVIEWER: Do the responsibilities of wife and mother interfere with your writing?

SEXTON: Well, when my children were younger, they interfered all the time. It was just my stubbornness that let me get through with it at all, because here were these young children saying, "Momma, Momma," and there I was getting the images, structuring the poem. Now my children are older and creep around the house saying, "Shh, Mother is writing a poem." But then again, as I was writing the poem, "Eighteen Days Without You"—the last poem in *Love Poems*—my husband said to me, "I can't stand it any longer, you haven't been with me for days." That poem originally was "Twenty-one Days Without You" and it became "Eighteen Days" because he had cut into the inspiration; he demanded my presence back again, into his life, and I couldn't take that much from him.

INTERVIEWER: When writing, what part of the poem is the prickliest part?

SEXTON: Punctuation, sometimes. The punctuating can change the whole meaning, and my life is full of little dots and dashes. Therefore, I have to let the editors help me punctuate. And, probably the rhythm. It's the thing I have to work hardest to get in the beginning—the feeling, the voice of the poem, and how it will come across, how it will feel to the reader, how it feels to me as it comes out. Images are probably the most important part of the poem. First of all, you want to tell a story, but images are what are going to shore it up and get to the heart of the matter —but I don't have to work too hard for the images—they have to come—if they're not coming, I'm not even writing a poem, it's pointless. So I work hardest to get the rhythm, because each poem should have its own rhythm, its own structure. Each poem has its own life, each one is different.

INTERVIEWER: How do you decide a length of line? Does it have something to do with the way it looks on a page as well as how many beats there are to a line?

SEXTON: How it looks on a page. I don't give a damn about the beats in a line, unless I want them and need them. These are just tricks that you use when you need them. It's a very simple thing to write with rhyme and with rhythmic beat—those things anyone can do nowadays; everyone is quite accomplished at that. The point, the hard thing, is to get the true voice of the poem, to make each poem an individual thing, give it the stamp of your own voice, and at the same time to make it singular.

INTERVIEWER: Do you ever find yourself saying, "Oh, yes, I've explored that in another poem," and discarding a poem?

SEXTON: No, because I might want to explore it in a new way . . . I might have a new realization, a new truth about it. Recently I noticed in "Flee on Your Donkey" that I had used some of the same facts in *To Bedlam and Part Way Back*, but I hadn't realized them in their total ugliness. I'd hidden from them. This time was really raw and really ugly and it was all involved with my own madness. It was all like a great involuted web, and I presented it the way it really was.

INTERVIEWER: Do you revise a great deal?

SEXTON: Constantly.

INTERVIEWER: Do you have any ritual which gets you set for writing?

SEXTON: I might, if I felt the poem come on, put on a certain record, sometimes the "Bachianas Brasileiras" by Villa-Lobos. I wrote to that for about three or four years. It's my magic tune.

INTERVIEWER: Is there any time of day, any particular mood that is better for writing?

SEXTON: No. Those moments before a poem comes, when the heightened awareness comes over you, and you realize a poem is buried there somewhere, you prepare yourself. I run around, you know, kind of skipping around the house, marvelous elation. It's as though I could fly, almost, and I get very tense before I've told the truth—hard. Then I sit down at the desk and get going with it.

INTERVIEWER: What is the quality of feeling when you're writing?

SEXTON: Well, it's a beautiful feeling, even if it's hard work. When I'm writing, I know I'm doing the thing I was born to do.

INTERVIEWER: Do you have any standard by which you judge whether to let an image remain in a poem, or be cut?

SEXTON: It's done with my unconscious. May it do me no ill.

INTERVIEWER: You've said, "When I'm working away on a poem, I hunt for the truth . . . It might be a poetic truth, and not just a factual one." Can you comment on that?

SEXTON: Many of my poems are true, line by line, altering a few facts to get the story at its heart. In "The Double Image," the poem about my mother's death from cancer and the loss of my daughter, I don't mention that I had another child. Each poem has its own truth. Furthermore, in that poem, I only say that I was hospitalized twice, when in fact, I was hospitalized five times in that span of time. But then, poetic truth is not necessarily autobiographical. It is truth that goes beyond the immediate self, another life. I don't adhere to literal facts all the time; I make them up whenever needed. Concrete examples give a verisimilitude. I want the reader to feel, "Yes, yes, that's the way it is." I want them to feel as if they were touching me. I would alter any word, attitude, image, or persona for the sake of a poem. As Yeats said, "I have lived many lives, I have been a slave and a prince. Many a beloved has sat upon my knee, and I have sat upon the knee of many a beloved. Everything that has been shall be again."

INTERVIEWER: There Yeats is talking about reincarnation.

SEXTON: So am I. It's a little mad, but I believe I am many people. When I am writing a poem, I feel I am the person who should have written it. Many times I assume these guises; I attack it the way a novelist might. Sometimes I become someone else, and when I do, I believe, even in moments when I'm not writing the poem, that I am that person. When I wrote about the far-

mer's wife, I lived in my mind in Illinois; when I had the illegitimate child, I nursed it—in my mind—and gave it back and traded
life. When I gave my lover back to his wife, in my mind, I grieved
and saw how ethereal and unnecessary I had been. When I was
Christ, I felt like Christ. My arms hurt, I desperately wanted to
pull them in off the Cross. When I was taken down off the Cross
and buried alive, I sought solutions; I hoped they were Christian
solutions.

INTERVIEWER: What prompted you to write "In the Deep
Museum," which recounts what Christ could have felt if he were
still alive in the tomb? What led you to even deal with such a
subject?

SEXTON: I'm not sure. I think it was an unconscious thing. I
think I had a kind of feeling Christ was speaking to me and telling
me to write that story . . . the story he hadn't written. I thought
to myself, this would be the most awful death. The Cross, the
Crucifixion, which I so deeply believe in, has almost become trite,
and that there was a more humble death that he might have had
to seek for love's sake, because his love was the greatest thing
about him—not his death.

INTERVIEWER: Are you a believing nonbeliever? Your poems,
such as "The Division of Parts" and "With Mercy for the
Greedy," suggest you would like to believe, indeed struggle to
believe, but can't.

SEXTON: Yes. I fight my own impulse. There is a hard-core part
of me that believes, and there's this little critic in me that believes
nothing. Some people think I'm a lapsed Catholic.

INTERVIEWER: What was your early religious training?

SEXTON: Half-assed Protestant. My Nana came from a Protestant background with a very stern patriarchal father who had
twelve children. He often traveled in Europe, and when he came
back and brought nude statues into his house, the minister came
to call and said, "You can't come to church if you keep these nude
statues." So he said, "All right, I'll never come again." Every
Sunday morning he read the Bible to his twelve children for two

hours, and they had to sit up straight and perfect. He never went to church again.

INTERVIEWER: Where do you get the "juice" for your religious poetry?

SEXTON: I found, when I was bringing up my children, that I could answer questions about sex easily. But I had a very hard time with the questions about God and death. It isn't resolved in my mind to this day.

INTERVIEWER: Are you saying then that questions from your children are what prompted you to think about these poems— that doesn't sound quite right.

SEXTON: It isn't. I have visions—sometimes ritualized visions —that come to me of God, or of Christ, or of the Saints, and I feel that I can touch them almost . . . that they are part of me. It's the same "Everything that has been shall be again." It's reincarnation, speaking with another voice . . . or else with the Devil. If you want to know the truth, the leaves talk to me every June.

INTERVIEWER: How long do your visions last? What are they like?

SEXTON: That's impossible to describe. They could last for six months, six minutes, or six hours. I feel very much in touch with things after I've had a vision. It's somewhat like the beginning of writing a poem; the whole world is very sharp and well defined, and I'm intensely alive, like I've been shot full of electric volts.

INTERVIEWER: Do you try to communicate this to other people when you feel it?

SEXTON: Only through the poems, no other way. I refuse to talk about it, which is why I'm having a hard time now.

INTERVIEWER: Is there any real difference between a religious vision and a vision when you're mad?

SEXTON: Sometimes, when you're mad, the vision—I don't call them visions, really—when you're mad, they're silly and out of place, whereas if it's a so-called mystical experience, you've put everything in its proper place. I've never talked about my religious experiences with anyone, not a psychiatrist, not a friend, not a priest, not anyone. I've kept it very much to myself—and I find this very difficult, and I'd just as soon leave it, if you please.

INTERVIEWER: A poem like "The Division of Parts" has direct reference to your mother's dying. Did those excruciating experiences of watching someone close to you disintegrate from cancer force you to confront your own belief in God or religion?

SEXTON: Yes, I think so. The dying are slowly being rocked away from us and wrapped up into death, that eternal place. And one looks for answers and is faced with demons and visions. Then one comes up with God. I don't mean the ritualized Protestant God, who is such a goody-goody . . . but the martyred saints, the crucified man . . .

INTERVIEWER: Are you saying that when confronted with the ultimate question, death, that your comfort comes, even though watered down, from the myths and fables of religion?

SEXTON: No myth or fable ever gave me any solace, but my own inner contact with the heroes of the fables, as you put it, my very closeness to Christ. In one poem about the Virgin Mary, "For the Year of the Insane," I believed that I was talking to Mary, that her lips were upon my lips; it's almost physical . . . as in many of my poems. I become that person.

INTERVIEWER: But is it the fact in your life of someone you know dying that forces you into a vision?

SEXTON: No, I think it's my own madness.

INTERVIEWER: Are you more lucid, in the sense of understanding life, when you are mad?

SEXTON: Yes.

INTERVIEWER: Why do you think that's so?

SEXTON: Pure gift.

INTERVIEWER: I asked you, are you a believing disbeliever. When something happens like a death, are you pushed over the brink of disbelieving into believing?

SEXTON: For a while, but it can happen without a death. There are little deaths in life, too—in your own life—and at that point, sometimes you are in touch with strange things, otherworldly things.

INTERVIEWER: You have received a great deal of fan mail from Jesuits and other clergy. Do any of them interpret what you write as blasphemy?

SEXTON: No. They find my work very religious, and take my books on retreats, and teach my poems in classes.

INTERVIEWER: Why do you feel that most of your critics ignore this strain of religious experience in your poetry?

SEXTON: I think they tackle the obvious things without delving deeper. They are more shocked by the other, whereas I think in time to come people will be more shocked by my mystical poetry than by my so-called confessional poetry.

INTERVIEWER: Perhaps your critics, in time to come, will associate the suffering in your confessional poetry with the kind of sufferers you take on in your religious poetry.

SEXTON: You've summed it up perfectly. Thank you for saying that. That ragged Christ, that sufferer, performed the greatest act of confession, and I mean with his body. And I try to do that with words.

INTERVIEWER: Many of your poems deal with memories of suffering. Very few of them deal with memories that are happy ones. Why do you feel driven to write more about pain?

SEXTON: That's not true about my last book, which deals with joy. I think I've dealt with unhappy themes because I've lived them. If I haven't lived them, I've invented them.

INTERVIEWER: But surely there were also happy moments, joyous, euphoric moments in those times as well.

SEXTON: Pain engraves a deeper memory.

INTERVIEWER: Are there any poems you wouldn't read in public?

SEXTON: No. As a matter of fact, I sing "Cripples and Other Stories" with my combo to a Nashville rhythm.

INTERVIEWER: What is your combo?

SEXTON: It's called "Her Kind"—after one of my poems. One

of my students started putting my poems to music—he's a guitar-
ist, and then we got an organist, a flutist, and a drummer. We call
our music "Chamber Rock." We've been working on it and
giving performances for about a year. It opens up my poems in
a new way by involving them in the sound of rock music, letting
my words open up to sound that can be actually heard, giving a
new dimension. And it's quite exciting for me to hear them that
way.

INTERVIEWER: Do you enjoy giving a reading?

SEXTON: It takes three weeks out of your life. A week before
it happens, the nervousness begins, and it builds up to the night
of the reading when the poet in you changes into a performer.
Readings take so much out of you because they are a reliving of
the experience, that is, they are happening all over again. I am
an actress in my own autobiographical play. Then there is the love
. . . When there is a coupling of the audience and myself, when
they are really with me, and the Muse is with me, I'm not coming
alone.

INTERVIEWER: Can you ever imagine America as a place where
thousands of fans flock to a stadium to hear a poet, as they do in
Russia?

SEXTON: Someday, perhaps. But our poets seem to be losing
touch. People flock to Bob Dylan, Janis Joplin, the Beatles—these
are the popular poets of the English-speaking world. But I don't
worry about popularity; I'm too busy.

INTERVIEWER: At first your poetry was a therapeutic device.
Why do you write now?

SEXTON: I write because I'm driven to—it's my bag. Though
after every book, I think there'll never be another one. That's the
end of that. Good-by, good-by.

INTERVIEWER: And what advice would you give to a young
poet?

SEXTON: Be careful who your critics are. Be specific. Tell almost the whole story. Put your ear close down to your soul and
listen hard.

INTERVIEWER: Louis Simpson criticized your poetry, saying,

"A poem titled 'Menstruation at Forty' was the straw that broke this camel's back." Is it only male critics who balk at your use of the biological facts of womanhood?

SEXTON: I haven't added up all the critics and put them on different teams. I haven't noticed the gender of the critic especially. I talk of the life-death cycle of the body. Well, women tell time by the body. They are like clocks. They are always fastened to the earth, listening for its small animal noises. Sexuality is one of the most normal parts of life. True, I get a little uptight when Norman Mailer writes that he screws a woman anally. I like Allen Ginsberg very much, and when he writes about the ugly vagina, I feel awful. That kind of thing doesn't appeal to me. So I have my limitations, too. Homosexuality is all right with me. Sappho was beautiful. But when someone hates another person's body and somehow violates it—that's the kind of thing I mind.

INTERVIEWER: What do you feel is the purpose of poetry?

SEXTON: As Kafka said about prose, "A book should serve as the axe for the frozen sea within us." And that's what I want from a poem. A poem should serve as the axe for the frozen sea within us.

INTERVIEWER: How would you apply the Kafka quote to your new book, *Love Poems?*

SEXTON: Well, have you ever seen a sixteen-year-old fall in love? The axe for the frozen sea becomes imbedded in her. Or have you ever seen a woman get to be forty and never have any love in her life? What happens to her when she falls in love? The axe for the frozen sea.

INTERVIEWER: Some people wonder how you can write about yourself, completely ignoring the great issues of the times, like the Vietnam war or the civil-rights crisis.

SEXTON: People have to find out who they are before they can confront national issues. The fact that I seldom write about public issues in no way reflects my personal opinion. I am a pacifist. I sign petitions, etc. However, I am not a polemicist. "The Fire Bombers"—that's a new poem—is about wanton destruction, not about Vietnam, specifically; when Robert Kennedy was killed, I wrote about an assassin. I write about human emotions; I write about interior events, not historical ones. In one of my love poems, I say that my lover is unloading bodies from Vietnam. If that poem is read in a hundred years, people will have to look up the war in Vietnam. They will have mixed it up with the Korean or God knows what else. One hopes it will be history very soon. Of course, I may change. I could use the specifics of the war for a backdrop against which to reveal experience, and it would be just as valid as the details I am known by. As for the civil-rights issue, I mentioned that casually in a poem, but I don't go into it. I think it's a major issue. I think many of my poems about the individual who is dispossessed, who must play slave, who cries "Freedom Now," "Power Now," are about the human experience of being black in this world. A black emotion can be a white emotion. It is a crisis for the individual as well as the nation. I think I've been writing black poems all along, wearing my white mask. I'm always the victim . . . but no longer!

BARBARA KEVLES

16. John Updike

Born on March 18, 1932, in Shillington, Pennsylvania, John Updike left his hometown in 1950 to attend Harvard University, from which he graduated in 1954. After spending a year at the Ruskin School of Drawing and of Fine Art in England, he returned to New York in 1955 and served for two years on the staff of *The New Yorker*, where a great many of his poems and stories have subsequently appeared.

Updike has published two collections of poetry, *The Carpentered Hen* (1958) and *Telephone Poles* (1963); and five collections of short stories, *The Same Door* (1959), *Pigeon Feathers and Other Stories* (1962), *Olinger Stories* (1964), *The Music School* (1966), and *Museums and Women* (1972). He is the author of seven novels: *The Poorhouse Fair* (1959); *Rabbit, Run* (1960); *The Centaur* (1963), which won the National Book Award in 1964; *Of the Farm* (1965); *Couples* (1968); *Rabbit Redux* (1971); *A Month of Sundays* (1975), and *Picked-Up Pieces* (1976).

He was the recipient of the Rosenthal Award of the National Institute of Arts and Letters (1960) and of the O. Henry Prize Story award (1967–68) and is a member of the National Institute of Arts and Letters. He lives with his wife and their four children in Ipswich, Massachusetts.

wore away
Whitewash washed off after two or three rains and after the
war some better chemical compound came out that
pretty well lasted until winter. In winter there could not be too much light.
And the Michigan snows towered around the glass walls, and within
there was a sound of dripping and a purring
in the pipes, the color of dirt, that travelled along the dirt floor.
Piet thought deliberately of the marsh house he
and Gallagher had sold to the Whitmans, with a possibility of the
renovation contract, and the

incalculable saving seemed wonderfully solid, like the phantoms
seen in a steroscope. A child cried out

From the voice he guessed it was Nancy. She,
who could tie her shoes at the age of three,
had lately, at the age of five, begun to suck her thumb
and talk about dying. I will never grow up and I will never ever in
my whole life die. He thought he should go to her but the cry
was not repeated and in her new mood the child preferred her
mother. The microscopic whirring tick of their
bedside clock flowed into his listening. A
truck passed on the road and his ears followed it
down the road, focussing on its vanishing point. As a child he had
dreamed of living beneath tracks, found nothing so

Manuscript page of *Couples*

John Updike

In 1966, when John Updike was first asked to do a Paris Review *interview, he refused: "Perhaps I have written fiction because everything unambiguously expressed seems somehow crass to me; and when the subject is myself, I want to jeer and weep. Also, I really don't have a great deal to tell interviewers; the little I learned about life and the art of fiction I try to express in my work."*

The following year, a second request won acceptance, but Updike's apprehension caused further delay. Should there be a meeting followed by an exchange of written questions and answers, or should this procedure be reversed? Need there be any meeting at all? (Updike fears becoming, even for a moment, "one more gassy monologist.") In the end, during the summer of 1967, written questions were submitted to him, and afterward, he was interviewed on Martha's Vineyard, where he and his family take their vacation.

A first view of Updike revealed a jauntiness of manner surprising

in a writer of such craft and sensibility. After barreling down
Edgartown's narrow main street, the author appeared from his
beat-up Corvair—a barefoot, tousle-haired young man dressed in
khaki Bermudas and a sweatshirt.

    Updike is a fluent talker, but obviously not a man who expects
talk to bridge the distance between others and his inner life. There-
fore, the final stage of this interview was his revision of the spoken
comments to bring them into line with the style of his written
answers. The result is a fabricated interview—in its modest way,
a work of art, and thus appropriate to a man who believes that only
art can track the nuances of experience.

INTERVIEWER: You've treated your early years fictionally and
have discussed them in interviews, but you haven't said much
about your time at Harvard. I wonder what effect you think it had.

UPDIKE: My time at Harvard, once I got by the compression
bends of the freshman year, was idyllic enough, and as they say,
successful; but I felt toward those years, while they were happening, the resentment a caterpillar must feel while his somatic cells
are shifting all around to make him a butterfly. I remember the
glow of the Fogg Museum windows, and my wife-to-be pushing
her singing bicycle through the snowy Yard, and the smell of wet
old magazines that arose from the cellar of the Lampoon and hit
your nostrils when you entered the narthex, and numerous pleasant revelations in classrooms—all of it haunted, though, by knowledge of the many others who had passed this way, and felt the
venerable glory of it all a shade keener than I, and written suffi-
ciently about it. All that I seem able to preserve of the Harvard
experience is in one short story, "The Christian Roommates."
There was another, "Homage to Paul Klee," that has been
printed in *The Liberal Context* but not in a book. Foxy Whitman,
in *Couples,* remembers some of the things I do. Like me, she feels
obscurely hoodwinked, pacified, by the process of becoming nice.
I distrust, perhaps, hallowed, very O.K. places. Harvard has
enough panegyrists without me.

INTERVIEWER: Did you learn much writing for the *Lampoon?*

UPDIKE: The *Lampoon* was very kind to me. I was given, beside the snug pleasures of club solidarity, carte blanche as far as the magazine went—I began as a cartoonist, did a lot of light verse, and more and more prose. There was always lots of space to fill. Also, I do have a romantic weakness for gags—we called ourselves, the term itself a gag, gagsters. My own speciality was Chinese jokes. A little birthday party, and the children singing to the blushing center of attention, "Happy Birthday, Tu Yu." Or coolies listening to an agitator and asking each other, "Why *shouldn't* we work for coolie wages?" Or—another cartoon—a fairy princess in a tower, her hair hanging to the ground and labeled Fire Exit. And I remember Bink Young, now an Episcopal priest, solemnly plotting, his tattered sneakers up on a desk, how to steal a battleship from Boston Harbor. Maybe, as an imperfectly metamorphosed caterpillar, I was grateful for the company of true butterflies.

INTERVIEWER: Have you given up drawing entirely? I noticed that your recent "Letter from Anguila" was illustrated by you.

UPDIKE: You're nice to have noticed. For years I wanted to get a drawing into *The New Yorker,* and at last I did. My first ambition was to be an animator for Walt Disney. Then I wanted to be a magazine cartoonist. Newly married, I used to draw Mary and the children, and did have that year in art school, but of late I don't draw at all, don't even doodle beside the telephone. It's a loss, a sadness for me. I'm interested in concrete poetry, in some attempt to return to the manuscript page, to *use* the page space, and the technical possibilities. My new book, a long poem called *Midpoint,* tries to do something of this. Since we write for the eye, why not really write for it—give it a treat? Letters are originally little pictures, so let's combine graphic imagery, photographic imagery, with words. I mean *mesh* them. Saying this, I think of Pound's Chinese characters, and of course Apollinaire; and of my own poems, "Nutcracker," with the word "nut" in bold face, seems to me as good as George Herbert's angel-wings.

INTERVIEWER: After graduating from Harvard, you served as a *New Yorker* staff writer for two years. What sort of work did you do?

UPDIKE: I was a Talk of the Town writer, which means that I both did the legwork and the finished product. An exalted position! It was playful work that opened the city to me. I was the man who went to boating or electronic exhibits in the Coliseum and tried to make impressionist poems of the objects and overhead conversations.

INTERVIEWER: Why did you quit?

UPDIKE: After two years I doubted that I was expanding the *genre.* When my wife and I had a second child and needed a larger apartment, the best course abruptly seemed to leave the city, and with it the job. They still keep my name on the staff sheet, and I still contribute Notes and Comments, and I take much comfort from having a kind of professional home where they consider me somehow competent. America in general doesn't expect competence from writers. Other things, yes; competence, no.

INTERVIEWER: How do you feel about being associated with that magazine for so many years?

UPDIKE: Very happy. From the age of twelve when my aunt gave us a subscription for Christmas, *The New Yorker* has seemed to me the best of possible magazines, and their acceptance of a poem and a story by me in June of 1954 remains the ecstatic breakthrough of my literary life. Their editorial care and their gratitude for a piece of work they like are incomparable. And I love the format—the signature at the end, everybody the same size, and the battered title type, evocative of the twenties and Persia and the future all at once.

INTERVIEWER: You seem to shun literary society. Why?

UPDIKE: I don't, do I? Here I am, talking to you. In leaving New York in 1957, I did leave without regret the literary demimonde of agents and would-be's and with-it nonparticipants; this world seemed unnutritious and interfering. Hemingway described literary New York as a bottle full of tapeworms trying to feed on each other. When I write, I aim in my mind not toward New York but toward a vague spot a little to the east of Kansas. I think of the books on library shelves, without their jackets, years old, and a countryish teen-aged boy finding them, and having them speak to him. The reviews, the stacks in Brentano's, are just hurdles to get over, to place the books on that shelf. Anyway, in 1957, I was full of a Pennsylvania thing I wanted to say, and Ipswich gave me the space in which to say it, and in which to live modestly, raise my children, and have friends on the basis of what I did in person rather than what I did in print.

INTERVIEWER: Do your neighbors—present in Ipswich, past in Shillington—get upset when they fancy they've found themselves in your pages?

UPDIKE: I would say not. I count on people to know the difference between flesh and paper, and generally they do. In Shillington I was long away from the town, and there is a greater element of distortion or suppression than may appear; there are rather few characters in those Olinger stories that could even remotely take offense. Ipswich I've not written too much about. Somewhat of the marsh geography peeps through in *Couples*, but the couples themselves are more or less adults who could be encountered anywhere in the East. The town, although it was a little startled at first by the book, was reassured, I think, by reading it. The week after its publication, when the Boston papers were whooping it up in high tabloid style, and the *Atlantic* ran a banshee cry of indignation from Diana Trilling, people like the gas station attendant and a strange woman on the golf course would stop me and say something soothing, complimentary. I work downtown, above a restaurant, and can be seen plodding up to my office most mornings, and I think Ipswich pretty much feels sorry for me, trying to make a living at such a plainly unprofitable chore. Also, I do participate in local affairs—I'm on the Congregational church building committee and the Democratic town committee, and while the *Couples* fuss was in progress, capped by that snaggle-toothed cover on *Time*, I was writing a pageant for our Seventeenth-century Day. Both towns in my mind are not so much themselves as places I've happened to be in when I was a child and then an adult. The difference between Olinger and Tarbox is much more the difference between childhood and adulthood than the difference between two geographical locations. They are stages on my pilgrim's progress, not spots on the map.

INTERVIEWER: What about your parents? They seem to appear often in your work. Have their reactions to earlier versions had an effect on later ones?

UPDIKE: My parents should not be held to the letter of any of the fictional fathers and mothers. But I don't mind admitting that George Caldwell was assembled from certain vivid gestures and plights characteristic of Wesley Updike; once, returning to Plowville after *The Centaur* came out, I was upbraided by a Sunday-school pupil of my father's for my outrageous portrait, and my father, with typical sanctity, interceded, saying, "No, it's the truth. The kid got me right." My mother, a different style of saint, is an ideal reader, and an ideally permissive writer's mother. They both have a rather un-middleclass appetite for the jubilant horrible truth, and after filling my childhood with warmth and color, they have let me make my adult way without interference and been never other than encouraging, even when old wounds were my topic, and a child's vision of things has been lent the undue authority of print. I have written free from any fear of forfeiting their love.

INTERVIEWER: Most of your work takes place in a common locale: Olinger. So it was interesting to see you say farewell to that world in your preface to the *Olinger Stories.* Yet in the following year you published *Of the Farm.* Why do you feel so drawn to this material?

UPDIKE: But *Of the Farm* was about Firetown; they only visit the Olinger supermarket. I am drawn to southeastern Pennsylvania because I know how things happen there, or at least how they used to happen. Once you have in your bones the fundamental feasibilities of a place, you can imagine there freely.

INTERVIEWER: That's not what I mean. What I meant to ask is not why you keep writing about Olinger per se, but why you write so much about what most people take to be your own adolescence and family. Numerous critics, for example, have pointed to similarities between *Of the Farm, The Centaur,* and stories like "My Grandmother's Thimble." "Flight," for example, seems an earlier version of *Of the Farm.*

UPDIKE: I suppose there's no avoiding it—my adolescence seemed interesting to me. In a sense my mother and father, considerable actors both, were dramatizing my youth as I was having it so that I arrived as an adult with some burden of material already half formed. There is, true, a submerged thread connecting certain of the fictions, and I guess the submerged thread is the autobiography. That is, in *Of the Farm,* although the last name is not the name of the people in *The Centaur,* the geography is not appreciably changed, and the man in each case is called George. *Of the Farm* was in part a look at the world of *The Centaur* after the centaur had indeed died. By the way, I must repeat that I didn't mean Caldwell to die in *The Centaur;* he dies in the sense of living, of going back to work, of being a shelter for his son. But by the time Joey Robinson is thirty-five, his father is dead. Also, there's the curious touch of the Running Horse River in *Rabbit, Run* which returns in the Alton of *The Centaur.* And somehow that Running Horse bridges both the books, connects them. When I was little, I used to draw disparate objects on a piece of paper—toasters, baseballs, flowers, whatnot—and connect them with lines. But every story, really, is a fresh start for me, and these little connections—recurrences of names, or the way, say, that Piet Hanema's insomnia takes him back into the same high school that John Nordholm, and David Kern, and Allen Dow sat in—are in there as a kind of running, oblique coherence. Once I've coined a name, by the way, I feel utterly hidden behind that mask, and what I remember and what I imagine become indistinguishable. I feel no obligation to the remembered past; what I create on paper must, and for me does, soar free of whatever the facts were. Do I make any sense?

INTERVIEWER: Some.

UPDIKE: In others words, I disavow any essential connection

between my life and whatever I write. I think it's a morbid and inappropriate area of concern, though natural enough—a lot of morbid concerns are natural. But the work, the words on the paper, must stand apart from our living presences; we sit down at the desk and become nothing but the excuse for these husks we cast off. But apart from the somewhat teasing little connections, there is in these three novels and the short stories of *Pigeon Feathers* a central image of flight or escape or loss, the way we flee from the past, a sense of guilt which I tried to express in the story, the triptych with the long title, "The Blessed Man of Boston, My Grandmother's Thimble, and Fanning Island," wherein the narrator becomes a Polynesian pushing off into a void. The sense that in time as well as space we leave people as if by volition and thereby incur guilt and thereby owe them, the dead, the forsaken, at least the homage of rendering them. The trauma or message that I acquired in Olinger had to do with suppressed pain, with the amount of sacrifice I suppose that middle-class life demands, and by that I guess I mean civilized life. The father, whatever his name, is sacrificing freedom of motion, and the mother is sacrificing in a way—oh, sexual richness, I guess; they're all stuck, and when I think back over these stories (and you know, they *are* dear to me and if I had to give anybody one book of me it would be the Vintage *Olinger Stories*), I think especially of that moment in "Flight" when the boy, chafing to escape, fresh from his encounter with Molly Bingaman and a bit more of a man but not enough quite, finds the mother lying there buried in her own peculiar messages from far away, the New Orleans jazz, and then the grandfather's voice comes tumbling down the stairs singing, "There is a happy land far far away." This is the way it was, is. There has never been anything in my life quite as compressed, simultaneously as communicative to me of my own power and worth and of the irremediable grief in just living, in just going on.

I really don't think I'm alone among writers in caring about what they experienced in the first eighteen years of their life. Hemingway cherished the Michigan stories out of proportion, I would think, to their merit. Look at Twain. Look at Joyce. Nothing that happens to us after twenty is as free from self-consciousness because by then we have the vocation to write. Writers' lives break into two halves. At the point where you get your writerly vocation you diminish your receptivity to experience. Being able to write becomes a kind of shield, a way of hiding, a way of too instantly transforming pain into honey—whereas when you're young, you're so impotent you cannot help but strive and observe and feel.

INTERVIEWER: How does Mrs. Updike react to your work? *Time* quotes you as having said she never entirely approves of your novels.

UPDIKE: Mary is a pricelessly sensitive reader. She is really always right, and if I sometimes, notably in the novels, persevere without her unqualified blessing, it is because somebody in me— the gagster, the fanatic, the boor—must be allowed to have his say. I usually don't show her anything until I am finished, or stuck. I never disregard her remarks, and she is tactful in advancing them.

INTERVIEWER: In your review of James Agee's *Letters to Father Flye*, you defend professionalism. Even so, are you bothered by having to write for a living?

UPDIKE: No, I always wanted to draw or write for a living. Teaching, the customary alternative, seemed truly depleting and corrupting. I have been able to support myself by and large with the more respectable forms—poetry, short stories, novels—but what journalism I have done has been useful. I would write ads for deodorants or labels for catsup bottles if I had to. The miracle of turning inklings into thoughts and thoughts into words and words into metal and print and ink never palls for me; the technical aspects of bookmaking, from type font to binding glue, interest me. The distinction between a thing well done and a thing done ill obtains everywhere—in all circles of Paradise and Inferno.

INTERVIEWER: You write a fair amount of literary criticism. Why?

UPDIKE: I do it (a) when some author, like Spark or Borges,

excites me and I want to share the good news, (b) when I want to write an essay, as on romantic love, or Barth's theology, (c) when I feel ignorant of something, like modern French fiction, and accepting a review assignment will compel me to read and learn.

INTERVIEWER: Do you find it helpful in your fiction?

UPDIKE: I think it good for an author, baffled by obtuse reviews of himself, to discover what a recalcitrant art reviewing is, how hard it is to keep the plot straight in summary, let alone to sort out one's honest responses. But reviewing should not become a habit. It encourages a writer to think of himself as a pundit, of fiction as a collective enterprise and species of expertise, and of the imagination as a cerebral and social activity—all pernicious illusions.

INTERVIEWER: I'd like to ask a bit about your work habits if I may. What sort of schedule do you follow?

UPDIKE: I write every weekday morning. I try to vary what I am doing, and my verse, or poetry, is a help here. Embarked on a long project, I try to stay with it even on dull days. For every novel, however, that I have published, there has been one unfinished or scrapped. Some short stories—I think offhand of "Lifeguard," "The Taste of Metal," "My Grandmother's Thimble"— are fragments salvaged and reshaped. Most came right the first time—rode on their own melting, as Frost said of his poems. If there is no melting, if the story keeps sticking, better stop and look around. In the execution there has to be a "happiness" that can't be willed or foreordained. It has to sing, click, something. I try instantly to set in motion a certain forward tilt of suspense or curiosity, and at the end of the story or novel to rectify the tilt, to complete the motion.

INTERVIEWER: When your workday is through, are you able to leave it behind or does your writing haunt your afternoons and echo your experience?

UPDIKE: Well, I think the subconscious picks at it, and occasionally a worrisome sentence or image will straighten itself out, and then you make a note of it. If I'm stuck, I try to get myself unstuck before I sit down again because moving through the day surrounded by people and music and air it is easier to make major motions in your mind than it is sitting at the typewriter in a slightly claustrophobic room. It's hard to hold a manuscript in your mind, of course. You get down to the desk and discover that the solution you had arrived at while having insomnia doesn't really fit. I guess I'm never unconscious of myself as a writer and of my present project. A few places are specially conducive to inspiration—automobiles, church—private places. I plotted *Couples* almost entirely in church—little shivers and urgencies I would note down on the program and carry down to the office Monday.

INTERVIEWER: Well, you're not only a writer but a famous one. Are you experiencing any disadvantages in being famous?

UPDIKE: I'm interviewed too much. I fight them off, but even one is too many. However hard you try to be honest or full, they are intrinsically phony. There is something terribly wrong about committing myself to this machine and to your version of what you get out of the machine—you may be deaf for all I know, and the machine may be faulty. All the stuff comes out attached to my name, and it's not really me at all. My relationship to you and my linear way of coping out loud are distortive. In any interview, you do say more or less than you mean. You leave the proper ground of your strength and become one more gassy monologist. Unlike Mailer and Bellow, I don't have much itch to pronounce on great matters, to reform the country, to get elected Mayor of New York, or minister to the world with laughter like the hero of *The Last Analysis.* My life is, in a sense, trash, my life is only that of which the residue is my writing. The person who appears on the cover of *Time* or whose monologue will be printed in *The Paris Review* is neither the me who exists physically and socially or the me who signs the fiction and poetry. That is, everything is infinitely fine, and any opinion is somehow coarser than the texture of the real thing.

I find it hard to have opinions. Theologically, I favor Karl Barth; politically, I favor the Democrats. But I treasure a remark

John Cage made, that not judgingness but openness and curiosity are our proper business. To speak on matters where you're ignorant dulls the voice for speaking on matters where you do know something.

INTERVIEWER: One of the things I've always thought would be difficult for famous writers is being constantly sent manuscripts by aspiring amateurs. Do you experience this, and if so, how do you treat them?

UPDIKE: I tend to lose them. The manuscripts. I remember myself as an aspiring writer, and you know, I never did this. I assumed that published writers had worked at it until they became worth publishing, and I assumed that that's the only way to do it, and I'm a little puzzled by young men who write me charming letters suggesting that I conduct an impromptu writing course. Evidently, I've become part of the Establishment that's expected to serve youth—like college presidents and the police. I'm still trying to educate myself. I want to read only what will help me unpack my own bag.

INTERVIEWER: While we're on the subject of your public role, I wonder how you react to the growing use of your fiction in college courses?

UPDIKE: Oh, is it? Do they use it?

INTERVIEWER: I use it a great deal. What do you think about it, as a writer? Do you think that it's going to interfere with the reader's comprehension or feeling for your work. I mean, do you go along with Trilling's idea, for example, that modern literature is somehow diluted by appearing in the social context of the classroom, or are you not concerned about this?

UPDIKE: No. Looking back on my own college experience, the college course is just a way of delivering you to the books, and once you're delivered, the writer-reader relationship is there. I read Dostoevsky for a college course and wept.

If what you say is true, I'm delighted. I do think it difficult to teach, as is done so much now, courses in truly contemporary writing. (At Oxford, they used to stop with Tennyson.) Of course, maybe I'm not so contemporary anymore; maybe I'm sort of like Eisenhower or—

INTERVIEWER: You're over thirty—you're over the hill.

UPDIKE: Don't laugh—most American writers *are* over the hill by thirty. Maybe I'm like Sherman Adams and Fats Domino and other, you know, *semi-*remote figures who have acquired a certain historical interest. We're anxious in America to package our things quickly, and the writer can become a package before he's ready to have the coffin lid nailed down.

INTERVIEWER: Well, let's think of another package now—not the package by time but by country. Are you conscious of belonging to a definable American literary tradition? Would you describe yourself as part of an American tradition?

UPDIKE: I must be. I've hardly ever been out of the country.

INTERVIEWER: Specifically, do you feel that you've learned important things or felt spiritual affinities with classic American writers such as Hawthorne, Melville, James, people of this sort?

UPDIKE: I love Melville and like James, but I tend to learn more from Europeans because I think they have strengths that reach back past Puritanism, that don't equate truth with intuition—

INTERVIEWER: In other words, you want to be nourished by the thing that you don't feel is inherently your tradition.

UPDIKE: Right. I'm not saying I can write like Melville or James, but that the kind of passion and bias that they show is already in my bones. I don't think you need to keep rehearsing your instincts. Far better to seek out models of what you *can't* do. American fiction is notoriously thin on women, and I *have* attempted a number of portraits of women, and we may have reached that point of civilization, or decadence, where we *can* look at women. I'm not sure Mark Twain *was* able to.

INTERVIEWER: Let's get into your work now. In an interview you gave *Life* you expressed some regret at the "yes, but" attitude critics have taken toward it. Did the common complaint that you had ducked large subjects lead to the writing of *Couples?*

UPDIKE: No, I meant my *work* says, "Yes, but." Yes, in *Rabbit,*

Run, to our inner urgent whispers, but—the social fabric collapses murderously. Yes, in *The Centaur,* to self-sacrifice and duty, but—what of a man's private agony and dwindling? No, in *The Poorhouse Fair,* to social homogenization and loss of faith, but—listen to the voices, the joy of persistent existence. No, in *Couples,* to a religious community founded on physical and psychical interpenetration, but—what else shall we do, as God destroys our churches? I cannot greatly care what critics say of my work; if it is good, it will come to the surface in a generation or two and float, and if not, it will sink, having in the meantime provided me with a living, the opportunities of leisure, and a craftsman's intimate satisfactions. I wrote *Couples* because the rhythm of my life and my oeuvre demanded it, not to placate hallucinatory critical voices.

INTERVIEWER: What do you mean by attributing the setting up of religious communities in *Couples* to God's destruction of our churches?

UPDIKE: I guess the noun "God" reappears in two totally different senses, the god in the first instance being the god worshiped within this nice white church, the more or less watered down Puritan god; and then god in the second sense means ultimate power. I've never really understood theologies which would absolve God of earthquakes and typhoons, of children starving. A god who is not God the Creator is not very real to me, so that, yes, it certainly *is* God who throws the lightning bolt, and this God is above the nice god, above the god we can worship and empathize with. I guess I'm saying there's a fierce God above the kind God, and he's the one Piet believes in. At any rate, when the church is burned, Piet is relieved of morality and can choose Foxy—or can accept the choice made for him by Foxy and Angela operating in unison—can move out of the paralysis of guilt into what after all is a kind of freedom. He divorces the supernatural to marry the natural. I wanted the loss of Angela to be felt as a real loss—Angela is nicer than Foxy—nevertheless it is Foxy that he most deeply wants, it is Foxy who in some obscure way was turned on the lathe for him. So that the book does have a happy ending. There's also a way, though, I should say (speaking of "yes, but") in which, with the destruction of the church, with the removal of his guilt, he becomes insignificant. He becomes merely a name in the last paragraph: he becomes a satisfied person and in a sense dies. In other words, a person who has what he wants, a satisfied person, a content person, ceases to be a person. Unfallen Adam is an ape. Yes, I guess I do feel that. I feel that to be a person is to be in a situation of tension, is to be in a dialectical situation. A truly adjusted person is not a person at all—just an animal with clothes on or a statistic. So that it's a happy ending, with this "but" at the end.

INTERVIEWER: I was impressed by the contrast between the presentation of oral-genital contacts in *Couples* and its single appearance in *Rabbit, Run*. Rabbit's insistence that Ruth perform the act is the cause of their breakup.

UPDIKE: No. Janice's having the baby is.

INTERVIEWER: If you say so; but I'd still like to know why an act that is treated so neutrally in the later book is so significant in the earlier one.

UPDIKE: Well, *Couples,* in part, is about the change in sexual deportment that has occurred since the publication of *Rabbit, Run,* which came out late in '59; shortly thereafter, we had *Lady Chatterley* and the first Henry Miller books, and now you can't walk into a grocery store without seeing pornography on the rack. Remember Piet lying in Freddy's bed admiring Freddy's collection of Grove Press books? In *Rabbit, Run* what is demanded, in *Couples* is freely given. What else? It's a way of eating, eating the apple, of knowing. It's nostalgic for them, for Piet of Annabelle Vojt and for Foxy of the Jew. In De Rougement's book on Tristan and Iseult he speaks of the sterility of the lovers and Piet and Foxy are sterile vis-à-vis each other. Lastly, I was struck, talking to a biochemist friend of mine, how he emphasized not only the chemical composition of enzymes but their structure; it matters, among my humans, not only what they're made of but exactly how they attach to each other. So much for oral-genital contacts.

About sex in general, by all means let's have it in fiction, as detailed as needs be, but real, real in its social and psychological connections. Let's take coitus out of the closet and off the altar and put it on the continuum of human behavior. There are episodes in Henry Miller that have their human resonance; the sex in *Lolita*, behind the madman's cuteness, rings true; and I find the sex in D. H. Lawrence done from the woman's point of view convincing enough. In the microcosm of the individual consciousness, sexual events are huge but not all eclipsing; let's try to give them their size.

INTERVIEWER: I'd like to move on to *The Centaur* now. If I'm right in regarding it as formally uncharacteristic, I wonder why you prefer it to your other novels?

UPDIKE: Well, it seems in memory my gayest and truest book; I pick it up, and read a few pages, in which Caldwell is insisting on flattering a moth-eaten bum, who is really the god Dionysius, and I begin laughing.

INTERVIEWER: What made you decide to employ a mythic parallel?

UPDIKE: I was moved, first, by the Chiron variant of the Hercules myth—one of the few classic instances of self-sacrifice, and the name oddly close to Christ. The book began as an attempt to publicize this myth. The mythology operated in a number of ways: a correlative of the enlarging effect of Peter's nostalgia, a dramatization of Caldwell's sense of exclusion and mysteriousness around him, a counterpoint of ideality to the drab real level, an excuse for a number of jokes, a serious expression of my sensation that the people we meet are *guises*, do conceal something mythic, perhaps prototypes or longings in our minds. We love some women more than others by predetermination, it seems to me.

INTERVIEWER: Why haven't you done more work in this mode?

UPDIKE: But I have worked elsewhere in a mythic mode. Apart from my short story about Tristan and Iseult, there is the St. Stephen story underlying *The Poorhouse Fair*, and Peter Rabbit under *Rabbit, Run*. Sometimes it is semiconscious; for example, only lately do I see that Brewer, the city of brick painted the color of flowerpots, is the flowerpot that Mr. McGregor slips over Peter Rabbit. And in *Couples,* Piet is not only Hanema/anima/Life, he is Lot, the man with two virgin daughters, who flees Sodom and leaves his wife behind.

INTERVIEWER: Yes, of course, the Tristan story is like *The Centaur,* but even if your other novels have underlying mythological or scriptural subjects, they don't obtrude as they do in *The Centaur.* So let me rephrase my question. Why *didn't* you make the parallels more obvious in the other books?

UPDIKE: Oh—I don't think basically that such parallels should be obvious. I think books should have secrets, like people do. I think they should be there as a bonus for the sensitive reader or there as a kind of subliminal quavering. I don't think that the duty of the twentieth-century fiction writer is to retell old stories only. I've often wondered what Eliot meant in his famous essay on *Ulysses.* Does he mean that we are ourselves so depleted of psychic energy, of spiritual and primitive force, that we can do little but retell old stories? Does he mean that human events, love, death, wandering, certain challenges overcome or certain challenges which sweep us under, have already attained classic narrative form? I don't quite know what Eliot meant. I do know that there is certainly for all of us some attraction in old stories. Mine is a generation not raised on the Bible. The Greek stories seem to be more universal coin, and they certainly have served to finance more modern creations than the Hebrew stories. (Although do read sometime Kierkegaard's splendid retelling of Abraham and Isaac in *Fear and Trembling.*) Freud, for one, named a number of states of mind after them.

I have read old sagas—*Beowulf,* the *Mabinogion*—trying to find the story in its most rudimentary form, searching for what a story *is*— Why did these people enjoy hearing them? Are they a kind of disguised history? Or, more likely I guess, are they ways of relieving anxiety, of transferring it outwards upon an invented tale and purging it through catharsis? In any case, I feel the need for this kind of recourse to the springs of narrative, and maybe my little buried allusions are admissions of it. It's funny, the things you don't know you're doing; I was aware of Piet as Lot and I was aware of Piet and Foxy as being somehow Tristan and Iseult, but I was not very aware of him as Don Juan. The other day I got a long, brilliant letter from a man at Wesleyan describing the book in terms of the Don Juan legend, pointing out numerous illuminating analogies. He thinks that Don Juans, historically, appear in the imperialist countries just as the tide turns: the classic Don Juan appears in Spain just as Spain has lost the Netherlands, and so Piet's activity somehow coincides with our frustration in Vietnam. All this is news to me, but, once said, it sounds right. I'll have to read the letter again. It elicited for me certain basic harmonies, certain congruences with prototypes in the Western consciousness that I'm happy to accept.

INTERVIEWER: Let's turn from myth to history. You have indicated a desire to write about President Buchanan. Yet, so far as I can see, American history is normally absent from your work.

UPDIKE: Not so; quite the contrary. In each of my novels, a precise year is given and a President reigns; *The Centaur* is distinctly a Truman book, and *Rabbit, Run* an Eisenhower one. *Couples* could have taken place only under Kennedy; the social currents it traces are as specific to those years as flowers in a meadow are to their moment of summer. Even *The Poorhouse Fair* has a President, President Lowenstein, and if one is not named in *Of the Farm*, it may be because that book, in an odd way, also takes place in the future, though a future only a year or so in advance of the writing—a future now in the past. Hook, Caldwell, the Applesmiths, all talk about history, and the quotidian is littered with newspaper headlines, striking the consciousness of the characters obliquely and subliminally but firmly enough: Piet's first step at seducing Foxy is clearly in part motivated by the death of the Kennedy infant. And the atmosphere of fright permeating *The Centaur* is to an indicated extent early cold-war nerves. My fiction about the daily doings of ordinary people has more history in it than history books, just as there is more breathing history in archeology than in a list of declared wars and changes of government.

INTERVIEWER: What about violence? Many critics complain that this is absent from your work—reprehensibly, because it is so present in the world. Why is there so little in your pages?

UPDIKE: There has been so little in my life. I have fought in no wars and engaged in few fistfights. I do not think a man pacifist in his life should pretend to violence in fiction; Nabokov's bloody deeds, for example, seem more literary than lived to me. Muriel Spark's have the quality of the assassinations we commit in our minds. Mailer's recent violence is trumpery, just like Leslie Fiedler's cry for more, more. I feel a tenderness toward my characters that forbids making violent use of them. In general, the North American continent in this century has been a place where catastrophe has held off, and likewise the lives I have witnessed have staved off real death. All my novels end with a false death, partial death. If, as may be, the holocausts at the rim of possibility do soon visit us, I am confident my capacities for expression can rise, if I live, to the occasion. In the meantime let's all of us with some access to a printing press not abuse our privilege with fashionable fantasies.

INTERVIEWER: Well, one thing I'm sure must impress everyone about your fiction: the factual accuracy. The way, for example, you can provide data for Ken Whitman's talk on photosynthesis as well as Piet's on architectural restoration. Do you actively research such material, or do you rely on what you already know?

UPDIKE: Well, a bit of both, and I'm glad you do find it convincing. I'm never sure it is. A man whose life is spent in biochemistry or in building houses, his brain is tipped in a certain way. It's terribly hard, I think, for specialists to convey to me, as I ask them more or less intelligent questions, the right nuance—it's hard for me to reconstruct in my own mind the mind of a man who has spent twenty years with his field. I think the attempt should be made, however. There is a thinness in contemporary fiction about the way the world operates, except the academic world. I do try, especially in this novel, to give characters professions. Shaw's plays have a wonderful wealth of professional types. Shaw's sense of economic process, I guess, helped him (a) to care and (b) to convey, to plunge into the mystery of being a chimneysweep or a minister. One of the minimal obligations a book has to a reader is to be factually right, as to be typographically pleasant and more or less correctly proofread. Elementary author ethics dictate that you do at least *attempt* to imagine technical detail as well as emotions and dialogue.

INTERVIEWER: I'd like to ask a question about *The Poorhouse Fair.* Many people have been bothered in that book by Conner's foolishness. He seems a bit easy as the butt of satire. Do you think there is much justification in that charge?

UPDIKE: I'd have to reread the book to know. It could be that I was too little in sympathy with what I imagine him to be standing for. Of course a writer is in no position to alter a reader's reaction. Performance is all, and if I didn't really give you flesh and blood, then nothing I can say now will substitute. But it occurs to me that Conner was a preliminary study for Caldwell in *The Centaur:* the bulging upper lip and a certain Irishness, a certain tenacity, a certain—they're both poor disciplinarians, I notice in thinking about them. I wasn't satirical in my purpose. I may have been negative, but satire, no. I'm not conscious of any piece of fiction of mine which has even the slightest taint of satirical attempt. You can't be satirical at the expense of fictional characters, because they're your creatures. You must only love them, and I think that once I'd set Conner in motion I did to the best of my ability try to love him and let his mind and heart beat.

INTERVIEWER: Isn't "The Doctor's Wife" an exception to your statement that you never satirize one of your characters?

UPDIKE: You think I'm satirizing the doctor's wife? I'm *criticizing* the doctor's wife. Yes, I do feel that in some way she is a racist, but I'm not trying, I don't think I'm trying, to make her funny because she's a racist.

INTERVIEWER: There's some satire in your poetry, isn't there? But I wonder why, with few exceptions, you only write light verse.

UPDIKE: I began with light verse, a kind of cartooning in print, and except for one stretch of a few years, in which I wrote most of the serious poems in *Telephone Poles*, I feel uncertain away from rhyme to which something comic adheres. Bergson's mechanical encrusted upon the organic. But the light verse poems putting into rhyme and jaunty metrics some scientific discovery have a serious point—the universe science discloses to us is farcically unrelated to what our primitive senses report—and I have, when such poems go well, a pleasure and satisfaction not lower than in any other form of literary activity.

INTERVIEWER: You've published work in all the literary forms except drama. Why haven't you worked in this form?

UPDIKE: I've never much enjoyed going to plays myself; they always seem one act too long, and I often can't hear. The last play I went to, I remember, was *A Delicate Balance;* I sat next to the wall, and trucks kept shifting gears on the other side of it, and I missed most of the dialogue. The unreality of painted people standing on a platform saying things they've said to each other for months is more than I can overlook. Also, I think the theater is a quicksand of money and people with push. Harold Brodkey, a splendid writer my age, disappeared for five years into a play that was never produced. From Twain and James to Faulkner and Bellow, the history of novelists as playwrights is a sad one. A novelist is no more prepared to write for the stage than a good distance runner is equipped for ballet. A play is verbal ballet, and I mean to include in that equation some strong reservations about ballet. Less than perfectly done, it's very tiresome. A play's capacity for mimesis is a fraction of a novel's. Shakespeare, and to a lesser extent Shaw, wrote their plays as "turns" and exercises for actors they knew—without Will Kempe, no Falstaff. Without this kind of intimacy, the chances of life creeping into a play are slight. On both sides of the footlights, I think the present American theater mainly an excuse for being sociable.

INTERVIEWER: But if I'm not mistaken, you once expressed a desire to write for the films and I think *Rabbit, Run,* in particular, is quite a cinematic novel. Do you have any such plans now?

UPDIKE: *Rabbit, Run* was subtitled originally, "A Movie." The present tense was in part meant to be an equivalent of the cinematic mode of narration. The opening bit of the boys playing basketball was visualized to be taking place under the titles and credits. This doesn't mean, though, that I really wanted to write for the movies. It meant I wanted to make a movie. I could come closer by writing it in my own book than by attempting to get through to Hollywood.

INTERVIEWER: Do you think the film has much to teach the novelist?

UPDIKE: I'm not sure. I think that we live in an eye-oriented era and that both the movies and the graphic arts, the painterly arts, haunt us, haunt word people quite a lot. I've written about our jealousy in my review of Robbe-Grillet and his theories. In brief, we're jealous because the visual arts have captured all the glamorous people—the rich and the young.

INTERVIEWER: Do you think there is a possibility of the novelist feeling at a disadvantage, that the instantaneousness and completeness of the image is making him somehow have to run to catch up? Have you ever felt that?

UPDIKE: Oh, sure. I think we are covetous of the success, the breadth of appeal. A movie does not really require much work. It pours into us, it fills us like milk being poured into a glass, whereas there is some cerebral effort needed to turn a bunch of mechanical marks on a page into moving living images. So that, yes, the power of the cinema, the awful power of it, the way from moron to genius it captivates us, it hypnotizes us . . . What I don't know is how relevant attempts to imitate this instantaneity, this shuffle of images, are to the novelist's art. I think that the novel is descended from two sources, historical accounts and letters. The personal letters, the epistolary novel, the novel of Richardson, which is revived now only as a *tour de force,* does have this cinematic instantaneity; the time is occurring on the page. But this is a minority current in the contemporary novel; we are held captive to the novel as history, as an account of things once done. The account of things done minus the presiding, talkative, confiding, and pedagogic author may be a somewhat dead convention; that is, like anybody who takes any writing courses, I was told how stale and awful it is when authors begin to signal, as Dickens did, over the heads of the characters to the reader. Yet I feel that something has been lost with this authority, with this sense of an author as God, as a speaking God, as a chatty God, filling the universe of the book. Now we have the past tense, a kind of a noncommittal deadness: God paring his fingernails. We may be getting the worst of both worlds.

Couples was in some ways an old-fashioned novel; I found the last thirty pages—the rounding up, the administering of fortunes —curiously satisfying, pleasant. Going from character to character, I had myself the sensation of flying, of conquering space. In *Rabbit, Run* I liked writing in the present tense. You can move between minds, between thoughts and objects and events with a curious ease not available to the past tense. I'm not sure it's as clear to the reader as it is to the person writing, but there are kinds of poetry, kinds of music you can strike off in the present tense. I don't know why I've not done a full-length novel in it again. I began tentatively, but one page deep into the book, it seemed very natural and congenial, so much so that while doing *The Centaur* I was haunted by the present tense and finally wrote a whole chapter in it.

INTERVIEWER: You speak with some regret about the present authorial disinclination to signal above the heads of the characters. I am interested in your evaluation of the success of three contemporary writers who seem to me to have maintained this willingness to signal to the reader directly. The first one I'd like to mention and get your reaction to is Robert Penn Warren.

UPDIKE: I'm sorry. I don't know Penn Warren's prose well enough to comment.

INTERVIEWER: How about Barth?

UPDIKE: Barth I know imperfectly, but I have read the first two novels and parts of the last two and some of the short stories. I also know Barth personally and find him a most likable and engaging and modest man. He and I are near the same age and born not too far from each other, he in Maryland and I in southeastern Pennsylvania. His work is partly familiar and partly repellent; I feel he hit the floor of nihilism hard and returns to us covered with coal dust. We are very close to an abyss as we traverse Barth's rolling periods and curiously elevated point of view. I guess my favorite book of his is *The Floating Opera*, which is like *The Poorhouse Fair* in ending with a kind of carnival, a brainless celebration of the fact of existence. As it stands now, Barth seems to me a very strongminded and inventive and powerful voice from another planet; there is something otherworldly about his fiction that makes it both fascinating and barren, at least for me. I'd rather visit Uranus than read through *Giles Goat-Boy*.

INTERVIEWER: What about Bellow?

UPDIKE: There is in Bellow a kind of little professor, a professor-elf, who keeps fluttering around the characters, and I'm not sure he's my favorite Bellow character, this voice. He's almost always there, putting exclamatory marks after sentences, making little utterances and in general inviting us to participate in moral decisions. This person—whom I take to be the author—contributes to the soft focus of Bellow's endings. The middles are so rich with detail, with charm and love of life; I think how in *Henderson the Rain King* he remembers rubbing oil into his pregnant wife's stomach to ease the stretch marks. It's this professor, this earnest sociological man who somehow wants us to be better than we are, who muddles the endings, not exactly happy endings, but they are endings which would *point the way*. He cares so—the way Bellow can conjure up a minor character and set him tumbling across the paragraph.

But the general question of authorial presence—I find it irksome when an author is there as a celebrity. In Salinger's later works and most of Mailer's work the author appears as somebody who counts, somebody who has an audience of teen-agers out there waiting to hear from him. This kind of return to before Chekhov I don't find useful, although authorial invisibility is also a pose. The proper pose may be the Homeric bard's one—he is there, but unimportantly there, there by sufferance of the king.

INTERVIEWER: What about the cultivation of pretense—playing around with it. I mean, what do you think of a writer like Barthleme?

UPDIKE: He was an art director of some sort and, just as Kerouac's work was a kind of action writing to answer action painting, so Barthleme's short stories and the one novelette seem to me to be an attempt to bring over into prose something Pop. I think, you know, on the one hand of Andy Warhol's Campbell's soup cans and on the other of the Chinese baby food that the Seven Dwarfs in *Snow White* are making. Then again you do get a hard-edge writing in a way. In one of his short stories he says that the hard nut-brown word has enough aesthetic satisfaction for anybody but a fool. I also think his stories are important for what they don't say, for the things that don't happen in them, that stand revealed as clichés.

Yes—I think he's interesting, but more interesting as an operator within a cultural scene than as a—oh, as a singer to my spirit. A quaint phrase that possibly betrays me.

INTERVIEWER: What of writers who've influenced you. Salinger? Nabokov?

UPDIKE: I learned a lot from Salinger's short stories; he did remove the short narrative from the wise-guy, slice-of-life stories of the thirties and forties. Like most innovative artists, he made new room for shapelessness, for life as it is lived. I'm thinking of a story like "Just Before the War with the Eskimos" not "For Esmé," which already shows signs of emotional overkill. Nabokov, I admire but would emulate only his high dedication to the business of making books that are not sloppy, that can be reread. I think his aesthetic models, chess puzzles and protective colorations in Lepidoptera, are rather special.

INTERVIEWER: Henry Green? O'Hara?

UPDIKE: Green's tone, his touch of truth, his air of peddling nothing and knowing everything, I would gladly attain to, if I could. For sheer transparence of eye and ear he seems to me unmatched among living writers. Alas, for a decade he has refused to write, showing I suppose his ultimate allegiance to life itself.

Some of O'Hara's short stories also show a very rare transparence, freshness, and unexpectedness. Good works of art direct us back outward to reality again; they illustrate, rather than ask, imitation.

INTERVIEWER: You mentioned Kerouac a moment ago. How do you feel about his work?

UPDIKE: Somebody like Kerouac who writes on teletype paper as rapidly as he can once slightly alarmed me. Now I can look upon this more kindly. There may be some reason to question the whole idea of fineness and care in writing. Maybe something can get into sloppy writing that would elude careful writing. I'm not terribly careful myself, actually. I write fairly rapidly if I get going, and don't change much, and have never been one for making outlines or taking out whole paragraphs or agonizing much. If a thing goes, it goes for me, and if it doesn't go, I eventually stop and get off.

INTERVIEWER: What is it that you think gets into sloppy writing that eludes more careful prose?

UPDIKE: It comes down to what is language? Up to now, until this age of mass literacy, language has been something spoken. In utterance there's a minimum of slowness. In trying to treat words as chisel strokes, you run the risk of losing the quality of utterance, the rhythm of utterance, the happiness. A phrase out of Mark Twain—he describes a raft hitting a bridge and says that it "went all to smash and scatteration like a box of matches struck by lightning." The beauty of "scatteration" could only have occurred to a talkative man, a man who had been brought up among people who were talking and who loved to talk himself. I'm aware myself of a certain dryness of this reservoir, this backlog of spoken talk. A Rumanian once said to me that Americans are always telling stories. I'm not sure this is as true as it once was. Where we once used to spin yarns, now we sit in front of the TV and receive pictures. I'm not sure the younger generation even knows how to gossip. But, as for a writer, if he has something to tell, he should perhaps type it almost as fast as he could talk it. We must look to the organic world, not the inorganic world, for metaphors; and just as the organic world has periods of repose and periods of great speed and exercise, so I think the writer's process should be organically varied. But there's a kind of tautness that you should feel within yourself no matter how slow or fast you're spinning out the reel.

INTERVIEWER: In "The Sea's Green Sameness" you deny that characterization and psychology are primary goals of fiction. What do you think is more important?

UPDIKE: I wrote "The Sea's Green Sameness" years ago and meant, I believe, that narratives should not be *primarily* packages for psychological insights, though they can contain them, like raisins in buns. But the substance is the dough, which feeds the storytelling appetite, the appetite for motion, for suspense, for resolution. The author's deepest pride, as I have experienced it, is not in his incidental wisdom but in his ability to keep an organized mass of images moving forward, to feel life engendering itself under his hands. But no doubt, fiction is also a mode of spying; we read it as we look in windows or listen to gossip, to learn what other people *do*. Insights of all kinds are welcome; but no wisdom will substitute for an instinct for action and pattern, and a perhaps savage wish to hold, through your voice, another soul in thrall.

INTERVIEWER: In view of this and your delight in the "non-committal luminosity of fact," do you think you're much like the "nouvelle vague" novelists?

UPDIKE: I used to. I wrote *The Poorhouse Fair* as an anti-novel, and have found Nathalie Sarraute's description of the modern novelistic predicament a helpful guide. I am attracted to the cool surface of some contemporary French novels, and, like them, do want to give inanimate or vegetable presences some kind of vote in the democracy of narrative. Basically, though, I describe things not because their muteness mocks our subjectivity but because they seem to be masks for God. And I should add that there is, in fiction, an image-making function, above image-retailing. To create a coarse universal figure like Tarzan is in some ways more of an accomplishment than the novels of Henry James.

INTERVIEWER: As a technician, how unconventional would you say you were?

UPDIKE: As unconventional as I need to be. An absolute freedom exists on the blank page, so let's use it. I have from the start been wary of the fake, the automatic. I tried not to force my sense of life as many-layered and ambiguous, while keeping in mind some sense of transaction, of a bargain struck, between me and the ideal reader. Domestic fierceness within the middle class, sex and death as riddles for the thinking animal, social existence as sacrifice, unexpected pleasures and rewards, corruption as a kind of evolution—these are some of the themes. I have tried to achieve objectivity in the form of narrative. My work is meditation, not pontification, so that interviews like this one feel like a forcing of the growth, a posing. I think of my books not as sermons or directives in a war of ideas but as objects, with different shapes and textures and the mysteriousness of anything that exists. My first thought about art, as a child, was that the artist brings something into the world that didn't exist before, and that he does it without destroying something else. A kind of refutation of the conservation of matter. That still seems to me its central magic, its core of joy.

CHARLES THOMAS SAMUELS

Notes on the Contributors

NATHANIEL BENCHLEY *(Introduction to John Steinbeck Interview)* has written a variety of novels, short stories, and articles, as well as a dozen or so books for young readers. His play *The Frogs of Spring* was produced on Broadway in 1953; a motion picture, *The Great American Pastime*, appeared in 1957; and his novel *The Off-Islanders* was made into the motion picture *The Russians Are Coming, The Russians Are Coming*. He lives in Siasconset, on the island of Nantucket, and is at present completing work on a biography of Humphrey Bogart.

TED BERRIGAN *(Interview with Jack Kerouac)* is the author of three books of poems: *The Sonnets* (Grove Press), *Many Happy Returns* (Corith Books), and *In the Early Morning Rain* (Cape Goliard–Grossman). He has also collaborated on two other books of poems: *Bean Spasms* with Ron Padgett (Kulchur Press), and *Back In Boston Again* with Tom Clark, Aram Saroyan, and Ron Padgett (Telegraphy Books). He has two books forthcoming, *Memorial Day* and *A Feeling for Leaving*. Formerly poet in residence at the University of Essex, he is currently poet ,in residence at Northwestern Illinois University. He lives in Chicago with his wife, the poet Alice Notley, and their two children.

PETER BUCKMAN *(Interview with Robert Graves)* is the author of *The Limits of Protest* and *Playground: a Game of Fiction*. He edited the anthology *Education Without Schools* and has just finished a biography of Lafayette. He lives in rural Oxfordshire with his wife and two small daughters.

RONALD CHRIST *(Interview with Jorge Luis Borges)* is the author of *The Narrow Act: Borges' Art of Allusion* (N.Y.U. Press) and the editor of *Review*, a journal devoted to Latin American literature in translation. In addition, he teaches English at Livingston College, Rutgers University, and directs the literature program at the Center for Inter-American Relations. He lives in New York and is working on a collection of essays concerned with style in Latin American fiction.

FRANK CROWTHER *(Co-editor of the John Steinbeck interview)* is a free-lance writer and producer who is currently working on a book, *Give Me a Ticket to Wherever It Is*. He resides in New York City and plans to return to Paris upon publication of the book.

JOHN CULLINAN *(Interview with Anthony Burgess)* has studied at Yale and Columbia, taught in New York and California, and spent 1973 as a research fellow at the University of Wisconsin, Milwaukee. He currently lives in Chicago and is working on a book about Anthony Burgess's novels.

WILLIAM FIFIELD *(Interview with Robert Graves)* is the author of *Modigliani* and is currently at work on *Conversations with Genius* (a considerable elaboration of talks with Graves, Picasso, Miró, Marcel Marceau, Dali, Cocteau, and so forth) to be published by

Morrow in 1976. His interview with Cocteau appeared in *Writers at Work*, Third Series, and has been released in French as a Caedmon Record Album, *Jean Cocteau: A Self-Portrait—A Conversation with William Fifield*. An O. Henry prizewinner in the short story, he lives in Spain.

HERBERT GOLD *(Interview with Vladimir Nabokov)* has published a number of novels: *Fathers, The Man Who Was Not With It, Salt*, and the most recent, *Swiftie the Magician* (1974). He is also the author of a literary autobiography, *My Last 2000 Years*, and stories and essays, including *The Magic Will* and *The Age of Happy Problems*. He lives in San Francisco with his wife and five children.

EDMUND KEELEY *(Interview with George Seferis)* has written four novels, *The Libation, The Gold-Hatted Lover, The Imposter*, and *Voyage to a Dark Island*, and published eight volumes of translation, including *Six Poets of Modern Greece, George Seferis: Collected Poems (1924–1955), C. P. Cavafy: Collected Poems*, and *Odysseus Elytis: The Axion Esti* (in collaboration with Philip Sherrard and George Savidis). He is currently at work on a critical study of Cavafy's poetry. He divides his time between Princeton, N.J. (where he is Professor of English and Creative Arts and Director of the Creative Writing Program at Princeton University), and Greece, where he does much of his writing.

BARBARA KEVLES *(Interview with Anne Sexton)* is working on a book recounting her reportorial experiences with radical feminists. Ms. Kevles has written for *Look, The Atlantic Monthly, New York, Good Housekeeping, Mademoiselle, Seventeen, Show, Film Culture, The Saturday Evening Post*, and various other mass and literary magazines.

LINDA KUEHL *(Interview with Eudora Welty)* is a free-lance writer and critic living in New York City. She has published in *The New York Times Book Review, Commonweal, The Christian Science*

Monitor, Modern Fiction Studies, Chicago Sunday Times, Boston Herald Traveler, and others. She has been a writing fellow at the MacDowell Colony, Yaddo, and the Virginia Center for the Creative Arts. In progress is a biography of Billie Holiday.

MICHAEL NEWMAN *(Interview with W. H. Auden)* as associate editor of *The Paris Review* is at work on *The Quantum Poetic,* a synthesis of art and science. Formerly a newsman for *The Washington Post* and *Daily News,* he has also published in *Poetry, The New York Times, Book World,* and *The New York Quarterly.* He studied poetry with Mr. Auden until the poet's death in 1973.

GEORGE PLIMPTON *(Co-editor of John Steinbeck Interview)* has been the editor of *The Paris Review* since its founding in 1953. He is the author of a number of books with a sports background, including *Paper Lion, Mad Ducks and Bears,* and *One for the Record.*

CHARLES THOMAS SAMUELS *(Interview with John Updike)* died on March 13, 1974, at the age of thirty-eight. He had been professor of English at Williams College, film critic of *The American Scholar,* and author of *John Updike, Encountering Directors,* and *The Ambiguity of Henry James.*

DAVID SANDERS *(Interview with John Dos Passos)* is a professor of English at Harvey Mudd College and the Claremont Graduate School. He has written recently on Dos Passos, Hemingway, John Hersey, and baseball.

W. I. SCOBIE *(Interview with Christopher Isherwood)* has had poetry published in *Encounter* and *London Magazine.* He lives in Santa Monica, California, where he writes for the *London Observer.*

PETER A. STITT *(Interview with John Berryman)* has had poems, essays, and reviews in *The New York Times Book Review, The Southern Review, The Minnesota Review, Shenandoah, The Carolina Quarterly, Concerning Poetry, The Ohio Review, Arizona Quarterly, Hawaii Review, Ann Arbor Review,* and others. He has just finished a study of the poetry of John Berryman. He is an assistant professor of American Literature at Middlebury College in Vermont.

EUGENE WALTER *(Interview with Isak Dinesen)* never left Mobile, Alabama, until he went as a cryptographer to the Andreanof Islands in World War II. He has won prizes for fiction and poetry, translation, and design and has worked with ten different literary magazines. After a three-year visit to New York and a five-year visit to Paris, he has settled in Rome, where he raises cats and irises.

ROBERT HUNTER WILBUR *(Interview with Conrad Aiken)* is currently director of public affairs for a private public-relations and trade-association management firm in Washington, D.C.; he was a public-affairs officer at the State Department and a speech writer for Arthur Goldberg when he was U.S. Ambassador to the United Nations. He has published articles on foreign affairs in *Vista* and *The New Republic* and is author of a Columbia doctoral dissertation entitled "George Santayana and Three Modern Philosophical Poets: T. S. Eliot, Conrad Aiken, and Wallace Stevens."